The New Certificate Geography Series

ADVANCED LEVEL

NORTH AMERICA

Pike's Peak. This mountain thrusts itself up nearly $1\frac{1}{2}$ miles above the High Plains, which are themselves more than a mile above sea-level in Colorado. The surrounding district was the goal of many nineteenth century gold-prospectors. Note the bare summit and pine-clad mountain slopes, characteristic of the Rocky Mountains.

The New Certificate Geography Series

ADVANCED LEVEL

NORTH AMERICA

F. S. HUDSON, B.A., F.R.G.S.

(Formerly Deputy Headmaster, and Head of Geography Department, King James's Grammar School, Almondbury, Huddersfield.)

THIRD EDITION

MACDONALD & EVANS LTD

8 John Street, London, WC1N 2HY

1974

First published August 1962
Reprinted December 1962
Reprinted June 1963
Reprinted May 1964
Reprinted (with corrections) July 1965
Reprinted (with corrections) December 1966
Reprinted February 1968
Second Edition July 1968
Reprinted 1969
Reprinted (with amendments) September 1970
Reprinted (with amendments) March 1972
Third Edition published January 1974
Reprinted August 1974
Reprinted November 1975

MACDONALD AND EVANS LIMITED

1974

ISBN: Hardcase Edition 0 7121 1407 6
ISBN: Paperback Edition 0 7121 1408 4

The New Certificate Geography Series

ADVANCED LEVEL

Africa
Australasia
The British Isles
Europe
Latin America
The Mediterranean Lands
Monsoon Asia
North America
The Soviet Union
The United States
of America

Printed in Great Britain by
Fletcher & Son Ltd, Norwich

AUTHOR'S PREFACE

THIS book has been written specifically for the needs of G.C.E. Advanced Level candidates, but it is hoped that it will also be found useful to students preparing for Scholarship Level examinations, and be of interest to members of the general public interested in North American affairs.

The greater part of the volume is taken up with a consideration of the general and regional geography of Anglo-America in both its physical and human aspects; but there is a comprehensive general section on North America as a whole, and chapters are included on Mexico, Central America, and the West Indies, because most teachers cover these lands in their "North America" syllabus. For a fuller treatment of these regions, students are referred to another book in this series: *Latin America*, by Dr Harry Robinson.

Statistical information, which embodies, for instance, material extracted from the 1960 census returns of the United States, is as up-to-date as possible. Special attention is paid to recent economic advances, but the value of the historical perspective is not disregarded.

The eighty specially drawn maps and sections are fully integrated with the text, and virtually all the place-names used in the text are incorporated in the maps. The photographic illustrations have been carefully chosen to reveal something of the complexity of the cultural landscapes and economic activities of the continent, and to illuminate significant aspects of its physical make-up.

Among the many books and articles consulted, I have found particularly valuable Jones and Bryan's *North America*, Miller and Parkins' *North America*, Paterson's *North America*, Shaw's *Anglo-America*, Taylor's *Canada*, and Putnam's *Regional Geography of Canada*. These books, and other sources, are listed in the "Short Guide to Further Reading" at the end of the book.

I am greatly indebted to my good friend, Dr Harry Robinson, for permission to reproduce illustrations which have appeared in sections on the Central American Mainland and the West Indies in his *Latin America*. Dr Robinson has also read the manuscript and made many useful suggestions. I should also like to thank Mr G. B. Davis, of Macdonald and Evans Ltd, for his helpful comments and skilful editing. Acknowledgments also go to the Canadian High Commissioner and the United States Information Service, who have been kind enough to supply me with most of the pictorial illustrations scattered through the text.

Finally, I must thank my wife for her continual interest in the progress of the book, and for all the moral support she has given me in its preparation.

F. S. H.

March 1962

Most temperatures in this book are given in degrees Fahrenheit. In view of the gradual substitution of the Centigrade scale by the Meteorological Office, the following list of equivalents may prove helpful.

°F	°C	°F	°C	°F	°C
0·0	−17·8	35·0	1·7	70·0	21·1
1·0	−17·2	36·0	2·2	71·0	21·7
2·0	−16·7	37·0	2·8	72·0	22·2
3·0	−16·1	38·0	3·3	73·0	22·8
4·0	−15·6	39·0	3·9	74·0	23·3
5·0	−15·0	40·0	4·4	75·0	23·9
6·0	−14·4	41·0	5·0	76·0	24·4
7·0	−13·9	42·0	5·6	77·0	25·0
8·0	−13·3	43·0	6·1	78·0	25·6
9·0	−12·8	44·0	6·7	79·0	26·1
10·0	−12·2	45·0	7·2	80·0	26·7
11·0	−11·7	46·0	7·8	81·0	27·2
12·0	−11·1	47·0	8·3	82·0	27·7
13·0	−10·6	48·0	8·9	83·0	28·3
14·0	−10·0	49·0	9·4	84·0	28·9
15·0	−9·4	50·0	10·0	85·0	29·4
16·0	−8·9	51·0	10·6	86·0	30·0
17·0	−8·3	52·0	11·1	87·0	30·6
18·0	−7·8	53·0	11·7	88·0	31·1
19·0	−7·2	54·0	12·2	89·0	31·7
20·0	−6·7	55·0	12·8	90·0	32·2
21·0	−6·1	56·0	13·3	91·0	32·8
22·0	−5·6	57·0	13·9	92·0	33·3
23·0	−5·0	58·0	14·4	93·0	33·8
24·0	−4·4	59·0	15·0	94·0	34·4
25·0	−3·9	60·0	15·6	95·0	35·0
26·0	−3·3	61·0	16·1	96·0	35·5
27·0	−2·8	62·0	16·7	97·0	36·1
28·0	−2·2	63·0	17·2	98·0	36·6
29·0	−1·7	64·0	17·8	99·0	37·2
30·0	−1·1	65·0	18·3	100·0	37·8
31·0	−0·6	66·0	18·9	101·0	38·3
32·0	0·0	67·0	19·4	102·0	38·9
33·0	0·6	68·0	20·0	103·0	39·5
34·0	1·1	69·0	20·6	104·0	40·0

PREFACE TO THE THIRD EDITION

THE success of the previous editions of this book, together with the many impressions which have been called for, has been most gratifying. Though every effort has been made at each reprint to keep the text up to date, the pace of change in North America is such that both publisher and author have decided that the time has now come to effect another full revision.

For this new edition, every chapter has been amended and several sections have been expanded. Account has been taken of the 1970 Population Census of the United States and the 1971 Census of Canada, and all production and trade statistics have been updated. New tables have been provided to illustrate the demographic and economic characteristics of Central America and the West Indies, and the graphs relating to the international trade of Canada and the U.S.A. are now based on 1970 figures. Virtually all the maps and diagrams have been redrawn; some have also been amended and their statistical basis revised. They now appear, for the first time, in uniform style.

In view of the extensive revision the book has undergone, it is the author's hope that the circle of its readers will be enlarged and that those already familiar with it will give it as warm a welcome as they gave earlier editions. Once again, the author would like to record his thanks to the publishers for their consideration and also for their expert editing and pilotage through the press.

June 1973   F. S. H.

CONTENTS

ix

PART THREE

THE UNITED STATES

PART FOUR

ANGLO-AMERICA

LIST OF ILLUSTRATIONS

LIST OF STUDY QUESTIONS

Part One

THE GEOGRAPHICAL FRAMEWORK OF NORTH AMERICA

Chapter I

NORTH AMERICA : PHYSICAL GEOGRAPHY

SIZE, POSITION, AND SHAPE

PHYSICALLY, North America extends from the Arctic Ocean to the Isthmus of Panamá, and politically to the frontier between Panamá and Colombia. It has a total area of nearly 9½ million square miles, of which the United States, Canada, and Mexico occupy almost 90%. The rest is taken up by Greenland, the West Indies, and Central America. Only Asia and Africa are larger continents.

Both Canada and the United States extend from the Atlantic Ocean to the Pacific. Mexico has the latter on its southern side, and the Gulf of California washes part of its western coast. On the east, this country descends to the Gulf of Mexico, an arm of the Atlantic. Between the West Indies and Central America is another extension of the Atlantic, the Caribbean Sea. (*See* Fig. 1.)

The latitudes of the different parts of the continent are significant. Most of Canada lies polewards of the 49th parallel, and the Arctic Circle (lat. 66½ degrees N.) passes through its northern territories and also through Alaska and Greenland. The Tropic of Cancer (lat. 23½ degrees N.) roughly bisects Mexico, and runs a few miles north of Cuba and through the Bahamas. The United States' most southerly town, Key West, off the southern end of the Florida peninsula, lies about 70 miles north of the Tropic. Only a small proportion of the North American mainland can be described as tropical; a somewhat larger part of the continent is arctic in character, but most of it has a temperate climate and vegetation.

Longitude 100 degrees W. divides the continent into roughly equal western and eastern parts. Alaska reaches almost to 170 degrees W., to face the Soviet Union across the narrow Bering Strait. On the other side, Newfoundland is less than 2000 miles from Ireland, and Greenland, approaching 10 degrees W., *i.e.* the longitude of western Ireland, is barely 1000 miles from Scotland and Norway.

Like Africa and South America, but less markedly, the mainland of North America tapers from north to south. The huge embayment of the Gulf of Mexico and the triangular shape of Mexico north of the Isthmus

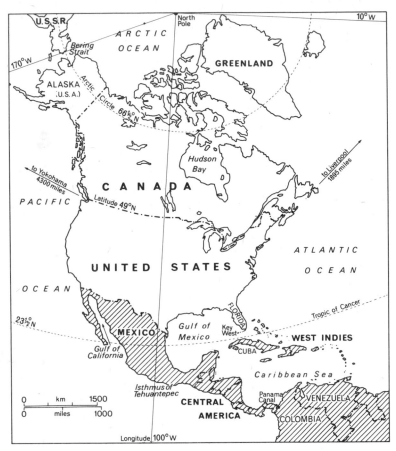

Fig. 1.—Geographical position of North America. Shaded portions represent Latin America.

of Tehuantepec exaggerate this tendency. In latitude 52 degrees N. the continental mainland is 3000 miles from east to west; in latitude 35 degrees N. (nearly 1200 miles farther south) it is still 2500 miles wide.

To the north and south of the continent are two extensive archipelagos: an arctic one and a tropical one (the West Indies), respectively. Greenland and Baffin Island dominate the former group, Cuba and Hispaniola the latter.

STRUCTURE, RELIEF, AND DRAINAGE

THE MAJOR STRUCTURAL DIVISIONS

Structurally, the North American mainland may be divided into four major divisions:

1. The Canadian or Laurentian Shield, in the north-east.
2. The Appalachian Mountains to the south and east, separated from the Atlantic by a recent coastal plain.
3. The Central Plains.
4. The Western Highlands, or Cordillera.

1. *The Laurentian Shield.* Geologically, the Laurentian Shield is the oldest part of the continent. Formed mainly of ancient crystalline rocks, rich in minerals of economic value, it was subject to several periods of earth-building movements before any other part of North America, except the Older Appalachians, came into being. Tilted upwards now on its southern and eastern edges, in southern Quebec and Labrador respectively, it descends unevenly to the Hudson Bay Lowlands, where it is masked by younger sediments, and extends beyond Canada southwards into the sterile Upper Lakes region and Adirondack Mountains of the United States. Its average height has been reduced to little more than 1000 ft by long-continued denudation.

2. *The Appalachian Mountains.* South-east of this geologically stable region, the Appalachians were folded, faulted, and intruded by igneous rocks in Palaeozoic times. There is an older zone in Newfoundland, the Maritime Provinces of Canada, northern New England, and the Piedmont area south of New York, and a newer, more highly folded zone farther west. The Appalachians have been greatly denuded, and the highest summits do not reach 7000 ft. Nevertheless, the mountains for a long time hemmed in the early Atlantic settlers and confined them to the coastal margins.

3. *The Central Plains.* These North American plains stretch from the Arctic Ocean to the Gulf of Mexico. They consist in the main of very gently folded sedimentary rocks, generally younger than those of the Appalachians, although a large inlier of more ancient rocks, structurally a continuation of the Appalachians, occurs in the Ozark–Ouachita region of the south-central United States. The youngest Plain sediments are those of the broad lowlands bordering the Gulf of Mexico and uniting with those of the Atlantic Plain. West of the Mississippi, the Central Lowlands rise gradually to about 5000 ft in the High Plains, which lead to the Rocky Mountain foothills.

4. *The Western Cordillera.* These highlands take up nearly a third of the total continental area, and measure 1000 miles across in latitude 40 degrees N. They form a highly complex system of young fold mountains which owe the main features of their structure to the recent Alpine orogeny (*i.e.* mountain-building movements). They were built up at various times during the late Mesozoic and Tertiary eras, mainly by pressures exerted from the east, and today form part of the circum-Pacific mountain belt. Folding movements with associated igneous activity raised up high ranges in the west, along the Pacific coast, and also in the east, where the Rocky Mountains form the principal rampart. Vertical uplift and subsidence, accompanied by faulting and regional fissure eruptions, were chiefly responsible for the sequence of inter-montane plateaus and basins which run all the way from the Yukon Basin in Alaska to the plateau of Mexico. The names of individual plateaus and basins are shown on Fig. 2.

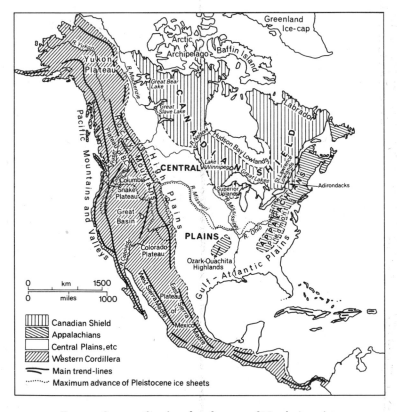

FIG. 2.—Structural and surface features of North America.

Many parts of the Western Cordillera are highly mineralised. On their flanks and in the Central Plains are the greatest oilfields in the world, including those of Kansas–Oklahoma–Texas, Mexico, and southern California. The position of these oilfields may be compared with the situation of the great Appalachian Coalfield, on the western slopes of the older Eastern Highlands.

THE PLEISTOCENE ICE AGE

Like Europe, North America underwent a recent Ice Age, whose later stages were contemporary with the appearance of Man on earth. The period probably lasted for about 500,000 years, and was marked by four or five glacial advances and retreats. From centres in the Cordillera, Keewatin area, and Labrador, ice-sheets moved southwards whenever the climate grew colder, but never passed beyond the line of the Missouri–Ohio rivers nor south of Long Island (New York).

The results of these repeated glacial invasions were various. From the Canadian Shield and Newfoundland, in particular, much soil was removed and many bare rocks were scraped and even hollowed out to produce thousands of depressions in which water has since collected to form lakes. Farther west and south, over considerable areas of the Central Plains, boulder clays (forming glacial till) were deposited. South of the Missouri, extensive areas are covered with outwash sands and gravels, and with fertile, wind-blown loess.

Sandwiched between the Mississippi water-parting on the south and the finally retreating ice-sheets on the north, great bodies of melt-water were held up for a time; today, in this region, lie the Great Lakes of North America, and the large lakes of Manitoba.

In the Cordillera, valley glaciation was widespread during the Pleistocene period, and in many of the lofty mountain ranges are U-shaped valleys, hanging valleys, cirques, morainic and rock-basin lakes, and other features of glaciated highland landscapes. A number of shrunken ice-fields and high-level glaciers still persist in the highest parts.

As is well known, Greenland is still cold enough to retain a large ice-cap, several thousands of feet thick in the centre. From it, valley glaciers debouch into the sea, and calve those castellated icebergs which may endanger North Atlantic shipping as they are carried southwards by sea currents. Baffin and other large Arctic islands have smaller ice-caps.

NORTH AMERICAN RIVERS

In no continent have rivers played a greater part in the human story than in North America. Used for transport long before Europeans began to move in, the larger ones still form very valuable highways, and may also be sources of hydro-electric power and of irrigation and industrial water. They flow variously into the Pacific (*e.g.* Canada's Fraser and the United States' Colorado), into the Atlantic (notably the St Lawrence), Hudson Bay (*e.g.* the Nelson), the Arctic (*e.g.* the Mackenzie), and the Gulf of Mexico (especially the Mississippi).

Several western rivers, particularly the Columbia, Sacramento, and Colorado, have recently been harnessed for power-generation and irrigation water supplies. In the east, the Tennessee, a number of the north-bank tributaries of the St Lawrence, and many short rivers falling abruptly from the Appalachians to the Atlantic coast plain have been dammed back to support power-stations, while the waterway of the Great Lakes–St Lawrence River, shared between Canada and the United States, has been so improved as to provide the greatest inland water route in the world.

It is worth while to compare the Mackenzie, Mississippi, and St Lawrence, the most notable rivers in North America. The first, flowing northwards for 2300 miles to the isolated Arctic Ocean, and collecting on its way much of the drainage both of the northern Rockies and the Shield, traverses a very thinly peopled region largely covered with coniferous forest. Though used to some extent as a highway in the relative absence of other means of communication, it is economically the least important of the three great rivers because of the undeveloped character of its basin. It suffers, too, from floods, which may inundate extensive areas in early summer.

By contrast, the Mississippi flows southwards to its delta by the warm waters of the Gulf of Mexico through well-developed farmlands, growing corn, cotton, and rice. From the west, the main river receives the great, muddy Missouri—longer than itself above the confluence—and several other mighty rivers including the Arkansas and the Red. From the Appalachians come the Ohio and its important tributary, the Tennessee. Owing to its very gentle gradient, the Mississippi meanders widely in its lower course, and deposits large quantities of solid material on its bed, which has been built up to a higher level than that of the flood-plain. Consequently, despite the construction of man-made levees, *i.e.* reinforced high banks, the river rises high enough in some years to overflow its confines and to flood wide areas of well-cultivated, populous country. Hence its floods cause far more damage than those of the Mackenzie.

As a routeway, the Mississippi was greatly used in the pioneer days of the later eighteenth and early nineteenth centuries. It still carries a fair amount of traffic, such as cotton, lumber, and petroleum. But since the building of transcontinental railways, the main traffic movements of the United States have been east–west; also, railways and roads now follow its valley, and provide quicker and more direct means of transport for supplies carried north–south.

The St Lawrence, draining the Great Lakes, flows eastwards into the Atlantic. It passes through the most densely-populated part of Canada, and also serves a highly-industrialised portion of the United States. Man's ingenuity in overcoming various obstacles to navigation—waterfalls, rapids, and shallows—has converted a natural waterway into a well-used 2000 mile routeway. At a number of places, notably Niagara and Cornwall, stations have been erected to convert part of the immense power of the river into electrical energy. The St Lawrence, with a more regular régime than either the Mackenzie or the Mississippi, does not overspill its bounds and periodically flood its valley.

THE CLIMATE

Owing to its wide latitudinal range, its great extent from east to west, and its varied relief, North America has many climates which differ in temperature, precipitation, and minor elements.

TEMPERATURE CONDITIONS

Almost all parts of the continent have warm or hot summers, average July temperatures varying from over 90° F in the south-west (where skies are normally clear and the noonday sun almost overhead) to 50° in the northern parts of the mainland. Only the Arctic margins and the highest mountain areas are cool. The Atlantic and Pacific coasts, especially where they are washed by the cold Labrador and Californian currents, are less warm than the interior, but even places like New York suffer from occasional prostrating heat waves when warm air moves up from the south.

In winter there are wider regional variations in temperature than in summer. On the northern mainland the mean January temperature is —20° F, but in the lowlands of Central America it exceeds 70°. Very striking is the large part of the continent with January temperatures below 32° F; equally significant is the relative mildness of the coastlands of the Alaskan panhandle and British Columbia, favoured by warm air masses from the Pacific. Continental air meanwhile prevails over the corresponding eastern coastlands, and even Atlantic air is fairly cool as it crosses the Labrador current before reaching North America. New York, as far south as latitude 40 degrees N., freezes in January.

Apart from small areas which benefit from the moderating influence of the Great Lakes, the continental interior has exceptionally cold winters, owing to its distance from warm seas and to the lack of any east–west relief barrier to stop the invasion of biting Arctic air. Only when an occasional *chinook* (*see* Fig. 32) descends the eastern slopes of the Rockies in Canada and the northern United States does a short mild spell ensue, due to the heating of descending air by compression.

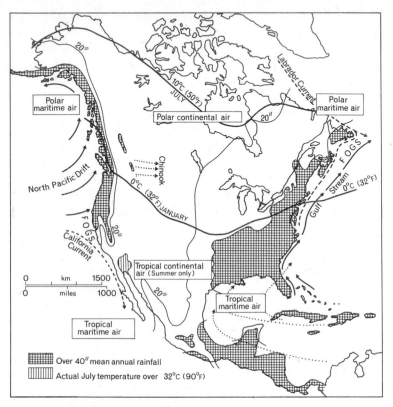

FIG. 3.—Climatic features of North America. Selected mean sea-level isotherms and mean 20-in. annual isohyets are marked. Solid arrows indicate warm ocean currents, broken arrows cold currents. The pecked lines over the Gulf of Mexico show the main hurricane tracks.

The mean annual range of temperature is extreme over most of North America except the west coastlands and the more tropical south. In parts of the northern interior the average range exceeds 80° F.

PRECIPITATION

Regional variations in precipitation are as marked as those in temperature. Westerly air streams bring heavy orographic rainfall throughout the year to the Pacific coast ranges of North America north of about

40 degrees N., while the north-east trades bring an equally heavy rainfall to the highlands of Central America and the West Indies. For example, Prince Rupert (British Columbia) has a mean annual rainfall of 103 in., Colón (Panamá) one of 127 in. By contrast, parts of the south-west United States and north-west Mexico, dominated by sub-tropical high pressures, are extremely dry. For instance, Yuma (Arizona) has only 3 in. of rain in an average year.

In summer the heated interior and south-east parts of the continent experience occasional convectional storms, but the greater part of the land-mass receives the bulk of its annual precipitation from temperate depressions or "lows." The rainfall, in other words, is of the frontal or cyclonic type. Depressions, born along the Polar front, cross the continent from west to east, most frequently in winter, and converge on the Great Lakes–St Lawrence corridor. In the eastern half of North America warm maritime air from the Gulf of Mexico frequently moves north and contributes to the formation of fronts in this region. Hence the mean annual precipitation of the continent tends to decrease moving westwards from the Atlantic to the Rockies, and also to be increasingly concentrated in the summer half of the year.

In central California there is a "Mediterranean" region of winter rain and summer drought, experiencing occasional winter "lows" from the Pacific, but subject to high-pressure conditions in summer, when the winds are mostly northerly and offshore. Farther south, however, along the west coasts of Central America, rainfall shows a marked summer maximum due to a monsoonal indraught from the Pacific. In winter anticyclones build up over this area, and the rains die away.

MINOR CLIMATIC ELEMENTS

While temperature and precipitation are the two principal climatic and meteorological elements, certain others merit consideration. It is important to know, for example, that the large number of hours of sunshine enjoyed by parts of California in summer has encouraged both fruit-drying and tourist industries, and played a part in the early development of the film-making industry. Conversely, the possibility of cold polar air sweeping southwards over the continent at any time of the year allows hardly any part of the United States to escape damaging frost from time to time. The fruit-growers of both California and Florida must always arm themselves against this threat by having ready in their orchards smudge-pots or other appliances.

Fogs, too, can be troublesome, especially to shipping and city transport. They are particularly common on the west coast of the United States and off Newfoundland and the north Atlantic coast of mainland Canada and the United States. The former are due to the chilling of warm maritime air as it moves over the cold Californian current, the latter due to the convergence of the warm Gulf Stream and the cold Labrador current.

The West Indies and the south and east coastlands of the United States may suffer from hurricanes, especially between June and October. These vehicles of destruction move from east to west along the trade-wind track in the Caribbean, and then curve north-eastwards in about latitude 20 degrees N. around the western end of the sub-tropical high over the Atlantic Ocean. Since the pressure gradient is exceedingly steep, hurricane winds may well exceed 100 miles per hour, and they are usually accompanied by torrential rains. Hence the passage of a hurricane is marked by a trail of ruin, in which crops, livestock, buildings, and people may all be involved.

REGIONS OF NATURAL VEGETATION, NATURAL SOIL, AND CLIMATE

Natural vegetation, soil, and climate are inextricably bound up together, since the latter is the main determinant of the other two. Consequently, if it is borne in mind that, when each of these distributions is separately mapped, there is some overlapping of boundaries—which does not matter much because boundaries are very seldom, if ever, linear in nature—it may be sufficient to divide the continent into broad regions of natural vegetation only, and to discuss their climate and soils at the same time. Two points must, however, be noted: (a) the pattern of both native vegetation and soil has been greatly affected by the activities of man as a feller of trees and as a cultivator; and also by the browsing of animals; (b) in high mountain areas there is a whole complex of climatic, vegetational, and edaphic forms which can be adequately analysed only by the intensive study of small areas.

Fig. 4 shows in a simplified form the natural vegetation regions of North America, an account of which follows. The large areas bearing a natural cover of forest should be noted.

1. *Tundra.* Here the mean annual temperature is lower than anywhere else in the continent save for parts of Greenland and a few mountain tops. Even the warmest month has an average temperature of less than 50° F. The winters are longer than elsewhere, and light snow normally carpets the ground for eight or nine months. The tundra is an area of

permafrost;* only the top few inches of infertile soil thaw out in the brief summer, when the ground becomes waterlogged. Only lowly forms of vegetation can thrive. They include mosses, sedges, and lichens, sporadic

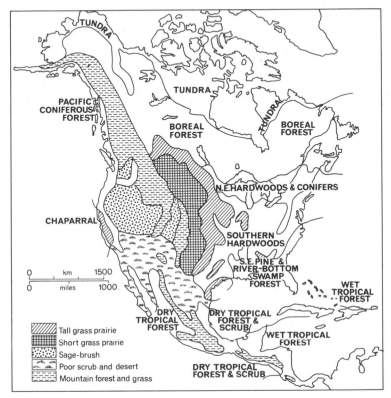

FIG. 4.—Natural vegetation of North America.

grasses (producing "Arctic Prairie"), and a few dwarf willows, birches, and other trees, which grow where the acid soils are deepest and where the summers are longest and warmest, *i.e.* along the water-courses and on the southern margins of the region.

2. *Northern coniferous forests.* In this region of "boreal" forests or *taiga*, as in the tundra, anticyclonic conditions are normal, except in the east, where Polar Front depressions bring both a heavy summer rainfall and a considerable winter snowfall. The summers are warmer and longer than in the tundra, and temperatures in some places may from time to time

* *I.e.* permanently frozen sub-soil.

exceed 60° F, but the winters are extremely severe. Soils, known as podsols, are thoroughly leached and markedly acidic. They bear only a thin layer of surface humus, mostly raw, and are of very low fertility, but they nourish an abundance of coniferous trees, including white spruce (the commonest), the balsam fir, and white and red pines. It should be noted that the taiga extends into the Upper Lakes region of the United States, where there is an important pine belt, and into northern New England and the Adirondacks.

3. *Pacific coniferous forests.* Bordering the Pacific Ocean in Alaska, British Columbia and the northern United States, and extending inland along the Sierra Nevada of California, is a region with a cool temperate, equable, moist climate. Dense coniferous forests—richer than those of the taiga, owing to the warmer, moister climate—clothe the windward slopes of the insular and mainland highlands. Among the more valuable trees are the Douglas fir, red cedar, and hemlock. On the Sierra Nevada flourish the giant sequoias, many of which are protected because of their great age and beauty.

4. *Mountain forests.* Because of their height, many Cordilleran ranges far from the sea have a heavier rainfall than lower areas, therefore forests—largely of conifers—may adorn them, though their tops may reach up to a zone of alpine flora and even permanent ice and snow.

The high Cordillera of Mexico and Central America and the higher parts of the West Indies similarly have a greater precipitation than adjacent areas, and usually carry forests of pine and cedar, though savanna occurs locally.

5. *North-eastern hardwood forests.* This region, in south-east Canada and the north-eastern United States, has a well-distributed precipitation, with severe but less prolonged winters than those of Region 2, and warmer summers. Soils are very mixed, but on the whole are less podsolised than those of the taiga. Native trees include deciduous hardwoods like beech, birch, maple, and oak, and—particularly on light, sandy soils—coniferous species like red and white spruce, pine, and hemlock. This forest is altogether richer in species than those already examined.

6. *Southern hardwood forests.* In this region the climate is transitional between that of Region 5 (cool temperate eastern margin) and that of Region 7 (warm temperate eastern margin). As in both these regions, rainfall is well distributed; the summers are rather hotter than those to the north, the winters very much warmer, but the growing season is shorter than to the south. The following six climatic stations are worth comparison, the first three situated on the Atlantic coast, the others farther west:

| Region | Temperature (° F) | |
	January	July
Boston 5	27	72
Washington . . . 6	34	77
Miami 7	66	82
Toronto . . . 5	22	69
St Louis . . . 6	32	79
New Orleans . . 7	54	84

The soils of the southern hardwood forests are usually brown or red, strongly weathered and moderately acid, with fair amounts of organic matter. They have responded well to cultivation when fertilised, but have become badly eroded in places, e.g. on the slopes of the Appalachians. Among native trees, the oak is dominant, but several species of pine are common in the south-east. In parts of the Appalachians, below the coniferous forest zone of mountain forests, there are chestnuts and yellow poplars, and in the north-west of the region hickory is locally important.

The southern hardwood forests extend in prongs up the valleys of the right-bank tributaries of the Mississippi, while tall-grass Prairie (see Region 10) thrusts eastwards along the better-drained interfluves.

7. *South-eastern pine and swamp forests.* The south-eastern United States is a region of very hot summers, mild winters (with rare frost), and a well-distributed rainfall of the frontal and convectional type. In the flat lands and river-bottoms, cypress, oaks, tupelos, cottonwoods, and red gums grow well. They are interspersed with coarse grasses and other undergrowth. Where soils are light and sandy, these trees are replaced by pines, notably the long-leaf varieties. Most soils are well-leached, and red or yellow in colour. They somewhat resemble those of the tropical regions, but being a little richer in minerals are not quite as infertile.

8. *Tropical forests, grasslands, and chaparral.* These hot regions occupy the oceanic coastlands of Mexico and Central America, and the lower parts of the West Indies. Their vegetation varies with the mean annual rainfall and the duration of the dry season. Where the rainfall is heaviest and the dry season shortest, tropical rain forests predominate, but elsewhere savanna and scrub forests (or tropical chaparral) appear, the density and size of the trees diminishing as the rainfall decreases.

9. *The Mediterranean region.* Owing to the great variety of its relief, which affects both temperature and rainfall, the Mediterranean region of

Central California, though experiencing ubiquitous summer drought, has many types of vegetation, ranging from the forests of "big trees" in the well-watered Sierra Nevada and northern Coast Ranges to chaparral (*i.e.* evergreen trees and shrubs, with stunted oaks and cherries, sumac and wild lilac) in the drier southern uplands, and bunch-grass in the central valley.

10. *Prairie regions.* Sandwiched between the pine forests of the Rocky Mountains and the hardwood and coniferous forests of eastern Canada and the United States are two great regions of natural cool temperate grassland: (*a*) the tall-grass Prairie in the east, with deciduous woodlands along the rivers; (*b*) the short-grass Prairie in the drier west, or Great Plains region. The line of division between the two is roughly the 20-in. annual isohyet. In both regions the rainfall is concentrated in the late spring and summer months, and the mean annual range of temperature is extreme.

In these Prairie regions the deep, lime-rich soils (mainly pedocals) are among the most fertile and friable in the world. In the moister east and north they are very dark in colour, owing to the large amounts of humus they contain, and they resemble the Russian black earths or *chernozems.* In the drier west, where there is less organic matter, the soils are mostly chestnut brown in colour.

11. *Temperate sage-brush.* Over most of the central and northern parts of the rain-shadow region of the intermontane basin and plateau country of the Western Highlands of the United States the rainfall is less than 20 in. yearly. It decreases southwards (just as it does along the Pacific coast). A few patches of pinyon and juniper woodland occur here and there (*e.g.* on the ridges of the Great Basin), but the vegetation is mostly that of mid-latitude steppes and deserts. Sage-brush, with grass in the shade of the bushes, is characteristic, but many areas are covered with drifting sands or occupied by shallow, salt-encrusted depressions known as *playas.*

12. *Tropical desert and semi-desert.* In the south-western United States, especially in the basin of the Lower Colorado River, and in north-western Mexico, including the peninsula of Lower California, pressures are usually high and winds are parallel to the Pacific coast; therefore the rainfall is very scanty. Temperatures show large seasonal and diurnal ranges. Large areas are occupied by plantless desert, but xerophilous vegetation, active only after occasional rainstorms, sprouts here and there. Various succulent plants like cacti and creosote bushes are typical.

The soils of this region are fertile, because aridity has preserved their soluble salts, but in places some of these have been drawn up to the surface to form the same kind of sterile alkali land that one may find in the temperate desert. This region, again, is of very limited agricultural value, except where irrigation water is available.

Much of the Mexican plateau has a better vegetational cover than the above-mentioned desert tracts, but even here bare, saline depressions (*bolsons*) appear. Generally speaking, however, there is fair grazing for beef cattle.

Chapter II

NORTH AMERICA : SOME ASPECTS OF HUMAN GEOGRAPHY

EUROPEANS did not begin their colonisation of North America before the sixteenth century. But agriculturally, industrially, and commercially, the continent is now as well developed as Europe herself. Moreover, the economic potential of this comparatively new land is probably greater than that of the old, as many North American resources are not yet fully utilised.

LAND UTILISATION

Originally, as we have seen in Chapter I, a large part of North America was forest-covered. Much of this forest remains, except in the north-eastern United States and the adjacent portions of Canada, where most of the hardwood timber has been removed, some of it too recklessly, in the interests of farming and settlement. The milder, southern skirt of the taiga, the Pacific forests of British Columbia, Washington, Oregon and northern California, and the Gulf–Atlantic pine belt are still being vigorously exploited for their valuable softwood timber and wood-pulp supplies, and forest conservation is now common practice. Hence the area of economically useful forest is diminishing at a slower rate than formerly, despite the continued reduction caused by fires and the spread of other forms of land utilisation. Altogether, North America produces a quarter of the world's forest products.

Most of the non-forested parts of the continent are in agricultural occupation. But farming is generally precluded in the tundra, and very limited in the taiga, by the brevity of the growing season. In the most mountainous areas, which suffer from steep slopes, cold weather, and thin soils, farming may also be impracticable. The principal areas of cultivation, therefore, lie in the comparatively warm, moist south-eastern quadrant of North America. Here climatic variety is reflected in a heterogeneous agricultural pattern. In the north pasture, fodder crops, and dairy cattle tend to dominate the scene, though spring-sown wheat is the main source of income in the western part of this region. Southwards, where the summers are longer and warmer, winter wheat and maize take precedence, and dairying largely gives way to the raising of beef and bacon. As the growing season lengthens still further, in the south-eastern United States, most farmers have come to depend upon cotton or tobacco, while along the hot Gulf shores rice and sugar-cane occupy considerable areas (see Fig. 49). Along the sandy Atlantic margins of the United States, truck-farming (the American name for market-gardening) is well developed, while on the tropical lowlands of Central America there are many banana plantations. The main economic crop of the West Indies is sugar-cane.

West of about longitude 100 degrees W., where the mean annual rainfall drops below 20 in., the grazing of cattle and sheep, largely on native grasses, generally replaces the cultivation of the soil as the dominant form of agricultural activity, though the main wheatlands of Canada lie west of this line (evaporation decreasing northwards). In a number of restricted areas in the west the availability of irrigation water has encouraged intensive cultivation. Near the Pacific, in the fertile valleys leeward of the Coast Ranges, fruit-growing tends to be the most impor-tant branch of farming. This is particularly true of the productive Central Valley of California.

The total agricultural production of the United States is far in excess of that of either Canada or Mexico, partly because of its more favourable climates. Its mid-latitudinal position excludes from it the very cold areas, but since it extends southwards almost as far as the Tropic, it can grow successfully a rich variety of crops. Its earth, in fact, has been so fruitful that it has often been abused, and large areas have become badly eroded as a result. Unfortunately, until very recently, soil conservation measures have lagged behind land spoliation.

MINERAL WEALTH AND POWER SUPPLIES

North America is not only rich in forest and agricultural land. Beneath its soils lie some of the world's most abundant mineral reserves, and many of its surface rivers, e.g. the St Lawrence, Columbia, and Colorado, are noted for their tremendous water resources. These mineral deposits and water-powers have already been extensively utilised, but in some areas they remain untouched. Their exploitation may be uneconomic owing to the small scale on which they occur or because of their inaccessible location, e.g. in the tundra.

For many years now, the United States has been the world's chief producer of petroleum, natural gas and hydro-electric power, and in most years it outrivals the U.S.S.R. in coal production. Canada is the second most important source of hydro-electric power, and a rapidly expanding producer of petroleum and natural gas. Mexico has long had productive oil-wells, but as it is poorly developed industrially has not yet gone very far in the utilisation of its other power resources.

The United States stands out as the world's foremost producer of lead, copper, molybdenum, vanadium, uranium, sulphur, salt, gypsum, and phosphates; Mexico leads in silver, Canada in nickel, zinc and asbestos, Jamaica in bauxite, and the continent as a whole ranks very high in the output of iron ore, potash and gold. Most of these minerals are located in either the Canadian Shield or the Western Cordillera, but it is the Central Plains and Plateaus which have the largest petroleum deposits (mainly in the west) and the greatest coal supplies (mainly in the east).

The continent as a whole accounts for about one-third of the world's mineral output, and is markedly deficient only in manganese, chrome, tin, and diamonds among the minerals of major economic value.

INDUSTRIAL DEVELOPMENT AND MANUFACTURING REGIONS

North America's importance as a source of mineral and power supplies is matched by the scope of its industrial development. Manufacturing regions, however, do not take up large tracts of country like vegetational and agricultural regions, and are much more irregular in their distribution (see Fig. 5). The main ones have assumed major significance only during the last century, and the minor ones only during the last generation or even the last two decades.

Thanks in the main to the early settlement of the eastern parts of Anglo-America, to the full-scale development of its large resources of coal, hydro-electric power, and iron ore, to the closeness of its transport network, and to the advantage man has taken of its natural harbours to build well-equipped ports, the main manufacturing region of the continent is situated in the north-east of the United States and the south-eastern fringe of Canada. It is roughly bordered on the north by the Shield and the highlands of New England, and on the south by a line joining St Louis to Baltimore. This region accounts for nearly two-thirds of the total volume of manufactures produced in North America. It includes most of the large steel and engineering works, the chief rubber, leather, woollen, and clothing establishments, many of the pulp- and paper-mills, some of the chief aluminium plants, the principal printing and publishing firms, many of the food-processing works, and some of the cotton and chemical factories. Here lie most of the very big cities of North America: New York, Chicago, Philadelphia, Detroit, Montreal, Toronto, Baltimore, Cleveland, St Louis, Boston, Pittsburgh, Milwaukee, and Buffalo. The very large and diversified population of the region (nearly half the combined population of Canada and the United States) provides not only a valuable source of labour but also one of the world's most prosperous internal markets.

During the present century a second significant manufacturing region has taken shape in North America, south-east of the main industrial region. It runs roughly parallel to the Atlantic coast from Richmond

FIG. 5.—Main cities and manufacturing regions of North America. Shaded portions indicate the major manufacturing areas.

in the north to Birmingham in the south, and spreads over much of the Appalachian Piedmont country; recently it has shown signs of expansion into the Tennessee valley. Steel and paper are made, and tobacco is processed, but the main industry is the manufacture of cotton and rayon textiles. The main source of power is falling water.

Large-scale industrial development is now taking place along the Gulf coast, notably in Texas, where oil-refining, base-metal smelting, and the manufacture of petro-chemicals are pre-eminent.

A number of small areas along the Pacific coast have also taken up many new industries, especially during the last twenty-five years. These areas include the Los Angeles Metropolitan area, the San Francisco–Oakland conurbation, and the Vancouver–Puget Sound–Portland district.

Outside the United States and Canada, manufacturing in North America is not very important except in and near to Mexico City.

THE SPREAD OF EUROPEAN SETTLEMENT IN NORTH AMERICA

When the first Europeans began to enter North America as traders, missionaries, and colonisers they did not go into an empty continent, but into one already occupied, at least in part, by Indians (or Amerinds) and Eskimos, both of whom had probably first set foot in the New World via the Bering Strait. The total population, however, was no

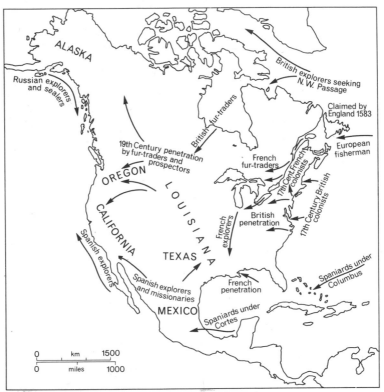

FIG. 6.—European penetration of North America.

more than a few million. Most of these people were devoted to hunting, though the Eskimos and the Pacific coast Indians were also sea-fishers, and a few groups in the interior had learnt how to grow such native crops as maize, pumpkins, and tobacco by shifting cultivation.

The newcomers came from various parts of western Europe, and entered North America by different routes (*see* Fig. 6). Following the voyages of Columbus, the Spaniards, interested in precious metals, penetrated Mexico, but their advance was keenly contested by the Aztec

Indians. Even after overcoming them, they were slow to expand, but by the early nineteenth century they had established a string of mission-stations which took them northwards into Texas and California. The Spaniards were also the first whites to occupy the large West Indian islands and the Central American region.

At the end of the sixteenth century French fur-traders and missionaries, and, at a rather later date, true colonists, moved into the continent via the St Lawrence, and eventually pushed beyond the Great Lakes into the Mississippi valley, where they established a line of fur-trading forts, including New Orleans (1719). They gave the name "Louisiana" to the whole of their possessions in the continental interior south and west of the Great Lakes.

Stirred by the example of the French, British fur-traders entered North America by way of Hudson Bay in the seventeenth century, and their fishermen occupied parts of what are now the Atlantic Provinces of Canada. Other people from the British Isles settled as colonists along the Atlantic fringe of what is now the United States, the southern groups importing Negro slaves from West Africa to help them develop planta-tions of tobacco and cotton. West of the coastal plain lay the Appa-lachians, a formidable barrier to movement into the interior, which, however, was crossed by pioneers in the mid-eighteenth century. Enter-ing the Ohio basin, these frontiersmen, for a time, had to strive for mastery with both the French and the native Indians.

Other Europeans, too, found a foothold along the east coast: Dutch, Swedes, and Germans in particular.

Following the Peace of Paris (1763),* which gave north-east America, including Canada, to the British, and the Declaration of Independence (1776), which initiated the freedom of the Atlantic colonists from British rule, American pioneers were able to continue—unmolested, save by Indian tribes—their migration over the Appalachians. After the Louisiana purchase (1803), which gave the United States the old French colony west of the Mississippi, the way lay open for a further advance, which took settlers from the forested lands to which they had been accustomed to the unfamiliar, open grasslands farther from the Atlantic seaboard. Eventually, explorers pointed the way through the difficult Western Cordillera, and the Pacific coast was reached. The way had been long, and often weary; it was bravely contested by the Indians, and only slowly had the frontier of settlement been driven westwards. Farms immediately west of the Appalachians were being established before 1800; by 1830 the tall-grass Prairies were partially occupied, and by 1850 the first gold-seekers had entered California. The frontier did not, however, disappear until

* The Peace of Paris ended the Seven Years' War between Britain and France.

about 1890, and many parts of the Western Highlands and High Plains were not settled until the present century.

Population spread across Canada more slowly owing to the wide barrier of the infertile Shield, and it was not until the 1880s that many migrants filtered into the Prairies. The first people to settle in Pacific Canada were lured there by the discovery of gold in 1858, but few made their homes there before 1890, after the Canadian Pacific Railway had reached Vancouver.

The main frontier of settlement is now no longer the west but the north. The taiga and tundra zones remain, for the most part, pioneer areas.

THE PRESENT POPULATION OF NORTH AMERICA

Compared with an Asiatic population of nearly 2100 million, and a European population of about 500 million, both exclusive of the U.S.S.R. (which itself exceeds 240 million), North America has the modest total of about 320 million, of whom almost exactly two-thirds live in the United States. Mexico has over 50 million, the West Indies more than 25 million, and Central America about 17 million. Canada supports little more than 20 million, Greenland less than 50,000.

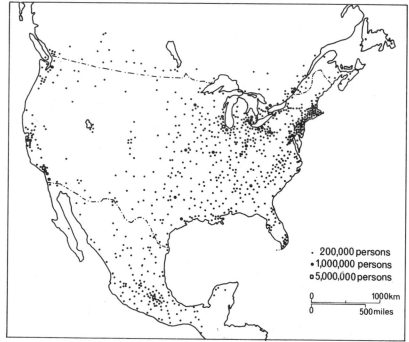

FIG. 7.—Distribution of population in North America.

Regional variations in population density reflect not only the influence of factors such as relief, climate, and accessibility but also the extent to which mineral and other resources have been utilised. The United States and Mexico have average densities of about 60 per square mile (not unlike that of the world as a whole), but Canada's density is only 6. These figures may be compared with those for the U.S.S.R. (28), England and Wales (over 800), and Australia (4).

People are very unevenly distributed through the continent (see Fig. 7). Ninety per cent of Canada, for example, is still virtually uninhabited; nearly all its people live along its narrow southern fringe, where the climate and soils are kindest. The United States is sparsely peopled in the

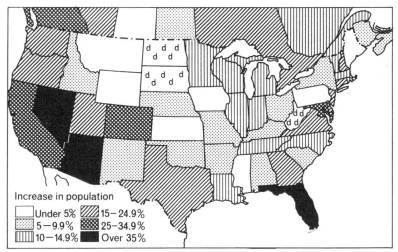

Fig. 8.—Percentage changes in the population of Anglo-America, 1960–70. d = 0–10% decrease in population; Alaska: increase of 33.6%; Newfoundland: increase of 14·0%; District of Columbia: decrease of 0·9%.

Cordillera, but densely populated in the east, where the moist climate favours cultivation, coal and iron have been developed as the basis for manufacturing industries, and the indented Atlantic coastline, facing Europe, has been utilised for port construction. In Canada and the U.S.A. the greatest rates of population increase are in the main being achieved by the Province of British Columbia and the western states of the United States (notably Alaska, Arizona, Nevada, and California) respectively (see Fig. 8).

In Mexico there is a pronounced concentration of population in the high, fertile, southern part of the Plateau, in which the capital is situated. The dry Pacific littoral and the north-western desert, and the hot, wet southern part of Yucatán, are very sparsely inhabited.

In Central America the high plateau areas again suit the Spanish and *mestizo* population more than the tropical coastlands. Nevertheless, high densities are found on the Pacific shores of Costa Rica and Salvador. Local densities are exceptionally high in the West Indies. In Puerto Rico, for instance, there is an uncomfortably high one of nearly 800 persons per square mile, consequently there is much emigration to the United States, especially to New York. In this city there are more opportunities for making a livelihood, but paradoxically even more crowding than in the homeland.

Many different national origins and languages are represented in North America. Both Canada and the United States are melting-pots of European nations, though people of British origin are most numerous. The west coastlands of both countries have proved attractive to Chinese and Japanese people, and 11% of the population of the United States is Negro. English is the official language of the Union, but both English and French are used in Canada.

By contrast, the European element in the population of Mexico and Central America is overwhelmingly Spanish in origin. In these lands, however, there has been much interbreeding with the native Indians, and a mestizo type has been produced. The Indians themselves, too, form a far larger element in the population than they do farther north. Most of the West Indian islands are strongly Negroid in character.

Spanish, of course, is the official language in Mexico and Central America (except in British Honduras) and also in Cuba, Puerto Rico, and the Dominican Republic. English is spoken in the British West Indies, French in the French West Indies and Haiti, Dutch in the Netherlands West Indies, Danish in Greenland.

Throughout the continent, many Indian dialects are spoken, and Eskimo tongues prevail in the tundra regions of Canada and Alaska, and along the fairly populous southern coastlands of Greenland.

STUDY QUESTIONS

1. Explain why the climates of the Pacific coastlands of North America differ from those of the Atlantic coastlands.

2. Describe the part played by air masses in determining the climate and weather of North America.

3. Discuss in relation to relief and climate the extent of boreal forests, Prairie grasslands, and deserts in North America.

4. Discuss the influence of relief and climate upon the pattern of agricultural activity in North America.

5. Illustrate the truth of the saying, "Go West, young man, go West," in relation to the evolution of settlement in North America.

PART TWO

CANADA

Chapter III

GENERAL PHYSICAL GEOGRAPHY

SIZE AND POSITION

WITH an area of about 3,850,000 square miles, Canada is the largest country in North America, and is the largest member of the British Commonwealth. The whole continent of Europe is smaller, and only two countries in the whole world—U.S.S.R. and China—surpass it in size. The Atlantic coast is more than 3000 miles from the Pacific, and it is farther from Vancouver to Halifax (Nova Scotia) than it is from Halifax to Liverpool.

The southernmost point of Canada is on Pelee Island (Lake Erie) in 41° 41′ N., the northernmost on Ellesmere Island in 83 degrees N. Canadian sovereignty actually extends over a sector of the Arctic Ocean to the North Pole. No part of the country has a climate warmer than cool temperate. Some of the ports are icebound in winter, and work on the land ceases for several months throughout the whole country with the modest exception of south-west British Columbia.

Canada's position in relation to the United States, the United Kingdom, and Russia is obviously important at the present time. The country is sometimes said to act as a hinge which helps to smooth relations between its neighbour to the south and the Mother of the Commonwealth. Northwards across the Pole, Canada faces the U.S.S.R., an aspect of its position which is vital to the United States as well as to Canada itself.

PHYSICAL FEATURES

STRUCTURE AND RELIEF

Reference to Fig. 2 will show that six structural regions may be recognised in Canada:

1. *Western Cordillera.* The main physical features of this region, shared with the United States and Mexico, trend roughly from north-west to south-east. Between the Coast Ranges and the Rockies is the dissected plateau of British Columbia, with the Upper Yukon Basin farther north.

25

2. *Appalachian Mountains.* This region, structurally older than 1, represents an extension of the main Appalachian region from the United States into the Maritime Provinces and Newfoundland. The main features trend from north-east to south-west; elevations—rarely more than 4000 ft—are generally much lower than those of the Cordillera, which have many summits exceeding 10,000 ft.

3. *Arctic Archipelago.* This region, unique to Canada, is largely mountainous, but belongs neither to the Cordilleran nor to the Appalachian system.

4. *Canadian or Laurentian Shield.* The Shield covers more than half of the country, and, as we saw in Chapter I, crosses the frontier into the United States. It consists mainly of a complex of resistant Pre-Cambrian rocks, round which the rest of the continent has grown. Round the southern shores of Hudson Bay, the Shield has been buried beneath undisturbed Palaeozoics, which form a coastal lowland.

5. *Great Lakes–St Lawrence depression.* Between the Shield and the Appalachians is a lowland trough consisting of a downfaulted belt of weak rocks, mainly Palaeozoic sedimentaries. Occupying the lowest parts are the Great Lakes, the River St Lawrence, and the lower courses of its tributaries.

6. *Central Lowlands.* This region, between the Cordillera and the Shield, extends north to the Arctic. Characterised by monotonous rolling plains, rising westwards, it is largely floored with almost horizontal beds of sedimentary rocks varying in age from Palaeozoic to Tertiary. Beneath these strata the Pre-Cambrian rocks of the Shield are buried.

SURFACE WATER

In recent geological times, as we have noticed (*see* Chapter I), Canada felt the full impact of the Pleistocene Ice Age. The effects of glaciation are still observable, *e.g.* in the incoherent drainage and lake-strewn character of northern Quebec and Ontario, in the glacial valleys of the Cordillera (*see* Fig. 9) and the fiords of British Columbia, in the drumlins and till soils of the Ontario Peninsula, and in the lacustrine deposits of Manitoba, where the present lakes, though large, are nothing more than remnants of the once extensive Lake Agassiz.

Six per cent of Canada's surface is occupied by fresh water, amounting in all to one-third of the world's fresh-water area. Any atlas map will show that the northern halves of Lakes Superior, Huron, Erie, and Ontario are in Canada, as are the whole of such large bodies of water as Great Bear Lake, Great Slave Lake, and Lake Winnipeg, but few atlases show more than a few of the thousands of small lakes in the Shield, and only large-scale maps reveal the many "sloughs" of the Prairie Provinces.

The Rocky Mountains form the main watershed in the country. Rivers like the Fraser, the Yukon, and the Columbia drain thence to the Pacific, but only the first of these is confined to Canada. The

[Courtesy: National Film Board of Canada

FIG. 9.—Athabaska Glacier, Albertan Rockies. A view from the Icefields Highway, Jasper National Park, of the Athabaska Glacier, issuing from the Columbia Icefield, source of the headwaters of the Athabaska, Saskatchewan and Columbia Rivers. Note the tributary cirque glaciers, the arêtes and the huge lateral moraine.

Mackenzie is the longest river flowing to the Arctic, the Nelson the longest to reach Hudson Bay. Other rivers make their way from the lower Shield watershed to Hudson Bay, which collects half the total drainage of Canada, or to the River St Lawrence.

CLIMATES OF CANADA

As has been noted, Canada's climates are not among the most favourable either to widespread agriculture or to international shipping. Though farming is rarely prohibited by aridity, the whole of the north suffers from a growing season which is too short for cultivation (*see* Fig. 10).

Everywhere, except in the extreme south-west, winter temperatures are below 32° F. North-eastwards from Vancouver, where the average

January temperature is 36° F, and north-westwards from Halifax, where the average is 24° F, midwinter temperatures decline to —25° F on the north-west side of Hudson Bay, and to —40° F in the northernmost Arctic islands, owing to the decreasing elevation of the midday sun and the increasing distance from oceanic sources of warmth.

Regional variations in July temperatures are smaller, though still largely controlled by the sun and the sea. The southern parts of the Lakes Peninsula (Ontario) and the southern valleys of British Columbia average 70° F, and nearly half the whole country averages more than

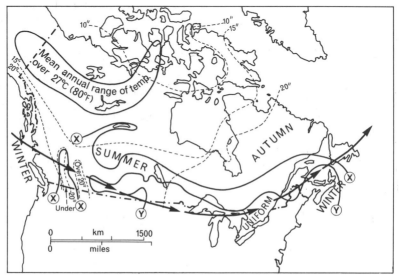

Fig. 10.—Climatic features of Canada. Selected mean annual isohyets are shown by broken lines and the most frequently followed storm track by arrows. Names of seasons refer to periods of maximum precipitation.

x–x = 100 frost-free day line.
y–y = 120 frost-free day line.

60° F. Occasional cold northers, however, penetrate all areas, and in the Arctic islands the average temperature of the hottest month may not exceed 35° F. The northlands, however, have one advantage: that of long hours of summer daylight. Hence vegetational growth is rapid, if short-lived. In the extreme north the midnight sun is visible for five months but, of course, in winter the night lasts for an equally long time.

Apart from the Pacific coastlands, Canada has an extreme or continental type of climate, e.g. Winnipeg has a mean annual range of temperature amounting to 70° F, parts of Yukon and the North-West

Territories one of 80° F. Even eastern oceanic provinces like Nova Scotia and Newfoundland have ranges of more than 35° F, since they are dominated by continental rather than by oceanic air masses.

Like January temperatures, Canada's mean annual precipitation tends to decrease moving north-eastwards from the Pacific coastlands and mountain flanks (which average 40 in. and 80 in. respectively), and also north-westwards from the Atlantic margins, where the figure is over 50 in. In the north generally, and also in parts of southern British Columbia and the southern Prairies, precipitation is usually less than 15 in. yearly, and may fall below 10 in.

The bulk of Canada's precipitation is of the cyclonic type, and is chiefly associated with the Polar Front, along which eastward-moving depressions develop as a result of the convergence of dry, cold Polar air masses and warm, tropical air masses. The latter originate in the Pacific, the Gulf of Mexico, and the Atlantic, and most commonly meet continental air masses in the Great Lakes–St Lawrence Gulf region. Convectional storms in summer, especially common in the heated interior, and orographic rain in British Columbia brought by Polar and Tropical maritime air, cause local increases in precipitation.

Except in the Pacific area of British Columbia and in the south-eastern quadrant of Canada, where precipitation is fairly well distributed through the year though tending to show a winter maximum, Canada's rainfall exhibits a marked maximum in summer or autumn, when average pressures in the interior are lower than at other times. Winter snowfalls are frequently heavy: the high Laurentians north of Quebec and certain parts of Newfoundland receive over 120 in., and most of even the drier portions of the interior generally have more than 40 in. of snow.

THE NATURAL VEGETATION OF CANADA

The climate of a country is mirrored in its natural vegetation, but locally changes are produced by variations in soils and drainage conditions. For example, in the boreal forests of Canada there are areas of *muskeg* (peat-swamp), and rocky districts may be covered with lichens.

Leaving aside local variations of this kind, it becomes possible to divide Canada into regions based on natural vegetation. The most significant boundaries are: (*a*) the July isotherm for 50° F, which roughly defines the northern limit of forest-growth, and (*b*) the line south of which there are six months with temperatures of at least 43° F—a line which, in eastern Canada, broadly separates the southern hardwood forests from the northern coniferous forests.

VEGETATION REGIONS

The following represents a simple scheme for dividing Canada into natural vegetation regions (see Fig. 11). It supplements the information conveyed in Chapter I.

1. *Western coniferous forests.* In this region the most luxuriant growth is that of western hemlock, western red cedar, and Douglas fir on the windward slopes of Vancouver Island and the Coast Range of British Columbia. Poorer forests are located: (a) in the dry, southern interior of the Province where yellow or ponderosa pinewoods alternate with a

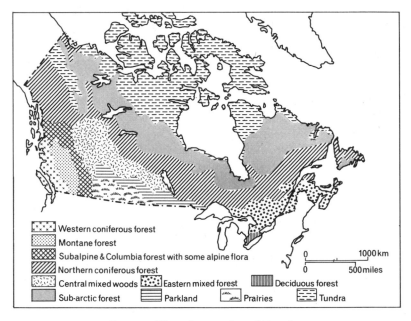

FIG. 11.—Natural vegetation of Canada.

steppeland vegetation of scrub and bunch-grass; (b) in the higher parts of the interior ranges, e.g. the Rockies and Selkirks, where forests of spruce and fir lie below the zone of Alpine tundra.

2. *Northern or boreal forests.* These forests, or taiga, include large stands of white and black spruce, balsam fir, white and red pines, jack pine and lodgepole pine, aspen poplar, and birches. The first three species in this list are particularly valuable as pulpwoods; the last two are hardwoods, though the aspen can be used for pulping.

3. *Hardwood and mixed forests of the Great Lakes–St Lawrence–Atlantic region.* Here there are more species than in any of the other forest regions.

Deciduous species—dominant in the south—include maples, beech, yellow birch, oaks, ash, elm, chestnut, and sycamore. Coniferous species —dominant in the cooler north—include pine, hemlock, white cedar, white spruce, and, in the Maritime region, red spruce. Smaller plants, such as raspberry, blackberry, blueberry, ferns, and bracken, are not uncommon.

4. *The Prairies.* In this region, as we have seen (p. 14), the grasses gradually become shorter moving westwards, as the mean annual rainfall diminishes. Except in some of the river valleys, and on occasional residual hills, trees are not naturally present.

5. *Central mixed woods.* This region covers most of the northern parts of the Prairie Provinces west of the boreal forests of the Shield. It suffers even less from evaporation than the northern Prairies, and is therefore able to support forests of white spruce, into which other trees like white aspen, Balm of Gilead (a fir from which Canada balsam is obtained), and white birch penetrate.

These mixed forests are divided from the Prairie grasslands by a transitional parkland or "aspen-grove" region, in which tall grasses are dotted with "bluffs" or clumps of aspen-poplar and other trees.

6. *Arctic tundra.* The tundra lies north of the tree-line, and is separated from the essential taiga by a transitional sub-Arctic zone where the trees are so scattered and stunted that the title "land of little sticks" has been bestowed upon it. The tundra itself—covering about a third of Canada— consists mainly of Arctic Prairie and heath interrupted by rocky areas carrying a very sparse cover of lichens, and in places Arctic ferns, crowberries, and other ground plants. The Arctic Prairie bears grasses, sedges, and various quick-growing flowering plants, while the heath is dominated by ground birch, heaths, bilberry, and cranberry.

A NOTE ON CANADIAN SOILS

It is not yet possible to classify Canadian soils satisfactorily on a regional basis owing to the lack of widespread pedological research. It can, however, be said that on the whole the best soils are those of the Prairies and adjacent parkland region. In the forested areas fertility generally deteriorates northwards. Mixed forests are usually floored with grey, wooded soils, whose upper or "A" horizon may be leached, but whose lower horizon is generally lime-accumulating. The podsols of the taiga, as we have seen in Chapter I, are excessively leached and are very infertile. Moreover, especially in the Shield, many soils are thin and stony, others waterlogged.

Chapter IV

GENERAL HUMAN GEOGRAPHY

DISCOVERY AND SETTLEMENT

EXPLORATION AND POLITICAL GROWTH

As we have seen (Chapter II), the indigenous people of Canada were Indian and Eskimo hunters and fishermen. A few of the former practised shifting agriculture in the south-east, but neither possessed domestic animals. Probably their way of life had not changed for centuries when the first Europeans discovered the country. These were Norsemen who had already made a home in Greenland, and who reached Canada in about A.D. 1000. Their voyages, however, were not followed up by settlement, and they were soon forgotten. It is possible that western Canada was discovered by the Chinese in the fifth century A.D., but the credit is usually given to the Danish navigator Bering, in Russian service, and the British sailors, Cook and Vancouver, each of whom sailed along the Pacific shores in the eighteenth century.

The first modern expedition to Canada was undertaken by John Cabot. He was a Venetian out from Bristol in search of the north-west passage to the East. In spite of ice and stormy seas, he succeeded in locating Newfoundland and Labrador in 1497. Prospects of settlement, however, he regarded as unpromising owing to the harsh climate and the lack of good soil. But Cabot reported most favourably upon the fishing-grounds off Newfoundland, and it was not long before a series of annual transatlantic expeditions were organised by fishermen from western Europe, including Basques, Bretons, Britons, and Portuguese.

Following the Venetian, in the sixteenth and early seventeenth centuries, many British explorers, *e.g.* Frobisher, Davis, Hudson, and Baffin, made important voyages of discovery, which revealed many of the straits and islands of the East Arctic Archipelago. It was, however, the celebrated voyage of Jacques Cartier which really led to the settlement of Canada. In 1535 the Frenchman sailed up the St Lawrence as far as the site of an Indian village now engulfed in Montreal; he was succeeded by a stream of French traders who were quick to enter into relations with Indian tribes for the barter of furs. One of Cartier's successors as explorer was the geographer Samuel de Champlain, whose travels resulted in the settle-

32

ment of farmers along the St Lawrence valley and in parts of Nova Scotia, where they were challenged by the British.

French fur-traders and Jesuit missionaries extended the Europeans' knowledge of the new continent by using the Great Lakes and the lakes and rivers of the Shield to penetrate deeper into the interior. There never came to be much permanent French settlement, however, beyond the St Lawrence valley lowlands, an area which came to be called Lower Canada, and is now the heart of Quebec Province.

Meanwhile, the British occupied the lowlands of New England (now the north-eastern United States), and established a few sporadic settlements in Newfoundland, the Maritime Provinces of Canada, and the coastlands of Hudson Bay. Fur-traders, pressing into the interior from their forts on Hudson Bay, clashed with the French, rival groups of fishermen strove with each other in Newfoundland, and the English traders of New York and New England came to blows with their French competitors in the Lake Ontario district and in Nova Scotia. In 1713 (Peace of Utrecht) France had to yield to Britain her claims to Hudson Bay, Newfoundland, and the mainland portion of Nova Scotia, but she was allowed to retain the small islands of St Pierre and Miquelon off Newfoundland, which she still holds. And, of course, the French continued to occupy the St Lawrence lowlands, where about 16,000 colonists were strongly entrenched in 1713.

The rivalry of Britain and France in Europe, and of British and French traders in North America, culminated in the Seven Years' War, as a result of which all Canada, except St Pierre and Miquelon, passed under British rule (Peace of Paris, 1763). The total white population was then about 65,000, but was shortly afterwards swelled by the advent of about 40,000 United Empire Loyalists, who left the United States (chiefly New England) for Upper Canada (Ontario) and New Brunswick after the American War of Independence. Immigrants from the British Isles also began to move in, very slowly at first, but by 1850 more rapidly. Avoiding the French-occupied districts in Lower Canada, and also the inhospitable Shield, they settled mainly in southern Ontario and the Maritimes, though one group, using the Hudson Bay entrance, founded an agricultural colony at Winnipeg, the first in the Prairies (1812). Farther north and west, fur-trading pioneers, with the help of Indian guides, gradually laid bare the secrets of the remoter parts of Canada. Prominent among them was Alexander Mackenzie, who, in the last decade of the eighteenth century, travelled down the river named after him to the Arctic, and made another journey across the Cordillera to the Pacific.

By 1867 the provinces of Upper and Lower Canada, Nova Scotia and

New Brunswick, joined together to form one self-governing Dominion of Canada. Three years later, Manitoba—the eastern part of what was then the North-West Territories—was created a province of the new Dominion. In the following year British Columbia entered on the promise of a transcontinental railway (completed, as the C.P.R., in 1885), and in 1873 Prince Edward Island came in.

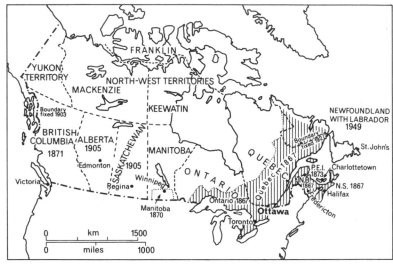

FIG. 12.—Political growth of Canada. The dates indicate the years when different provinces entered the Dominion. The shaded area shows those provinces which formed the Dominion in 1867. The cities named are the provincial capitals.

P.E.I. = Prince Edward Island.
N.B. = New Brunswick.
N.S. = Nova Scotia.

With the opening-up of the interior grasslands to agricultural occupation, following the building of railways, two more Prairie Provinces—Saskatchewan and Alberta—were formed (1905). The remaining northern part of the North-West Territories for long remained under the direct control of the Hudson Bay Company, which had been founded in 1670. But it is now divided, for administrative purposes, into Yukon (the far north-west) and the Districts of Mackenzie, Keewatin, and Franklin. These Arctic territories remain very thinly peopled, though Yukon experienced an influx of several thousands during the Klondike gold-rush, which began in 1897, and the other districts have recently achieved some importance as mineral-producing areas. Newfoundland, which includes Labrador, became a Canadian Province in 1949 (see Fig. 12).

Canada is now a completely independent country within the British Commonwealth. The central government, sitting at Ottawa, is in the hands of a Governor-General (the Queen's representative), who is supported by an upper and lower house (Senate and House of Commons). Each of the ten Provinces has a Lieutenant-Governor and an elected Parliament. The North-West Territories and Yukon are administered chiefly from Ottawa, just as the Northern Territory of Australia is from Canberra.

THE POPULATION

In 1850 Canada still had less than 3 million people, in 1900 5 million. Of the latter, only 8% lived in the Prairies, only 4% in British Columbia.

Since 1900, over 8 million immigrants have moved into Canada, not only from the British Isles but also from the United States, and—largely as farmers—from Scandinavia, Poland, Ukraine, Germany, Russia, and the Netherlands. Between 1900 and 1914 alone, 3 millions entered; the tide of immigration surged again after the First World War, and once more after the Second. In 1960 the 2-millionth post-war migrant came into the country.

At the 1971 census the total population of Canada was 21,586,311. Nearly three persons out of four live in the eastern provinces, the Prairie Provinces have about 16%, British Columbia about 10%. The provincial and territorial breakdown is as follows:

Territory	1961 census	1971 census	% increase, 1961–71
Ontario	6,236,092	7,703,106	23·5
Quebec	5,259,211	6,027,764	14·6
British Columbia	1,629,082	2,184,621	34·1
Alberta	1,331,944	1,627,874	22·2
Saskatchewan	925,181	926,242	1·1
Manitoba	921,686	988,247	7·1
Nova Scotia	737,007	788,960	7·0
New Brunswick	597,936	634,557	6·1
Newfoundland, incl. Labrador .	457,853	522,104	14·0
Prince Edward Island . . .	104,629	111,641	6·7
North-West Territories . . .	22,998	34,807	51·3
Yukon	14,628	18,388	25·7

Included in the population of Canada are about 180,000 Indians and 12,500 Eskimos. Of the total population, over 25% are French-speaking, and a minority of these can also speak English. Two-thirds speak English only, and just over 1% can speak neither English nor French, the two official languages. As regards national origins, nearly half are of British stock (though mostly Canadian-born) and nearly 30% are of French stock. The latter are virtually all of Canadian birth, as there has been no significant immigration from France since 1763. A considerable minority of the population (over 10%) stems from other parts of Europe, especially Germany, Italy, Ukraine, the Netherlands and Poland.

The average density of population is less than six per square mile, but most of the country still has less than one per square mile. More than half the population lives within 100 miles of the United States frontier, and well over 90% are gathered south of a line only 200 miles away. Cold climates and sparse communications still keep people away from northern Canada, so that—despite the Government's efforts to develop the north—the country continues to suffer from "top-heaviness."

Well over half the Canadians are concentrated in southern Quebec and southern Ontario, densities being highest in the St Lawrence Lowland and in the Lakes Peninsula. Most of the rest inhabit three widely separated areas: (a) the Atlantic coastlands and valleys of the Maritimes and Newfoundland; (b) the Pacific coastlands and southern valleys of British Columbia; (c) the southern parts of the Prairie Provinces.

Increasingly, the people of Canada are living in cities. In 1901 only 37% of Canadians were urban-dwellers, and there were only two cities (Montreal and Toronto) of over 100,000 people. In 1971, by contrast, nearly 75% lived in towns and cities, i.e. in places of more than 1,000 people, and there were twenty-two settlements housing more than 100,000. Ontario, Quebec, and British Columbia have the highest urban densities. Prince Edward Island, New Brunswick, and Saskatchewan are still predominantly rural. The growth of mining and manufacturing in Alberta and Nova Scotia has recently encouraged more urbanisation in these provinces.

The growth of population in Canada is becoming rather less marked, owing to a slightly reduced birth-rate and a diminution in the flow of immigrants. Between 1956 and 1961 about 2·16 millions (13·4%) were added to the total, but only 1·55 (7·8%) between 1966 and 1971. More and more people are following secondary and tertiary occupations, a development reflected in the rapidly growing urban population.

THE ECONOMY

Ever since the first Europeans began to migrate to Canada in the sixteenth and seventeenth centuries, the country has been mainly a source of primary products, at first chiefly fish and furs, later lumber, wood-pulp, wheat, precious and base metals. To these commodities may be added fruit and dairy produce, and, chiefly since the Second World War, natural gas, petroleum, uranium, and iron ore.

While Canada continues to produce and export all these commodities in large quantities, manufacturing has become much more important during the present century, and Canada has now gone farther towards industrial maturity than any other country in the British Commonwealth except the United Kingdom, though it remains a long way behind the United States in this respect.

FISHING

The fishing industry shares with fur-trading the honour of being the oldest commercial industry of Canada; both still play a considerable part in the country's economy, and both are largely dependent on foreign markets.

In most years 60–70% of Canada's fishery products are exported, largely to the United States. Dried fish is sent to Caribbean and Latin American countries, and tinned fish to western Europe.

There are several distinct fishing-grounds:

1. *North-west Atlantic.* This region includes the inshore lobster, herring, and other fisheries of the Atlantic Provinces and the more distant "Banks" cod fisheries. Over half Canada's fish comes from these eastern sources. Lobster has now surpassed cod as the most important individual catch, so that in some recent years Nova Scotia, the main lobster-fishing province, has earned more money from fishing than Newfoundland, traditionally concerned chiefly with cod.

2. *North-east Pacific.* This region produces some of the best salmon in the world, and also considerable quantities of herring and "deep-sea" fish, especially halibut. The value of salmon may reach 40% of the total Canadian catch of fish.

In both Atlantic and Pacific waters Canada undertakes conservation measures, especially as regards lobsters, oysters, and salmon, in order to maintain stocks. The use of fish hatcheries is growing, and more of the catch is being marketed by quick-freezing methods. The fleets of the more backward Atlantic area are being modernised, and much labour is being freed by the increased use of capital.

3. *Inland fisheries.* Fur-trappers have long valued Canada's rivers as sources of fish, and many sportsmen enjoy fishing week-ends and summer angling holidays, but commercial fishing in the interior has been slow to develop. Fair catches are now, however, being secured from the Manitoban Lakes, and Great Slave Lake. They include whitefish, eel, and blue pickerel. Fishing in Lakes Erie and Ontario has suffered from both the ravages of the sea lamprey and from chemical pollution, neither of which

is as yet controlled, though the Canadian Government has banned, as from 1972, the disposal in both the lower Lakes of certain chemicals found in industrial effluent.

FUR-TRADING

Just as the fish of the Newfoundland Banks drew many adventurers to the Atlantic shores of Canada, so did fur-bearing animals draw many traders and trappers to the mainland forests.

The fur-trapping industry remains chiefly in the hands of the Hudson Bay Company, which continues to employ many Indian and half-breed trappers and some whites and Eskimos, despite the spread of settlement and the extension of lumber and pulp industries, which destroy the natural habitat of fur-bearing animals. In northern Canada, outside scattered mining centres, it still forms the main, and over wide areas the only, commercial activity.

The development of fur-ranching has reduced the dimensions of the industry. The first ranch (a fox-farm) was set up in Prince Edward Island in 1894, and the idea of breeding animals instead of hunting them in the wild spread thence to every province in the country. Today there are 3000 Canadian ranches, many of them with hundreds of animals, which produce not only fox furs (now somewhat declining in fashion) but also mink, chinchilla, raccoon, marten, fisher, and nutria. Beaver, musk-rat (for musquash fur), and certain other species are still obtained almost entirely from trapping. About 6 million pelts are taken yearly from animals of all kinds, and farm-raised furs account for rather more than half the total by value. The main advantage of ranch-produced pelts is that the animals can be humanely killed, exactly when their furs are in the best condition, without damaging the pelt.

Winnipeg, the headquarters of the Hudson Bay Company in Canada, is the principal fur-collecting city. Exports go mainly to Europe and the United States, though Canada herself has a sizeable fur-manufacturing industry which produces goods worth more than 50% of her export furs.

THE LUMBERING AND WOOD-PULP INDUSTRIES

Prior to the European occupation of Canada, probably more than 60% of the surface was forest-covered. Even today, when more than 10% of the original forest has been cut or destroyed by fire, insects and disease, the forested area exceeds that of any other country except the Soviet Union (which has more softwoods) and Brazil (most of whose forests yield tropical hardwoods).

Over half of Canada's forests are productive, but not all are at present accessible to commercial enterprises. Three-quarters of the productive forests consist of softwoods, of which the most valuable species are the spruces, Douglas fir, and white pine. The principal hardwoods are the deciduous maple, poplar, birch, and beech.

Canada comes fourth among world producers of sawn timber, the United States and the U.S.S.R., and recently Japan, leading her. She is the world's principal exporter, however, and sends to other countries, especially the United States and Britain, three times as much as her chief rival, Sweden. The saw-mills of the Pacific Province of British Columbia account for about 60% of the country's output of commercial lumber, and most of the plywood and shingles.

Canada's position in the pulp and paper industry is even more outstanding. She produces 40% of the world's newsprint, and exports 90% of her production, the great majority of it to the United States. She also ships much pulp. The manufacture of wood-pulp and paper is Canada's largest industry whether we consider the value of production, the number of employees (about 350,000), the capital invested, the wages paid, or the amount of power consumed (about a quarter of Canada's hydro-electric power).

Between them, Quebec and Ontario account for three-quarters of Canada's output of newsprint, though there are important mills also in British Columbia and Newfoundland. The Prairie Provinces produce little, and Prince Edward Island none at all.

Favouring the development of Canada's pulp and paper industry have been the following factors, particularly applicable to mill-sites in southern Quebec and Ontario:

1. Accessibility to a large supply of softwood timber, notably spruce.

2. The availability of large supplies of cheap hydro-electricity.

3. The abundance of water for converting timber into pulp and paper.

4. The existence of relatively cheap and efficient communications, by water and land, for collecting the timber and chemicals required by the industry, and for distributing the finished articles.

5. The nearness of an almost insatiable market, the United States.

AGRICULTURE

Owing to her low population density, Canada is in the fortunate position of producing a surplus of farm products, with which she can help to feed people in more densely populated lands such as Britain. Apart from the Prairies and a few other very restricted areas north of lat. 50 degrees, however, the only important tracts suited by relief, climate, and soil to farming are confined to a narrow belt close to the United States. Here are the Ontario Lakes Peninsula, the St Lawrence Lowlands, Prince Edward Island, and a few coastal and valley districts in southern British Columbia and the Maritime Provinces. Between them, the Prairies and the Great Lakes–St Lawrence Lowland produce 90% of Canada's agricultural output.

Extensive grain-farming dominates the agricultural economy of the Prairies, though the drier parts are used for large-scale cattle- and sheep-ranching, the more populous for mixed farming and dairying. Large amounts of wheat, and smaller quantities of barley, rapeseed and animal products are exported from the Prairies each year.

Farmers in the more thickly peopled areas of eastern and western Canada concentrate upon intensive mixed farming and dairying. Specialised fruit-farms occur in the warmer districts, e.g. the Okanagan valley in the southern part of the British Columbian interior, the lake shores of south-eastern Ontario, and the Annapolis valley in Nova Scotia. Apples are Canada's chief fruit, followed by strawberries, peaches, grapes, blueberries, raspberries, cherries, pears, plums, apricots, and logan-berries. Most of the small fruits are grown for local consumption, the larger fruits have a wider distribution, and apples are the chief export. The number of fruit-processing and freezing plants is growing, and more use is being made of mechanical sprays to safeguard the higher-quality fruits from disease.

Though, as we have seen, an increasing proportion of Canadians are living in urban areas, 10% of all gainfully employed Canadians work on the land. Since the 1930s, small increases have taken place in the total cultivated acreage, and the output per man has grown by 100%. Yet the manpower employed in agriculture has declined. How is it that the farm output has increased while the number of farm-workers has fallen? Crop varieties have been improved, fertilisers more generously applied, there has been a general upgrading of stock, but the main reason is extended mechanisation and electrification. As tractors have multiplied, horses have been reduced in number. Not all parts of Canada have benefited from these recent improvements. On the Isle of Orleans below Quebec, for instance, one may still see oxen pulling old-fashioned ploughs.

The typical Canadian farm—if one exists—is operated only by a farmer and his family, though a little hired labour may be called in at busy periods, especially harvest-time. Hence the size of farms tends to be governed by the area an average family can manage. It may be only about 15–20 acres if a fruit-farm, 100–150 if a dairy or mixed farm, 320–640 (depending largely on soil and rainfall) if a Prairie grain-farm, up to

10,000 acres if a sheep or cattle ranch. The average farm size is slowly increasing, except in the Prairies, where mixed farms are becoming more numerous, and now averages well over 300 acres.

Canada still possesses potentially useful cultivable land. The most promising areas are the Mackenzie and Liard valleys, and the central parts of the British Columbian plateau, where, over fairly wide areas, climatic and soil conditions are suitable for the extension of agriculture, but where means of transport are inadequate and from which markets are distant. The recent piling-up of grain surpluses in the Prairies, which have enjoyed a long series of excellent harvests, is not at present conducive to the development of these lands. Farm intensification is going ahead more quickly than the extension of farm acreages.

MINES AND POWER SUPPLIES

As a primary industry, mining takes second place only to agriculture in the Canadian economy. When considering the spacing of these activities, it is important to notice that, broadly speaking, minerals occur in areas not well suited to agriculture, namely in the Canadian Shield, the Cordillera, and the Appalachians. Only in the case of Prairie coal, petroleum and potash are large mineral deposits located in important farming areas, i.e. in the sedimentary basin between the Rockies and the Shield.

The value of minerals produced in Canada increases yearly. Canada, however, like the United States, has its ghost towns, notably in the Klondike district of Yukon, and the minerals which are most valuable at one time are not necessarily those which are most rewarding at another. Since the Second World War, for example, petroleum, uranium, and iron ore have all made phenomenal advances, while coal and silver have declined.

For many years, Canada has led the world in the production of nickel, chiefly from the Sudbury deposits in Ontario, and of asbestos from the Eastern Townships of Quebec. She has recently attained first place also in zinc. Other leading minerals include potash (from southern Saskatchewan), the platinum metals (largely a by-product of nickel-smelting), gold and silver, cobalt, uranium, gypsum, copper, lead and iron ore. The last-named is drawn chiefly from the Ungava (Labrador–Quebec border) deposits and from Steep Rock, Ontario.

The search for minerals during the last 30 years has taken Canadians into many of the more remote parts of the country, especially into the thinly peopled Shield. When the size or richness of the deposits has justified it, equipment has been flown in by charter aircraft, and roads and railways have followed. Pioneer towns like Uranium City, Schefferville

(p. 58) and Yellowknife (a gold-mining centre—*see* Fig. 13) have almost literally sprung to life, and new names have begun to appear in our atlases.

In the past Canada has been largely dependent economically upon the United States, which has supplied her not only with manufactures, petroleum, cotton, and other sub-tropical products but also with manpower. The position is changing somewhat, and the United States is now beginning to look to Canada, not simply for increasing quantities of

[*Courtesy: National Film Board of Canada.*

FIG. 13.—Yellowknife, N.W.T. This town is a gold-mining centre on the north shore of Great Slave Lake. Note the rocky, lake-strewn background of the intensely eroded Shield.

timber, wood-pulp, nickel, and other minerals the northern country has worked for years but also for uranium, iron ore, and petroleum, which Canada scarcely produced before the War. American companies are playing the major part in the production of these new Canadian minerals.

For a country which has scarcely stepped beyond the threshold of modern industrial development, Canada has abundant, if not altogether well-distributed, power supplies. In 1950 coal furnished over half her total energy requirements, but today it provides less than a quarter. Her chief fields are in Cape Breton Island (Nova Scotia), Alberta, and British

Columbia. The place of coal is being increasingly taken by petroleum and natural gas, the production of which, especially in Alberta, has grown enormously since the new discoveries near Edmonton in 1947. Today, petroleum is Canada's most valuable mineral. Thousands of miles of pipeline have been laid down, and Canadian petroleum (and also gas) are now being distributed to refineries in all parts of Canada except the lower St Lawrence valley and the Atlantic Provinces. Canada has indeed become the main centre of oil production in the British Commonwealth, and has even found markets in the United States.

Water power (known simply as "hydro" in Canada) has long been the chief source of electricity in the country. The capacity now approaches 30 MW, an amount equivalent to 60 million tons of coal. Canada is second only to the United States as a source of this form of energy, and is surpassed only by Norway in production *per capita*. Apart from the recently completed Kemano and Peace River projects in British Columbia, the largest power-stations are located close to the high southern edge of the Shield in Quebec, at Niagara, and along the River St Lawrence. Large amounts are used by the saw-milling, pulp, and paper industries, and also by the large aluminium works in Quebec and at Kitimat (British Columbia). Probably little more than a third of Canada's vast potential has yet been realised.

The first commercial power-stations to use nuclear fuels have now been built in Canada (Ontario and Quebec), and the country has several mines producing uranium, especially important being those at Elliot Lake (near the Georgian Bay lobe of Lake Huron) and those at Uranium City (on the north shore of Lake Athabaska). Uranium has been exported to the United States, mainly for defensive purposes, and is at present going to the United Kingdom and Spain, chiefly for commercial purposes.

MANUFACTURING INDUSTRIES

Owing, no doubt, to the obvious importance of primary products among Canadian exports, it is not generally realised that manufacturing now comes first among Canadian industries, both in employment and in the value of the output. In fact, as many Canadians find work in manufacturing as in farming, forestry, mining, and fishing combined.

Canada, however, is not a manufacturing country of long standing. Until the present century the only large fabricating industries were those concerned with the processing for sale of various domestic foodstuffs and raw materials, *e.g.* wheat (milled into flour), meat (prepared and packed), milk (converted into butter and cheese), timber (made into planks, shingles, pulp, and paper), copper and nickel (smelted), and salmon (canned).

Since 1900 not only have the above industries grown larger, but others—in many cases based on imported materials or on newly discovered domestic supplies—have been added. Canada has now a steel industry half as large as that of Britain, and she turns out a great variety of metal goods, including motor cars, aircraft, and farm machinery. Associated with the vehicle industry is the manufacture of tyres and other rubber goods. Her aluminium industry (based on imported bauxite and alumina) is one of the largest in the world. The advance of domestic oil production has led to the building of about forty refineries and a number of petrochemical plants, which produce fertilisers, nylon, synthetic rubber, paints, explosives, detergents, etc. Cotton and wool are imported and converted into textiles and clothing, and there is a rayon industry.

Manufacturing industries, like other occupations in Canada, are unevenly scattered over the country. The chief region—producing 80% of the total products—is the Great Lakes–St Lawrence area in Ontario (the chief single manufacturing province) and Quebec (the second). Both Provinces have important food-processing, textile, and engineering industries, but Ontario turns out nearly all the motor vehicles, Quebec most of the aluminium, pulp, and paper. Montreal and Toronto lead all other Canadian cities in factory production.

Outside Ontario and Quebec, the principal manufacturing districts are (a) the Vancouver area, concerned largely with saw-milling and timber using industries, shipbuilding, fish-canning, and oil-refining; (b) the larger Prairie cities, using mainly local materials in their oil refineries, chemical works, and food-processing plants; (c) scattered centres in the Atlantic Provinces, manufacturing paper, processing fish, and repairing ships.

The main reasons for the modern industrial expansion of Canada may be enumerated as follows:

1. The abundance of native raw materials from farms, mines, and forests.

2. The rapid growth of Canada's population, with its high living standards, which has created not only a considerable labour supply but also a rich domestic market.

3. The proximity of the American market (especially for newsprint and metals), the well-organised shipping facilities to other markets across the Atlantic and Pacific, and the development of a close network of domestic communications in the populous zone of Canada.

4. The expansion of power supplies through the development of coal-mining, petroleum and natural gas production, and hydroelectric power generation.

5. The growth of both domestic and United States' capital investment, encouraged by Canada's political stability.

6. The opportunity presented by the two World Wars and subsequent rehabilitation periods, when the older European manufacturing industries were unable to satisfy all their customers at home and abroad.

Chapter V

REGIONAL GEOGRAPHY : NEWFOUNDLAND AND LABRADOR

CANADIAN REGIONS

REGIONS are not easy to define, even when only a single criterion, *e.g.* physiography, climate, or natural vegetation, is employed. The task becomes almost impossible when all these, and other, more human considerations are taken into account.

Since the international frontier runs from east to west, whereas most other geographical trend lines go from north to south, the individuality of many Canadian areas extends into the United States. For instance, Canada shares the Western Cordillera, the Central Lowlands, and the Northern Appalachians with the United States. Moreover, areas of similar economy may be located on either side of the frontier. Hence the Prairie farmer of Saskatchewan, for example, has a far greater community of interest with the wheat farmer of North Dakota, who lives in a similar physical, climatic, and economic region, than with either the Polar Eskimo, the Shield miner, or the salmon-fisher of the Pacific coast, who all live in the same country as himself, but in different environments.

Yet Governments play such an important part in human life that the existence of international boundaries cannot be ignored. We may even be tempted to base our study of Canadian regions upon political units, *i.e.* upon the ten provinces of Canada, as D. F. Putnam and D. P. Kerr do in *A Regional Geography of Canada*. It is true that certain groups of provinces, if not so much single provinces, do have some personality of their own, as is shown by group-names such as "Prairie Provinces" and "Maritime Provinces," and it is also a fact that various statistics, *e.g.* population data, are normally available only for political units. But the choice of purely administrative divisions is not usually satisfactory because most provincial boundaries are astronomical lines which have no other natural significance, and also because within any one province there may be found several climatic, vegetational, pedalogical, and economic types, *e.g.* Ontario's Lakes Peninsula is distinct in every way (except administratively) from Ontario's Northland.

In his book, *Canada*, Griffith Taylor expresses the view that the major natural regions of Canada are best defined in terms of physiography. His minor regions (twenty in all) are obtained by examining the human response to environment, including density of population and the history of settlement. Thus his Western Mountains, Central Downfold, and the Eastern Shield and its margins each are said to have a populous zone, a transition zone, and a pioneer zone. He adopts as separate regions the Tundra mainland and the Arctic Archipelago.

It is interesting to compare Griffith Taylor's scheme with that of the Geographical Branch of the Department of Mines and Technical Surveys, which divides up Canada as follows: (1) Arctic Canada, *i.e.* the

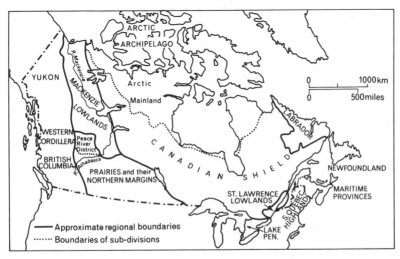

FIG. 14.—Geographical regions of Canada. The regions marked on this map are those used in this book.

Tundra; (2) Mackenzie Lowlands; (3) Laurentian Forest; (4) Prairie Pioneer Fringe; (5) Eastern Pioneer Fringe; (6) Gulf Region, *i.e.* Maritime Provinces and Newfoundland; (7) Great Lakes and St Lawrence Lowland; (8) Prairies; (9) Yukon; (10) Pacific Pioneer Fringe, *i.e.* northern British Columbia; (11) Southern British Columbia. In this attempt to define the natural regions of Canada, one of the most striking facts is the omission of any mention of the Canadian Shield as a distinctive unit.

Every classification has its limitations, and regional boundaries in such a new, developing country as Canada are constantly in a state of flux.

In this book the following regions, based partly upon structure, partly upon climatic and other natural factors, partly on economic life, have been chosen as a basis for a study of the regional geography of Canada:

1. Newfoundland, with Labrador as a sub-region.

2. The Maritime Provinces and the Highlands south of the St Lawrence.

3. The Great Lakes and St Lawrence Lowlands, including the lower Ottawa valley.

4. The Canadian Shield, including, as a sub-region, the Tundra part of the Canadian mainland.

5. The Prairies and their northern pioneer margins.

6. The Mackenzie Lowlands, north of Region 5.

7. The Arctic Archipelago of Canada.

8. The Pacific margins and Cordillera of British Columbia and Alberta.

9. The Cordillera of Yukon.

These regions are shown on Fig. 14.

NEWFOUNDLAND—PHYSICAL ASPECTS

Politically, Newfoundland includes Labrador. The latter belongs structurally to the Canadian Shield, of which it is in part the upturned eastern edge. It is, however, more akin to Newfoundland in some ways than to the rest of the Shield, since its outlook and people are essentially maritime. Hence it will be included in the present chapter, even though in the south it extends landwards into more typical Shield country.

Newfoundland and Labrador, with the Maritime Provinces of Nova Scotia, New Brunswick, and Prince Edward Island, are often referred to as the "Atlantic Provinces of Canada."

SIZE, POSITION, AND STATUS

The island of Newfoundland is not much smaller than England, and is nearer to the British Isles than one might imagine. Indeed, St John's, the capital, commands the western end of the shortest North Atlantic shipping route; the airport of Gander has a direct link of less than 2000 miles with Shannon in the Irish Republic; and many submarine cables, for telegraphs and telephones, terminate on the island.

Besides being at one end of a relatively short oceanic crossing, Newfoundland points the way to Canada. It stretches athwart the Gulf of St Lawrence, leaving two relatively narrow passages for ships proceeding up the river estuary: (a) the Strait of Belle Isle, about 10 miles across; (b) Cabot Strait, less than 70 miles across. To the south-east of Newfoundland is a large continental shelf forming a broad platform submerged by shallow water. Called in the main the "Grand Banks," this relic of the Canadian mainland is as large as Newfoundland itself, and is covered with an accumulation of rock waste transported thence in summer by icebergs floating down with the Labrador current from the Greenland coast. (*See* Fig. 15.)

Seven years after John Cabot discovered Newfoundland in 1497, West European fishermen began to pay regular visits to the Banks, but not until 1621 was there any permanent white settlement on the island. Despite opposition from the French, who valued the area for the

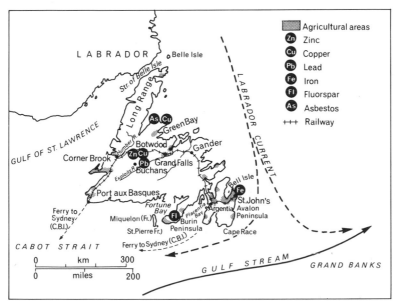

FIG. 15.—Newfoundland: general features.

temporary summer fishing-bases it afforded, Sir Humphrey Gilbert claimed Newfoundland for Queen Elizabeth in 1583, and the English were the first to settle it.

Newfoundland was granted its first Parliament in 1833, and, with Labrador, it formed a self-governing colony from 1854 to 1934. Unfortunately, during the twentieth century it did not earn enough money to pay for capital improvements such as railways, roads, and adequate community services. Its public debt grew, until by 1933 the Government found itself unable to meet the annual interest on its external loans, and it was obliged to revert to its former status as a dependency of Britain. From 1934 to 1949 it was ruled from London by six financial commissioners (three of them Newfoundlanders), and was helped by subsidies from the United Kingdom. During the Second World War, however, when a number of American air and naval bases were built there, Newfoundland recovered its prosperity, and in 1949 its people were given the chance to decide the colony's future by a referendum. Should it become independent again, should Commission rule continue, or should it join the Federation of Canada? By a narrow majority, the Newfoundlanders chose to throw in their lot with Canada, and on April 1st, 1949, their country, along with Labrador, became Canada's tenth province.

Newfoundland today, though much better off than it was in the 1920s and 1930s, lags behind most of the rest of Canada in transport services, health, and material prosperity, but all these are slowly improving.

PHYSICAL GEOGRAPHY

Like the Laurentian Shield, most of Newfoundland consists of a glaciated plateau of Pre-Cambrian rocks, though Lower Palaeozoics—belonging to the Appalachian system—outcrop in the west and occupy large parts of the Gander and Exploits valleys.

As in the Appalachians, the main relief features trend from northeast to south-west. Notable is the Long Range, 300 miles long, which exceeds 2000 ft in elevation. Most of the island is over 1000 ft high. Pleistocene ice-sheets stripped much of the ground of its soil and contributed to the formation of muskeg and the thousands of lakes which together cover one-third of the surface. The many coastal fiords are another legacy of the Ice Age. Only where lowland areas are floored by Palaeozoic sediments is there generally much soil; consequently, both commercial forests and agricultural areas have a very restricted distribution.

Climatically, as well as physiographically, Newfoundland has been ill served by nature. Though insular, the region does not greatly benefit from its Atlantic location, even though its latitude, on the whole, is more southerly than that of the British Isles. Winter temperatures are unpleasantly low, as the island is dominated by Polar continental air masses, but even when air moves in from the sea it is usually chilled by its passage over the cold waters of the Labrador current. Warm air from the Gulf Stream rarely penetrates Newfoundland, but the mingling of air from the two opposed currents produces fog, which is almost endemic over the Banks and in coastal areas to a distance of about 20 miles inland. At Cape Race half the days in the year are usually foggy. Visibility is especially poor in summer, when Atlantic air reaches the island most frequently.

Summer temperatures are about the same as in Scotland, but the growing season lasts only four to five months in most places. Only in the Corner Brook district, in the south-west, do July temperatures exceed

60° F. In winter temperatures everywhere are below 32° F, and rarely rise above freezing-point for four months. Except in the south, the shores are ice-bound at least in February and March. Belle Isle, in the north, has a January average of only 9° F. In most places the average annual range of temperature is 35°–40° F.

Precipitation is well distributed, though there is a winter maximum. Winter snowfalls are very heavy, and exceed 120 in. in the central parts of the island. Most of the precipitation, whether rain or snow, is of the frontal type, and is associated with the passage of depressions down the St Lawrence valley *en route* to the north Atlantic. It is heaviest, taking the year as a whole, in the south and east, lightest in the north-west, and generally exceeds 30 in. annually.

Climatic statistics for St John's are typical of much of the island:

	J.	F.	M.	A.	M.	J.	Jy.	A.	S.	O.	N.	D.
Temperature (°F) .	24	23	28	35	42	50	56	59	54	45	38	29
Precipitation (in.) .	6	6	5	4	3	4	4	4	3	6	6	5

Mean Annual Temperature: 40° F; Mean Annual Range of Temperature: 36° F; Mean Annual Precipitation: 56 in.

Though climatic conditions favour the growth of coniferous forests in Newfoundland, only about a quarter of the surface is in fact well forested, because of the absence of soil in many upland tracts, the wide occurrence of poorly drained terrain, favouring muskeg, the elevation of the highlands, leading to tundra, and the extensive areas of fresh water.

The commonest forest trees are spruce, balsam fir, and tamarack. The two former are associated with the better-drained valley slopes. Apart from the birch, which is widespread, almost the only deciduous species are confined to the south-west, where summers are warmer than elsewhere.

NEWFOUNDLAND—THE ECONOMY

THE FISHERIES

Fish from the surrounding seas still represent the only widespread resource of the Newfoundlanders. Fishing is the oldest industry, and remains the most important. Directly and indirectly, it provides the livelihood of nearly half the people. Normally, the island lands more fish annually than any other Canadian province, but the value of the catch (largely cod) is generally exceeded by that of Nova Scotia (mainly lobster) and British Columbia (chiefly salmon).

Between March and September, fishermen leave the outports to seek

cod, haddock, mackerel, hake, and other fish, which throng the Grand
Banks at this time of the year. Braving the perils of icebergs, sudden
storms, and fog, some of them still use the old-fashioned "banker," *i.e.* the
traditional schooner, and catch their prey by long-lines, carefully paid
out from the small "dories," or boats carried to sea in the mother ship.
Delivered periodically to the banker, the fish are salted down and
then taken ashore, where they are washed and dried in the open air
on platforms and shelves known as "flakes" (*see* Fig. 16). Fish dried in this

[*Courtesy: National Film Board of Canada.*

FIG. 16.—Drying cod, Newfoundland. The fishermen shown in the photograph are placing cod
to dry on "flakes" at Pouch Bay, one of the
numerous inlets along the Newfoundland coast.

way are exported to the Caribbean and Latin American countries, and
even to the Roman Catholic countries of southern Europe, where Friday
is a meatless, but not a fishless day.

Slowly, the Banks fisheries are being modernised and made more
efficient, and the life of the sailors is being eased. After the stunning
Titanic disaster of 1912, an International Ice Patrol was established to
warn ships of the whereabouts of icebergs. More effective coastguard
services have been introduced, and since the Second World War the
development of radar devices has helped. Schooners are steadily being

replaced by larger, faster, diesel-powered vessels, many of which carry trawl-nets. Refrigerated chambers are being installed, and centralised freezing and processing plants are being provided in the main settlements. Fresh, deeply frozen cod, in the form of small fillets or "fish sticks," are being increasingly marketed in North America and even in Europe.

Besides fishing on the Banks, many Newfoundlanders visit the waters off Labrador. Others, operating mainly in winter and spring from Fortune Bay on the south coast of the island, go out with the purse seine fleet in search of inshore herring, second only to cod in the quantities caught. Lobsters are potted on the rocky south and west coasts. Salmon are hunted off the east coast, and in some of the rivers sportsmen and tourists try their skill.

In March and April a number of fishermen move north in search of seals, whose pelts make good handbags and motor-cycle seats, and whose fat provides an illuminant for some of the older lighthouse lamps as well as a soap-making material. An occasional arctic whale is brought ashore.

Closely associated with Newfoundland's fishing industry are the skills of barrel-making, rope manufacture, boat-building, the extraction of fish and seal oils, the canning of lobster, and the preparation of fish glue and fertiliser.

It may be asked why the fishing industry has continued to occupy so many Newfoundlanders for so long a time. The main reasons for this are:

1. The 6000-mile coastline, with its numerous inlets, provides ample shelter and anchorage for thousands of craft.

2. The meeting of the Labrador current and Gulf Stream in the vicinity of the Grand Banks appears to stimulate the growth of plankton, on which large numbers of fish feed.

3. The shallow waters surrounding the island provide excellent breeding-grounds for fish, as the sun can penetrate nearly to the sea-bed. Also, the sea-bed is smooth and can easily be reached by fishing-gear.

4. Despite a shortage of capital, the traditional skills of the fishermen are still valuable, and it has never proved impossible to find a market.

5. The physical geography of the island precludes much agriculture and internal development.

6. The forests of Newfoundland provide plenty of wood for various ancillary industries and items of equipment.

THE PULP AND NEWSPRINT INDUSTRIES

Newfoundland has a very large number of small saw-mills, which are especially numerous on and near to the west and east coasts, but the manufacture of pulp and paper affords more employment.

In 1909 Lord Northcliffe, wishing to possess his own supply of news-print for his newspaper, the *Daily Mail*, launched the Anglo-Newfound-land Development Company, which purchased 2500 square miles of forests and established the first large paper-mill in Newfoundland. This mill was situated at the hydro-electric power site of Grand Falls, which has since become the site of the island's largest inland town. The original factory has now been extended, the forest concession augmented, and the port of Botwood firmly established on the Exploits River to export the Company's products. In 1923 a larger paper-mill—now owned by Bowaters—was built at Corner Brook on the Humber River. Near it today, at the head of Deer Lake, stands Newfoundland's largest hydro-electric power-station, and round it stretches a well-forested region ex-tending into the northern peninsula. Corner Brook has become the second largest city and port in the province.

These large paper-making concerns benefit considerably from the physical character of Newfoundland. High-level lakes, in narrow valleys, and the well-distributed rainfall favour the generation of water power, and the highly-accidented coast has allowed the building of mills on or near deep water and at the same time close to rich spruce forests. Cutting is done mainly in late summer and in winter, to some extent by part-time fishermen, and river log-drives begin in early May. But much timber is now transported along company roads, and some moves to the mills by rail.

FARMING

Owing to its rugged relief, inclement climate, and sterile soil, New-foundland is ill suited to commercial farming, and less than 1% of the surface is under crops, chiefly hay, oats, and vegetables. Real agri-culture, in fact, is restricted to the vicinity of towns, where there is a regular demand for milk and vegetables, and small fruits like goose-berries, raspberries, and strawberries. The rise of Corner Brook has stimulated efforts somewhat in the Humber valley, but the Newfound-landers must import much of their food.

Most fishermen in the small outports work small plots of potatoes and other vegetables in summer, and may also provide themselves with eggs and milk. A few mink-ranches have been started, and small flocks of sheep are grazed.

MINING AND MANUFACTURING

Until recently there were two important mining areas in Newfound-land: (*a*) Bell Island, in Conception Bay, about 12 miles north-west of St John's; (*b*) the Middle Exploits River district, near Buchans.

In the former district valuable deposits of iron ore had been worked since 1893 at the very large Wabana mine in the northern part of the island. The ore is rich but highly phosphoric and was mined both on the island and under the sea. Most of it was sent to Sydney, Cape Breton Island, for smelting, but occasional shipments were made to Britain. High operating costs and competition from the newer Labrador ironfield caused the Bell Island mines to close in 1966.

In the Exploits River district silver, lead, and zinc, together with gold and copper, have been produced since 1928. Production expanded greatly during the Second World War.

A little coal has been worked in south-west Newfoundland, but the seams are thin and faulted. In the Burin Peninsula over 90% of Canada's fluorspar is produced. Most of it is used in electric steel-furnaces, but it is sent out of Newfoundland for this purpose, and some of it finds a place in the chemical industry. Other minerals are only now coming into production on a commercial scale. They include copper and gold (from Tilt Cove and other northern coastal districts), asbestos (Baie Verte), and gypsum (west coast). Oil exploration teams are at present active on the Grand Banks.

Apart from the production of sawn timber, pulp and paper, and the manufacture of articles associated with the fishing industry, Newfoundland has little importance as a manufacturing area. Since it became a province of Canada in 1949, however, a few plants have been erected for the production of cement, gypsum wallboard, plywood, machinery, knitted goods, leather products, batteries, and chocolate.

ST JOHN'S

Easily the largest settlement, and with a population of 130,000, including its suburbs, St John's has a long, deep, ice-free, and almost land-locked harbour on the north-east side of the Avalon Peninsula, but is somewhat restricted for very large liners. It is approached via the "Narrows," a 300-yard-wide passage set between high cliffs which guard the harbour entrance. Passenger connections are maintained with New York, Halifax, and Liverpool. The city is the chief general port of the country, and the only significant seat of general manufacturing. Imports —which far exceed exports—include textiles, flour, metal goods, petroleum, and coal. Among exports are fish and fish products, and some paper (in winter, when Botwood and Corner Brook are frozen up).

St John's has the distinction of being North America's oldest city: it was founded in 1580. Its buildings, mostly of wood, are confined to the north-west of the harbour, as hills rise very steeply from the south-east shore. One of its newest structures is a small oil refinery, dependent on

Venezuelan petroleum. A larger refinery is now under construction at Come-by-Chance, a deep-water site at the head of Placentia Bay on the south coast, and seat of a new pulp and paper mill.

NEWFOUNDLAND—A SUMMARY OF THE HUMAN GEOGRAPHY

Physically, the Newfoundland interior is so unattractive to settlement that the total population of the island is less than half a million. Most people live on or close to the coast in over 1000 small fishing villages known as "outports," e.g. Harbour Grace, Bonavista, and Carbonear. Nearly all the rest are concentrated either in the capital or in the paper-milling city of Corner Brook. Most of the people are engaged in fishing, some in forestry, a few in mining. A mile inland, the greater part of Newfoundland remains an unproductive wilderness.

A circuitous railway, hugging the coastlands, and roughly paralleled by a motor highway, the eastern part of the Trans-Canada Highway, links St John's with most of the other settlements, e.g. Corner Brook, Grand falls, and Gander. It terminates at Port aux Basques, in the far south-west, a ferry-port for Sydney, Cape Breton Island. A short spur leads to Argentia in the south-east, another ferry-port. The rails have never served either the south coast as a whole or the northern peninsula, and have recently been closed to passenger traffic. Many Newfoundlanders, however, have for long communicated with each other mainly by sea.

LABRADOR—PHYSICAL AND HUMAN GEOGRAPHY

PHYSICAL GEOGRAPHY

Labrador is nearly four times as large as Newfoundland. Visible from the latter's northern peninsula, it extends for 600 miles from the Strait of Belle Isle to Cape Chidley. It is very narrow in the north, but broadens out in the south to take in the whole of the Churchill (Hamilton) River Basin. The intensely fiorded coast is backed in the north by the high, serrated, cirque-cut peaks of the Torngat Mountains, which reach 5500 ft. The interior consists mainly of smoother glaciated country, somewhat resembling, in the south-west especially, the Finnish Lake Plateau.

Labrador lies within roughly the same latitudes as the British Isles, but the climate is very much colder: indeed, the average annual temperature is below 32° F. Most of the air masses affecting it come from the continental interior, while the seas are frozen up during the long winter and are chilled by icebergs in summer.

North of Hamilton Inlet—a magnificent fiord 150 miles long—the vegetation is mostly tundra, though the interior bears a few dwarf trees. To the south there are forests, largely of stunted spruce and balsam fir, interspersed with lakes, muskeg, and rock outcrops. Stands of good timber, however, clothe the relatively deep soils of the Churchill valley. (*See* Fig. .17.)

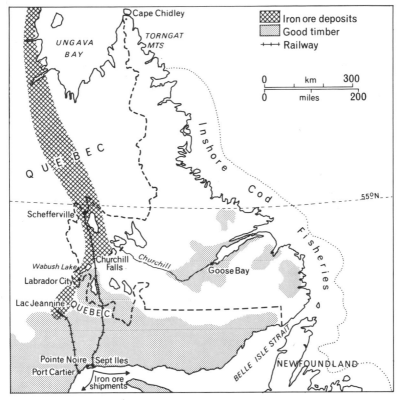

FIG. 17.—Labrador: general features.

THE PEOPLE

Labrador has a population of little more than 10,000, a reflection of its harsh climate, which earned for it Cartier's brief condemnation: "the land God gave to Cain."

About 2000 of the people are Eskimos. They are semi-nomadic, generally inhabiting a fixed, wooden house in the winter, near a mission station, and erecting small huts or simple tents during the warmer weather, when they may travel fairly widely. They engage in both fishing and trapping. Their catches include fox, seal, caribou, salmon, sea-trout, and cod. They may also collect the eggs of sea-shore birds, *e.g.* puffins and guillemots.

In the interior, mainly in the taiga, but partially in the tundra, are small groups of Cree Indians, most of whom are completely nomadic. They may occasionally visit the coast, where they trap birds and fish, but they spend much of the year inland, where they hunt caribou, foxes, hares, and porcupines.

Whites are more numerous today than either Eskimos or Indians. They include missionaries and traders, trappers and fishermen. Some take part in the Banks cod-fisheries, others concentrate on the trapping of commercially valuable animals, *e.g.* marten, mink, beaver, ermine, musk-rat, and fox. Most live in permanent dwellings in small villages dominated by a Grenfell Association hospital and school, and perhaps a trading-post. These tiny settlements often have small gardens producing cabbages, lettuces, and potatoes; such vegetables may have to be started under glass, as the growing season is very short.

MODERN DEVELOPMENTS

It is likely that Labrador will always be a "negative" land, but three recent developments have brought it into closer relation with the outside world. The first has been the establishment, during the Second World War, of the large Goose Bay airport at the head of Hamilton Inlet. Its *raison d'être* was the need to transport American aircraft across the Atlantic, and to be ready to repel a possible German attack on North America. Though it suffers less from fog than the similar base at Gander, Newfoundland, the latter has become a more prominent Atlantic terminal owing to its somewhat more accessible situation in relation to international air routes.

The second recent development has been the working and shipment of iron ore from large deposits on the Labrador–Quebec border, which now produces two-thirds of Canada's iron ore. The mineral beds are located in a trough extending southwards from Ungava for over 400 miles in a belt about 50 miles wide. The main workings, which started in the early 1950s, when fears were beginning to be expressed that the Lake Superior ores were approaching exhaustion, are round the new town of Scheffer-ville, on Knob Lake. This settlement, which has replaced the original site at Burnt Creek, had a population of 3000 in 1959. In the neighbourhood— a cold region of tundra, stunted spruce and muskeg—haematite and other ores are being dug out from just beneath a thin cover of glacial drift. They are transported southwards in summer along a specially built 360-mile railway, to the newly equipped deep-water port of Sept Iles (Seven

Islands), on the St Lawrence, whence they can be moved to Baltimore and the Lake Erie steel cities as cheaply as ores from Minnesota.

Associated with these developments, three hydro-electric power-stations have been erected near the Sept Iles railway. A road has been constructed to join the iron rails to Churchill (formerly Grand) Falls, on the Churchill (formerly Hamilton) River, 115 miles from Knob Lake. The largest power station in the western hemisphere has now been built to tap the enormous energy of these Falls. Its eventual capacity, which may be realised by 1976, is intended to exceed 5 million kw. Quebec has contracted to purchase most of this power, some of which may be transmitted over a phenomenal distance of 800 miles to Montreal. A proportion, however, should be available for the development of a local pulp and paper industry.

The working of iron ore in the Ungava trough is now accelerating. A promising start has been made with the exploitation of ores in two areas near the southern end of the iron belt, viz. the Carol Lake–Lake Wabush (Labrador) area, and the Lac Jeannine (Quebec) district. Ores from the former area—obtained by an international consortium—are being up-graded at a local beneficiation plant using hydro-electric power from a tributary of the Churchill River and then railed to Mile 224 on the Sept Iles Railway, whence they can reach Pointe Noire, a near neighbour of Sept Iles. They are shipped thence up the St Lawrence River, mainly to Hamilton (Ontario) and Buffalo (New York) but also to Europe. In the vicinity of Lake Wabush a second Schefferville, Labrador City, is now rising. So many miners are now at work in the vicinity of Schefferville, Carol Lake, Wabush, and Lac Jeannine, that outgoing shipments of iron ore, upgraded concentrates, and pellets amounted to more than 30 million tons in 1970.

Additional information about the Lac Jeannine ores, which lie outside Labrador, will be found in p. 95.

Chapter VI

THE MARITIME PROVINCES AND THE HIGH-LANDS SOUTH OF THE ST LAWRENCE

THE MARITIME PROVINCES—GENERAL PHYSICAL CHARACTERISTICS

IN relation to the great size of Canada, the three Maritime Provinces are of pocket-size (*see* Fig. 18). All together, they cover only about the same area as England and Wales. New Brunswick, the largest, adjoins Quebec on its northern side and Maine (United States) on its western. The narrow Chignecto isthmus, only 17 miles wide, attaches it to the peninsula of Nova Scotia, the second of the Maritime Provinces. Cape Breton Island, joined to Nova Scotia politically (and also, since 1955, by a bridge), is physically divided from the major part of the province by the Strait of Canso. The third of the Maritime Provinces, Prince Edward Island, is often referred to by the mainlanders simply as the "Island," a characteristic it shares with Vancouver Island in the far west. It is the smallest of all Canadian provinces, and is separated from its two neighbours by Northumberland Strait, in 1970 bridged and tunnelled for road and rail traffic.

Structurally, the Maritime Provinces, together with the Notre Dame and Shickshock Mountains in south-eastern Quebec, form a northern extension of the Appalachian system. The main relief features, therefore, trend from south-west to north-east. Most of the rocks are of Palaeozoic age; they have been folded and crushed, in parts metamorphosed, and in places disrupted by igneous intrusions, *e.g.* in the central highlands of New Brunswick and the uplands of Nova Scotia. Landscapes are generally rugged and hilly, but elevations do not usually greatly exceed 500 ft except in the Gaspé peninsula (Quebec Province), central New Brunswick, and western Nova Scotia. Prince Edward Island is particularly low-lying: in places only coastal dunes keep out the sea, but in other parts there are cliffs.

The effects of recent glaciation are evident in the widespread development of morainic surfaces, in the distribution of erratics, and in the diversion of some of the drainage. The St John, in New Brunswick, is the only major river: it is 400 miles long.

Climatically, the region may be regarded as transitional between the St Lawrence Lowlands and Newfoundland, especially with regard to temperature conditions. Precipitation, mostly frontal in type, is well distributed and generally heavy, and winter snows are considerable in the interior. Early summer fogs are common on the coastlands. The strong tides and Gulf Stream Drift keep the harbours open in winter,

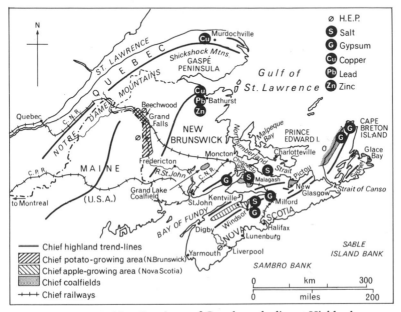

FIG. 18.—Maritime Provinces of Canada, and adjacent Highlands.

but land temperatures fall below freezing-point for three or four months, and in the middle of New Brunswick may average only 10° F in the coldest month. Summer temperatures, however, are as high as those of the British Isles; hence the mean annual range of temperature is extreme, though generally less so than in the St Lawrence lowlands.

Climatic figures for Halifax illustrate these points. A comparison should be made with St John's, Newfoundland (p. 51).

	J.	F.	M.	A.	M.	J.	Jy.	A.	S.	O.	N.	D.
Temperature (° F) .	24	24	31	40	49	58	65	65	59	49	40	29
Precipitation (in.) .	6	5	5	5	4	4	4	4	4	5	6	5

Mean Annual Temperature: 44° F; Mean Annual Range of Temperature: 41° F; Mean Annual Precipitation: 57 in.

THE MARITIME PROVINCES—GENERAL ECONOMY

Despite their early settlement (Port Royal, Annapolis, Nova Scotia, was established by the French in 1605), the Maritime Provinces have not made the same material progress as most other parts of Canada. In fact, they have been described as "the land that was passed by," since the main stream of immigration into the Dominion flowed up the St Lawrence. It has been suggested that in their economy, no less than in their structure, the Maritimes are more akin to the northern parts of New England (United States) than to the rest of Canada, though resemblances with Newfoundland are not lacking. The general standard of living, though a little higher than in Newfoundland, is still lower than that enjoyed by a majority of the North American people. Mineral and forest resources are important, but not fully exploited; agriculture, owing largely to the paucity of good soils, is not yet very widespread nor intensive; and new industries are needed. The area suffers from being rather isolated, and it is feared that the increasing use of the St Lawrence Seaway (*see* Chapter VII) may harm the main ports and make this region still more of a backwater. Perhaps, too, it is unfortunate that the Maritimes, unlike other provinces, have no northland to develop.

FOREST INDUSTRIES

The original cover of mixed temperate "Acadian" forest, in which coniferous trees predominated, has been removed only from Prince Edward Island. The highlands of southern Quebec, over three-quarters of New Brunswick, and over half of Nova Scotia are still clothed with spruce and fir, birch, maple, and beech.

Every part of the region, except Prince Edward Island, has its saw-mills and its pulp and paper factories. In the eighteenth and nineteenth centuries, when Nova Scotia was an important maritime power, much timber was cut for shipbuilding. Today, it is largely used for structural purposes, the value of sawn timber being rather less than that of pulp and paper.

New Brunswick is the chief lumbering province. Many of its mills are located on the coast or at or near to power-sites on the St John River, *e.g.* at Grand Falls, Beechwood, Fredericton, and St John. Nova Scotia has many similar sites, *e.g.* at Liverpool on the Mersey and at Port Hawkesbury. There has been talk of harnessing the power of the tides at the head of the Bay of Fundy, where the average spring rise of 50 ft is the highest in the world, but any such scheme is considered uneconomic at the present time.

In New Brunswick thousands of maple-trees are tapped annually for their sugar, and in the untouched forests some fur-trapping is carried on.

AGRICULTURE

Away from the forested areas, mixed and dairy farming are practised in the Maritime Provinces, and in a few districts specialised vegetable- and fruit-growing have become important.

Prince Edward Island is almost entirely given over to farming. In fact, the province is often called the "Garden of the Gulf" or the "Million Acre Farm." Eighty-five per cent of the area is utilised either for crop-growing or for pasture. It resembles the Channel Islands in breeding

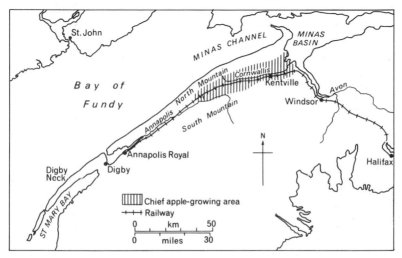

FIG. 19.—Annapolis–Cornwallis Valley, Nova Scotia.

pedigree cattle and producing seed-potatoes. Oats and hay are widely grown on the island and, like the less important barley and turnips, are chiefly fed to stock. Pigs and poultry are only a little less important than dairy-cattle as farm animals. The province has several advantages for farming: a rolling, lowland relief; a well-distributed rainfall; an adequately long, warm growing season for cool temperate produce; fairly fertile red soils (derived from Permian rocks); and the availability of sea-weed and mussel mud (rich in lime) for fertilising the ground. Most of the farms are of moderate size: they average a little less than 100 acres, of which about two-fifths are in field crops.

In the other parts of the region agricultural areas are very scattered. Farmers avoid the obvious "negative" areas, i.e. the rocky uplands, the tracts of thin, sterile soil, and the swamps, and seek out the broader valleys, lower plateaus, and coastal basins. Many rural-dwellers have wood-lots from which they derive fuel and fence-wood, and perhaps even commercial timber, pulp-wood, and pit-props.

The plateau of the middle St John valley, extending over the Maine border, rivals Prince Edward Island as a potato-growing district; the lower St John valley produces apples and poultry; the shorelands of

[Courtesy: High Commissioner for Canada.

FIG. 20.—Annapolis Valley. The Annapolis Valley is one of the most productive strips of farmland in the Maritime Provinces.

Northumberland Strait, in New Brunswick, are concerned mainly with dairying. Nova Scotia has two significant farming districts: (a) The dyked lands on the northern lowland. These were formerly tidal marshes, but have long been devoted to dairying and the cultivation of fodder crops, vegetables, and small fruits. (b) The Annapolis–Cornwallis valley, where apples, potatoes, oats, dairy-farming, and poultry-keeping are all significant, and where small acreages are given over to the cultivation of flowers and salad crops (see Fig. 19).

The Annapolis–Cornwallis valley is a very interesting region (see Fig. 20). It is about 80 miles long, and varies in width from about 4 to 10 miles. About a quarter of the agricultural area is taken up with orchards, bearing mainly apples, but also some pears, cherries, plums, and small fruit. The valley has a sheltered location between North Mountain (of Triassic trap rocks) and South Mountain (of granite); it experiences a warm and sunny late summer, when warm winds approach it from the Bay of Fundy; its red, sandy soils are warm and more fertile than most podsols; and it is linked by rail with Halifax, whence fruit can be shipped to Britain. Unfortunately, the apple market collapsed during the Second World War. As a result, Kentville and other packing centres now convert much of the fruit into bottled apple juice; and other agricultural activities, notably poultry management, have developed at the expense of fruit-farming.

In 1894 Prince Edward Island pioneered silver-fox farming, which has spread thence to the other two Maritime Provinces (and, in fact, all over Canada). The export of fox, mink and animals for breeding and recent changes in fur fashions have caused some depression in the industry, though the eastern provinces possess several advantages: the availability of farm-labour in winter; the presence in most of the soils of a hard-pan which prevents deep burrowing; the ranch vegetation of light woodland with a ground covering of blueberry and heaths; and the severity of the winters, which assists the growth of rich furs.

THE FISHING INDUSTRY

Like Newfoundland, the Maritime Provinces are well placed to take advantage of the large numbers of fish which frequent both inshore and more distant Banks waters, and are even nearer populous markets in Quebec, Ontario, the Prairie Provinces, and the eastern United States. The types of fish caught and the methods of catching them resemble those of Newfoundland, but more trawlers are employed. Lobsters and oysters, however, are more important in the economy of the Maritimes. The former are trapped in the Bay of Fundy, in Northumberland Strait, and off the south-west coast of Nova Scotia. The latter are particularly plentiful in Malpeque Bay, Prince Edward Island, where they are either dredged up from the sea-bed or cultured within hollow concrete blocks. All the provinces have lobster canneries which send part of their output as far as the United Kingdom, and many fresh lobsters are sold in the United States.

Nova Scotia, with its long, indented coastline thrust out towards several submarine Banks, lands more fish than New Brunswick and Prince Edward Island. Its ports include Lunenburg, the chief, where a huge new processing plant was erected in 1965, Yarmouth, Digby, and Halifax.

THE MINING INDUSTRY AND THE MANUFACTURE OF IRON AND STEEL

The Maritime Provinces possess useful resources of several minerals.

Nova Scotia produces a third of Canada's coal. The chief mines are on the north and west sides of Cape Breton Island. In the Glace Bay district submarine mining is carried on for 2 miles off the coast as well as on land. Other mines are situated on the mainland, especially at Pictou and Cumberland; the Pictou seam, 39 ft thick, is one of the thickest in the world. Since these Nova Scotian deposits are virtually the only ones on the Atlantic coast of North America, they can find a market as far up the St Lawrence as Montreal, above which they enter into strong competition with Pennsylvanian supplies, and also in New England. But a considerable proportion of the output is taken by the iron and steel industries of Sydney, on Cape Breton Island, and Trenton, near New Glasgow, in the Pictou district. Both works obtain their iron ore chiefly from the Ungava trough (*see* p. 59), and their limestone from Nova Scotia, Maine, and western Newfoundland. Nova Scotia and New Brunswick have several engineering industries, *e.g.* shipyards and repair works in Halifax, axle and shaft industries in Trenton, and nail, screw, and bolt-making shops in St John.

As in Britain, the increasing use which is being made of imported petroleum for generating power is causing a contraction of the coal-mining industry, and uneconomic mines are gradually being closed under a modernisation programme. There is also competition, especially in Quebec, from hydro-electric power.

New Brunswick has a number of small coal-mines, notably in the Grand Lake district; most of the output is used locally, *e.g.* in thermal electric plants.

Other minerals are worked in Nova Scotia and New Brunswick, but not, be it noted, in Prince Edward Island. They include natural gas (Moncton district, New Brunswick), rock salt (Windsor and Malagash, Nova Scotia), and gypsum (near Milford and Windsor, Nova Scotia, and on the shores of Cape Breton Island). The latter, of which Nova Scotia produces over 80% of Canada's large supply, is largely marketed in the United States, which sends plaster of Paris back to Canada. In the 1950s, large deposits of zinc, lead, silver, and copper were discovered near Bathurst in the north of New Brunswick, and are now being smelted locally. Near by, a large fertiliser plant has been opened. These developments are giving a fillip to the broadening of New Brunswick's economy. The discovery of oil off Sable Island in 1972 is encouraging Nova Scotia's aspirations, already widened by the opening of an oil refinery and new paper-mill in the south-west of Cape Breton Island.

THE MARITIME PROVINCES—POPULATION AND MAJOR CITIES

THE POPULATION

Owing partly to their contiguity to Quebec, partly to the share both Britain and France took in the original settlement of Acadia, partly to their position next door to New England at the time of the American War of Independence, and partly to the varied nationalities of nineteenth- and twentieth-century immigrants, the population of the Maritime Provinces is very mixed.

In Prince Edward Island about a third of the population of about 110,000 is of Scottish origin, nearly 30% is of English stock, just under 20% of Irish stock, and 15% of French origin. The people here are predominantly rural, and there has been very little increase in the total in the last century.

Nova Scotia has nearly 800,000 people. Nearly 80% are of British descent, 12% are French, 4% German. Scots are numerous in Cape Breton Island, which they entered in considerable numbers after the '45 Rebellion and the subsequent eviction of many Highland crofters. The province has more Negroes than any other Canadian province: many entered, with British aid, after the War of Independence, others came in later from Jamaica.

New Brunswick has a large minority of French-speaking people in its total population of 630,000: almost two in five of its people speak that tongue, which is most common in the north and east.

Though population densities are higher in the Maritimes than in any other Canadian provinces considered as a whole, the average number of persons per square mile is only about 30, and many of the inland areas of New Brunswick and Nova Scotia are virtually empty. Moreover, there tends to be as much emigration to other parts of Canada and to the United States as immigration into this eastern region: an indication of its economic backwardness.

THE MAIN CITIES

Halifax, the capital and chief port of Nova Scotia, with a metropolitan population exceeding 200,000, of which half lives in the city itself, is the largest settlement in the Maritime Provinces. It is built on a peninsula which divides its 12-mile-long harbour into an inner and outer part.

Halifax has been the chief naval station of eastern Canada for 200 years. Ice-free, and capable of accommodating the largest ocean liners, over 600 miles nearer Liverpool than is New York, and serving as the eastern terminus of the Canadian National Railway, it has become eastern Canada's main winter port as well as the principal foreign outlet of its own province. Its imports include crude petroleum (refined in the city) and various manufactured articles; its exports are dominated by fish, forest products, apples, and wheat, the latter drawn from the Prairie Provinces and stored in large grain elevators prior to shipment. Manufactures include shipbuilding and repairing, fish- and food-processing, and aircraft construction. Dalhousie University is situated in Halifax.

St John, the chief port of New Brunswick, with nearly 90,000 people in the city itself and more than 100,000 in the metropolitan area, has a similar trade and winter port function to Halifax, but its maritime position is less favourable, and its harbour inferior. Large ships are dependent on the tide, which, when high, reverses the falls of the St John River at this point, so that traffic movement tends to be concentrated at half-tide, when neither the river nor the marine current is too strong. St John is the eastern terminus of the Canadian Pacific Railway,.and, like Halifax, is free from ice in winter. It is believed that its trade might be augmented were a canal to be cut through the narrow Chignecto isthmus, a project which would give it a direct outlet to the Gulf of St Lawrence. St John's main industries are pulp- and paper-milling, shipbuilding and repair work, sugar-refining and the manufacture of railway rolling-stock. North America's first deep water terminal for giant oil-tankers was opened near St John in 1970. Half this oil is being transhipped to east coast refineries, the rest piped to a new refinery at St John itself.

Moncton is the second largest city in New Brunswick. It stands at the head of navigation on the Petitcodiac River, which is subject to a tidal bore, but its main traffic is by rail, not water. All trains moving between Nova Scotia and the rest of Canada must pass through it, and it possesses therefore important marshalling-yards and has become the headquarters of the Atlantic region of the C.N.R. It also has a large airport. Local supplies of natural gas have assisted the development of various small industries, including textile, timber and metal manufacturing, and the processing of foodstuffs.

Fredericton and *Charlottetown*, the capitals of New Brunswick and Prince Edward Island respectively, are both small cities. The former, built on a low river terrace 90 miles up the St John River, of which it is the head of navigation, was founded, like St John, by United Empire Loyalists who migrated into Canada as an outcome of the American War of Independence. They chose Fredericton as their capital because they felt it was safer than St John from potential attack by hostile rebels from the south. It has a few wood-processing, textile, and footwear works, but most of its working inhabitants are civil servants. The Cathedral and University are important institutions.

Charlottetown has a good harbour on Northumberland Strait, but has little seaborne trade. It is the chief trading centre of Prince Edward Island, and possess food-processing works. The Federal Government's intention to build a combined tunnel, bridge, and causeway across Northumberland Strait will increase its importance. The city was the scene of the conference, in 1864, which led to the union of the existing British North American colonies. It therefore lays claim to be the birthplace of Canada, but its own province did not join the Dominion until 1873.

THE HIGHLANDS SOUTH OF THE ST LAWRENCE LOWLAND

Sandwiched between New Brunswick and Maine on the south-east, and the St Lawrence Lowland on the north-west, is an extension of the Appalachian plateau country. West of Maine are the Notre Dame Mountains, whose higher parts reach nearly 4000 ft, while to the north of New Brunswick, in the Gaspé peninsula, are the Shickshock Mountains, which top 4000 ft. The latter descend to the sea in spectacular cliffs, which reach 1000 ft in height; some of these cliffs are bird sanctuaries.

The highlands are still forested, and carry only very small populations. But on the seaward margins of the Breton-like Gaspé, wherever there are narrow terraces, small settlements have been established. Their inhabitants are mainly French-speaking fishermen and farmers, who grow potatoes and raise dairy-cows. Most of them have been accustomed to an almost self-sufficient life, but two recent developments are likely to break down their isolation: (a) the construction of a scenic motor-road along the entire coastal margin, which is already attracting summer tourists to the area; (b) the discovery and exploitation of large copper deposits, near Murdochville. A copper smelter has been built, and some gold and silver are being recovered as by-products.

Chapter VII

ONTARIO AND QUEBEC : THE GREAT LAKES AND ST LAWRENCE LOWLANDS

THE PROVINCES OF QUEBEC AND ONTARIO

As a preface to this chapter, it is appropriate to consider the general character of the two provinces of Quebec and Ontario which share the Great Lakes–St Lawrence region in Canada.

Quebec, with 15·5% of the total area of the country, is Canada's largest province. It is twice the size of France, from which over 80% of its population is derived. Only its St Lawrence Lowland, however, is densely settled, since nine-tenths of the province is underlain by the rocky, inhospitable Shield; south of the river the rugged Appalachian region also deters close settlement.

The natural wealth of Quebec includes furs and fish, timber, minerals, water power, and agricultural land. For a long time rural life was dominant, but 80% of the population is now urban or of a non-agricultural rural type, and more than two-thirds of the provincial income is derived from manufacturing. It is the leading part of Canada for hydro-electric power generation, and for the manufacture of pulp and paper, aluminium, cotton textiles, women's clothing, and footwear.

Ontario, covering 10·7% of Canada's area, has a greater population than Quebec, in fact, one in every three Canadians lives in this province. Like its neighbour, well over 80% of its area is virtually empty northland ("New Ontario"), where only a few people dwell in lumber camps, mining townships, fur-trappers' cabins, and on the farms of the Cochrane Clay Belt (*see* Chapter VIII).

As in Quebec, too, the people of Ontario live mainly in towns and cities. Two-thirds of the population, however, are of British origin. Generally speaking, European settlement followed that of Quebec, and was mainly subsequent to, and consequent upon, the establishment of British rule over Canada.

Southern Ontario accounts for about two-fifths of the total commodity production of Canada, and half the output of Canadian factories. Manufacturing is concentrated upon the production of metal goods like steel, motor cars, and general machinery, though there are also textile, chemical, rubber, furniture, and other works. Nearly half the working people are employed in transport, trade, finance and the professions, an indication of its economic maturity.

Both Ontario and Quebec are favoured, in those parts which are densely-settled, *viz.* the St Lawrence Lowland, lower Ottawa valley, and Lakes Peninsula, by a longer growing season than most of Canada enjoys, fairly good soils, an undulating relief, nearby forest resources, accessibility to power supplies and economic minerals, excellent transport and contiguity to the United States.

THE GREAT LAKES AND ST LAWRENCE LOWLANDS—PHYSICAL ASPECTS

PHYSICAL GEOGRAPHY

Broadly speaking, the Great Lakes and St Lawrence valley may be regarded as an arm of the Central Lowlands of North America. The region occupies a depression between the Canadian Shield and the Appalachian Mountains, which approach each other most closely below Quebec (*see* Fig. 21). Though most of the underlying rocks are of Palaeozoic sandstones, shales and limestones similar to those of the Appalachians, the region was undisturbed by mountain-building movements, and the only patches of relatively high ground are in the Eastern Townships of Quebec, where the Monteregian Hills form a series of old, denuded intrusions 700–1400 ft high.

At the close of the Ice Age the area was invaded by the sea, which for a time extended up the downfaulted valleys of the Ottawa and the Saguenay, and also up the Richelieu–Champlain valley. Hence extensive tracts of the present lowlands are floored with marine sediments. Moreover, since the Great Lakes were much larger towards the end of the Ice Age than they are now, their shores in places are occupied by lacustrine sands, silts, and clays. In the Ontario Lakes Peninsula many glacial deposits, notably boulder clay (or till), gravelly moraines, and occasional eskers and kames mantle the surface and emphasise its undulating character. Some erosional features are also present, *e.g.* glacial overflow channels. Across the peninsula runs the Niagara Cuesta, up to 1000 ft higher than the plains at its base.

The Great Lakes were formed during the latter part of the Pleistocene period in a trough lying between the water-parting north of the Mississippi drainage system and the retreating ice-sheets to the north. Together, they occupy about 100,000 square miles; Lake Superior is the largest body of fresh water in the world.

The infant River St Lawrence (actually the St Louis River) flows into

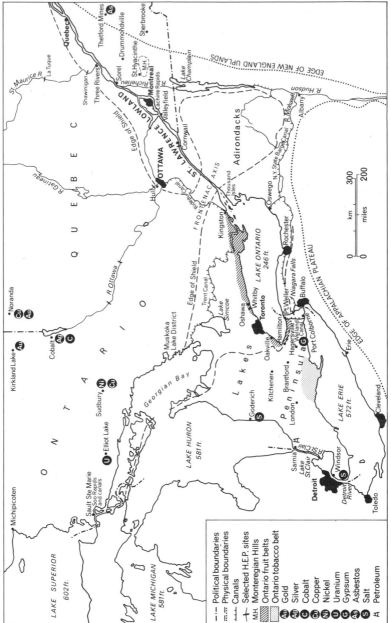

FIG. 21.—Great Lakes–St Lawrence Lowland and its margins. The broken line running through the Lakes Peninsula indicates the Niagara Cuesta.

the extreme western end of Lake Superior, in U.S. territory. This lake, however, receives most of its inflow from the Canadian Lake Nipigon. From a surface level of 602 ft, Lake Superior discharges into Lake Huron via the rapids of St Mary's River, or the "Sault Ste Marie." Lake Huron, like Lake Michigan 581 ft above sea-level, drains into Lake Erie via the shallow River St Clair, Lake St Clair, and Detroit River. From Lake Erie (572 ft O.D.*) to Lake Ontario (246 ft), there is a very steep descent. In a distance of 26 miles the Niagara River, crossing the Cuesta mentioned above, drops 326 ft, half of which is accounted for by the Niagara Falls and half of the rest by the rapids of the 7-mile gorge produced by the gradual recession of the Falls.

Below Lake Ontario, the St Lawrence flows north-eastwards through a series of rapids, the last of which are the Lachine at Montreal. Near this city the St Lawrence Lowland attains its maximum breadth of about 70 miles, and the long Ottawa tributary enters on the left bank, the River Richelieu, draining Lake Champlain, on the right.

In the course of the 160 miles separating Montreal from Quebec, the St Lawrence gradually descends to sea-level (see Fig. 22). The incoming tide dies out at Three Rivers (Trois Rivières), where the powerful St Maurice reaches the main river after a rapid descent from the Shield. At Quebec the St Lawrence narrows markedly, and its valley becomes very restricted. Below the isle of Orleans, however, it soon widens to 20 miles, a figure which is greatly exceeded long before it reaches the Gulf. Despite this change in the character of the river, the riparian lowland never re-asserts itself beyond Quebec. The banks, however, are broken where the deep, rejuvenated Saguenay and other tributaries, such as the Bersimis and the Manicouagan, have cut passages through the high Shield wall.

Though normally highest in May, following snow-melt, and lowest in October, the St Lawrence has one of the most regular régimes of any Canadian river, and discharges a greater volume of water than any other.

THE CLIMATE

The region under study has a cool temperate, extreme type of climate with a well-distributed precipitation, including a heavy winter snowfall. Districts close to the Lakes, especially those in the south of the Lakes Peninsula, have somewhat milder winters than other parts of the region. Here the spring and fall are quite warm, the diurnal temperature range is smaller than elsewhere, and the winter snowfall is comparatively light, particularly in the Niagara Peninsula.

The region as a whole is dominated by Polar continental air masses, which reduce temperatures below freezing-point in January. When this

* O.D.=Ordnance Datum.

arctic air meets milder maritime air from the Gulf of Mexico or the Atlantic, depressions are formed which generally move eastwards along the St Lawrence corridor to bring rain and unsettled weather. Precipitation averages 40 in. a year in the St Lawrence Lowland, and 30–40 in. in the Lakes Peninsula, July temperatures average 65° to 74° F (Pelee Island, in Lake Erie), January temperatures 10° to 25° F. On Pelee Island there are 175 frost-free days, only 130 at Ottawa and Quebec.

A comparison between the climatic statistics of Toronto and Montreal is instructive:

Toronto	J.	F.	M.	A.	M.	J.	Jy.	A.	S.	O.	N.	D.
Temperature (° F) .	22	21	30	42	54	64	69	67	60	49	37	27
Precipitation (in.) .	2·8	2·4	2·4	2·3	2·8	2·7	2·7	2·8	2·7	2·6	2·6	2·5

Mean Annual Temperature: 45° F; Mean Annual Range of Temperature: 48° F; Mean Annual Precipitation: 31·4 in.

Montreal	J.	F.	M.	A.	M.	J.	Jy.	A.	S.	O.	N.	D.
Temperature (° F) .	13	15	25	41	55	65	69	67	59	47	33	19
Precipitation (in.) .	3·7	3·2	3·7	2·4	3·1	3·5	3·8	3·4	3·5	3·3	3·4	3·7

Mean Annual Temperature: 42° F; Mean Annual Range of Temperature: 56° F; Mean Annual Precipitation: 40·7 in.

THE GREAT LAKES AND ST LAWRENCE LOWLANDS—THE ECONOMY

LAND UTILISATION

Originally, the region under study was well wooded with mixed temperate trees. Probably less than 10% of this native forest survives, mostly in the form of copses and wood-lots on farms, owing to the spread of settlement and agriculture. Forestry is an important means of employment only on the Shield and Appalachian borders of the region, though the St Lawrence and tributary valleys have many saw-mills, pulp-works, and paper-mills. Wood-turning and carving are significant village industries in winter, when it is too cold to work in the fields, and the collection of maple-sugar is widely carried on in spring on many farms.

The warm summers, well-distributed rainfall, and fairly long growing season, the varied and generally productive soils, and the close settlement of both the Lakes Peninsula and the St Lawrence Lowland, favour mixed farming and dairying.

"Strip-farms"—a survival of the earliest forms of French land-holdings in Canada—are characteristic of Quebec. The original landlords, or seigneurs, were granted blocks of land along the St Lawrence which they shared out among their tenants, each of whom originally received a river frontage of about a furlong. Back from the river lay a tract of cultivated land and a stretch of pasture: farther from the water was the natural forest, from which fuel and timber might be obtained. These "long lots," or "rangs," with their fenced fields, wooden houses and farm buidings, Roman Catholic churches and schools, and connecting roads, are less self-sufficing today than they were in the seventeenth and eighteenth centuries. They usually have a surplus of dairy produce, especially milk and cheese, and may also grow fruit, especially apples, and truck crops, such as potatoes, tomatoes, and lettuces for urban markets, *e.g.* on the lake silts and fine alluvium of the Montreal Plain and the Champlain valley. Some tobacco is grown on warm, light soils in the Montreal Plain round Joliette, and apple orchards are numerous in the Monteregian Hill country, where gravelly slopes assist both air and water drainage. Dairying is the chief branch of agriculture in the Ottawa valley.

In the Lakes Peninsula, as in the valley lowlands, dairying and fruit-farming are characteristic. In this "English" part of Canada the farms are laid-out on the usual North American grid-iron plan, 95% of them are electrified, the majority are highly mechanised and methods of production are the most intensive in the country.

Most holdings carry cattle and pigs, and grow oats for feeding; there is a surplus of milk, cheese, butter, and bacon. Some farms yield winter wheat, maize (generally cut green for silage except in the south), sugar-beet, vegetables, and apples. Truck-farms are numerous because of the existence of large, nearby markets and the close network of roads and railways. Near the shores of Lakes Erie and Ontario, the fertile lacustrine silts, the comparatively low latitude, and the relatively high spring and fall temperature minima have encouraged good crops of early potatoes and other market-garden produce, *e.g.* carrots, asparagus, celery, cucumbers, tomatoes, strawberries, and raspberries. In the Niagara Fruit Belt, round the favoured western edge of Lake Ontario, grapes, apricots, and peaches do well. In south-west Ontario, in the central parts of the north shorelands of Lake Erie, the existence of sandy soils has stimulated the cultivation of tobacco. Leaf is exported to the United Kingdom.

Generally speaking, dairying is dominant in the eastern parts of the Lakes Peninsula, mixed farming in the west, truck-farming and horticulture in the south. The poorest areas are the poorly drained patches which occur between drumlins; the northerly parts, near the Shield; the higher, rougher ground of the Niagara Cuesta.

MINING AND MANUFACTURING

The lowland area under study has few minerals of outstanding economic value, though the richly mineralised southern parts of the Shield are very accessible to manufacturers in both the Lakes Peninsula and in the St Lawrence valley (*see* Chapter VIII).

South-western Ontario contains Canada's oldest oilfield (first worked in 1857), and there is still a small output of petroleum and natural gas from the neighbourhood including that from new wells in Lake Erie. 60% of Canada's salt is obtained from deep wells at Windsor, and from mines at Goderich and Lake Ojibway (near Windsor), and gypsum is worked at Hagersville. The largest asbestos mines in the world are those of Thetford Mines, Black Lake, and Asbestos in the Eastern Townships of Quebec, which yield over 50% of the "free" world supplies. This fire-resisting mineral is found in veins in serpentine rock only lightly overlain by soil. It is largely exported to the United States, where it is used in the manufacture of heat insulators, brake linings, and building materials.

The Lakes Peninsula, dominated by Toronto and Hamilton, and the St Lawrence Lowland, under the ascendancy of Montreal, form the chief manufacturing region, not only in Canada but in the whole of the British Commonwealth outside the United Kingdom. It has several advantages:

1. A large, well-educated labour supply.

2. A populous market with much purchasing-power.

3. Proximity to the United States. Bridges join Windsor to Detroit, and Sarnia to Port Huron; others cross the Thousand Isles district of the St Lawrence River, and span the "Soo" rapids and the Niagara River. Ships carry Pennsylvanian coal across both Lake Erie and Lake Ontario. Many United States firms have found it profitable to establish branch factories both in Southern Ontario and Quebec.

4. Easy access to the rich forest and mineral resources of the southern parts of the Shield.

5. A close network of communications, and access to overseas markets and sources of supply through the Great Lakes and St Lawrence Seaway (*see* below).

6. The relatively low cost of electrical power. This is supplied partly by large hydro-electric stations at Niagara and along the St Lawrence and its tributaries, *e.g.* the Ottawa, St Maurice, Saguenay and Manicouagan; partly by coal, obtained either from Nova Scotia or from Pennsylvania; partly by petroleum, imported via the St Lawrence or brought by pipeline from the Prairies.

7. The large agricultural output of the region itself, which has led to the establishment of many works concerned with the processing of foodstuffs, *e.g.* the canning and quick-freezing of fruit and vegetables; the manufacture of biscuits and breakfast cereals; the preparation of cheese, condensed milk, and meat; the making of boots and shoes.

Apart from such large manufacturing cities as Montreal, Toronto, Hamilton, Quebec, and Windsor, many smaller centres, most of which are also market towns, have significant factories. The chief one is London (on the River Thames), the seat of the University of Western Ontario; it cans both fruit and vegetables, makes biscuits and breakfast foods, and produces footwear, farm implements, and radio sets. Kitchener makes motor-car tyres, furniture, and various food products, and Brantford turns out agricultural machinery. Sarnia, located where Lake Huron gives way to the St Clair River, and close to Canada's first oil-well, now benefits from a position on the Inter-Provincial pipeline. It has become the centre of Canada's "Chemical Valley": besides refining oil, it produces soap and detergents, drugs, fertilisers, synthetic rubber, and plastics.

In the St Lawrence Lowland textiles are manufactured at St Hyacinthe, Sherbrooke, Drummondville, Valleyfield, Cornwall, and Kingston. The latter is the oldest city in Ontario, and the seat of Queen's University, the Royal Military College, and an Anglican Cathedral. Most of these towns manufacture more than textiles, *e.g.* Kingston builds ships and locomotives and makes aluminium; Cornwall, paper, furniture, and chemicals; Sherbrooke, machinery. Of the many towns manufacturing pulp and paper, the chief is Three Rivers near which a new steel mill has recently been built. Sorel, at the mouth of the Richelieu, has shipyards and also produces titanium dioxide from the ilmenite deposits worked at Allard Lake, lower down the St Lawrence.

THE GREAT LAKES–ST LAWRENCE WATERWAY

One of the greatest economic assets available to Ontario and Quebec is the Great Lakes–St Lawrence shipping route and its associated water-power resources, which they share as far downstream as Cornwall with the United States.

As a means of communication, various parts of the natural waterway suffer from certain obstacles, chief of which are winter ice, summer fog, river waterfalls, rapids, and shallows. To a very large extent, the first two remain to be overcome; the others, through man's ingenuity, have been conquered.

Normally, the St Lawrence is closed to shipping from December to April owing to frost. Below Quebec, the river never freezes over completely, but floating ice keeps ships in port. The Gulf of St Lawrence is beset by frequent fogs in early summer, though radar devices have reduced the risk of collisions. Rapids (the " Soo " falls) occur between Lakes Superior and Huron; parts of the Rivers St Clair and Detroit are naturally shallow; the rapids along the Niagara River and the 160-ft-high falls present an impassable barrier between Lakes Erie and Ontario; while navigation along the St Lawrence between Kingston and Montreal was formerly impeded by a whole series of rapids.

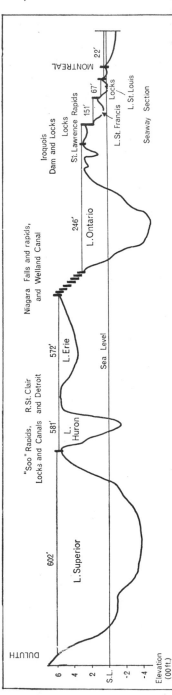

FIG. 22.—Section through the Great Lakes and along the St. Lawrence. The principal obstacles to navigation and the means of circumventing them should be noted.

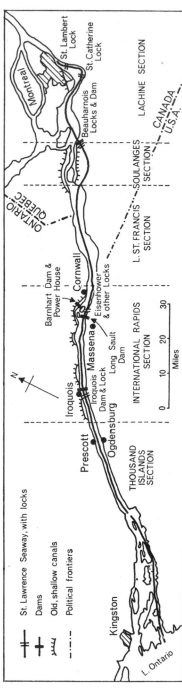

FIG. 23.—St Lawrence Seaway.

The following operations should be noted: Thousand Islands and L. St. Francis sections: dredging; International Rapids section: new waterway to replace old canals; Soulanges section: improvement to Beauharnois Power Canal; Lachine section: new ship canal.

Thanks to many engineering projects which have been carried out during the last 130 years, a 27-ft-deep channel is now available throughout the 2300 miles which separate lake ports such as Duluth and Chicago from the open Atlantic (*see* Fig. 23). The "Soo" Canals (two in the United States, one in Canada) allow of an easy passage from Lake Superior into Lake Huron; the rivers between Huron and Erie have been dredged so as to maintain a deep channel; circumventing the Niagara hazard is the Welland Canal, equipped with eight locks, and extending 27 miles between Port Colborne and Port Weller. Prior to 1959, when the St

[*Courtesy: National Film Board of Canada.*

FIG. 24.—Iroquois Lock, St Lawrence Seaway. A ship is shown in the most westerly of the seven new Seaway locks. The Iroquois Lock can handle vessels up to 715 ft in length. The Iroquois Control Dam is in the background.

Lawrence Seaway was opened, there was a bottleneck to large ships between Kingston and Montreal, as the sole means of water communications available was a series of narrow canals only 14 ft deep. Now, however, thanks to the co-operation of Canada and the United States, a completely new, deep shipping channel (equipped with seven locks) has been constructed (*see* Fig. 24) and the older canals are gradually being closed.

Below Montreal, a 35-ft channel is kept open by tidal action, assisted by dredging.

Prior to the completion of the St Lawrence Seaway, only the very smallest sea-going ships could ascend the river above Montreal. The usual vessels plying between Kingston and the Upper Lakes were specially built "lakers," up to 730 ft long, 72 ft broad, and capable of carrying 28,000 tons. These "lakers" can now descend to Montreal. Moreover, ocean-going ships of 9000 tons can now travel all the way from Europe to any of the Lake ports, e.g. Chicago, Toronto, and Hamilton, each of which has recently enlarged its harbour and wharfing facilities to handle the increased traffic the Seaway is bringing. It must, however, be remembered that the waterway is open for less than eight months each year, ships using it must pay tolls, and there is severe congestion in the Welland Canal. To help reduce this congestion, a new 8-mile by-pass round the central town of Welland has been made. The feasibility of deepening and widening the Canal is also being studied.

The main eastbound traffic on the Great Lakes is iron ore, transported from the Superior deposits to iron and steel centres on the Lakes, whence it may also be sent by rail to Pittsburgh and other consuming localities. Considerable quantities of limestone, petroleum, sand and gravel, lumber, wheat and maize are also shipped eastwards. Upstream, coal and petroleum and some manufactures are important cargoes. There has been a marked increase in the amount of iron ore sent upriver from Sept Iles and other new St Lawrence ports in recent years.

MINOR CANALS

A number of narrow canals, less than 10 feet deep, were constructed in the nineteenth century to improve the natural communications of the region under study. None of them carry very much traffic today, owing to the development of rail and road communications, but they are attractive to tourists. They include:

1. The Carillon and Grenville Canals along the Ottawa valley, which link the Canadian capital with Montreal.

2. The Rideau Canal between Ottawa and Kingston.

3. The Trent River Canal system, using an old glacial overflow channel between Georgian Bay and Lake Ontario, via Lake Simcoe.

4. The Chambly Canal, joining the River Richelieu to Lake Champlain, which in turn is linked to the navigable Hudson.

HYDRO-ELECTRIC POWER DEVELOPMENTS

Quebec and Ontario have developed 80% of Canada's hydro-electric power supplies, the former accounting for over half the total. Many of the largest stations are situated on the Ottawa, St Maurice, Saguenay, Manicouagan, and Bersimis Rivers, and will be treated in the next chapter.

Along the course of the Great Lakes–St Lawrence Waterway, as we have seen, there is a number of rapids and waterfalls, most of which have now been harnessed to generate industrial power. Use has long been made of the power of the Niagara falls and Lachine rapids. At Niagara both Canada and the United States have installed several large generators from which electricity is transmitted to such cities as Toronto, Hamilton, and Buffalo. Near Montreal, the Beauharnois power-station has been recently enlarged and is producing 2 million horsepower. Even bigger is the new Barnhart power-house, at Massena, which is shared by Ontario and New York State; its construction was an integral part of the engineering work concerned with the St Lawrence Seaway. It yields 2·2 million horsepower and is encouraging industrial expansion in both Canada and northern United States.

While hydro-electricity continues to be the main source of power in both Ontario and Quebec (both provinces having new schemes on hand in their Shield areas), it should be noted that Ontario in particular also has a number of large coal-fired stations, including Lambton, near Sarnia (2000 MW) and Lakeview, near Toronto (2400 MW) and is planning others (*e.g.* at Nanticoke on Lake Erie). She is building a powerful oil-fired plant near Kingston and is also developing nuclear power generation (*see* p. 97).

MAJOR CITIES

THE ST LAWRENCE LOWLAND

Quebec and Ontario can boast of having seven out of the eleven most populous cities in Canada. In the St Lawrence Lowland there are two of them, Montreal and Quebec, both in the province of Quebec. The former —the largest of all Canadian cities—has a population of well over a million, with over 2½ millions in its metropolitan area. In the 1971 census the latter numbered 480,000 in its metropolitan area.

Montreal.—The French planted a settlement here in 1642. Never did they choose a finer position (*see* Fig. 25). The site lay 1000 miles upriver, where the Lachine rapids halted navigation; on an island dominated by the 770-ft-high Mount Royal (Mont Real), which gave it excellent defences; and close to : (*a*) the confluence of the Ottawa River, which provided an early route into the interior; (*b*) the junction of the Richelieu, which led to the Hudson corridor through the Appalachians, at the southern end of which New York was established.

A natural route focus, therefore, Montreal came to command both land and water routes: it came to be not only the child of the Atlantic and St Lawrence but the offspring also of the interior, including the Prairies. The city has spread east of its island site on to the mainland, with which it is connected by bridges. The Lachine rapids, by-passed in the nineteenth century by a 14-ft canal (now closed) driven through the island, and in the 1950s by the 27-ft Seaway channel, are of less consequence than formerly, but the city remains the head of navigation for large ocean-going ships.

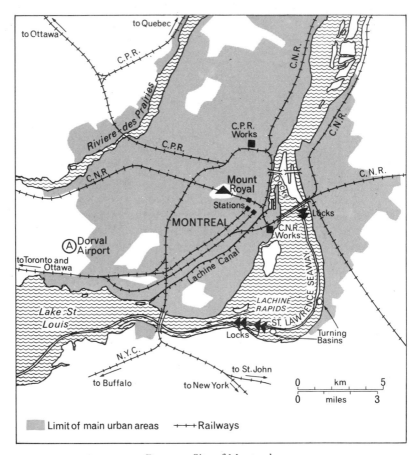

FIG. 25.—Site of Montreal.

Docks front the St Lawrence on the eastern and southern sides of Montreal's island. Into them ships come upriver with coal, petroleum, tropical products like sugar, and various manufactures; by rail, road, and river from the west and north come grain, flour, dairy produce, pulp and paper, metals, fruit, and furs. Montreal is perhaps the world's greatest grain port, and has some of North America's largest elevators. No other Canadian city conducts as much foreign trade.

It leads all other Canadian cities, too, as a manufacturing centre. It benefits from easily transported Cape Breton coal, the hydro-electric power of Beauharnois and various stations in the Shield and imported petroleum. Most factories are located along the harbour front, along the Lachine Canal, and in the railway zone. As the headquarters of both the C.P.R. and the C.N.R., it has built large railway works. It also manufactures ships, aircraft, clothing, tobacco, and electrical apparatus, some pulp, paper, chemicals, and leather. It refines sugar, copper and petroleum and

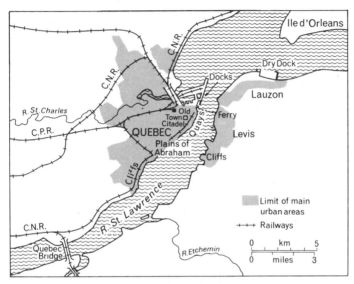

FIG. 26.—Site of Quebec.

processes various foodstuffs. To help relieve traffic congestion in the city, an underground railway system ("Montreal Metro") was inaugurated in readiness for "Expo 67," the great exhibition of 1967.

Montreal is a very important banking city. With two Universities, a Cathedral, and a number of theatres, it ranks first in Canada as a cultural and entertainments centre. Two-thirds of its people speak French and live mostly in the east. English-speaking residents dwell mostly in the west, on the slopes leading up to Mount Royal. There are important Jewish and Italian minorities.

Quebec, founded by Champlain in 1608, is the capital of the province (*see* Fig. 26). Though having a sheltered harbour at the confluence of the Charles River, and an even better defensive position than Montreal— where the Heights of Abraham overlook the "Narrows" (at a point where the river dwindles to a width of $\frac{3}{4}$ mile)—it has no natural nodality, and has not achieved the commercial importance of Montreal. It stands at the threshold of the St Lawrence Lowland and is connected to Montreal and the interior by rail and river. Just above the city is the lowest bridge across the St Lawrence: it carries the C.N.R. line to Halifax (Nova Scotia). Quebec ships timber, pulp and paper, and, along with its satellite, Levis, on the east bank of the St Lawrence, manufactures boots and shoes, textiles, tobacco, pulp and paper and miscellaneous foodstuffs. Just south of it, at St. Romuald, Canada's largest oil refinery has been erected recently. There are shipyards at Lauzon, opposite Quebec. Though iced over in winter, it is possible to keep open the port by efficient ice-breakers.

Quebec retains more of its ancient French character than Montreal, and is a less cosmopolitan city, 85% of its population being French Canadian. It is popular with tourists, as it still looks more like a European rather than an American city. It is the seat of the French-speaking, Roman Catholic, Laval University, and has an important Cathedral.

ONTARIO

Excluding the Canadian capital, Ottawa, Ontario has three large cities: Toronto and Hamilton, on the shores of Lake Ontario, and Windsor, on the Detroit River near the Lake St Clair entry. Their populations are as follows (Statistics from the Dominion Bureau of Statistics):

	1961 census		1971 census	
	City	Metropolitan Area	City	Metropolitan Area
Toronto	672,407	1,824,589	712,000	2,628,043
Hamilton	273,991	395,189	309,000	495,523
Windsor	114,367	193,365	203,000	258,643

Toronto, founded in 1793, is the capital of Ontario, not only politically but also commercially, industrially, and culturally. It grew up at one end of an old Indian portage route which led, via Lake Simcoe, to Georgian Bay, a route now followed in part by one of the main C.P.R. lines from Montreal to western Canada. Its name, of Indian origin, signifies "meeting-place"; its aptness today is shown by the convergence here of land and waterways including a number of new express ways. There is a very good harbour, where a small bay is sheltered by a sandy hook on the north-western shore of Lake Ontario. Power for manufacturing is derived partly from the Niagara power-station, partly from its own very large thermal-electric station, fed with Pennsylvanian and Nova Scotian coal. It has very important meat-packing, electrical, and clothing industries, and also manufactures machinery (including farm implements), aircraft, and paper. It has large printing and publishing works and houses a famous University.

Within 50 miles of Toronto are situated a quarter of all the manufacturing plants in Canada. Among satellite towns are Whitby, which makes rubber tyres, Oakville and Oshawa, which manufacture motor cars.

Hamilton is mainly concerned with heavy industry. Importing Pennsylvanian coal, limestone from the Niagara Cuesta and iron ore from Steep Rock and the Ungava trough, it has become Canada's leading steelmaking centre. It also manufactures farm tractors and textile machinery, motor-vehicles, chemicals, rubber goods, electrical apparatus, canned goods and pottery. Its harbour is large and sheltered, and approached by a short canal cut through the sandy beach which divides it from the western reaches of Lake Ontario.

Gradually, Hamilton and Toronto are growing towards each other, and the western side of Lake Ontario is coming to be known as the Mississaga conurbation.

Windsor, though dwarfed by Detroit, to which it is linked by bridges and tunnels, is the greatest automobile-manufacturing city in Canada. Most of its works are branches of American corporations. Windsor also makes salt and chemicals, two industries based mainly on the thick salt deposits which underlie and surround the city.

THE CAPITAL OF CANADA

Ottawa is situated on the Ottawa River, where the Chaudière Falls mark the head of navigation (*see* Fig. 27). On the high right bank of the river close to the confluences of the Rideau and Gatineau, Ottawa became the capital of the Dominion of Canada in 1857. It had been founded, under the name Bytown, only in 1827, when Colonel By was given the job of building the Rideau Canal to Kingston. In 1857 it was the chief lumbering centre of Canada. Today, most of its working people are employed in the Civil Service. It still mills timber and pulp (though less now than the French-Canadian city of Hull, opposite), and has important printing and publishing works, served by hydro-electric plants on the upper Ottawa and Rideau Rivers. It is accessible to some of the best forest land in the Shield, and is well placed on the edge of the fertile lowland extending down-river to the Montreal Plain. A dignified city, it attracts many tourists. The residential population of the city and suburbs in 1971 was over 600,000.

The reasons why such a relatively insignificant city was chosen by Queen Victoria to be the capital of Canada were probably as follows:

1. It lay on the border between French-speaking Lower Canada and English-speaking Upper Canada.

[*Courtesy: Photographic Survey Corporation Ltd., Toronto.*

FIG. 27.—Aerial view of Ottawa. This view, taken from the south-east, shows the Parliament Buildings (on high ground overlooking the river), Union Station (bottom left), Canadian War Memorial (left centre). Across the river is Hull, where a large papermill may be seen. Steeply pitched "chateau-style" roofs are a notable feature of Ottawa's official architecture.

2. Its choice represented a compromise between the rival claims of older, more important cities: Quebec, Montreal, Toronto, Kingston.

3. It was regarded as a "safe" city, well away from the American frontier at a time when the United States and Canada were less friendly than they are today.

4. It was accessible by rail and water to the older settlements, and its population was a fair mixture of most of the ingredients in the contemporary population of Canada: English, Scottish, Irish, and French.

Chapter VIII

THE CANADIAN SHIELD

PHYSICAL ASPECTS

THE EXTENT OF THE SHIELD

The Canadian or Laurentian Shield includes certain areas studied elsewhere in this book: Labrador, and the Upper Lakes country and Adirondack Mountains of the United States. In the west it forms parts of the Mackenzie Basin.

The western boundary, dividing the Shield from younger sediments, is masked in places by glacial deposits, and is hard to define in detail. Broadly, it runs southwards parallel to the lower Mackenzie from a point on the Arctic coast east of the delta. It cuts through the centre of such "Glint Line" lakes as Great Bear and Great Slave, passes through the western end of Lake Athabaska, and then swings south-eastwards to follow the eastern margin of Lake Winnipeg. Having crossed into the United States to include the Lake Superior Highlands, it traverses the northern edge of the Lakes Peninsula between Georgian Bay and Lake Ontario, and then forms the northern rim of the St Lawrence Lowlands. In the Thousand Isles district the Shield crosses the St Lawrence along the "Frontenac" axis and broadens out in the Adirondacks (*see* Fig. 21).

PHYSICAL GEOGRAPHY

As we saw in Chapters I and III, most of the Shield forms a saucer-shaped plateau bitten into by Hudson Bay and its southern extension, James Bay. The surface is diversified by residual mountains, hummocky patches of glacial material, thousands of lakes, and an indeterminate drainage pattern. The basic rocks include granite (often in the shape of huge batholiths), lava, quartzite, limestone, slate, and gneiss.

Climatically, most of the Shield is unsuited to close human settlement. Polar air masses are usually in occupation: they bring very long and severe winters, which greatly restrict the length of the growing season. Precipitation is generally light and shows a summer or autumn maximum. It is heaviest in the east and south, where there are more frequent incursions of Polar maritime air from the Atlantic.

From the human point of view, the climate deteriorates northwards.

The southern parts may have a growing season of more than a hundred days, and at least five months in which the average temperature exceeds 45° F. (At North Bay, a typical southern station, the January average temperature is 10° F, July 66° F.) But north of the main line of the C.N.R., only July may be free from frost. West of Hudson Bay, in these latitudes, the mean annual precipitation is only 10–15 in., to the east it averages 20–40 in. The winter snowfall, like the summer rainfall, increases eastwards. The Laurentides (a winter-sports region north of Quebec exceeding 3000 ft in altitude) may well have more than a hundred inches of snow in the year.

Polewards of the 50° July isotherm, the growing season is generally less than 40 days, the mean annual temperature only 12° F. There may be only one month with a mean temperature exceeding 43° F. West of Hudson Bay, and north of 60 degrees N. lat., is Keewatin, the "Home of the North Wind," which is usually in the grip of cold, heavy, Polar air. Here winters last from mid-September to mid-June. The mean annual precipitation averages only 10 in., but on the other side of the Bay it is generally more than 15 in.

NATURAL VEGETATION

In contrast with the Great Lakes–St Lawrence Lowland, most of the natural vegetation of the Shield remains. Its luxuriance declines north-wards with the increasing length of the cold season, and often varies within the same climatic zone according to the depth of the soil. About 10% of the whole surface consists of bare rock, and part of the rest is so ill-drained as to carry only muskeg.

In the south, e.g. on the margins of Lake Superior and Georgian Bay, there are mixed forests into which temperate hardwood species, e.g. maple, oak, and yellow birch, have penetrated from the Lakes Peninsula. Within the heart of this southern region, the dominant conifers are white pine, red pine, white cedar, and hemlock.

North of this narrow zone of mixed forests lie the more extensive northern or boreal forests, sometimes called the taiga. Here, over wide areas, the white spruce is the main species, but balsam fir is prominent in the east, black spruce in the west, and there are frequent stands of pine, especially on areas of light soil.

Between the taiga and the tundra is a transitional, sub-arctic forest, sometimes called the "land of the little sticks," because, although the trees are broadly of the same species as those of the boreal forests, they are very stunted and scattered. Cranberries are common among ground plants.

North of the "tree-line," which roughly corresponds with the 50° F

July isotherm, the vegetation is of the tundra type. Formerly called the "Barren Lands," now more commonly "Arctic Pastures," this region may carry ground birch, heather, bilberry, and cranberry in its better-drained uplands; and grasses, sedges, and flowering plants like the arctic poppy, lupin, daisy, and arctic wallflower on the plains, but in rocky districts there are only very low-lying plants like lichens, saxifrages, and crowberries. All the tundra plants are inured to permafrost conditions, and must go through their annual cycle of growth very rapidly during the long days of the brief summer.

THE LAKES AND RIVERS AND THEIR EFFECTS ON HUMAN GEOGRAPHY

The drainage of the Shield is largely to Hudson Bay, via the River Nelson (1660 miles) and smaller rivers like the Churchill, Albany, and Moose. In the east the watershed is much nearer the St Lawrence than Hudson Bay, therefore the rivers entering the St. Lawrence are shorter than those flowing into the Bay, and have a swifter course down the border escarpment: among the chief are the Ottawa, St Maurice, and Saguenay. The north-western parts of the Shield drain to the Mackenzie via Great Bear, Great Slave, and Athabaska Lakes. In the north-east rivers like the Hamilton have independent outlets to the north Atlantic, and other streams seek Ungava Bay.

In many ways the rivers and lakes of the Shield have had much to do with the development of the region. Some of them have been instrumental in laying bare mineralised rocks; many of them have been used for driving logs; in some cases their water-power resources have been utilised. Since the seventeenth century fur traders have used them for navigation, and taken advantage of the many low portages between opposing streams. Indian fishermen value many of the rivers and lakes for their fish, and recently commercial fisheries have been developed on the larger lakes. In summer many tourists travel along the railways and highways of southern Quebec and Ontario in search of river and lakeside picnic places, where they have an opportunity of studying animals and wildfowl in their natural habitat, e.g. in the Muskoka Lake country east of Georgian Bay, and in the Algonquin Provincial Park south of the River Ottawa.

THE ECONOMY OF THE SHIELD

FOREST OCCUPATIONS

The northern parts of the Shield are remote, and the quality of the timber is poor, therefore forestry is most important in the south. In the Prairie Provinces and the west generally, however, little timber is cut save what will satisfy local demands, *e.g.* for fencing poles and telegraph poles, and there are few pulp-mills. The chief timber-working areas lie in southern Quebec and Ontario, but even these areas lag far behind British Columbia in their output of sawn timber. Many of the best forests in the far south have gone, and the principal saw-mills today are situated near hydro-electric power sites in the valleys of the Ottawa, Saguenay, and St Maurice, in the Abitibi district and along the northern margins of the upper lakes.

The real wealth of the south-eastern forests lies in their pulpwood, especially spruce and balsam fir. Pulp-mills are very numerous in Quebec and Ontario, though scattered in their distribution and rarely giving rise to large settlements. The leading region is the St Maurice valley, where there are large mills at Shawinigan, La Tuque, and Three Rivers, the latter being in the St Lawrence Lowlands. In the Saguenay–Lake St John valley milling centres include Port Alfred, Chicoutimi, and Kenogami. Hull is the chief milling-town in the Ottawa valley. In Ontario the factories at Port Arthur and Fort William (incorporated in the new city of Thunder Bay, 1969), Kenora, Iroquois Falls, and Kapuskasing are among the most important.

Reafforestation and other conservation measures are now common practice, and the Shield forests are no longer the diminishing asset they once were. Steps which are being taken to preserve what remains of the timber and pulpwood include:

1. The issue of licences for felling.
2. The restriction of cutting to trees of a defined size.
3. The establishment of a Forest Protection Service (1924), designed to check fires and insect-infestation.
4. The setting apart of forest reserves, where neither trees nor animals can be interfered with.

The Shield forests are valuable as a source of furs as well as of wood. Trapping—the oldest Shield industry—is almost entirely controlled by the Hudson Bay Company, which operates many trading-posts throughout the region. Some are situated on Hudson and James Bays, others at significant river confluences or on strategic portages. To them, Indian, half-breed, Eskimo and white trappers take their catches of musk-rat, beaver, mink, squirrel, fox, rabbit, marten, ermine, and other skins. Despite the growing attraction of other means of livelihood, and despite the development of fur-ranching throughout the Dominion, trapping remains an important occupation.

Conservation measures, which help to maintain the stock of fur-bearing animals include:

1. The enforcement of trapping restrictions, including the provision of closed seasons.

2. The close study of the annual catch.

3. The creation of wild life sanctuaries.

SOILS AND AGRICULTURE

Agriculture has been very slow to develop in the Shield for the following reasons:

1. The severity of the climate, which in the north prohibits cultivation altogether, and in the south restricts it to the growing of crops which mature quickly and may withstand slight frost.

2. The poverty and thinness of most of the soils. The best soils are the grey wooded earths of the southern mixed forests, which have fair amounts of humus and a little lime-accumulation in the lower or B horizon; and the lacustrine and marine silts of the so-called "Clay Belts" (see below). Unfortunately, the most promising pedological areas may be those most attractive to lumber companies. Even where the latter are not interested, the problem of clearing trees and the need for careful drainage may deter prospective farmers.

3. The inadequacy of communications, except in a few areas.

4. The small size of local markets (generally mines and lumber camps), and the difficulty of competing with more favoured areas in distant markets.

Even where farms have been established in the Shield, many of the occupants may be part-time workers in mines, lumber camps, and pulp- and paper-mills, especially in winter.

Two farming regions stand out at present:

1. The Cochrane Clay Belt (*see* Fig. 28).

2. The Clay Belt of the Saguenay Basin (*see* Fig. 29).

The first is the larger and more firmly established. It covers an area, shared between Quebec and Ontario, threaded by the C.N.R. Its soils— derived from the decay of the glacial lake Ojibway—are deep and reasonably fertile, but in places they are overlaid with peat. Though requiring forest-clearance and drainage, the land is good enough to have attracted many pioneers since the First World War, as the local lumber camps, paper-mills (*e.g.* at Kapuskasing), and gold-mines (*e.g.* at Porcupine and Noranda) furnish a fair market.

The climate, as well as the soil, is satisfactory for oats, barley, roots, potatoes and other vegetables, and hay. Dairying is successfully undertaken. At Cochrane—the chief trading centre for both farmers and

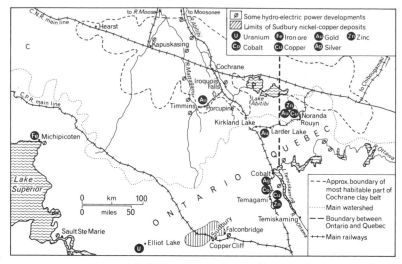

Fig. 28.—Cochrane Clay Belt and adjacent areas.

foresters—the July temperature reaches 64° F, there are five months with average temperatures exceeding 43° F, and out of a mean annual precipitation of 29·5 in., 15·9 in. comes in the five warmest months. Unhappily, the harvest is often wet. Agriculturally speaking, the Cochrane Clay Belt remains part of Canada's "pioneer fringe": much forest has been cut-over without cultivation starting, and some farms have already been abandoned.

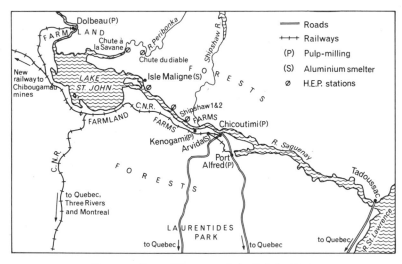

Fig. 29.—Part of Saguenay–Lake St John Basin.

Conditions are roughly similar round Lake St John, near the head of the deep, glaciated Saguenay valley. The soils are mainly marine silts left behind by the former Champlain Sea; in places they have been covered by alluvium brought down by the headwaters of the Saguenay. The most prosperous farms lie on the well-drained clays of the southern lake shores. Dairying, with supporting feed crops and potatoes, is the chief activity. A market is provided by workers at the local pulp-mills, aluminium works, and hydro-electric power-stations.

Two less densely settled, more sporadically farmed areas occur on the pockets of clay in the Shield:

1. The "Little Clay Belt" of the Ontario–Quebec border, between the C.P.R. and C.N.R. main lines. The chief farming districts here lie south of Cobalt and round Temiskaming.

2. Small tracts close to the C.P.R. main line, *e.g.* the districts: (*a*) round Sudbury; (*b*) north-east of Sault Ste Marie; (*c*) west of Thunder Bay; (*d*) east of the Lake of the Woods.

Most of the ground on these farms, which specialise in dairying and vegetable-growing, requires both intensive drainage and manuring. Most have wood-lots from which pulp-wood is collected. Rural densities are increasing only slowly.

MINERAL WEALTH

Nickel and copper. The Shield is richer in minerals than any other part of Canada: it is, in fact, one of the world's most opulent areas. But the character of the rocks is not such as to lead to the formation of coal or petroleum, therefore little industrialisation is to be expected. The working of particular ores has depended in the past upon land communications as well as the size of the deposits, therefore the older mines were only opened-up as railways spread. Newer finds, however, have been to some extent exploited as a result of aerial surveys and the flying-in of supplies. Even now, little has been done to exploit the mineral resources of the tundra.

Among the earliest of Canada's minerals to be worked were the Sudbury nickel–copper sulphide deposits, occupying a basin about 35 miles from east to west, and 17 miles from north to south, north of the city (*see* Fig. 28). From 1886 to 1955 the Sudbury mines accounted for about 80% of the world's nickel production. Canada still produces nearly 40% and the Sudbury deposits still furnish her main supplies. The ores are in the form of sulphides of nickel, copper, and iron, and are easily worked by either open-cut methods or deep mining. Small proportions of other metals are separated out during various stages of the extraction processes.

They include cobalt, silver, gold, iron, the metalloids selenium and tellurium, and the platinum metals. The main smelter is at Copper Cliff, 4 miles from Sudbury; refining is undertaken at Sudbury and Port Colborne, using Niagara hydro-electric power, and at Clydach, near Swansea, in South Wales, using coal.

Other nickel deposits are worked: (*a*) near Falconbridge, 14 miles northeast of Sudbury, where there is a smelter; (*b*) near Lynn Lake, northern Manitoba, whose nickel and copper are refined at Fort Saskatchewan, near Edmonton, with the help of natural gas; (*c*) at and near Thompson, a rapidly growing town of 25,000 people in Manitoba, 400 miles north of Winnipeg, on a new branch of the Hudson Bay Railway; there is a large smelter and refinery at Thompson, powered by hydro-electricity generated on the Nelson River (Fig. 35).

The United States is the chief market for Canadian nickel, and has stockpiled large amounts since 1945 due to its value in the manufacture of armour-plate, stainless steels, and jet engines.

Besides leading all Canadian areas in the output of nickel, Sudbury also heads the list of copper-producers. Second is normally Noranda, the seat of Quebec's chief base-metal smelter in the Rouyn–Noranda gold–copper-mining district near the Ontario border (see below). By-products are zinc, lead, silver, selenium and tellurium.

Other copper deposits are located: (*a*) near Flin Flon and Snow Lake, joined by rail to the Pas, and housing a base-metal refinery powered by a hydro-electric station on the Churchill River; (*b*) at Manitouwadge Lake, 200 miles north-west of Thunder Bay (Ontario), recently linked by rail and road to both the C.P.R. and C.N.R. main lines; (*c*) at Chibougamau (Quebec Province), where developments have been aided by a branch of the C.P.R. main line; (*d*) at Lake Temagami (Ontario), 60 miles north-east of Sudbury, where the ores are of particularly high grade; (*e*) near Timmins (Ontario), where vast deposits were discovered in 1964.

Zinc, mainly for galvanising, and silver are associated with all these copper deposits and gold is an important by-product of most of the workings.

Gold-mining. Canada's principal gold deposits lie in the Shield, and it is mainly due to their exploitation that the country holds third place as a world producer. The richest fields are in eastern Ontario and the adjacent parts of Quebec, especially at Porcupine, Larder Lake, Kirkland Lake, Rouyn, and Noranda (*see* Fig. 28). Each mine is favourably located with regard to railway communications and hydro-electricity. Timmins and Rouyn, like Sudbury, have become important commercial centres for the miners.

Other gold-mines in the Shield are sporadically distributed. They in-

clude Red Lake and Thunder Bay (Ontario) and Yellowknife (on Great
Slave Lake, N.W.T.). The latter, where gold-mining began in 1938, is
typical of many towns which are just leaving the pioneer stage and
entering that of maturity (see Fig. 13). With a population of about 3700,
it now has the usual amenities, e.g. schools, churches, hotels, shops. There
is a five-hour air link with Edmonton, and a new road has reached the town
from the western end of Great Slave Lake. Periodically, trappers come in
from the surrounding forest to the fur-trading post there. Some milk and
vegetables are produced locally, and commercial fishermen are active on
the lake, but much food must be brought in from more southerly areas.
A small hydro-electric power-station has been built on the Snare River
near by to supply electricity for the mines and also for domestic and other
needs.

Iron ore and uranium production. Both iron ore and uranium are alike in
having been unimportant among the Shield minerals of Canada until
recent years, though both are of great value today.

The principal iron-ore deposits in the Shield have long belonged to
the United States, where the Upper Lakes district is still the world's chief
source. Canada has worked the small deposits at Michipicoten (Ontario)
for a considerable period, but only recently has her production greatly
expanded with the exploitation of deposits in the Ungava trough along
the Labrador–Quebec border (see Chapter V) and at Steep Rock (Ontario), where high-grade haematite occurs beneath the lacustrine silts of a
specially drained Lake. Some of the Michipicoten ore goes to the furnaces
at Sault Ste Marie, while the Steep Rock ores are marketed largely in
Hamilton and the United States.

The Bethlehem Steel Corporation of the United States is developing,
with the aid of a beneficiation process, the use of the low-grade magnetite
ores of Marmora (Ontario) for their Buffalo furnaces. The U.S. Steel
Corporation is working and similarly concentrating the large haematite
deposits at Lac Jeannine in the southern part of the Ungava trough,
125 rail miles from Port Cartier on the St Lawrence, which is rapidly
becoming a second Sept Iles (see Fig. 17).

Other recent developments in Canadian iron ore production include
the extraction of iron oxide pellets from: (a) the Copper Cliff nickel and
copper smelter; (b) Hilton Mine (Quebec Province), 35 miles north-west
of Ottawa; and (c) the gold-mining districts of Kirkland Lake, Red Lake
and other places. Many of these concentrates are sent to Hamilton
(Ontario), Canada's leading steel town.

Since the Second World War, when nuclear fission was accomplished,
the world demand for uranium, chief of the nuclear fuels, has been
intensified. It is, therefore, important to note that the Shield possesses

some of the greatest supplies in the world.

Pitchblende, a source of uranium, was discovered in 1930 on the eastern shore of Great Bear Lake, 30 miles from the Arctic Circle. It was then valued for its content of radium, used in the treatment of cancer, but later the mining town of Port Radium became better known for its uranium. More important deposits have been opened up since 1945, especially near the shore of Georgian Bay, where the new town of Elliot Lake has been erected (*see* Fig. 30). Other workings have been developed

[*Courtesy: Sudbury Daily Star.*

FIG. 30.—Aerial view of Elliot Lake townsite. Set in typical Shield country, amid lakes and forest, Elliot Lake is one among many new mining towns in Canada. It has a refinery for the production of uranium oxide.

in the Beaverlodge area of north Saskatchewan, where Uranium City, containing many buildings from the abandoned town of Goldfields, has been established, and in the Bancroft area of east Ontario, and a large find of high-grade ore has recently been announced at Wollaston Lake in east Saskatchewan.

Canada's first nuclear electricity supply station (200 MW) was opened at Douglas Point on Lake Huron in 1966. It has been followed by a large station (2000 MW) at Pickering near Toronto and by a small one at Gentilly below Trois Rivières in Quebec. A fourth station—at Bruce, close to Douglas Point—is now under construction: when fully operational (in 1979?) it should have the remarkable capacity of 3000 MW. Like the others, it will rely on natural uranium and use heavy water as a moderator.

Minor Shield minerals. 80% of Canada's silver production is obtained from the treatment of base-metal ores. Cobalt, mined with silver round the town of that name, and also produced at the nickel-working centres of Sudbury, Lynn Lake, and Thompson, has long been valued as a source of blue pigment, but has recently gained importance as a metal used in the manufacture of high-speed cutting tools and jet engines. "Cobalt bombs" are now employed in the treatment of cancer, and the value of the mineral in the diet of sheep and calves is recognised. Titanium, another source of pigment, is also needed, when alloyed with steel, by the aircraft industry. It is obtained from the ilmenite deposits of Allard Lake (Quebec Province), north of the forested Anticosti Island, and is smelted at Sorel, near Montreal.

Small amounts of zinc, as we have seen, are extracted from the ores of Noranda, Flin Flon, and Manitouwadge. Likely to prove more important in the long run are the lead-zinc deposits of Pine Point, on the south side of Great Slave Lake, whose development is being encouraged by the extension of the Mackenzie Highway and Great Slave Lake Railway to this locality (*see* Chapter X). Other recently initiated projects include (*i*) the exploitation of zinc deposits in the Lake Mattagami area of northwestern Quebec, and (*ii*) the opening-up of asbestos finds at Sugluk (Saglouc) on Hudson Strait.

THE ALUMINIUM INDUSTRY OF QUEBEC

Aluminium can be produced economically only with large supplies of cheap power, such as may be obtained from falling water. Hence the suitability of such river-sites as those provided by the powerful Saguenay and St Maurice in their steep descent over the high upturned edge of the Shield in southern Quebec. This region—together with the new works at Kitimat (British Columbia)—is now the third most important producing area in the world (after the United States and the U.S.S.R.) and the principal exporter. About 85% of the output is exported, about half going to the United Kingdom, most of the rest to the United States.

The first Canadian smelter was opened in 1904 at Shawinigan, where a very large hydro-electric power-station was built on the St Maurice

River. This smelter is now dwarfed by one at Arvida, constructed in 1926 on the Saguenay, and similarly based on "hydro" (*see* Fig. 29). A third smelter has recently gone into operation at Baie Comeau, on the north bank of the St Lawrence, near the mouth of the Manicouagan River, which supplies power both for this plant and also for towns in the St Lawrence lowland. (In all, the Outardes–Manicouagan complex yields over 6000 MW.). Other works are located at Isle Maligne, at the outlet of Lake St John, and at Beauharnois, near Montreal. Power from several stations on the upper Saguenay and the neighbouring Peribonka is now available to Arvida and Isle Maligne. But Canada produces none of her own raw materials. She imports bauxite or alumina from British Guiana, Jamaica, and Guinea, petroleum coke from Texas, cryolite from Greenland, and fluorspar from Newfoundland. Many of these supplies are unloaded at Port Alfred, a tidewater harbour on the Saguenay.

HYDRO-ELECTRIC POWER RESOURCES

Though possessing no coal or petroleum, the Shield, with its storage lakes, numerous rivers of steep gradient, and resistant rock foundations, has very abundant water-power resources. About half Canada's available supplies have been developed in Quebec; Ontario follows her among Canadian provinces.

Besides building various stations on the St Maurice, Saguenay, and other rivers, Quebec has recently tapped the vast resources of the Manicouagan, Outardes, and Bersimis Rivers, from which power is now being transmitted to Gaspé by cable under the St Lawrence River and even as far as Montreal. The River Ottawa and its tributaries have long supplied power to Ottawa and Hull, but not until 1953 was a very large station built on any of these rivers. Now a number of large stations on the Ottawa are able to transmit power as far as Toronto. Other stations in Ontario are located on such rivers as the Nipigon, English, Mattagami and Michipicoten, from which electricity is distributed mainly to pulp- and paper-mills.

The construction of power-stations along the Nelson (*e.g.* at Kettle Rapids, Manitoba) and Churchill Rivers is now beginning.

Other promising sites have been located on the Albany and Moose, and Quebec is now studying the feasibility of developing the resources of those rivers (especially La Grande) entering James Bay from Ungava; in all, they are thought to have a potential of 15,000 MW.

COMMUNICATIONS

Though the rivers and lakes of the Shield are still used for transport, their use is generally confined to canoes. One of the great deterrents to economic development is the lack of railways, especially in the Arctic zone. Both the C.N.R. and C.P.R. main lines traverse the boreal section of the Shield, but they have few branches. Two points on Canada's north coast, Churchill and Moosonee, however, are in rail communication with the more populous south of Canada.

The Hudson Bay Railway (*see* Fig. 35) runs from the timber-milling town of The Pas, in west Manitoba, to the Bay. It was completed in 1929 to provide an additional outlet for Prairie wheat. The original intention was to terminate the line at Port Nelson, but in view of Churchill's better harbour, it was diverted when 100 miles from its goal.

Churchill, for many years simply a Hudson Bay fort, has a very large grain elevator on the eastern side of the Churchill River estuary, but has never exported as much wheat as the railway sponsors expected. Hudson Strait is open to shipping only from late July to early October, and even then high insurance rates are demanded from shippers in view of the risk of meeting ice-floes. It has also been difficult for Churchill to find suitable return cargoes. A recently inaugurated liner service direct to Manchester and the introduction of an air service via the port from Vancouver to Amsterdam may stimulate its trade.

The Ontario Northland Railway, owned and operated by the Ontario Government, joins Cochrane to the new port of Moosonee, built on the Moose River estuary 4 miles from the old, but still small, Moose Factory. The harbour is open for five months, but James Bay is shallow, and Moosonee remains little more than a supply-point for local fur-trading posts. It may, however, become an outlet for the Clay Belt.

Since the Second World War new railways have been built in the Shield to serve newly developed mining districts, *e.g.* the Labrador–Quebec ironfield, the Lynn Lake nickel–copper mines, the Chibougamau gold–copper deposits, and the Pine Point lead–silver mines. Suggestions have been made for lines from Lake St John to Labrador, and even for one from Churchill to the Pacific!

Highways are being slowly extended, though few have yet been made north of the C.N.R. main line. Aircraft are the usual means of transport in the northlands. Most small towns have airports or at least airstrips, and are served by charter flights if not by scheduled services. Air transport is widely used for surveying and also for ferrying in supplies, not only to pioneer mining districts but also to the chain of strategic radar and meteorological stations newly established in the Arctic zone. The value and population of the Shield are bound to increase if it becomes possible to establish commercial air links between North America, on the one hand, and Russia and China, on the other, since most of the quickest routes will cross this region.

A SUMMARY OF THE HUMAN GEOGRAPHY OF THE SHIELD

Structurally, the Shield is the ancient core round which the rest of North America has grown. But socially and economically, this is far from a heartland. Until the last few years, human beings—apart from small, nomadic bands of Indians and white fur-trappers in the forests, and Eskimo hunters and trappers in the tundra—have shunned this region owing to its severe climate, barren soils, and tenuous communications. In the present century, however, the discovery of widespread mineral deposits, the harnessing of the extensive water resources, the growth of air transport, and the realignment of strategic concepts are combining to give the Shield a "new look." These changes are increasing its importance, not only to Canada but also to the United States. Geographers are now beginning to envisage a "mid-Canada corridor" including Churchill Falls, the Schefferville mines, Athabaska tar-sands and Yukon mines among the development centres.

A NOTE ON THE HUMAN GEOGRAPHY OF ARCTIC CANADA

Arctic Canada, *i.e.* that part of the country which lies north of the tree-line, embraces more than a quarter of the entire territory of the Dominion. It includes the Arctic Archipelago, which will be discussed in Chapter X, northern Labrador, and the northern parts of the Mackenzie Basin and Yukon, as well as the Shield mainland.

Structurally and physically, the Arctic part of the Shield resembles the more southerly parts, but because of contrasts in climate and vegetation, there are variations in human life. Even fewer whites have been drawn to the tundra than to the boreal forests, mining operations have scarcely begun, modern transport, save by air, is virtually non-existent, and economically the whole region yields little but furs, though, according to some enthusiasts, it may have a future as a large grazing area which might supply reindeer-meat to the world's population.

The life of the native people, the Eskimo, has been influenced by their contacts with white Canadians. Traditionally, they are sea-hunters, trappers, and fishers, dependent for their food and clothing upon the natural fauna. Their traditional modes of transport are by dog-sledge on land, one-man *kayak* of seal-skin, and family *umiak* on water. Their impedimenta include wooden-shafted harpoons with narwhal barbs, darts and spears of driftwood and bone; threads of animal sinew, and soapstone lamps. They may own a semi-permanent home of stone, turf, or logs; on hunting expeditions they may erect a winter snow-house or *igloo* and a summer tent or *tupik* of caribou skin spread over a framework of Arctic willow or driftwood.

Today, these smiling people often make the hunting of the white fox for sale to white traders their main occupation. The introduction of a money economy has led many of them to adopt a diet of coffee, bread, jam, and tinned foods in preference to warmth-giving fish and blubber. With the adoption of the more efficient rifle, the art of harpoon-making is in danger of being lost. Kayaks have largely been displaced by motor boats. With a more settled life have come permanent frame-houses, perhaps heated with petroleum. The Canadian Government is now establishing permanent village communities and Eskimo co-operatives, *e.g.* at George River on the eastern side of Ungava Bay, where a fishing co-operative and fish-freezing plant has been set up. Some Eskimos have found work in Government defence establishments. Most have become Christianised, and have been encouraged to accept Government health, educational, and social services.

No longer do a majority of the Eskimo live close to their environment. Some have become impoverished nomads, too dependent upon the vagaries of the fur trade. Many have contracted white diseases, and some moral degeneration has set in. Poor clothing and undernourishment are noticeable. Despite the well-intentioned efforts of the Government, supported recently by the work of an Eskimo Affairs Committee, on which sit three Eskimos in Ottawa, these people are in real danger of losing their identity as a distinct cultural group (*see also* Chapter XXIX).

Chapter IX

THE PRAIRIE PROVINCES : THE PRAIRIES AND THEIR NORTHERN MARGINS

THE three Prairie Provinces, Manitoba, Saskatchewan, and Alberta, include not only the Canadian portion of the North American Prairies but also parts of the forested Shield, Mackenzie Basin, and Rocky Mountains. The Provinces are roughly of equal size, and cover about a fifth of Canada's territory. All have many lakes, but only Manitoba has a seacoast (on Hudson Bay).

European settlement mostly post-dates the construction of railways. Colonists have hardly ventured yet into the north, except in the Peace River district and in sporadic mining centres in the Shield, *e.g.* Flin Flon, Uranium City, and Lynn Lake. There are also a few fur-trading posts in the north, and there is the small port of Churchill, on Hudson Bay.

Farm production dominates the economic life of the Prairie Provinces, but the urban population is now growing at the expense of the rural, and the post-war development of the rich petroleum and natural-gas resources is bringing a more varied economy, especially to Alberta.

PHYSICAL GEOGRAPHY

STRUCTURE AND RELIEF

The region under study forms the southern part of the plains area between the Shield and the Cordillera. The rocks are nearly horizontally bedded Cretaceous sediments, with some Palaeozoics in the Red River lowland of Manitoba, and some Tertiary residuals. Over wide areas, the solid rocks are covered with glacial drift and lacustrine deposits, as, for example, in the Vale of York and its offshoot, the Vale of Pickering, in England.

On the whole, the relief is that appropriate to a region of plain and plateau, but two escarpments, producing three levels or steps and a number of residual hill masses, modify its general character (*see* Fig. 31).

In the east the South Manitoba Lowland forms the first Prairie level. Averaging about 800 ft in altitude, it consists of the fertile lacustrine plains of the Red River valley and the Manitoban Great Lakes, though between Lake Winnipeg and Lake Manitoba outcrops of bare rock and peaty hollows occur. The lakes are remnants of the pre-glacial Lake Agassiz, which was held up by decaying ice-sheets to the north and the Minnesota water-parting in the south. Bounding the area on the west are the scarps of various flat-topped hills of Cretaceous age, averaging 1200–2000 ft in elevation, and penetrated by such rivers as the Red Deer and Assiniboine. They include Pasquia Mountain, Porcupine and Duck Mountain, Riding Mountain (the site of a National Park), and Pembina Mountain. Most of these hills are wooded.

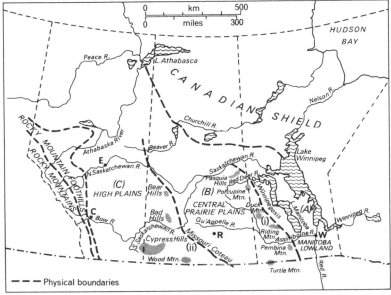

FIG. 31.—Main surface features of Canadian Prairies.

I, II = Prairie escarpments.   A, B, C = Prairie levels.
Many lakes, for example along the Churchill River, have been omitted from this map.
The cities marked by initial letters should be identified.

The second Prairie level, averaging 1500–2000 ft, comprises the un-dulating plateau of south-west Manitoba and Saskatchewan, and in the main forms the dip-slope of the Cretaceous hill masses noted above. The central part is the highest, though the Tertiary remnant of wooded Turtle Mountain is prominent in the south. The western margin is de-fined by a somewhat irregular escarpment known as the Missouri Coteau, which is continued southwards into the United States. It includes the Bear and Bad Hills of south-central Saskatchewan, and roughly follows a line running north-west to south-east from North Battleford to Estevan.

The third Prairie step, roughly 2000–4000 ft in height, is composed of the High Plains of south-west Saskatchewan and Alberta. It rises irregularly to the Rocky Mountain foothills, which may be said to begin west of a line from Calgary to Lethbridge. In the south high Tertiary remnants, such as Wood Mountain and the Cypress Hills, furnish examples of scrubby, gravelly "bad lands" topography.

A few large rivers, notably the North and South Saskatchewan, and their headstreams, cross the High Plains in deeply trenched valleys. These two rivers unite before flowing into Lake Winnipeg, whence all but the southern part of the entire Prairie region is drained north-eastwards via the Nelson River into Hudson Bay. All the Prairie rivers, but especially the Red, are subject to spring flooding due to snow-melt and early summer rains. But in late summer they may be reduced to semi-dry, gravelly channels. Surface depressions are frequently filled with shallow bodies of water known as "sloughs."

NATURAL VEGETATION AND SOILS

Three main regions of natural vegetation, each with its characteristic soils, can be recognised in the area under study: (a) grasslands; (b) parkland; (c) mixed woodland (see Fig. 11).

The grasslands are of the cool temperate variety. In the more humid east there is a tall-grass zone, or true Prairie, consisting largely of porcupine grass, green spear grass, rough fescue, and northern wheat grass. Its soils are deep and granular, black or dark brown in colour, very rich in humus and admirably adapted to wheat-growing. In the drier west there is a short-grass zone, sometimes referred to as steppe country. Prominent among its native grasses are blue grama, June, and Prairie blue grass. Lining the riverways, as in the tall-grass zone, are "bluffs" (i.e. clumps) of poplar and willow. The soils are lighter in colour than those of the true Prairie, as they are poorer in humus, but they are very fertile nevertheless. They may be used successfully for grain-farming, but since their organic content is quickly exhausted under cultivation, they may become eroded, as happened in the dry years of the 1930s. They are best suited to grazing. In the driest parts (south-west Saskatchewan and south-east Alberta) the vegetation degenerates into semi-desert, with a poor cover of sage and prickly pear cactus.

North, east, and west of the grasslands, where the rainfall is slightly heavier, lies a region of parkland, or aspen-grove, which carries bluffs of aspen and black poplar interspersed with occasional maples, oaks, elms, and ashes, and patches of tall grass. This region, which includes the Peace River district, is mostly used for mixed farming. Its soils are deep and very dark brown, even black in colour. They generally contain more organic matter and surface nitrogen than the Prairie soils, and though rather more leached, bear the heaviest crops.

Between this Park Belt and the boreal forests of the Shield is a zone of mixed woodland, in which the poplar is a common deciduous tree, the white spruce and jack pine notable conifers. The gradual deterioration in soil fertility and the shortening of the growing season reduce the attractiveness of this region to farmers, and agriculturally this is a pioneer zone.

THE CLIMATE

The climate of the Prairies and their northern margins is everywhere of the cool temperate continental type. July temperatures are higher than those obtaining in similar latitudes in eastern Canada, and the growing season—over 110 days in the south, 90 days in the Peace River district— is longer. Temperatures in the winter better reflect the interior location of the region. In the eastern part of the Prairies the thermometer may fall to —70° F on some days and there are no mild spells, but the west is occasionally warmed by a *chinook*, *i.e.* a body of air funnelled eastwards down

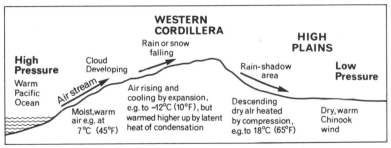

FIG. 32.—Mechanism of chinook wind.

the Rocky Mountain valleys during the passage of a "low," and undergoing heating by compression (*see* Fig. 32). Calgary may, in fact, on occasion, be 40°–50° F warmer than a place at the same altitude on the western side of the Rockies. Even Calgary, however, like Winnipeg, has five months below 32° F, and seven below 43° F, and both suffer from severe arctic blizzards which not only chill the air but also severely reduce visibility. Night frosts occasionally occur even in summer, but temperatures of 110° F are not unknown. Both the spring and fall seasons are brief: winter passes very quickly into summer, summer into winter.

Everywhere, the maximum precipitation comes in summer, up to half the year's supply normally falling in June, July, and August. September, the chief harvest month, usually has a lower rainfall than May. Winter snows may average 3–5 ft; the melting period coincides with the onset of April showers. Most of the rainfall is cyclonic, but in summer thunderstorms develop when warm, moist, Gulf air moves towards an interior low-pressure system.

Broadly speaking, the mean annual precipitation declines westwards from about 20 in. at Winnipeg to 16 in. at Calgary, but the Rocky Mountain foothills usually have about 20 in. The driest parts are in south-east Alberta and south-west Saskatchewan, where the mean annual rainfall is less than 13 in.

The region has abundant sunshine, and the sensible severity of the winters is mitigated by low atmospheric humidity.

The following climatic statistics for Winnipeg, Calgary, and Edmonton will repay study:

Winnipeg

(alt. 760 ft)	J.	F.	M.	A.	M.	J.	Jy.	A.	S.	O.	N.	D.
Temperature (° F) .	−4	0	15	38	52	62	66	64	54	41	21	6
Precipitation (in.) .	0·9	0·7	1·2	1·4	2·0	3·1	3·1	2·2	2·2	1·4	1·1	0·9

Mean Annual Temperature: 35° F; Mean Annual Range of Temperature: 70° F; Mean Annual Precipitation: 20·2 in.

Calgary

(alt. 3400 ft)	J.	F.	M.	A.	M.	J.	Jy.	A.	S.	O.	N.	D.
Temperature (° F) .	12	15	25	40	49	56	61	59	51	42	28	19
Precipitation (in.) .	0·5	0·6	0·7	0·8	2·3	2·9	2·6	2·5	1·3	0·7	0·7	0·5

Mean Annual Temperature: 38° F; Mean Annual Range of Temperature: 49° F; Mean Annual Precipitation: 16·1 in.

Edmonton

(alt. 2100 ft)	J.	F.	M.	A.	M.	J.	Jy.	A.	S.	O.	N.	D.
Temperature (° F) .	5	11	24	41	51	57	61	59	50	41	25	14
Precipitation (in.) .	0·9	0·6	0·7	0·8	0·8	3·2	3·5	2·4	1·4	0·7	0·7	0·7

Mean Annual Temperature: 37° F; Mean Annual Range of Temperature: 56° F; Mean Annual Precipitation: 16·5 in.

THE ECONOMY

GENERAL AGRICULTURAL FEATURES

From southern Manitoba, agriculture has gradually spread north towards the boreal forest, and west towards the Rockies. Between 1900 and 1950, the cultivated area grew from four to 40 million acres. Today, the percentage of cropped land falls to 20 only in the dry belt of Palliser's triangle (p. 114) and in the pioneer fringe of the mixed woodland zone.

The earliest settlers practised subsistence farming, but with the spread of railways, extensive wheat-farming became dominant, in response to the growing demand for bread in western Europe. During the present century, there has been a trend towards more agricultural diversification.

Wheat remains the chief cereal, but oats and barley are also widely grown. About 95% of Canada's wheat comes from the Prairie Provinces, which grow nearly half as much as the whole of the United States. Saskatchewan accounts for about 60% of the total crop. Nearly all of the Prairie wheat is spring-sown owing to the severity of the winters. About a quarter is retained for Canadian use, the rest is exported.

Oats, mostly grown as an animal feedstuff, and barley, mainly used for malting, often succeed wheat in Prairie fields. In Manitoba, where cattle are numerous, oats occupies roughly the same acreage as wheat, but it is a relatively minor crop in Saskatchewan, where wheat is often followed by fallow. Barley, too, is more important in Manitoba than elsewhere. Requiring lower ripening temperatures, both oats and barley can be grown farther north than wheat.

Rye and maize are minor cereals. The former is raised by east European farmers, both for bread and whisky distilling; the latter is cultivated, with irrigation, in south-west Alberta, and, without irrigation, along the southern margin of Manitoba.

Non-cereal crops include sugar-beet (the chief irrigation crop), vegetables and fruit (cultivated close to most farm-houses), tobacco and alfalfa (grown on a small scale, with irrigation), linseed, soybeans, rapeseed and sunflowers (all of which became important during the war years, when there was a shortage of vegetable oils).

While two-thirds of the cash income of the Prairie farmers still comes from wheat, an increasing amount is derived from the sale of cattle and their products, e.g. beef, milk, cheese, and butter; pigs; and from the marketing of poultry and eggs. Mixed farming, based on cattle, pigs, wheat, and oats, is extending. The reasons for this are mainly as follows:

1. The growth of population in the Prairies, notably in the Park Belt, which supports the three largest cities.

2. The growth of the British war-time market for animal products.

3. The drawbacks of the "wheat madness" system, and the piling-up of grain surpluses. It is now realised that monoculture weakens the soil and encourages weeds and plant diseases. The practice of fallowing is markedly uneconomic and conducive to soil erosion, and farmers are likely to suffer when they depend too much upon a single saleable commodity.

Prairie landholdings are normally square or rectangular in shape. The unit is the mile-square section of 640 acres, subdivided into quarter-sections. The size of the individual farms is related to soil, climate, and agricultural economy. A Park Belt mixed farm may average only 160 acres, a sub-humid grain-farm 320, a semi-arid one 640. Ranches in dry grazing areas may carry over 500 head of cattle and run up to 10,000 acres.

All Prairie farms are highly mechanised, and tractors are commoner than horses. Combines are particularly useful to farmers without hired labour because the gap between the ripening of the grain and the onset of autumn frosts is narrow.

THE AGRICULTURAL REGIONS

Reference to Fig. 33 will reveal a number of agricultural regions in the Prairies.

1. *The main wheat-growing region.* Wheat occupies at least half the total cropland in much of the true Prairie country, especially in those parts where the mean annual rainfall exceeds 15 in. In the short-grass zone it may be grown by dry-farming even if the annual rainfall is only 12 in.

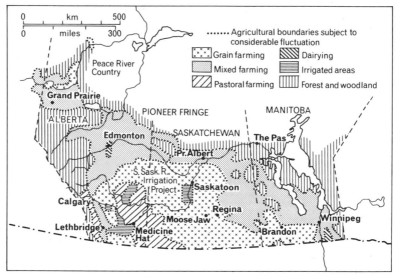

FIG. 33.—Agricultural regions of Canadian Prairies.

2. *The mixed farming region.* This region, mainly in the Park Belt, forms a horse-shoe enclosing the Wheat Belt on three sides. Locally, oats and barley may be more important than wheat, dairy-cattle are usually more numerous than beef-herds, and pigs and poultry are notable side-lines.

3. *The ranching areas.* These are found: (*a*) in the short-grass Prairie zone of south-west Saskatchewan and south-east Alberta; (*b*) in the

higher parts of the High Plains, and in the Rocky Mountain foothills; (c) in the Cypress Hills. Beef-cattle, especially Herefords and Shorthorns, are the main animals. In the west the *chinook* (or "snow-eater") quickly bares the ground of snow in spring, thereby reducing the amount of winter feed required, but watering may be difficult. Sheep—grazed on the driest and roughest land—are declining in number, partly due to the small demand for lamb and mutton.

4. *The irrigated areas.* Irrigation-farming is very limited in extent, and is chiefly found in south-west Alberta, *e.g.* in valleys such as the Bow near Calgary and Lethbridge, where the mean annual rainfall is under 15 in. Green vegetables and soft fruits (some of which are canned at Lethbridge), sugar-beet, alfalfa, tobacco, maize, and wheat are the chief crops. Recently Saskatchewan has completed two large irrigation projects, involving the damming of the South Saskatchewan River near Outlook, south of Saskatoon, and the damming on a smaller scale of the Upper Qu'Appelle River, east of Regina. The large South Saskatchewan Dam has an attached power-station to free the province from its present dependence upon thermal electricity, and the 140-mile long lake created by the dam is beginning to attract tourists and also assist flood control.

5. *The pioneer fringe.* This area, north of the mixed farming belt, is attracting a few pioneers who are rearing cattle and pigs and growing oats and potatoes, but as yet very few farms have been laid out north of Prince Albert (Saskatchewan) and The Pas (Manitoba).

THE PRAIRIE WHEAT INDUSTRY

The Prairies offer the following advantages to the wheat-farmer:

1. An undulating terrain, with a cover of natural grassland. Once the steel plough had been introduced, such ground could be easily cultivated without the burden of preliminary forest-clearance.

2. A suitable climate, which favours the production of a hard, glutinous grain, rich in protein.

3. A deep, mostly loamy soil, rich in nitrogen, with a good content of phosphorus and potassium, and able to retain its richness for a long time without fertilising. (Fertilisers are now being used to increase yields and reduce fallow).

4. Cheap land.

5. Excellent rail transport through the farm lands and between the Prairies and the ports.

6. Large, reliable markets at home and overseas, notably in the United Kingdom, which normally takes one-third of the exports, other countries in western Europe, Japan and South Africa and, more recently,

China and the U.S.S.R., especially when, as in 1963–4, 1965–6 and 1971–2, harvests in those countries are poor.

7. Good facilities for the movement of wheat, e.g.: (a) country elevators, the small storage-houses found at every Prairie railway station;* (b) terminal elevators, large storage buildings located mostly at the ports; (c) special box-cars on the railways, and specially designed ships called "whalebacks" on the Lakes; (d) grading facilities, notably at Winnipeg; (e) bulk-handling methods.

8. Special research facilities, which have enabled Canada to produce varieties of wheat which are resistant to drought and disease, and which are capable of maturing early, e.g. in less than 90 days. Among rust-resistant species are Thatcher, Apex, Renown, Selkirk and Manitou; early maturing types include Garnet and Prelude. The evolution of drought-resistant strains has enabled farmers to grow wheat in parts of the semi-arid Palliser's triangle, and the use of quick-maturing varieties has permitted the extension of wheat-growing into the Peace River district.

Large-scale wheat-growing, however, has its drawbacks, as we have seen. The equation of supply and demand has not yet been solved. While there have been phenomenal harvests during the last twenty years, and huge stocks of grain remain unsold, individual farmers are periodically liable to be hit by various natural catastrophes which destroy their crops. Among these are late spring frosts, night frosts in August, hailstorms, spring blizzards, grasshopper plagues, rust disease, damage by mice and gophers, drought, dust-storms. The last two may be widespread and may result in soil erosion and the loss of humus. In 1935, to combat these perils and provide general farm assistance, especially to owners of marginal land in Palliser's triangle which had suffered from recurrent drought, the Prairie Farm Rehabilitation Act was passed. It recommended, inter alia, the retention of stubble on the land instead of burning it, a reduction in the amount of summer-fallowing and dry-farming to conserve the soil, the encouragement of livestock by sowing deep-rooted grasses and improving watering facilities, and the introduction of contour ploughing, and strip-cropping, i.e. the division of farmland into strips bearing crops, stubble, and fallow so as to prevent soil blowing. Better weed and pest control is also being practised.

The movement of the wheat from the Prairies to the ports. Though situated much farther from the coast than the corresponding wheatlands of Argen-

---

* These buildings are often referred to as "Prairie cathedrals." Most of them are owned by farmers' co-operatives.

tina and Australia, the Canadian Prairies have well-organised and abundant transport facilities to both Atlantic and Pacific waters.

The eastward routes pass through Winnipeg, whence most wheat is passed on to the numerous terminal elevators at Fort William and Port Arthur (Thunder Bay), prior to shipment through the Lakes to Buffalo and New York, Kingston and Montreal. Some moves directly by rail to Montreal, the greatest Canadian grain port, or Quebec. When the St Lawrence freezes, outlets are found at Halifax, St John, and Portland (Maine). Even Philadelphia and Baltimore may be called upon to export Canadian grain, as well as surpluses from the United States.

The Hudson Bay route from Manitoba to Churchill was noted in Chapter VIII. This route may save 1000 miles compared with that to Montreal, but it is normally open only from late July to early October, so that it does no more than supplement the other eastern routes.

Vancouver is the chief Pacific outlet, Prince Rupert being subsidiary to it. Both ports are open all the year, and are nearer to the main wheat areas than Atlantic ports. The westward routes, however, involve heavy freight charges over the Western Cordillera, as well as a long voyage via the Panamá Canal to Europe, though the Japanese market is very accessible.

POWER AND MINERAL RESOURCES OF THE PRAIRIES

The Prairies are as richly endowed with petroleum, natural gas, and coal, as with cultivable land, but apart from small stations on the Winnipeg, Saskatchewan, and Bow Rivers, little has yet been done to develop hydro-electricity.

Coal. All three Prairie Provinces have extremely large reserves of coal. The chief mines are in Alberta, *e.g.* near Crows Nest Pass, Lethbridge, and Drumheller, where deeply trenched rivers have revealed seams of subbituminous and bituminous coals. In the Rocky Mountain foothills the deposits include anthracite, but the seams are badly disturbed and the output small. South Saskatchewan and Manitoba possess Tertiary lignites, some of which are worked by strip-mining and used in local power-stations.

The total Prairie coal production, including lignite, has declined in favour of natural gas and petroleum, but is now showing signs of revival with the signing of long-term contracts with Japanese steel-mills. (*See also p. 132.*)

Petroleum. In the last few years petroleum has become one of Canada's leading minerals, and the Prairie region produces virtually all of it (Fig. 34). Canada is now self-sufficient in petroleum, even though she consumes more oil per head than any other country save the United States, and she is able to sell some in the American Middle West and far North-west.

For over 30 years after its discovery in 1914 the Turner Valley field, near Calgary, was Canada's only significant producer. Most of the wells, however, are now more than ½ mile deep, therefore the discovery of petroleum in other localities has been providential for the industry. In 1944 a small field was opened at Lloydminster (Alberta), but it was in 1947 that the first major strike was made, at Leduc, 20 miles south of Edmonton. Other finds followed, e.g. at Redwater and later at Pembina, 75 miles south-west of Edmonton, and an oil boom set in.

[Courtesy: George Hunter, Toronto.

FIG. 34.—Aerial view of oil-well near Edmonton, Alberta. Oil-wells now punctuate many of the Prairie farmlands round Edmonton, and are also growing in number in Saskatchewan.

New deposits are still being located, e.g. in the last year or two at Rainbow Lake, north-west Alberta. Alberta now produces 70% of Canada's petroleum, most of the rest coming from newly developed wells in west Saskatchewan, south-west Manitoba and the Peace River district in British Columbia. The total Canadian production is now more than 55 million metric tons.

A growing number of pipelines distribute oil to Prairie refineries and beyond. The 2000-mile-long "Interprovincial" Line carries it, partly through U.S. territory, to Sarnia and Toronto, and the 700-mile "Trans-Mountain" Line takes it to Vancouver and north-west Washington (United States).

Growing out of the establishment of oil-refineries at Edmonton, Calgary, Moose Jaw, Regina, Winnipeg and other places, is a widening range of petro-chemical industries producing, for example, fertilisers and plastics.

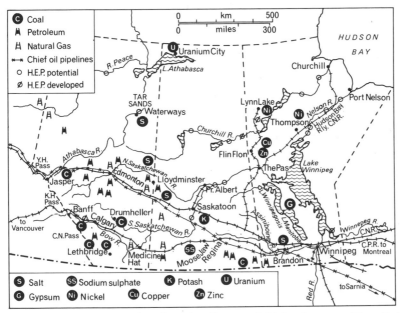

FIG. 35.—Power resources, minerals, main railways and chief settlements of Canadian Prairies. The railways of the Peace River country are shown on Fig. 36.

Natural gas deposits are often associated with petroleum supplies. Alberta has used this source of power since 1883, and Medicine Hat was gas-lit by 1900. But both output and the range of commercial utilisation have expanded in the last few years. Alberta produces 90% of Canada's output; much of the rest comes from western Saskatchewan and the Peace River district of British Columbia. Only the United States and the Soviet Union produce and use more natural gas than Canada. An important by-product recovered at a number of plants, chiefly in Alberta, is sulphur, obtained by cleansing natural gas. Canada is now a leading exporter of sulphur.

From Alberta, gas pipelines link up with the northern mountain states of the United States, Winnipeg, and the American Middle West. From the Peace River District, a pipeline serves Vancouver and is joined southwards to the American Pacific system, but the longest line (2300 miles) passes through Regina, Winnipeg, and Thunder Bay *en route* to Toronto (for Detroit and Boston) and Montreal.

Other resources of the Prairies. Excluding coal, petroleum, and natural gas, the chief mineral resources of the Prairie Provinces lie in the Shield (*see* Chapter VIII). The Prairies themselves furnish: (*a*) rock salt deposits, *e.g.* at Unity (Saskatchewan), Neepawa (Manitoba), and Elk Point (Alberta); (*b*) sodium sulphate, found in various alkali lakes in south Saskatchewan, notably Chaplin Lake; (*c*) potash, near Saskatoon, Regina, and elsewhere in south-east Saskatchewan: these appear to be the largest and richest deposits in the world, but have only been broached since 1962; the output has now surpassed that of East Germany, and exports are going to the U.S.A., Japan, and Europe, though there is now growing concern about overproduction; (*d*) gypsum, quarried at Gypsumville in the Manitoba Lowland. All these minerals are important chemical raw materials.

Forests are not widespread nor very valuable in the region, but there are a few lumbermen and pulp-mill operators in the Peace River district and the northern mixed woodland. The marshes of the Saskatchewan River delta form a natural habitat for many musk-rat, from which "musquash" furs are obtained, but fur-ranching is more important than trapping. There are commercial fisheries on the Manitoban Great Lakes.

PRAIRIE SETTLEMENTS

THE GROWTH OF SETTLEMENT

Prior to the advent of white people, the Prairies and Park Belt were occupied by members of various Indian tribes, the main group being the Blackfeet. They had acquired the horse, probably from Mexico, before making contact with white immigrants, and they used it on hunting expeditions.

The earliest Europeans to enter the region—in the eighteenth century—were fur-traders, of both French and British origin. The first true agricultural settlement was founded in 1812, when the Earl of Selkirk established a colony of evicted crofters from the Western Highlands of Scotland in the Red River valley. Early attempts at cultivation, however, were marred by clashes with fur-traders and Indians, and the first crops suffered from mice and grasshoppers, river floods and late frosts.

Meanwhile, the native bison were rapidly being slaughtered, both by

Indians and whites, who valued their meat and hides. Killings were intensified when the Indians acquired the repeating rifle, and reached a peak when the builders of the "Iron Horse" entered the region in the 1880s. Buffalo are now confined to certain national parks, notably the Wood Buffalo Park west of Slave River, northern Alberta.

It was the railways which really drew settlers to the Prairies, though the report of Captain John Palliser to the British Colonial Office had some effect. This officer, who is best remembered for the famous triangle of semi-arid land he located in south-west Saskatchewan and south-east Alberta—examined the Prairies between 1857 and 1860. It was not until 1878, however, that the first railway reached Winnipeg, from St Paul and Chicago, to be followed in four years by the C.P.R. line from Port Arthur. By 1885, a through route to Vancouver had been made. Branch lines followed and settlers flocked in to the Park Belt. Later, railways were built farther north: they are now incorporated in the C.N.R. Between 1896 and 1913, a million colonists moved into the Prairie Provinces. They took up farm-sites laid out by the Government who at first offered them free of charge.

By 1931 the Prairie Provinces had a combined population of about 2,300,000. In 1956—despite the wheat bankruptcies of the 1930s, which led to much farm abandonment—the population was 2,900,000 and in 1971 over 3,500,000. Alberta has shown the greatest increase. Many of the twentieth-century immigrants have been French Canadians and people from the mainland of Europe, e.g. Ukraine, Poland, the Netherlands, and Germany. These minority groups, notably Slavs, tend to inhabit their own villages, to wear the costume of their homeland, and to worship in their own churches.

In the present century motor highways have been added to railway lines to assist the movement of people and farm produce. But less than 20% of the roads are properly surfaced, and bulk commodities like grain continue to be transported over long distances in rail box-cars, not on lorries. Aircraft are commonly used for long-distance passenger transport: most cities have large airports; Edmonton, in fact, boasts three!

THE SMALLER URBAN CENTRES

To the rectangular fields of the Prairies, their oil derricks, wind-pumps, farms and farm-buildings, straight roads, railway lines, and country elevators, we must add urban centres as essential elements of the Prairie scene. Acting as local centres of trade, culture, and entertainment are numerous small towns, most of which are equipped with garages, farm machinery showrooms, food-packing and processing works. All are of modern growth, and all are built on a grid-iron pattern, occasionally modified by a river siting.

Among the larger towns are Saskatoon, the seat of Saskatchewan University, which has flour-mills, meat-packing works, and oilseed-crushing plants; Moose Jaw, with an oil refinery as well as meat-packing plants and flour-mills; and Brandon, with large flour-mills and stockyards, dairies and breweries.

THE MAJOR CITIES

The great urban centres are the three provincial capitals, Winnipeg, Regina, and Edmonton, and the city of Calgary. The following table gives an idea of their growth during this century, and illustrates the rapid growth of the Albertan cities.

Population

	1901	1931	1961	City	1971 Metropolitan Area
Winnipeg .	42,000	217,000	260,000	246,000	540,000
Edmonton .	4,000	78,000	274,000	438,000	496,000
Calgary .	4,000	83,000	242,000	403,000	403,000
Regina .	2,200	53,000	110,000	139,000	141,000

Winnipeg is Canada's fifth city, outstripped by Vancouver in the 1920s and by Ottawa–Hull in the 1960s. A settlement of wide and windy streets, it is situated on a flat, too-easily flooded plain, at the confluence of the Red and Assiniboine Rivers. Its importance derives from its situation rather than its site. Lying in the narrow gap of open country between Lake Winnipeg and its surrounding bush on the north, and the international frontier on the south; and sprawling almost halfway between Vancouver and Montreal, it has become the hub of central Canada. It commands the eastern approach to the Prairies, at a place where the C.P.R. and C.N.R. main lines converge before again dividing and throwing out their numerous Prairie branches, and it is in easy touch with the American Middle West. It boasts the largest privately owned (C.P.R.) railway marshalling yards in the world.

Though chosen by the French as a fur-trading centre in 1738, and becoming later the site of Selkirk's 1812 colony and the Hudson Bay Company's Fort Garry (1835), its population numbered only 213 in 1870. In that year it was chosen capital of the new province of Manitoba, and subsequently it came to house the provincial university. But its growth has been mainly conditioned by the building of railways and the development of the Prairies as a farming region.

Winnipeg is the chief distributing and grading centre for Prairie wheat; the commercial centre of the mixed farming region of southern Manitoba; the principal fur market in Canada and the administrative head-quarters of the Hudson Bay Company in Canada. It has many light in-dustries, *e.g.* the manufacture of flour, leather, farm machinery, electrical equipment, clothing, and needles. It also manufactures railway rolling stock and has large meat-packing, brewing, printing, and publishing works.

Edmonton has recently overtaken Calgary as the largest Albertan city. Founded in 1808 as a fur-trading post on the North Saskatchewan River, its growth has been phenomenal during the last thirty years. Though a gateway to the west via the Yellowhead Pass, it is more im-portant now as an entrance to the north. It is, in fact, symptomatic of the increasing attention Canada is paying to its Northlands that the city is expanding so rapidly. Edmonton is also the capital of Alberta and the seat of its university.

Edmonton's local power resources, mainly petroleum and natural gas nowadays, formerly coal (once mined in the city itself), have assisted the older industries, *e.g.* meat-packing, flour-milling, and the preparation of dairy products, as well as the newer, *e.g.* the manufacture of chemicals and rayon. The city has long been an important Park Belt market for wheat, cattle, hogs, and furs.

Calgary is newer than Edmonton, but more compact in its lay-out. It was established as recently as 1875 as a mounted-police fort at the con-fluence of the Bow and Elbow Rivers. Situated on the C.P.R. main transcontinental line at the meeting-place of arable field, ranch and irrigated plot, and close to coal-mines, oil-wells, and natural-gas resources, it has become both a busy commercial city and an industrial centre. Many people are employed in its flour mills, meat-packing works, breweries, oil refineries, engineering shops and petro-chemical plants but two-thirds of the employed population are engaged in tertiary occu-pations.

Regina had to await the coming of the C.P.R. to receive its first real settlers, in 1882. It was the first headquarters of the then North-West Mounted Police, who found a suitable site on the small Wascana Creek. Regina's industries include flour-milling, meat-packing, and oil-refining. In 1960 the first steel-rolling mill in Saskatchewan was set up there, and the city hopes to find useful a small deposit of iron ore located in north-east Saskatchewan.

THE PEACE RIVER COUNTRY

The Peace River country, which is physically and economically part of the Albertan Park Belt, extends into British Columbia. It consists of undulating country averaging 2000–3000 ft in altitude, diversified by a few flat-topped hills of 3000 ft. Though in a fairly high latitude (c. 56° N.), its summers are almost as warm as Edmonton's, but its winters are colder: the January average at Peace River is —9° F. The growing season is somewhat longer than that of areas immediately north and south of it, since the Cordillera are lower in this latitude and oceanic air can therefore enter it more easily. The mean annual rainfall is only 12–15 in., but three-quarters of it generally comes from May to September, i.e. when the farmer needs it most.

Widespreading woodlands, patches of muskeg, and broad penetrations of Prairie grasses diversify the scene. The farming population, which only began to move in after 1910, has found it can successfully cultivate early maturing strains of wheat, oats, and barley, and can make the raising of cattle, pigs, poultry, vegetables, clover, and alfalfa a paying proposition. A railway and a few roads have been made to link the farms with Edmonton, and a new road and railway to Prince George in central British Columbia enables Vancouver to be reached. Dawson Creek (British Columbia) and Grande Prairie (Alberta) are the main centres for local business (see Fig. 36).

A few hardy pioneers are now penetrating the Hay River valley to the north and the woodland and muskeg to the south of the occupied territory, but the most significant recent development has been the exploitation, especially near Dawson Creek, Fort St John and Fort Nelson, of oil and natural gas deposits and the extraction of sulphur from natural gas. Further progress is resulting from damming the Peace River in the Rocky Mountain Trench below the confluence of the Finlay and Parsnip Rivers, and the erection of a large hydro-electric power station which should soon be supplying 2300 MW.

Chapter X

THE MACKENZIE LOWLANDS AND THE ARCTIC ARCHIPELAGO

THE MACKENZIE LOWLANDS—PHYSICAL ASPECTS

PHYSICAL GEOGRAPHY

The greater part of the Mackenzie Basin (Fig. 36) forms the northern portion of the Central Plains of North America, but the eastern section belongs structurally to the Shield, and the headwaters of the main left-bank tributaries lie in the Western Cordillera. Economically, the south-western part of the Basin, *i.e.* the Upper Peace River country, forms an outlier of the Prairies (*see* Chapter IX).

The River Mackenzie, at least 2300 miles long, is one of the world's major rivers. It is the second longest in North America, and drains one-sixth of Canada. Most of its course is through an area of nearly horizontally bedded rocks largely concealed under a Pleistocene overlay of sand, gravel, and clay. Its source is in the Athabaska River, which rises in the Columbia icefield and forms the main approach to the Yellowhead Pass. This headstream flows into the south-west end of Lake Athabaska, which is linked to the Great Slave Lake by the Slave River. The name "Mackenzie" is restricted to that part of the drainage-line which emerges from the west end of Great Slave Lake and runs north-westwards into the Arctic. It reaches the ocean by means of an extensive delta, the northern half of which is floored with glacial deposits.

Many of the tributaries of the Mackenzie are great rivers. They include the Peace and the Liard, both of which thread the northern reaches of the Rocky Mountain Trench (*see* Chapter XI) before breaking through the mountains in wide corridors, lower than the Yellowhead Pass. North of the Liard confluence, the Keele River, rising in the 7000-ft-high Mackenzie Mountains, on the Yukon Frontier, joins the main river on the left bank, and lower down, on the right, the Great Bear Lake—the largest lake entirely in Canada—contributes its outflow via the river of the same name.

CLIMATE AND NATURAL VEGETATION

The climate of most of the Mackenzie Lowlands is of the sub-arctic or boreal type, but the coastal fringe lies in the arctic or tundra zone. Fort

Norman, where the Great Bear River enters the Mackenzie, is fairly typical: its January average temperature is —18° F, July 64° F. It should be noted that, owing to the penetration of Pacific air, the latter figure is

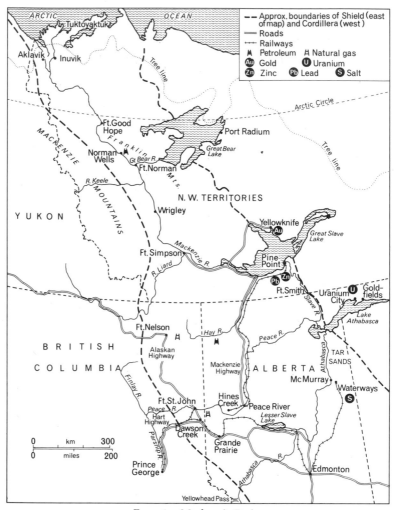

FIG. 36.—Mackenzie Basin.

higher than that for Edmonton. Even Aklavik, on the delta, has a July mean of 57° F, and the benefit of over 18 hours of daylight between April 21st and August 21st.

The precipitation is light: 15 in. normally in the south, only 10 in. in the north-east. There is a maximum in summer, when most maritime air invades the region, and the winter snowfall is not heavy.

The northern parts of the Mackenzie delta are occupied by tundra. Elsewhere there are boreal forests, in which the white spruce is supreme, though trees such as jack pine, aspen, poplar, willow, and birch are not uncommon. Some of the river-flats are marshy, and there are many lakes and areas of muskeg away from the watercourses.

THE MACKENZIE LOWLANDS—THE ECONOMY

AGRICULTURAL ACTIVITIES

Round most of the small settlements some gardening is practised, though commercial farming is restricted to the Peace River district (*see* Chapter IX). Potatoes, cabbages, and other vegetables can be grown, even at Aklavik, and lettuces, radishes, perhaps even strawberries may be raised, especially if started in greenhouses. A few dairy cattle are kept on clover, hay, and alfalfa. Oats, generally cut in early September, while still green, may be cultivated on a small scale.

Griffith Taylor has referred to the Mackenzie Basin as the "last frontier of potential arable lands in the Dominion." The region as a whole certainly possesses more favourable conditions for agriculture than the Shield, owing both to a more genial climate and deeper soils. Warm summers penetrate the lowlands in remarkable fashion: Wrigley (lat. 63 degrees N.) has a spring as early as Gaspé (lat. 49 degrees N.), and even the delta has a growing season of at least 80 days, though unseasonable frosts are apt to occur.

The agricultural development of the Peace River district suggests that success may attend the efforts of farmers taking up land even farther north. The agricultural frontier is actually extending now into the Hay River valley, and the Canadian Government has set up an experimental farm at Fort Simpson (lat. 62 degrees N.) to examine the relations between climate, soils and crops in the Mackenzie Lowlands. For the present, however, food is still imported into the region despite the small demand, and much is still eaten from cans.

FORESTRY OCCUPATIONS

Some timber has long been cut for fuel (*e.g.* for burning on river steamers in days before oil came into use), and also for building purposes, but there has been little commercial exploitation of the forests. There is, however, much good timber in the valleys, and new logging areas are slowly being taken up between the River Athabaska and the Lesser Slave Lake. The wealth of spruce and the hydro-electric power potential of the region may lead to the growth of a pulp and paper-making industry in the future. But at present there are few roads and railways, and labour is scarce. Also, the Mackenzie floods widely in spring and flows away from populous areas rather than towards them.

Fur-trapping is still the leading forest occupation, and most of the settlements are Hudson Bay Company depots, where Indians, halfbreeds, whites, and Eskimos all exchange their furs for consumer goods.

The Indians are often fishermen as well as trappers. Some act as guides for hunting and fishing parties, and for surveyors. Commercial fisheries are well developed only on Great Slave Lake, which yields whitefish, pike, and lake trout, marketed in Edmonton and even the United States.

SETTLEMENTS, COMMUNICATIONS, AND PETROLEUM

Originally established as fur-trading "forts," most of the settlements house Christian missions and units of the R.C.M.P. They are mostly linked together by air and water. The only group of settlements at all adequately served by rail and road are those in the Peace River agricultural district.

Since the War, however, the south-western fringe has been threaded by the Alaska Highway (*see* Chapter XI), and the more central parts by the newer Mackenzie Highway, which strikes north from the Peace River country to Hay River, on the southern shore of Great Slave Lake. Extensions now put Yellowknife and Fort Simpson in touch with the Prairies. New roads also link the Hay valley with Fort Smith and the base-metal mining centre of Pine Point (*see* Chapter VIII).

Until recently the railhead was Waterways (lat. 57 degrees N.), which has been joined to Edmonton since 1920. North of this small town there were no railways at all until 1965, when a line from Peace River to Hay River and Pine Point, running close to the Mackenzie Highway, was completed. This line is already stimulating forestry occupations, the northward extension of farming, and the production of lead and zinc at Pine Point.

Traditional modes of transport—by river in summer, and dog-sledge in winter—must still be relied upon in most areas. The Mackenzie, open in mild years from May to October, carries spruce-bark canoes, and also diesel-powered tugs, which drive steel barges. Its channel, however, is shifting and apt to be obstructed by sand-bars and fallen trees. Rapids just above Good Hope (lat. 66 degrees N.), where the valley narrows between the Mackenzie and Franklin Mountains, impede its use as a through waterway, though a skilled pilot can negotiate them.

Fort Smith is the head of continuous navigation on the main river. It is situated at a point where resistant Shield rocks cross the river to form rapids. At the head of navigation on the Athabaska stands McMurray, one of the oldest fur-trading centres in the whole region. It is 3 miles from Waterways, where salt wells have encouraged the canning of lake and river fish, and the opening of a small chemical works. Another trading centre is Fort Norman, at the confluence of the Great Bear and the Mackenzie. Forty miles north is Norman Wells, named after local petroleum deposits worked since 1920. A small refinery produces oil suitable for use both on river steamers and at the mines of Yellowknife and Port Radium. During the Second World War, the 4-in. "Canol" pipeline, 600 miles long, was laid thence to Whitehorse (Yukon) to serve military vehicles using the Alaska Highway, but it is now in disuse.

Interest in oil production, however, has recently been given a fillip with discoveries in the upper Hay valley (Rainbow Lake), near Lesser Slave Lake (Nipisi) and in the Mackenzie delta, and pipelines have been laid to Edmonton from the two former localities.

Besides those at Norman Wells, petroleum supplies are to be found in the Athabaskan tar-sands of north Alberta which are believed to contain enough oil to supply the needs of the whole world for at least a generation. After a long period of research they are now being worked commercially on a small scale. A recovery plant has been erected near McMurray and oil, bitumen and sulphur are being extracted. A pipeline to take naphtha, kerosene and gas oil southwards to Edmonton has been laid.

One of the most interesting settlements in the entire Mackenzie Basin is the township of Aklavik, on the Mackenzie Delta, 122 miles within the Arctic Circle. It is accessible to shallow-draught river vessels and has a mixed population of about 1000. In the last few years the peril

[Courtesy: National Film Board of Canada.

FIG. 37.—Inuvik, N.W.T., in its early stages. This town is replacing Aklavik as the principal centre of Canada's Western Arctic area. Buildings—mounted on stilts—are still being added. Note the vegetational setting, the flatness of the terrain, and the Mackenzie distributaries.

of building in a zone of deep permafrost has revealed itself here. The town, built on low, unstable ground, is gradually sinking as the thin cover of silt on which it rests thaws out in summer or is melted by domestic heat. Moreover, lateral erosion by the Mackenzie is slowly eating into the site. Consequently, in 1954 Canadian scientists chose a new site, "Inuvik," 35 miles away, on higher ground and accessible to a more navigable river channel. Here, a new town, erected on stilts, is rising, and an airstrip has been constructed. By 1961, enough progress had been made for the Federal Prime Minister to perform an inauguration ceremony.

Near Aklavik, a group of Eskimo has been instructed in the herding of reindeer. Several of these Asiatic animals were introduced into Alaska at the turn of the century, and between 1929 and 1934, with the help of Lapp experts, over 2000 of them were transported to the eastern side of the Mackenzie delta, where they now number about 10,000. They provide a permanent supply of milk and meat, material for clothing, domestic necessaries like needles and thread, and a means of conveyance additional to the traditional dog-sledge. Their introduction has allowed some Eskimos to adopt a less migratory life than was formerly practicable.

In view of the fact that only small vessels can reach Aklavik, a new port, Tuktoyaktuk, has been established on the Arctic coast. It conducts a little trade brought to it in summer by coastal steamers, which are of deeper draught than river steamers so that they can negotiate oceanic waters though they do not venture as far as the Pacific or Atlantic.

THE ARCTIC ARCHIPELAGO—PHYSICAL AND HUMAN GEOGRAPHY

PHYSICAL GEOGRAPHY

North of the Canadian mainland is a group of Arctic islands covering half a million square miles, *i.e.* about half the total area of the Canadian Arctic. Some of these islands, notably Baffin, are among the world's largest, as well as the most northerly. Ellesmere Island, extending to lat. 83 degrees N., reaches almost as near to the North Pole as Greenland. All the islands rise from the continental shelf of the Arctic Ocean.

The landscape usually has an undulating surface and is covered with tundra, but the eastern parts of Baffin, Devon, and Ellesmere Islands are mountainous, with summits of 10,000 ft in the latter. These highlands bear ice-caps, which in Baffin and Ellesmere are divided from each other by long fiords down which glaciers move to the sea.

The climate is polar rather than simply arctic. The average annual temperature is much lower than on the mainland and may reach only

0° F. The precipitation, mostly snow, is generally under 10 in., and may be less than 5 in. in the far north, though the eastern side of Baffin receives quite heavy orographic downpours.

HUMAN GEOGRAPHY

In such a region man is repelled by climate and inaccessibility, and it is not surprising that many areas remain unexplored. Ice joins the islands to the mainland in winter, and even in August it covers the middle reaches of the northern part of Baffin Bay, the McLintock Channel between Victoria Island and Prince of Wales Island, and most of the waters in the north-west. The first navigation of the historic North West Passage from the Atlantic to the Pacific dates only from 1903–6, when Amundsen, conqueror of the South Pole, sailed it from east to west. During the War years, Captain Larsen, in the *St Roch*, made a complete journey east-wards in 1940–42, and westwards between August and October 1944. In contrast with the Russian Arctic, there is no regular through route for shipping in the Canadian Arctic.

Prior to the present century, the population of the Arctic Archipelago was almost wholly Eskimo. The nomadic hunting of sea-mammals, and of the grazing caribou and musk-ox was virtually the only occupation. New ideas have been introduced by Hudson Bay traders, missionaries, employees of the R.C.M.P. and government officials, and modern medical and educational services have been started. Baffin Island houses more Eskimos than other islands: here, the Bay has important posts at Frobisher Bay (which is also a military base and growing airport) and Pangnirtung, the latter on Cumberland Sound.

Economically, the Arctic Archipelago is unlikely ever to achieve much significance. Major deposits of oil, and natural gas have been located on Melville Island, coal on Victoria Island and Banks Island, gas on King Christian Island, oil on Ellesmere Island and lignite and iron in the north of Baffin Island, but these products are far from scarce in more accessible parts of Canada.

Strategically, however, like the Arctic mainland, the region is assuming importance because of its position with respect to Arctic air routes. Several airstrips have been laid down and a number of radar and weather stations have been erected since North American relations with Russia worsened after 1945. The population of the region, though extremely scanty, is now greater than it has ever been. Increasingly, the native people are coming into contact with other Canadians. Many are taking part in Anglo-America's Arctic defence programme, as they show an aptitude for mechanical work and in very low temperatures can use their hands more easily than whites.

Chapter XI

THE CORDILLERA OF BRITISH COLUMBIA AND YUKON

REFERENCE has already been made (in Chapters I and III) to the general structural and physical character of the Western Cordillera of North America, and especially to those parts of it which lie within British Columbia and Yukon. It should be noted that, while many features are common to both province and territory, the mountains of Yukon are cut off from the sea by the "Alaskan panhandle." On the frontier between Yukon and Alaska, rising from the lofty, glaciated St Elias Range, lies Canada's highest mountain, Mt Logan, a giant of 19,850 ft (*see* Fig. 99).

BRITISH COLUMBIA—PHYSICAL ASPECTS

THE PHYSIOGRAPHY OF THE BRITISH COLUMBIAN CORDILLERA

British Columbia is Canada's third largest province, over three times the size of the British Isles. Most of it lies within the Cordillera, but there is, in the north-east, a part of the more low-lying Peace River district, which has already been considered (*see* Chapter IX).

With a width of about 500 miles, the Cordillera are narrower than in the United States, but an equal number of longitudinal divisions, here trending from north-west to south-east, may be recognised (*see* Fig. 39). Going eastwards from the Pacific, they are as follows:

1. The "skerry guard" of rugged, offshore islands, including the Queen Charlotte group in the north, and Vancouver Island in the south. The latter, nearly 300 miles long, reaches a height exceeding 7000 ft.

2. The "Inside Passage," *i.e.* the sheltered waterway extending from Puget Sound to Hecate Strait.

3. The highly fiorded coast and the narrow lowlands on the eastern side of Vancouver Island, and on the mainland opposite.

4. The glaciated Coast Range, still in places occupied by small ice-caps, and dissected by the transverse gorges of the plateau rivers, *e.g.* Skeena, Nass, and Fraser. Mount Waddington, at 13,260 ft, stands

higher than any peak in the Canadian Rockies, though the general elevation of the range is lower.

5. The Plateau of British Columbia, 300 miles wide. It averages about 3000 ft in altitude, but is diversified by a number of higher, north-south ranges, and is dissected, especially in the south, by several long, incised, longitudinal valleys such as those of the Columbia, Kootenay, and Okanagan, each of which is marked by ribbon lakes.

6. The rugged, glaciated ranges of the Columbia System, including the parallel Selkirk, Purcell, and Monashee Ranges. These mountains are represented in the northern part of the province by the Stikine Mountains.

7. The Rocky Mountain Trench, a remarkable 1000-mile-long depression developed along a gigantic fault line which can be traced into Yukon and Montana. Only 2-10 miles across, it contains the upper courses of the Columbia and Fraser, and also the headstreams of the Liard and Peace.

8. The Rocky Mountains, which British Columbia shares with Alberta. These spectacular highlands, composed of many ice-capped ridges separated by high, parallel valleys, attain well over 10,000 ft in such mountains as Robson (12,972 ft), Columbia (12,294 ft), and Assiniboine (11,870 ft). The Rockies support many National Parks where visitors may enjoy magnificent scenery, various outdoor sports, including trail-riding in summer and ski-ing in winter, and glimpses of abundant and varied wild life.

THE CLIMATE

Since British Columbia has such a diverse topography, it is a province of numerous micro-climates rather than one with two or three well-defined climates, but it is impossible to go into too much detail.

The dominant influences are latitude, ocean, and relief. The former, 49 degrees to 60 degrees N., is roughly comparable with that of the British Isles, and the Pacific influence resembles that of the Atlantic. But the height and position of the highlands limit the zone of "West European type" climate to the coastal margins. The Plateau has a climate more like that of eastern Europe in that its seasonal range of temperature is extreme, its precipitation light and concentrated in summer. The deeply trenched interior valleys—shut away from western maritime air streams—may barely receive 10 in. of rain annually. Indeed, apart from the fact that the coastlands have the mildest winters and the most equable temperatures in Canada, the most significant aspect of British Columbia's climate is the variation in the amounts of rainfall along an east-west line (see Fig. 38). Victoria, in the lee of Vancouver Island, has 27 in. yearly;

Vancouver, on the windward side of the Coast Range 59 in. (with a winter maximum), Kamloops, at 1200 ft on the Plateau, receives just over 10 in. The Selkirk Mountains, though a little lower than the Rockies, usually experience heavier summer rain and deeper winter snows, as they are nearer the source of maritime air.

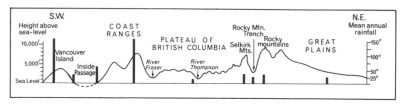

FIG. 38.—Simplified section across southern British Columbia. This section illustrates the connection between relief and precipitation characteristic of a region where the main physical features lie athwart the principal wind-tracks. Precipitation is shown in vertical columns.

The mountains of Vancouver Island and the Coast Range of British Columbia are the wettest parts of Canada: on average, they receive upwards of 200 in. of rainfall annually.

Climatic statistics are appended for Vancouver on the coast, and Kamloops, on the plateau, for comparison:

Vancouver	J.	F.	M.	A.	M.	J.	Jy.	A.	S.	O.	N.	D.
Temperature (° F) .	36	38	42	47	54	59	63	62	56	49	43	48
Precipitation (in.) .	8·6	6·1	5·3	3·3	3·0	2·7	1·3	1·7	4·1	5·9	10·0	7·8

Mean Annual Temperature: 48° F; Mean Annual Range of Temperature: 27° F; Mean Annual Precipitation: 59·8 in.

Kamloops	J.	F.	M.	A.	M.	J.	Jy.	A.	S.	O.	N.	D.
Temperature (° F) .	23	26	38	50	58	64	70	68	58	48	35	28
Precipitation (in.) .	1·0	0·8	0·3	0·4	0·9	1·2	1·1	1·1	0·8	0·6	1·0	0·9

Mean Annual Temperature: 47° F; Mean Annual Range of Temperature: 47° F; Mean Annual Precipitation: 10·1 in.

NATURAL VEGETATION

In keeping with its climatic variety, British Columbia exhibits nearly all those types of natural vegetation which are appropriate to a cool temperate region. But forests are dominant: they cover nearly two-thirds of the province. The islands and windward slopes of the Coast Range carry the richest forests in Canada, though the highest parts bear tundra and perpetual snow. The biggest trees, which may reach 300 ft in height and have a base diameter of 14 ft, are found in the mild south, at fairly low levels. Here are giant Douglas firs, western hemlock, and western red cedar. In the north, e.g. in Queen Charlotte Islands, spruce trees are numerous. The Selkirks and Rockies have pine forests, with some red cedars and hemlocks, but the bottomlands of the Rocky Mountain Trench are chiefly occupied by parkland.

Most of the British Columbian Plateau is clothed with light, open forests of spruce and balsam, with some fir in the south and ponderosa pine in the north. The trees in the north, however, are rather stunted. On the lower, drier parts of the plateau, steppe grassland tends to replace forests, and some areas are covered only with sage-brush and cacti.

BRITISH COLUMBIA—THE ECONOMY

FORESTRY OCCUPATIONS

Commercial interests in British Columbia make great use of its forest wealth, as the finest timber is close to open water and water power for milling is abundant. Spruce is cut in the north for pulping and papermaking, and there are saw-mills and a few pulp-mills in the valleys and mountains of the south-east and in the middle Fraser and Thompson valleys. But the principal lumber camps, saw-mills, pulp-mills and hydro-electric power-stations are located along the seaward margins of the Coast Range and on Vancouver Island. Altogether, British Columbia depends on her forests for a third of her income. Her saw-mills cut about 70% of Canada's lumber, and there is a considerable output of processed timber, e.g. doors and window-frames, shingles (for house-building), veneers and plywood, pit-props, railway sleepers and furniture. The main markets are the Prairies, the United States, Japan, Europe and South Africa.

FARMING

Less than 1% of British Columbia is under cultivation. The reasons are obvious: a lack of flat lowland, the aridity of the Plateau, the excessive rainfall of the coastlands, and the lack of a railway network and large nearby markets.

The best agricultural areas are the lower Fraser valley and the south-eastern plains of Vancouver Island, close to Vancouver, Victoria, and New Westminster. Dairy-farming, vegetable-growing, poultry-rearing, and the cultivation of small fruits like strawberries are the main activities. Though the alluvial plains of the Fraser, however, are fertile enough, careful draining and dyking are often necessary.

Elsewhere, apart from the Peace River country, the only significant areas under crops are the deep valleys in the southern part of the Plateau. Here orchard-farming, largely in the interests of overseas markets, is intensively practised. At Penticton, Kelowna, and Vernon in the Okanagan, and at Nelson in the Kootenay valley, large quantities of apples, and smaller amounts of pears, cherries, plums, even peaches, apricots, and grapes are packed each year and dispatched to the coast or the Prairies by rail and road. Some of the orchards are situated on lacustrine benches and deltas; all benefit from long, hot, sunny summers; and there is plenty of irrigation water available to supplement the meagre rains. Dairying and vegetable-growing are also carried on.

The better-grassed parts of the Plateau near the railways, and the warmer, more southerly pastures of the Rocky Mountain Trench are used to some extent for cattle- and sheep-ranching, *e.g.* round Kamloops and Cranbrook. Extensive areas round Prince George are naturally suited to mixed farming, but poor transport has until recently been a deterrent, and the soils are more podsolised, the growing season shorter, than in southern British Columbia; consequently little land has yet been taken up except for ranching.

THE FISHERIES

By value, British Columbia's fisheries usually account for 30-40% of the total annual catch of Canada, and the province generally leads all others. The principal fish is the salmon, normally netted near the mouths of rivers like the Fraser, Nass, and Skeena in summer, when the fish are in their finest condition and ready to swim up the rivers on the annual run to the spawning-grounds. In the interests of conservation, many salmon are allowed to ascend the rivers (where some may be taken by Indian fishermen) and fish hatcheries are maintained.

Fresh salmon are marketed in the cities of both western Canada and the United States, but about two-thirds of the catch is canned and sent to the United Kingdom and other countries. Canneries, located mainly on coastal inlets, employ more people than the fishing-vessels.

Beyond the coastal waters, halibut, herring, and other cool-water fish are caught, generally by long-lines or trawls. Fresh halibut is sold in many parts of North America, but the largest markets are so distant as to limit the scope of the industry, despite the vitamin-rich oil which is obtained from this kind of fish.

MINERALS AND POWER SUPPLIES

Though gold was the magic mineral which first lured settlers to British Columbia, it is of relatively little value today. There are, however, small mines in the Coast Range and on some of the Plateau ridges.

The leading metals today are zinc, lead, and silver, which are extracted at various places in the Kootenays and within the great upper bend of the Columbia, including the Sullivan mine near Kimberley. This is one of the largest and richest mines in the world, and even outrivals that of

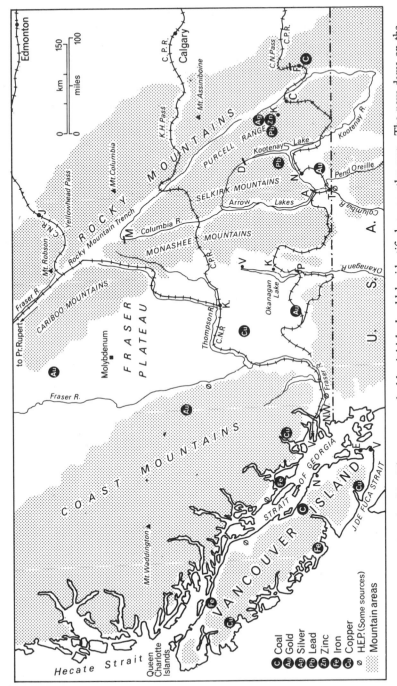

FIG. 39.—Southern British Columbia. The towns marked by initials should be identified on an atlas map. The new dams on the Columbia River and its tributaries should be noted. (A.: Arrow Dam; D.: Duncan Dam; M.: Mica Dam.)

Broken Hill, Australia. It was discovered in 1892 but became important only after 1918. It now produces half Canada's lead and half its zinc. The ores, which also contain iron (not at present utilised), are smelted at Trail. This town is situated on a number of terraces above the Columbia River, from which it obtains hydro-electric power. It boasts the world's largest lead and zinc smelter and also concentrates the copper deposits of the Coast Range, Vancouver Island, the Fraser plateau and Britannia Beach (north of Vancouver), as well as Yukon minerals. The sulphur dioxide emitted from the smelter was formerly allowed to escape. There were, however, complaints that it was destroying much of the surrounding vegetation, and it now helps to make sulphuric acid and ammonium sulphate. By-products derived from the works include antimony, bismuth, cadmium, indium, tin, tungsten, silver, and gold.

Iron ore is worked on Vancouver Island, on the Queen Charlotte Islands and on Texada Island, 50 miles north-west of Vancouver. There is a steel rolling mill at Vancouver, but most of the ore is shipped to Japan. Asbestos is mined in small quantities in the far north, and nickel in the lower Fraser valley. A mineral which has recently become prominent is molybdenum, now being worked in several places.

Four main sources of power are available for British Columbian industry: coal, petroleum, natural gas, and hydro-electricity. The first has long been worked in the Crows Nest Pass district and formerly also near Nanaimo. In the former area the seams are thick and the quality good, and contracts have been recently agreed for the export of coal to Japan from the purpose-built deep-water port of Roberts Bank, south of Vancouver.

Vancouver is now a terminus of oil and gas pipelines from fields in the Peace River District and from the larger fields of central Alberta. The city's oil-refining capacity is greater than that of Edmonton and it has a larger gas-fired electricity station.

Many parts of the province are rich in water power, relatively little of which (c. 5000 MW) has so far been developed. Even so, British Columbia stands third after Quebec and Ontario as a Canadian producer. The generation of "hydro" is favoured by the well-filled, steeply graded rivers and the growing industrial market. Prior to the last twenty years, however, all the developments have been comparatively small. Then, in 1951, work started on the Kemano project, 120 miles south-east of Prince Rupert (see Fig. 40). A large dam, 300 ft high, was erected across the Nechako River, a tributary of the Fraser, so as to impound a large lake. This lake overflows through a 10-mile tunnel burrowing through the coast range to the power-house at Kemano, built underground to make it safe from avalanches and from possible aerial attack. Transmission lines convey electricity thence to Kitimat, where a new, giant aluminium plant, rivalling Arvida, Quebec Province, has been built. The effective head of water at Kemano is 2400 ft; 2¼ million horsepower will ultimately be generated, of which about half is now available. The Kitimat plant produced its first ingots, for sale to the United States, in 1954. Alcan's own vessels are bringing alumina direct from Jamaica via the Panama Canal, and a railway has been laid between Kitimat and Terrace, to link up with the through C.N.R. line.

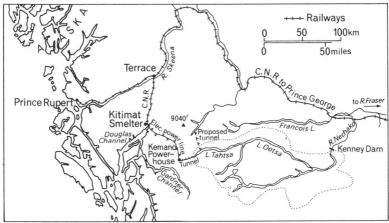

FIG. 40.—Kemano–Kitimat scheme. Drainage within the area enclosed by dotted lines has been reversed, and the volume of lakes has been enlarged. Many minor lakes have been omitted for the sake of simplicity.

The year when Kitimat produced its first aluminium ingots also saw the initiation of a plan to build a large hydro-electric power-station on the Pend d'Oreille River, south of Trail. More far-reaching are the joint plans prepared by the Government of Canada and the United States in 1964 for a comprehensive Columbia River scheme which may ultimately supply more than 12 million horsepower to the two countries, and also assist the United States irrigation water and flood-control projects. It should also be noted that the Government of British Columbia is harnessing the power of the Peace River for provincial use (*see* p. 118).

COMMUNICATIONS

Like other large Canadian provinces, British Columbia is served both by the Canadian National and Canadian Pacific Railways. Both approach western Canada from Winnipeg. The former, taking the more northerly course, reaches the Rockies via Saskatoon, Edmonton, and the small tourist resort of Jasper, and crosses the mountains at the Yellowhead Pass (3718 ft), which is overlooked by Mount Robson, the crowning peak of the Canadian Rockies. It then forks. One line follows the Rocky Mountain Trench alongside the upper Fraser as far as Prince George and then finds an easy way over the Plateau before descending the Skeena valley to Prince Rupert; the other strikes southwards down the North Thompson valley as far as Kamloops, and then follows successively the South Thompson and the gorge and flats of the lower Fraser to Vancouver.

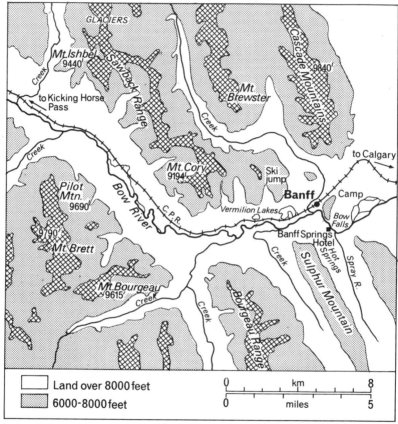

FIG. 41.—A small part of the Rocky Mountains near Banff, Alberta.

The main C.P.R. line attains the Rockies after passing through Regina, Calgary, and Banff (Fig. 41). The latter is the administrative headquarters of Canada's oldest National Park (established in 1885). Beyond it, the journey is very spectacular. The Great Divide (at 5337 ft, where · Alberta gives way to British Columbia) is surmounted by two spiral tunnels designed to reduce the gradient; the Kicking Horse Pass (5329 ft) and a short stretch of the Columbia valley in the Trench follows; then, to shorten the route, the track passes through the 5-mile Connaught Tunnel, which pierces the Selkirks. After crossing a number of Plateau ridges and skirting the picturesque Shuswap Lake, the line reaches Kamloops. Thenceforwards it roughly parallels the C.N.R. route along the Thompson and Fraser valleys before turning north to Vancouver.

In the extreme south of British Columbia a very circuitous C.P.R. line from Lethbridge and the Crows Nest Pass (4450 ft) serves Trail and various valley orchards before terminating at Vancouver. A few branch lines, e.g. a track along the Rocky Mountain Trench from the Kicking Horse Pass to the Crows Nest Pass, traverse the valleys themselves, and provide some communication between western Canada and the United States.

It should be noted that there are only two railways in the northern half of British Columbia: one from Dawson Creek to Prince George, and one from Fort St John to Fort Nelson. Highways, too, are few in this pioneer zone apart from a stretch of the Alaska Highway (see p. 139) and some offshoots. In southern British Columbia the main road is the western portion of the recently completed Trans-Canada Highway, which broadly follows the C.P.R. main line. The Hart Highway links Vancouver with Prince George and Fort St John (on the Peace River), and Prince George, a growing town with pulp and paper mills and an oil refinery, is also in road communication with Prince Rupert.

The many coastal settlements of British Columbia are joined together by the Inside Passage shipping route, and there are, of course, frequent ferries between Vancouver and Victoria.

BRITISH COLUMBIA—SOME ASPECTS OF HUMAN GEOGRAPHY

THE PEOPLE

Owing largely to physiographic and climatic disadvantages, and to the very thin spread of communications, three-quarters of British Columbia's 2 million people live in only one-twentieth of its total area, i.e. in Vancouver and the lower Fraser valley, in Victoria and adjacent parts of Vancouver Island, and in a few of the valleys of the southern interior. Most of the wealth of these people comes from forests and mines, and from manufactures dependent on the primary products of the province, e.g. timber, minerals, fish, and farm produce.

Since British Columbia is farther from Europe than any other Canadian province, and is naturally shut off from the rest of the country by the Rocky Mountains, it is not surprising that white settlers should have been late in reaching it. Captain Cook landed on Vancouver Island in 1778, and Captain George Vancouver took possession of it for England in 1792, but it was the fur-traders from beyond the Cordillera, led by such men as Mackenzie, Fraser, and Thompson, who pioneered its modern development. The discovery of gold in the Fraser valley caused a spurt in its population growth in 1858, and the 1860s saw the beginnings of commercial salmon-fishing, lumbering, and farming. But not until 1871, when the area was promised a railway link with the east, did the colony join the Canadian Federation. The railway (the C.P.R.) finally reached Vancouver in 1885, and since then development has been rapid. Indeed, in the last 30 years the growth of population has been at a faster rate than in any other province in Canada.

Most of the British Columbians are of British stock. Among others are families descended from Japanese and Chinese parents. Many of these Orientals are employed in the fisheries, lumber camps, and city catering establishments. Native Indians may still be found in the remoter parts, particularly in coastal districts.

THE MAIN SETTLEMENTS

Apart from certain small settlements in the Peace River country, *e.g.* Dawson Creek, and a few notable interior valley towns in the south, *e.g.* Penticton, Trail and Kamloops, the main urban centres of British Columbia lie on the coasts. The most important are Vancouver, Victoria,

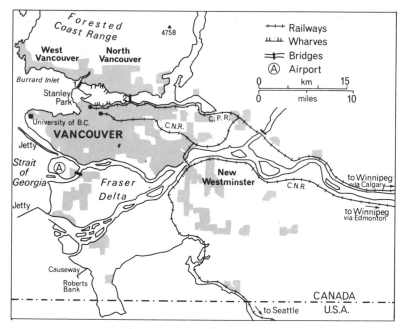

FIG. 42.—Site of Vancouver.

1 = Lions Gate Bridge; 2 = Second Narrows Bridge. It should be noted that plans exist to build a tunnel and another bridge across Burrard Inlet to assist freight movements. Shading indicates built-up areas.

New Westminster, Nanaimo, and Prince Rupert.

Vancouver is by far the largest. With North Vancouver, the city population in 1971 was 426,000, the metropolitan population over a million, *i.e.* half the population of the province. Yet in 1862 it was simply a "hole in the forest," and even in 1900 it housed only 10,000 people. Its growth has been a mirror of the growth of the province as a whole, though it has also owed much to its contacts with the Prairies, for both Saskatchewan and Alberta are nearer to it than they are to Montreal.

[*Courtesy: National Film Board of Canada.*

FIG. 43.—Aerial view of Vancouver. This view, taken from the south-east, shows Stanley Park and Lions Gate Bridge at the seaward end of Burrard Inlet. In the right centre is the passenger shipping terminal, and beyond Burrard Inlet are the forested Coast Mountains. Compare Fig. 42.

It has a very beautiful site—mountain-rimmed and forest-girt—along the 98-mile shoreline of ice-free Burrard Inlet, north of the Fraser delta (*see* Figs. 42 and 43). Near the seaward end of the inlet, close to the provincial University buildings, a part of the original forest has been preserved in Stanley Park, whence the Lions Gate Bridge carries traffic to North and West Vancouver. The docks, on which so much of the city's prosperity depends, are located on either side of Burrard Inlet between this bridge and a second one farther up. To these docks, the C.P.R. and several roads bring timber and wood-pulp, metals, fruit, and wheat for export. The latter can be stored in several large elevators. Into the harbour come ships from Europe and industrial North America (via the Panamá Canal) with manufactures, and steamers from Japan and the Far East bring rice, silk, and sugar.

Vancouver manufactures many goods for both domestic and overseas markets, e.g. pulp, sawn timber, flour, refined petroleum and sugar, canned salmon, and fruit. There are important shipyards and printing and publishing works. A recent stimulus has been given to industrial development by the construction of petroleum and gas pipelines (see p. 132), though much hydro-electricity is still used. Tertiary occupations are numerous and the city has many towering blocks of both offices and flats.

Vancouver maintains her contacts with the outside world not only by rail, road, and sea, but also by air. Her airport is the most used one in western Canada, and puts her into touch with Montreal, Seattle, San Francisco, Los Angeles and many cities in Latin America and Europe. The metropolis is spreading rapidly southwards and south-eastwards to the Fraser River and New Westminster.

New Westminster, though the third city of the province, has a population of little more than 30,000. The deltaic bars of the Fraser make it difficult of access for shipping, so that its water-borne trade is small. It is mainly an industrial city and manufactures pulp, sawn timber, paper and furniture as well as canning fruit and salmon.

Prince Rupert is British Columbia's second port, but it falls far behind Vancouver in its trade, since it is too distant from the populous parts of the province. It has, however, an excellent, almost landlocked, harbour on an island at the mouth of the Skeena, which provides a route into the interior. It has wheat elevators, though it has never exported very much grain, and has pulp- and timber-mills. More significant are its fish-freezing and fish-canning works, for the city is the chief halibut-fishing port in western Canada, and the Skeena is a valuable source of salmon.

Victoria, the capital, with nearly 200,000 people in its metropolitan area in 1971, is older than Vancouver. It has a harbour at the south-eastern end of the "Island," and it repairs ships and manufactures wood products, but its main functions are administrative, residential, and recreational. The pace of life is much slower than in Vancouver, and the reputation it enjoys for being the most "English" of all Canadian cities is jealously guarded by some of its older inhabitants.

Close to Victoria, as distances go in Canada, are Nanaimo, to the north, a growing fishing port and trading and industrial city, and Esquimalt to the south, an important naval base on a magnificent, deep, sheltered harbour on Juan de Fuca Strait, leading south-eastwards to Puget Sound (Washington) and northwards to Georgia Strait between Vancouver and Victoria.

YUKON TERRITORY—PHYSICAL AND HUMAN GEOGRAPHY

The northern part of British Columbia has already been referred to as a pioneer zone. Even more so is Yukon Territory, which has a population of less than 20,000; its chief administrative centre, Whitehorse, houses fewer than 5000. Its position is isolated between the Plateaus of Alaska and British Columbia, and it is cut off from the Pacific by the Alaskan panhandle. Its climate, sub-Arctic and Arctic, is less genial than that of the neighbouring Mackenzie Lowlands owing to its higher average elevation. It suffers from a very extreme range of temperature (80° F in the north-east) and its mean annual temperature is below freezing-point. Moreover, the famous "frost-hollow" of Snag recorded Canada's lowest ever in 1947: a minimum of −81° F (see Fig. 99).

The Yukon, however, is not without its human geography. Much of the area is covered with light forests of white spruce in which trappers have been active for nearly 200 years, though commercial lumbering has never become important. The first real population influx came between 1896 and 1898, when the "sourdoughs" flocked to the Klondike (a tributary of the Yukon) to work the placer gold deposits of Bonanza Creek and Eldorado Creek. Dawson City became the gold seekers' metropolis. Sixty years ago it had a population of over 30,000; today, only 750 people inhabit the "ghost town," and the only miners are employees of a gold-mining company which raises alluvial deposits by mechanical dredgers. There appear to be no lode deposits.

The other major event in Yukon's history took place during the struggle against Japan in 1942, when U.S. Army Engineers built the Alaska Highway, to serve at first as a connecting link between a chain of airfields on the "North-West Staging Route." The road—which is now chiefly used in summer by commercial vehicles trading with Alaska —follows a pre-existing way from Edmonton to Dawson Creek and Fort St John, continues northwards along the eastern side of the northern Rockies past Fort Nelson (British Columbia), and enters Yukon at Watson Lake. It then makes for Whitehorse. Finally, it proceeds west across the Yukon Plateau into Alaska, and its terminus at Fairbanks.

Reached by the Mayo Highway striking north from Whitehorse are the rich mines of Keno Hill, which are exploited for their silver, lead, and zinc. The ores have to be sent on a long haul to Trail for refining.

Other mineralised areas include Ross River (zinc, lead and copper), Kluane Lake (nickel and copper), Clinton Creek (asbestos) and Carmacks (coal). A little hydro-electric power has been developed at Whitehorse and Mayo Landing, and a major scheme, combined with a metal smelter, has been suggested on the Teslin River, near the British Columbian boundary.

Whitehorse, the main town in the Yukon, is a route focus. It stands on a terrace at the head of navigation on the Yukon, which is, however, little used nowadays for transport. Besides its position in respect to the Alaska and Mayo Highways, it is the terminus of Yukon's only railway (from Skagway, Alaska). There is also a road link to Skagway. Its airport maintains regular services with Vancouver and Fairbanks. Close to it a few vegetables are grown (as they are round Dawson and Watson Lake), and a very few dairy-cattle and horses are fed on hay and green grain, but the whole of the Territory has only a few thousand acres of farmland.

STUDY QUESTIONS

1. Canada: "Land of Tomorrow" or "Queen of the Snows." Which do you consider is the more fitting title?

2. Attempt an explanation of the distribution of (a) agricultural, (b) manufacturing areas in Canada.

3. Draw comparisons and contrasts between Newfoundland and the Maritime Provinces of Canada.

4. Discuss the manufacturing activities of Quebec and Ontario in relation to supplies of power and raw materials.

5. Why do you think Toronto and Montreal have become the largest cities in Canada?

6. Compare and contrast the agricultural production of the Ontario Lakes Peninsula with that of the Canadian Prairies.

7. Why has wheat, rather than some other cereal, become the dominant crop of the Prairie Provinces?

8. Critically assess the advantages and disadvantages of the Peace River country and the Cochrane Clay Belt for commercial agriculture.

9. Write an essay on "Changing Alberta." Do you think its economic production will ever surpass that of England?

10. By reference to Canada, explain what is meant by a "zone of pioneer settlement."

11. Why are the Canadian northlands unattractive to settlement? Do you consider they will always remain so?

12. Discuss the role played by minerals in the opening-up of Canada's northlands.

13. What effect has the relief of British Columbia had upon its human geography?

14. Draw maps to illustrate the position and economic activities of the following Canadian cities: Toronto, Winnipeg, Calgary, Windsor, Halifax.

PART THREE

THE UNITED STATES

Chapter XII

GENERAL PHYSICAL GEOGRAPHY : A COMPARISON WITH CANADA

SIZE AND POSITION

INCLUDING Alaska, which was incorporated as a State in 1959, the United States has an area of just over 3½ million square miles, and is therefore smaller than Canada by about 300,000 square miles. It covers more ground, however, than the whole of Oceania, and almost as much as Europe. The State of Alaska alone is nearly five times the size of the British Isles, Texas is five times the size of England, and California three times the size. Like Canada, therefore, the country is of almost continental proportions.

No part of the United States is as close to Europe as the Atlantic Provinces of Canada, and western Canada is nearer Japan than any part of the western United States except Alaska. The widely separated Atlantic and Pacific coasts of the United States have been brought into contact with each other by transcontinental road, rail, and air routes, and also by the Panamá Canal shipping route.

The latitudes of the United States—49 degrees N. to 25 degrees N.—are much more favourable than Canada's for agricultural endeavour, and the resultant temperate and sub-tropical, even, hot climates have proved far more suited to close settlement. None of the ports suffers from ice in winter except those on the Great Lakes, and, as a navigable waterway, the Gulf of Mexico compares more than favourably with Canada's Arctic Ocean.

STRUCTURE, RELIEF, AND DRAINAGE

Over a third of the United States is taken up with the Western Cordillera, which here are much wider than in Canada; indeed, they broaden not only southwards from Canada but also northwards from Mexico, until in latitude 40 degrees N., they are about 1000 miles across. The Skerry Guard of Canada's Pacific coast is continued into Alaska, but

south of Vancouver Island it is replaced by the Coast Ranges of the mainland. South of Puget Sound, the Inside Passage of the north-west is
raised to form the longitudinal lowlands of Washington, Oregon, and
central California. The Coast Ranges of Alaska and British Columbia
become the Cascades, succeeded in California by the block mountains
of the Sierra Nevada. The eastern framework of the Cordillera is again
known as the Rocky Mountains. These, however, are much more
extensive in the United States than in Canada; especially is this the case
in Colorado, where several summits top 14,000 ft. In Alaska, on the side
farthest from the Pacific, the Cordillera are bordered by the Brooks and
Endicott Ranges, which roughly parallel the Arctic coast.

As in Canada, there are intermontane plateaus and basins between the
Pacific ranges and the Rocky Mountains. Three such regions are prominent: the Snake–Columbia Plateau in the north-west United States, the
Great Basin, an area of inland drainage in the west-central United States,
and the Colorado Plateau in the south-western United States. Alaska
shares the Yukon Basin with north-west Canada (see Fig. 2).

The middle part of the United States is occupied by interior plains
similar to those of central Canada. West of about 100 degrees W. longitude, they exceed 3000 ft in height, and are known in part as the High
Plains. East of the Mississippi, they rise very gradually towards the
Appalachian Plateaus. Their surface is modified by the upstanding
character of certain ancient mountain areas, notably the Black Hills of
South Dakota and Wyoming, and the Ozark Plateau and associated
highlands of Missouri and Arkansas, but in the main they consist of almost undisturbed sediments. Nearly all the drainage finds its way into
the Mississippi, which leads to the warm waters of the Gulf of Mexico.
The Canadian plains, it will be remembered, are chiefly drained northwards by the Mackenzie and the Nelson to the cold waters of the Arctic
Ocean and Hudson Bay.

Bordering the Gulf of Mexico and extending northwards up the
Mississippi flood-plain, and eastwards and northwards again along the
Atlantic margin of the United States, as far north as the Hudson, are
broad expanses of recent coastal lowland, consisting of marine and river-
ine sediments. By contrast, Canada has no Atlantic Coast Plain, but only
pockets of lowland in the Maritime Provinces.

The Canadian Shield, as we have already seen, trespasses into the
United States to take in the uplands round Lake Superior and the Adirondack Mountains of New York. South-west of the latter, the old block
and fold mountains of the now greatly eroded Appalachian System
extend as far as the southern States of Alabama and Georgia, but fail to
sever the Gulf Plain from the Atlantic Plain. East of the Adirondacks,

beyond Lake Champlain, are other elements of the Appalachians, which, as we have seen (Chapter III) continue into south-eastern Canada.

Four of the Great Lakes are shared between the United States and Canada. The fifth—Lake Michigan—is entirely confined to the former. A short stretch of the frontier between the two countries follows the St Lawrence River, but, before Montreal is reached, Canada claims all the river, and virtually the whole of its lower drainage basin.

CLIMATES OF THE UNITED STATES

Though the Rocky Mountains act as the principal watershed in the United States, as they do in Canada, the main climatic divide lies farther east. It broadly follows the 100 degrees W. line of longitude (Figs. 1 and 3). To the west, as far as the Pacific mountains, the mean annual rainfall is generally less than 20 in., and the natural vegetation, except on high ground, is grassland or desert scrub, more suited to extensive ranching

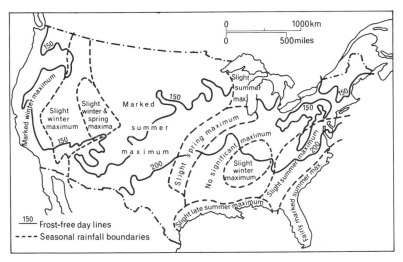

Fig. 44.—Climatic features of the U.S.A. Names of seasons refer to periods of maximum precipitation.

than to any other form of land occupance. To the east of the line, the rainfall everywhere exceeds 20 in., the natural vegetation is nearly all forest, and mixed farming, intensive dairying, and cultivation are widely practised. Paradoxically, it is in the far north-west of Washington, in the western half of the United States, that the heaviest rainfall is experienced outside Alaska: over 140 in. in the Olympic Mountains.

Almost the whole of the Appalachians and Atlantic coast plain receives over 40 in. of well-distributed frontal rainfall each year. The driest parts of the whole country are in the south-west, where pressures are generally high, at least in winter, and where surrounding mountain ranges hinder the passage of maritime air both from the Pacific and the Gulf of Mexico. Here, in southern California and south-western Arizona, the mean annual rainfall is less than 5 in. Along the Pacific coast the precipitation steadily increases northwards: San Diego has 9·6 in., San Francisco 22·2, Portland 43·8. The most notable feature of the climate of central California is its Mediterranean character of "winter rain, summer drought."

Temperature conditions vary as widely as those of precipitation. Among the most significant characteristics are the following:

1. The great extent of winter cold, revealed by the course of the 32° F isotherm for January, and caused by the dominance of Polar continental air.

2. The winter mildness of the Pacific shores of Oregon and Washington, even those of Alaska, compared with the frigidity of the Atlantic coastlands north of Cape Hatteras; this is due to the fact that while the former are influenced greatly by maritime air and the warm Pacific Drift, the latter suffer from continental air and the "Cold Wall."*

3. The extreme temperature range, not only of the interior but also of the north Atlantic margins.

In these three respects the reader will note that there are close resemblances between the United States and Canada. There are, however, certain interesting temperature conditions which are more peculiar to the United States. They include the following:

1. The great heat experienced in the south-west in the summer (Death Valley, California, has recorded 134° F).

2. The relatively cool summers of the central coastlands of California, produced by the cool Californian current, the prevailing north winds and the frequent fogs.

3. The almost tropical climate of the Florida peninsula, washed by the Gulf of Mexico and the Atlantic.

4. The tendency for all parts of the Central Plains to experience sudden cold snaps in winter, and occasional prostrating heat waves in summer, owing to the lack of any major relief barrier to the penetration of either icy Arctic winds or scorching Gulf winds.

* The continuation southwards of the cold Labrador Current.

NATURAL VEGETATION AND SOILS

VEGETATION REGIONS

The main regions of natural vegetation in the United States have already been described (Chapter I), and it has been pointed out earlier in the present chapter that grasslands and scrub dominate the western half of the country, forest the eastern. It should, however, be noted that the richest stands of softwood timber are to be found, as in Canada, on the well-watered Pacific Highlands. Washington, Oregon, and northern California are the leading sources of saw-mill timber in the United States, as

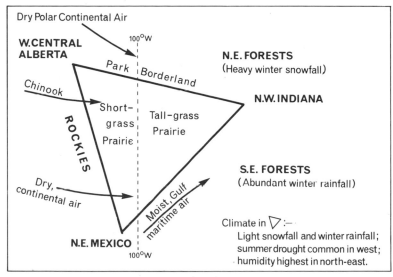

FIG. 45.—Eastward penetration of Tall-Grass Prairie, U.S.A.

British Columbia is in Canada. The coastal margins of Alaska, too, are mild enough to carry large coniferous trees, but much of the interior and the north, especially those parts away from the river valleys, is covered only with sparsely distributed, stunted trees or tundra. In the eastern United States the dominant trees are hardwoods, whereas in Canada they are softwoods, but valuable pine forests are found in the Upper Lakes region and in parts of the Gulf–Atlantic plain.

One of the most interesting features of the distribution of grassland vegetation in the United States is the way in which a salient of the North American Prairies is driven well beyond the 100 degrees W. longitude line to an apex in Indiana (see Fig. 45). It has been argued that grassland may have been produced in this relatively humid area by the repeated burning-off of timber by Indians before the coming of white people, but the true explanation may be a climatic one. The region experiences only a light winter rainfall and suffers much in summer from periodic droughts accompanied by scorching winds. Eastward-moving depressions normally follow tracks either to the north or to the south of this belt.

AMERICAN SOILS

The United States displays not only a greater variety of natural vegetation than Canada but also a greater diversity of regional soil groups. The reason, of course, is a wider climatic range. The richest soils are those of the Prairies, which are more extensive in the United States than in Canada. Of the poorest soils, podsols are more common in Canada, and in the United States tundra soils are confined to scattered mountain areas.

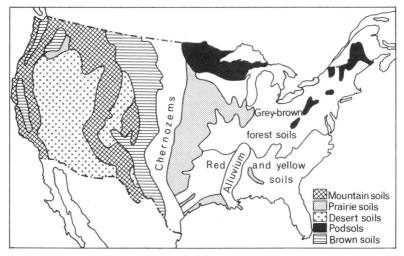

FIG. 46.—Generalised soil map of the U.S.A. This map should be compared with Fig. 4.

Broadly, soils in the western half of the United States belong overwhelmingly to the pedocal, or lime-accumulating group, while those in the moister eastern half of the country are mostly pedalfers, or acid soils. In the former, there is a general upward movement of water through the soil; evaporation produces an accumulation of lime and other soluble constituents which are drawn nearer the surface as aridity increases until—in desert soils—they may actually crystallise out upon it to form alkali incrustations. In damper, forested areas, such as those in the eastern

United States, soluble salts tend to be washed downwards: a process known as leaching; and the resultant soils are rich, not in calcium, but in aluminium (Al) and iron (Fe). Except in very dry areas, pedocals tend to be richer in organic matter (humus) than pedalfers, because grasses are more readily converted into humus than the leaves of trees.

Three main types of pedocals may be recognised in the United States: (1) black earths or *chernozems*; (2) brown and chestnut soils; (3) grey desert soils (*see* Fig. 46).

Black earths or chernozems occupy a broad belt which roughly corresponds to the central parts of the Prairies. The upper or "A" horizon, very rich in humus, is dark grey to black in colour; the dark-brown, "B" horizon, about 3–4 ft below the surface, has a marked accumulation of calcium carbonate which adds to the fertility of the soil, and endears it to the wheat-farmer.

Brown and chestnut soils, a little poorer in humus, and with a rather shallower "A" horizon, are typical of the drier "short-grass Prairie" region of the High Plains. These soils are again fertile, but, owing to their smaller water content, are best-suited to pasture. Grain, however, has often been planted on them, and serious wind erosion has resulted in the "Dust Bowl" of Kansas and Oklahoma.

Grey desert soils are found in the southern parts of the intermontane plateaus in the Western Cordillera (Fig. 47). They are very thin and deficient in organic matter, and the zone of carbonate accumulation is actually on the surface or only a few inches below it. Salt-encrusted surfaces are widespread, but in areas where salts have not crystallised out, irrigation-farming may be very successful owing to the complete absence of leaching.

The American pedalfers fall into four main classes:

1. *Prairie soils* are characteristic of the damper, eastern parts of the "tall-grass Prairie" country east of the chernozem zone. Though pedalferic, these soils are not greatly leached, their organic content is high, they are generally deep and friable, and, since they enjoy a more assured rainfall, are even safer for cultivation than the *chernozems*, and require comparatively little manuring.

2. *Grey-brown forest soils* are common to the northern zone of deciduous hardwood forests in the north-eastern United States. They have a shallow horizon of well-integrated humus, but soluble bases have been leached into the "B" horizon, so that their reaction is acidic. Most of the forest cover has been cleared, and mixed farming is characteristic, though much fertilisation is necessary for sustained yields.

3. *Podsols* are much more severely leached and usually carry only a

thin cover of humus, mostly raw. They are associated with the coniferous forests of upland areas, *e.g.* in northern New England, the Upper Lakes region, and the Pacific north-west. They are markedly acidic, and the "B" horizon is so indurated with iron as to hinder the penetration of

[*Courtesy: U.S. Information Service.*

FIG. 47.—Desert vegetation, Arizona. Here, at the foot of the Ajo Mountains, is a varied array of succulents, including the giant saguaro or organ cactus (*left*) and the prickly pear (*foreground*).

plant-roots, unless it is broken by deep-ploughing. Podsols remain largely under forest or "cut-over" land, though some dairying and the growing of oats and potatoes may be successful if the land is generously fertilised.

4. *Red and yellow soils* are typical of the south-eastern United States, where the natural vegetation is mostly southern hardwoods. Heavy rainfall and high temperatures have caused much leaching, and the organic content is rather low and quickly dispersed. These soils soon deteriorate under cultivation, and many of them, under continuous cotton-growing, have become exhausted and badly eroded. To maintain crop-yields rotations and heavy manuring are essential.

In each of the major soil zones there is a number of readily distinguishable types, including immature ones characteristic of areas where denudation is very active, *e.g.* mountainous regions. Glaciation has exerted important effects, stripping soils from the uplands of New England and the Upper Lakes region, and laying down moraines and outwash sands and gravels. Post-glacial lacustrine soils are found in many parts of the Dakotas. The soils of the Columbia Plateau have been enriched by lava flows, those of the Mississippi flood-plain with recent alluvium, and the Blue Grass region of Kentucky and the "Black Belt" of Alabama have soils richer in lime than those of the mature soil zones in which they lie.

Chapter XIII

GENERAL HUMAN GEOGRAPHY

SETTLEMENT AND POLITICAL GROWTH

EARLY SETTLEMENTS

The English were the pioneer settlers of the United States. Naturally, they first occupied the Atlantic margins. Among them were the "Company" colonists of Virginia who disembarked at Jamestown in 1607 following Raleigh's unsuccessful attempts at colonisation in the reign of Queen Elizabeth, and the Puritan colonists of New England, who made their first landing in 1620 at Plymouth, near the present city of Boston. Other parts of the Atlantic coastline north of Georgia were settled by English, Scots, and Irish, and by a few groups of Germans, Swedes, and Dutch, during the remaining years of the seventeenth century. Long before Georgia was established (1732), the British had come to control the whole of the east coast plain except for Florida, where a number of Spaniards were in occupation. The latter had also spread to some extent from Mexico into New Mexico.

The northern Atlantic colonists learnt from the native Indians how to grow maize in forest clearings, they sought the abundant fish of the coastal waters, and gradually became skilled boatbuilders, traders, and manufacturers. Many of the southerners, meantime, finding the summers too hot for gentlemen to do hard physical work out of doors, depended much more at first upon supply ships from home to support them. Later, they began to import negro slaves from the West Indies and West Africa to help them develop plantations of tobacco, sugar, rice, and eventually cotton.

For a long time, all the colonists tended to look back to Europe rather than forward to the interior of their new homeland. One reason for their attitude was the way in which their settlements were hemmed in by the Appalachian barrier. In Canada the French had no difficulty in rounding these mountains and were able to use the Great Lakes and various low portages as a means of ingress to the Mississippi basin. Not until 1750, however, did British pioneers manage to find a way across the Appalachians by ascending the valleys of the Susquehanna and Potomac, which led them into the Ohio basin. They were followed by a stream of travellers entering the fertile Blue Grass country of Kentucky by a more southerly route through the historic Cumberland Gap. The frontier lands west of the Appalachians and east of the Mississippi were awarded to Britain, along with French possessions in Canada, as a result of the Seven Years' War (1756–63).

THE THIRTEEN STATES

Thirteen years after the Peace of Paris, *i.e.* in 1776, the 2 million or so people who lived in the thirteen colonies of what is now the United States, felt sufficiently strong and self-reliant to declare their independence of Britain. The latter, having unsuccessfully contested the issue, was compelled to recognise the new republic of the United States of America in 1783. Its area—about 800,000 square miles—was less than a quarter of what it became by 1959.

By 1800 a new and much easier route through the Appalachians had been found. This was the Hudson–Mohawk gap, a lowland corridor leading to Lake Erie from New York. For a long time it had been held by a powerful confederacy of Iroquois Indians, but now it was ready to serve British colonists seeking their fortune in the central plains of the new republic. By 1825 it was equipped with the Erie Canal, which, like the trans-Appalachian roads from Philadelphia, Baltimore, and Washington, conveyed many settlers into the interior, and provided them with a much-used trade-route to the Atlantic.

THE GROWTH OF THE UNITED STATES

Meanwhile, between the Mississippi and the Rockies, lay the vast French colony of Louisiana. Though it was very sparsely settled, it represented a political threat to the westward march of the American frontiersmen. The United States, however, persuaded Napoleon to sell it to them in 1803, and it therefore became possible for American farmers and hunters to infiltrate into this new area without losing their national identity. A second purchase, in 1819, gave the republic Spanish Florida. As the Central Plains began to fill up, a new trading outlet became possible. This was the Mississippi River route, which for a time diverted a considerable volume of trade from the older Atlantic outlets. The historic stern-wheelers, however, lost most of their traffic later in the nineteenth century after the construction of transcontinental railways.

As far west as the Mississippi, most settlements were made in forest clearings in a humid land, and pioneering people had no difficulty in obtaining supplies of water, fuel, and constructional timber. Beyond the great river, the land was drier, and grassy rather than wooded, and its soils were difficult to break before the invention of the steel plough.

The Indians in these western plains, too, seemed to be more hostile than their fellow men farther east. But many land-seeking adventurers, and also mineral prospectors, dared to follow the moister valleyways and make their way out west. Following in the tracks of fur-traders and explorers, at first on horseback or on foot, later in their covered wagons ("Prairie schooners"), the majority overleapt Louisiana and pressed on to the better farmlands near the Pacific, *e.g.* the Willamette and Californian valleys. In the 1830s and 1840s, as this movement was proceeding via the Oregon, California, and Santa Fé trails (*see* Fig. 89) some of the transitional semi-arid land was set apart as reserves for Indian buffalo-hunters. Many of these reservations, however, were subsequently whittled down.

In 1821 a number of ranchers had established themselves in Texas, which came to be regarded as a "Cattle Kingdom." Unfortunately, this territory was claimed by Mexico, which had recently gained its independence from Spain. War followed, and between 1845 and 1848 Mexico was compelled to cede to the United States all the territories north of its present border. At about the same time the United States and Britain reached agreement on the use of the 49th parallel as the frontier of the American north-west, and the Americans were free to settle Washington and Oregon without troubling about the political consequences.

Few Americans made their homes in either the High Plains or the Western Cordillera before the present century, but hopes of a promised land brought Mormon cultivators into Utah under Brigham Young in 1847. A number of ranchers, using the "open-range" system of grazing, began to utilise the short-grass Prairies in the 1860s, and a few gold-seekers were attracted to Nevada, Colorado, Montana, and Idaho during the second half of the nineteenth century. But the total population out West remained very small.

After 1830 transcontinental migrations were facilitated and multiplied by the gradual westward spread of railways, but it was not until 1869, when the Union Pacific line from Omaha to San Francisco was completed, that it became possible to travel from coast to coast by modern transport. By 1884, a year before the first of Canada's transcontinental railways was finished, three additional American lines—the North Pacific, South Pacific, and Santa Fé—reached the Pacific coast. Railway construction also facilitated the political growth and unification of the United States. As different parts of the country became settled, states were created, *e.g.* Kentucky in 1792, Tennessee 1796, Ohio 1803, Indiana 1816, Iowa 1846, California 1850, Kansas 1861, Colorado 1876, Arizona and New Mexico 1912 (*see* Fig. 48).

Since 1912, two new states have been added to the United States. They are Alaska, purchased from Russia in 1867, and the Pacific islands of Hawaii, both of which territories achieved statehood in 1959. There are now fifty stars on the American flag, together with the original thirteen stripes.

THE POPULATION OF THE UNITED STATES

At the end of the War of Independence (or American Revolution), *i.e.* in about 1780, the United States had a population of between 2 and 3 millions, of whom about 90% were of Anglo-Saxon stock, most of the

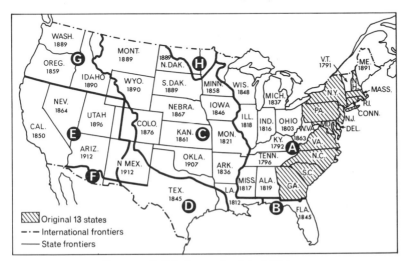

FIG. 48.—Political growth of the U.S.A.

The dates indicate the year of admission to the Union.

A. The United States, 1783.
B. Florida bought from Spain, 1819.
C. Louisiana, bought from France, 1803.
D. Texas, annexed from Mexico, 1845.
E. Ceded by Mexico, 1848.
F. Gadsden purchase, from Mexico, 1853.
G. Oregon Territory, recognised by British Treaty, 1846.
H. Ceded by Britain, 1818.

Alaska, bought from Russia in 1867, became a State in 1959; Hawaii also became a State in that year.

rest being of negro origin. By 1850 (when Canada had barely reached 3 millions), the total was 23 millions. From then until 1920 well over 30 million immigrants entered the country. They came not only from the British Isles but from most other European countries as well, *e.g* from Germany and Scandinavia, and later from the poverty-ridden lands of southern Italy and the Slav countries. By immigration and natural increase the population swelled to 105 millions. Another 75 millions have been added since 1920, and in 1960 the total population amounted to 180 millions. In 1970 it reached 205 millions.

America now restricts immigration by means of a quota system, which favours nationals from north-west European countries; she now accepts about 250,000 new arrivals each year, compared with four or five times that figure in the first decade of the present century. Well over 90% of the present-day Americans, whatever their origin, were born in the United States, and nearly all have been assimilated into the American way of life. In 1970 there were 22 million people of negro blood, but even these are Americans rather than Africans. About 450,000 men and women are of Chinese or Japanese origin excluding those who live in Hawaii. While over half the negroes inhabit the south, where their roots are, the Orientals are concentrated in the Pacific states, notably California. The aboriginal Indians number half a million, and there are small Mexican minorities in the border states.

Chiefly for reasons of relief, rainfall, and the distribution of coal and iron resources, but connected also with the importance of the North Atlantic trade-route, the configuration of the east coast, and the closeness of the rail and road network, most of the Americans still live in the older, eastern half of the country (see Fig. 7). In the western half people have congregated markedly in the farming and industrial areas round Puget Sound, San Francisco, and Los Angeles. In the mountain states, suited in the main only to extensive ranching, the population is very sparse, the only nuclei being in the vicinity of irrigated plots and mining districts. Alaska, with only 300,000 people, is the most notably empty state, owing to its remote situation and its generally inhospitable climate.

The average density of population in the United States in 1970 was about 57 per square mile. But this figure masks the high densities of states such as New Jersey (915), Rhode Island (782), Massachusetts (688), Connecticut (605), New York (367), and Pennsylvania (260). All these states are well-established manufacturing and trading areas, with intensive farms outside the many large cities. By contrast, Alaska has only 0.5 persons per square mile, Wyoming 3.4, Nevada 4.4, Montana 4.7, New Mexico 8.3, Idaho 8.5, South Dakota 8.6, and North Dakota 8.7. All these thinly settled states are in the Cordillera or western plains, and all suffer from at least partial aridity.

The United States is no more urbanised than Canada, despite the greater importance of manufacturing and trade in the former's economy. Canada has two cities with more than a million people, the United States has six: New York, Chicago, Los Angeles, Philadelphia, Detroit, and Houston. Another twenty or so cities have more than a million people in their central parts and metropolitan areas. More than 70% of the population may be classed as urban, and over half the total live on 7% of the total area. Only about one in twenty Americans actually lives on a farm. The percentage working in tertiary occupations, *e.g.* trade, transport, government, and the professions, is very high: a factor largely responsible for the present tendency for people to move from country to city.

We noticed in the first section of this chapter that the American frontier, from about 1750 to 1850, gradually moved westwards. In keeping with that movement, the "population centre," though lagging, has crept away from the Atlantic. By 1970, it had reached south-central Illinois. In 1950 California became the second most populous state in the Union. Ten years later it had a population of $15\frac{1}{2}$ millions, as against New York's $16\frac{1}{2}$. By 1964, with over 18 millions, it overtook New York.

THE ECONOMY

AMERICAN ECONOMIC STRENGTH

Economically, the United States is the strongest country in the world. Among the reasons for its pre-eminence are the following:

1. The great size of the country, combined with its favourable position in the temperate belt.

2. Its varied climates and soils, which are almost everywhere favourable for some form of agriculture.

3. Its oceanic setting and long coastline, which have not only encouraged the development of important fisheries but also the establishment of ports and shipping routes.

4. Its wealth of timber, both softwood and temperate hardwood.

5. Its rich mineral resources, notably coal, petroleum, iron, sulphur, phosphates, and copper.

6. Its large, healthy, varied population, hard-working, well-educated, and enterprising.

7. Its readiness to take advantage of Europe's example, and the freedom it has enjoyed from external attack, which allowed it to advance industrially at times when Europe was plunged into war.

8. The large amount of internal capital it has been able to build up to enable it to establish large-scale production techniques, typified by the conveyor-belt and the extension of automation.

9. The close network of communications it has laid down, especially in the eastern half of the country, and the advantage it has taken of the Great Lakes and Mississippi River as navigable waterways.

10. The use of a proportion of its capital for the development of

irrigation facilities and hydro-electric power plant, and for the setting-
up of industrial undertakings in other countries, notably in Canada.

11. The stability of its governments, whether Democratic or Republican in their political affiliations.

AGRICULTURE

The United States has six times as much "improved" farmland as
Canada, and its total agricultural output surpasses that of any other
country in the world. It grows nearly half the world's maize, more than
enough wheat for its requirements, and enough rice to satisfy its needs.
It grows sugar-cane in Louisiana, sugar-beet in Colorado, apples in
Washington and New England, pineapples in Florida. Its dairy-cattle
yield 20% of the world's milk, cheese and butter, and its pig industries
are among the foremost in the world. About 25% of the world's cotton
is grown in the United States, and no other country produces more
tobacco. Though permitting this abundance and variety of agricultural
production, however, the climate of the United States does not allow it to
grow such tropical products as tea, coffee, cocoa, rubber, and jute.

The United States has nearly 3 million farms, averaging nearly 400
acres each. As in Canada, the number is tending to decline, the average
acreage to increase.* Most of the holdings are highly mechanised and
electrified, and fertilisers are freely used, but intensive practices are only
widespread in the north-east, the Pacific lowlands, and the irrigated
districts of the western plateaus.

Like other countries, the United States has its agricultural problems.
One concerns farm surpluses. It has had difficulty in disposing of its
recently accumulated stocks of wheat and cotton. Another concerns soil
erosion. In places this is a serious handicap, and steps have had to be taken
to keep it in check. The loss of topsoil due to accelerated erosion is very
widespread in the United States. Such widely separated areas as the
Columbia Plateau in the north-west and New England in the north-east
have suffered from it. But there are two regions where the land has been
almost irretrievably ravaged: the High Plains, especially the notorious
"Dust Bowl," and the cotton-growing lands of the "Old South." In the
first region the severity of soil erosion has been largely due to the mis-
guided attempts to cultivate wheat in an area of marginal rainfall, which
has led to the blowing away of enormous quantities of fertile topsoil. In
the second region the traditional monocultural system of continuous
cotton-growing has resulted in the removal of soil from large areas of
sloping ground by heavy rain-storms. In both areas, and also in others
less seriously affected, soil conservation measures have recently been put

* There were 5 million farms in the United States as recently as 1955.

into operation. These include the adoption of contour-ploughing techniques, strip-cropping, the introduction of improved crop rotations, the extended use of manures, the planting of new grasses and soil-binding, leguminous plants, the transference of land from arable to pasture, the encouragement of mixed farming, and the planting of trees and the erection of small dams across rain-carved gullies.

"There is no typical American Farm," wrote Haystead and Fite in their book, *The Agricultural Regions of the United States*. But the most typical crop is corn, or, as we generally say, maize, which, like potatoes and

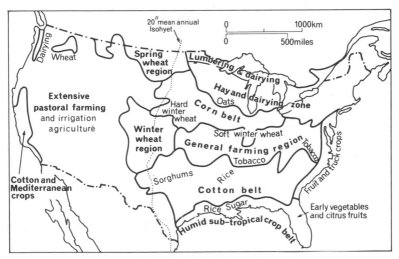

FIG. 49.—Agricultural Regions of the U.S.A.

tobacco, is native to the Americas. Maize in the United States is "something like sheep in Australia, tea in Ceylon, or rubber in Malaya," say the same authors. Though grown in every state of the Union, it is most important in the Corn Belt (*see* Fig. 49). This agricultural region is also the principal source of beef and pork. North-west of the Corn Belt, in the cooler part of the Prairies, spring wheat is the leading crop, while to the south winter wheat is widely grown, especially in the drier west of the plains. Winter wheat is also important on the Washington Plateau. Altogether, the United States produces far more wheat than Canada, and has recently been a strong competitor in world markets.

The north-eastern United States—a cool area of very varied topography and soils, and with a well-distributed precipitation—is favourable for mixed farming and dairying; and the Atlantic and Gulf Coast Plains, with nearby urban markets in the one case, and warm winters in the other, are widely suited to market-gardening, or truck-farming, as it is called in North America. California and Florida specialise in citrus fruits; and districts close to the Great Lakes, and benefiting from their moderating climatic influence, have become important for apples, peaches, apricots, and grapes. The main areas of tobacco cultivation lie on either side of the Middle Appalachians, *e.g.* in Kentucky on the west side, and in the Carolinas on the east side.

FORESTRY

When the first Europeans entered the United States about half the present area was forest-covered. As in Canada, however, much timber has been destroyed in the east, both by cutting and by fire, and in some places it has simply been replaced by "cut-over" land, *i.e.* by land under less valuable secondary trees. More care is now being taken of what remains of the former vast forest resources, the emphasis being placed, not as formerly upon the "mining" of trees, but upon "farming" them.

Over a quarter of the country is still under forest, which, as we saw in Chapter I, ranges from the mangroves and swamp-forests of Florida to the huge Douglas firs and redwoods of the Pacific States, and from the hickory, walnut, and oak of the east central states to the pines of Minnesota and the Rocky Mountains.

Though lumbering contributes less than 1% to the national income of the United States, the country leads the world in the production of temperate hardwoods, largely used for furniture-making, and is second only to the Soviet Union in its output of softwoods, which provide timber for constructional purposes and also wood-pulp for the manufacture of paper and rayon. The magnificent coniferous forests of Oregon, Washington, and northern California provide the largest quantities of sawn timber, but the pine forests of the Gulf–Atlantic–Appalachian region also contribute much, and the Upper Lakes region and northern New England furnish some. It is notable that the total softwood production greatly exceeds that of Canada; indeed, each of the three western states just mentioned cuts more than British Columbia, Canada's leading producer of sawn timber. The United States' appetite, however, is so voracious that she imports large quantities, despite the presence of near-virgin forests in Alaska. The position is similar with regard to wood-pulp and newsprint.

THE FISHERIES

Each year the United States lands more fish than Canada. In fact, until recently, when overtaken by Peru, the U.S.S.R., and China, only the Japanese have caught more. Like her northern neighbour, America has fisheries on both Atlantic and Pacific coasts as well as inland fisheries (chiefly on the Great Lakes), but she also benefits from the Gulf stocks. Most of her catch is consumed within her own borders.

In the Atlantic the cool, shallow waters off New England yield ocean perch, herring, flounder, lobster, cod, hake, haddock, halibut, mackerel, and other fish of the type caught off the Atlantic Provinces of Canada, and fishermen out from ports such as Boston and Gloucester often visit Canadian banks. Farther south are the unrivalled oyster and crab fisheries of Delaware and Chesapeake Bays, which, however, have recently shown signs of overfishing.

The Pacific fisheries yield heavy catches of halibut, tuna, and salmon. The latter is caught not only in Puget Sound and the Columbia River but also off Alaska, which has numerous canneries and leads British Columbia as a supplier of this commodity. Farther south, off California, tuna, sardine, and mackerel are the principal fish obtained. The first two are tinned in many coastal towns, and help to give California first place among all the states in the Union which are engaged in commercial fishing. Menhaden are netted in large quantities along the coasts of the Gulf of Mexico and off the middle and south Atlantic shores. Though generally too bony for human consumption, menhaden are valuable in that they supply an oil which acts as a substitute for linseed and other vegetable oils, e.g. in the manufacture of tin-plate and linoleum. Many are also converted into manure and fish-meal. Other fish caught in Gulf waters are shellfish such as oysters and shrimps, red snapper, and grouper. Sponges are collected by divers off Florida, but disease and depletion have reduced the haul in recent years.

As in Canada, fishing in the United States is not entirely a commercial undertaking, but is also a popular sport. In summer many tourists in many parts of the country try their luck in river and lake.

POWER SUPPLIES

The United States has not only very large reserves of coal, petroleum, natural gas, water power, and nuclear fuels, but she has been so active in their exploitation that she has come to lead the whole world in the production of all of them. Indeed, though the percentages for which she is responsible are falling, she manages even now to account for nearly 25% of the world's petroleum output, 20% of the coal, and over 25% of the hydro-electric power, and at least 25% of the uranium. Moreover, her developed reserves are well distributed in relation to utilisation. Most of the petroleum and natural gas deposits are located in the sedimentary basins on the flanks of the Cordillera, in California on the western side, on the High Plains and Gulf Coast Plain on the eastern side; the principal coalfields are in the eastern United States, the main producing areas being in the Appalachian Plateau region, where the world's largest coalfield is located (*see* Fig. 50). Hydro-electric power has been developed on the Tennessee River and on the "Fall Line" between the Appalachians and the Atlantic Coast Plain, on rivers such as the Columbia, Sacramento, and Colorado which drain to the Pacific, at Niagara Falls, on the River St Lawrence, and at many sites in New England. Uranium is produced in Colorado and several other Mountain States, and thorium in southern California and South Carolina.

The extraction of petroleum began in the United States, as in Canada,

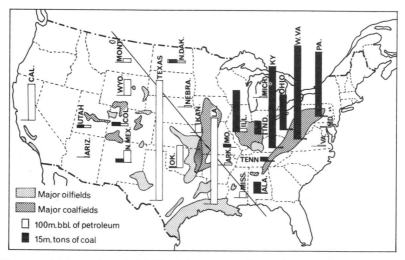

Fig. 50.—Major coal- and oilfields of the U.S.A. The production of coal and oil by States, 1970, is shown by vertical columns. Areas south-west of the bold line crossing the map produce nearly 95% of U.S.A.'s petroleum, areas north-east over 98% of the nation's coal.

a century ago, but the output remained small before the advent of the motor car. The invention of the aeroplane gave a later fillip to the industry and ships began to find it more serviceable than coal. It now also commands a large market in manufacturing areas, where it is valued not only as a source of power but also as a raw material. The first field to be worked in the United States lay in Pennsylvania, which still yields small amounts of high-grade oil ideal for lubrication. Other fields in the eastern half of the country include those of Ohio, Indiana, Michigan, and Illinois, but none is of major importance today. Fortunately, these eastern states possess exceptionally large supplies of bituminous coal, and north-east Pennsylvania boasts the most important anthracite field in the world.

Petroleum is also worked in the Rocky Mountain foothill zone, notably in Wyoming, where it competes with scattered coal deposits, but in neither case is the output very significant.

There are considerable reserves of coal and lignite in the south-western and southern interior of the United States, but few mines have been opened because it is this area which supports the world's greatest oil-producing industry at the present time. Two very extensive fields, each with thousands of wells, may be recognised: the Gulf Coast field of southern Texas and Louisiana, and the adjoining Mid-Continent field of northern Texas, Oklahoma, and Kansas, spreading into New Mexico (*see* Fig. 50). Already these fields supply more than two-thirds of North America's petroleum, but the industry is still expanding in response to an almost insatiable market. A forest of derricks has recently appeared in the Gulf of Mexico itself, and there is still plenty of "wild-catting," *i.e.* speculative drilling. Natural gas may be associated with petroleum, and today thousands of miles of gas pipelines as well as oil pipelines radiate from such states as Texas to refineries and manufacturing plants in the populous north-eastern parts of the United States. Even remote cities, such as Philadelphia and New York, are served by pipelines from the Texas oilfields, though petroleum is also conveyed to Atlantic cities by tankers operating from Gulf ports such as Houston.

Third among the United States' chief petroleum-producing regions is southern California, which accounts for about one-eighth of the total U.S. output. California has no coal, but her oil supplies and the hydro-electric power she obtains from Boulder Dam, on the Colorado, from the Shasta Dam on the Sacramento, and other sources, have given her an opportunity to develop industrially. It is significant, too, that California has more motor cars in relation to the population than any other state. (The United States as a whole has more than any other country.)

In view of her vast domestic supplies, it is perhaps surprising that the United States imports petroleum, chiefly from Venezuela. But it is not astonishing that she is the world's leading exporter of refined petroleum. She also has a surplus of coal, which she is able to market without difficulty in Ontario and Europe.

MISCELLANEOUS MINERALS

It is not only with coal and other mineral fuels that the United States is richly-endowed. She also possesses large iron-ore reserves and she produces nearly one-sixth of the world's current supply.* She also accounts for 70% of the world's output of molybdenum, 50% of the vanadium,

* Just as the advance of Near Eastern countries as petroleum-producers is reducing the relative output of the United States, so the advance of the Soviet Union as a producer of other minerals, especially coal and iron, is reducing the relative importance of the United States in this field also.

nearly 40% of the titanium, and more than 12% of the tungsten. But so vast is her steel and alloy-steel industry that she has to import many metals, including nickel (from Canada), manganese, chromium, and cobalt. Like Canada, she mines some cobalt and also small amounts of manganese and chromium, but her production of nickel is negligible.

The United States produces little asbestos, antimony and mica, and industrial diamonds and tin are virtually absent. But she comes first in the world as a producer of copper, lead, cadmium (a by-product of zinc, lead- and copper-smelting), sulphur (30%) magnesium (50%), salt (30%), phosphates (40%) and gypsum. The country has almost a monopoly of helium (formerly used in airships, now mainly for inflating meteorological balloons), and her very large output of sulphur, potash, salt, and phosphates greatly assists her chemical industry. She is also an important source of gold, silver, and bauxite.

The principal seat of iron deposits in the United States is the "ranges" located in the ancient rocks of the Canadian Shield close to Lake Superior and Lake Michigan. These ranges, e.g. the Mesabi, furnish 80% of the iron ore produced in the country. The rock is a fairly rich haematite, easily worked by open-cut methods, and accessible to Lakes shipping. But supplies are beginning to dwindle, and a lower-grade ore, taconite, is being broached. Other haematite deposits are mined in the Birmingham district on the Alabama coalfield, and rich magnetite ores are worked in Pennsylvania and in the Adirondack Mountains (New York State). Minor quantities of iron are obtained from a few of the Mountain States.

The main supplies of the other metallic minerals are drawn either from the Mountain States or from the Ozarks. The outstanding contributors are Colorado, Utah, Arizona, and Idaho, but all the western states except Oregon are of importance. Metal-refining, i.e. the separation out of the different metals after smelting the concentrates, may be carried out at some distance from the mining districts, e.g. in Pennsylvania, where zinc is treated, Connecticut, where uranium is concentrated, Tacoma on Puget Sound, where copper is smelted and refined. These localities benefit from cheap electricity, and can easily receive imported raw metals.

Non-metallic minerals are especially important in the Gulf States, which yield not only petroleum and natural gas, but also sulphur, salt, and helium. Salt is also produced in New York, Michigan, Ohio and Utah. Tennessee and Florida account for most of the phosphates, New Mexico and California for the bulk of the potash. Both these minerals are important sources of agricultural fertilisers.

THE MANUFACTURING INDUSTRIES

Although the United States, as we have seen, has a great wealth of agricultural land, forests, fisheries and minerals, all of which give employment to many people, it is in the field of manufacturing that she has made her greatest impact on the outside world. Among the factors which have given her pride of place among the industrial countries of the world are the following: (a) plentiful, easily-exploited supplies of coal, petroleum, natural gas and water power; (b) large resources of iron and other metals; (c) a wealth of timber and cultivated products; (d) an abundant and varied labour supply; (e) a large and rich domestic market; (f) an excellent system of communications.

We noticed in Chapter II the location of the principal manufacturing regions, but said little of the actual industries carried on in them. At least the following manufactures employ more than a million workers: (a) iron and steel, and other primary metals; (b) machinery; (c) food; (d) textiles and clothing. Other very important industries include the manufacture of electrical equipment, printing and publishing, chemical manufacture, lumber- and paper-making, the production of leather and footwear, pottery and glass, furniture and tobacco.

Food industries are the most widespread. They include meat-packing and grain-milling, the preparation of dairy produce, and the canning and preserving of fruit, vegetables, and fish.

The iron and steel industry, which is capable of producing well over 100 million tons of steel a year, is as large as that of the whole of western Europe, though the latter exports more than twice as much steel. The United States industry was successively dominant in: (a) New England; (b) the anthracite coalfield region of eastern Pennsylvania; (c) western Pennsylvania; (d) the Lake cities, e.g. Chicago and Gary, Cleveland, Toledo and Buffalo. Today, the main steel-making centres are the shores of Lake Erie and Michigan, Pittsburgh and its satellites, the Birmingham district of Alabama, and the north-east coast (see Fig. 70). New England and eastern Pennsylvania now concentrate on engineering and the electronics industry, though the manufacture of steel has not entirely deserted them. Round all the major steel-making cities large quantities of machinery and machine-tools are turned out.

Apart from the manufacture of aircraft, which has become most important in the west, especially in California, the vehicle industry, like the iron and steel industry, is concentrated in the north-east. Detroit holds first place as a motor-car manufacturing city, but by no means stands alone. Places as far apart as St Louis, Kansas City, Atlanta, and Los Angeles all have large plants. Shipbuilding is less important than in

Japan, Britain, Germany, and Sweden, but there are yards in many Atlantic cities, at Oakland and Tacoma on the Pacific coast, at Beaumont and Mobile on the Gulf Coast, and on the shores of the Great Lakes. Locomotive building tends to be concentrated on railway foci, *e.g.* Chicago, Detroit, New York, and Philadelphia.

The United States leads the world in the manufacture of cotton, rayon, and nylon. There are two significant textile-manufacturing areas: an older one in eastern New England, still dominating the wool industry, but, remote from the American Cotton Belt, making fewer cotton goods than formerly; a newer one in the Southern States, manufacturing two-thirds of the cotton tissues, and also much rayon and nylon. Paterson (New Jersey) and Scranton (Pennsylvania) process imported silk, but the advance of synthetic fibres has reduced the scale of this industry. The clothing industry is associated with many large cities, in particular New York and Los Angeles, both of which have become world fashion centres.

Certain major problems, apart from endemic ones such as labour and markets, are currently afflicting American industrialists. First is the growing cost of anti-pollution measures and the objections frequently lodged nowadays by "conservationists" to the siting of new factories, river dams, power stations, etc., especially when they are proposed in areas of natural beauty. Concern for the environment is growing among the American public who are increasingly demanding reductions in the volume of industrial smoke, noxious effluents such as those emanating from smelter and chemical plants, motor-vehicle exhaust fumes, factory waste, etc. To meet these demands—even partially—is placing both financial and technological burdens on manufacturers.

Industrialists have also begun more fully to realise that the country's reserves of fossil fuels are finite. In the last few years, the rate of discovery of new sources of natural gas in the U.S. has fallen below the rate of consumption, and—but for the recent discovery of large oil deposits on the remote north coast of Alaska—the same would doubtless be true of oil in a few years. Partly to counteract this problem of contracting oil and gas supplies, the United States, after a slow start, is now pressing rapidly forward with the generation of nuclear electricity. She is already operating plants in several power-hungry states, *e.g.* New York, New Jersey, Pennsylvania, Illinois, Minnesota, California and others, and many more are planned. But—as in Britain and mainland Europe—doubts have appeared, *e.g.* about (*i*) the most efficient type of plant, (*ii*) the relative costs of nuclear and other sources of electricity, (*iii*) the safety of nuclear plants, (*iv*) the least damaging way of disposing of radio-active waste.

Chapter XIV

NEW ENGLAND

THE REGIONS OF THE UNITED STATES

As in Canada, so in the United States, geographical regions are easy to define only in terms of large physical areas, if excessive fragmentation is to be avoided. The regions on which this book is based are shown on Fig. 51, but the writer does not claim that either his divisions or his boundaries are wholly satisfactory.

PHYSICAL ASPECTS

NEW ENGLAND AS A GEOGRAPHICAL REGION

Most geographers recognise New England as a distinctive region, even though many of its characteristics, *e.g.* structure, relief, climate, soils, and natural vegetation, are shared with adjacent parts of the United States and Canada. It occupies the north-eastern section of the United States, and consists politically of the fairly large state of Maine, which takes up half the total area, the smaller states of Vermont and New Hampshire, and the "pocket" states of Massachusetts, Connecticut, and Rhode Island. The whole region covers less than 2% of the total area of the country, but houses nearly 6% of its population.

In the west the boundary is fairly well defined along the margin of the Hudson valley and Lake Champlain lowland. In the south and east the coast is a sufficiently clear border, though many New Englanders make a living from the sea. In the north, however, the mountains of northern New England pass imperceptibly into those of south-eastern Quebec and New Brunswick.

As its name suggests, the region has something of the character of old England. Its size is not dissimilar, and it is alike in its very varied relief, with high, glacially eroded land mainly in the north and west, and lowland in the south and east. It is again a land of natural forest, though most of its people now find employment in intensive farming, fishing, manufacturing, and trade. It was the pioneer industrial area in North America just as old England was in Europe. A large number of its settlements, whether farmsteads, villages, or market towns, bear English names; its villages often have greens overlooked by country churches, and its

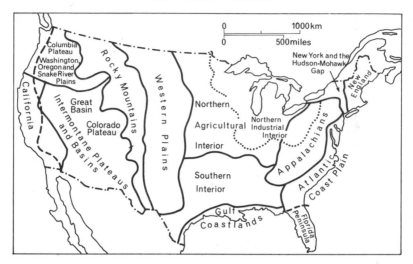

FIG. 51.—Geographical regions of the U.S.A. The regions marked on this map are those used in this book. Dotted line shows approximate boundary of industrialised area; broken lines indicate sub-regions.

towns, notably Boston, frequently have narrower and more winding thoroughfares than are usually found in American urban centres. New England supports the two oldest universities in the United States: Harvard, founded in the Cambridge suburb of Boston in 1636, and Yale, established at New Haven in 1701.

Many of New England's early industries, like those of old England, are now tending to "run down." The population, derived originally from England, has become more cosmopolitan in the last century: Poles, Italians, Irish, and French Canadians are numerous, and there are now more Roman Catholics than Protestants. But the life of the region still tends to be directed by the " real New Englanders," *i.e.* the descendants of the old colonists who have so profoundly affected the moral, cultural and industrial traditions of the nation as a whole.

STRUCTURE AND RELIEF

Physically, New England forms part of the Appalachian region, although in the west the main trend-lines run from north to south rather than in the more general north-east to south-west direction.

The rocks, which are mainly of early Palaeozoic age, were folded and fractured earlier than those south of the Hudson River, and were later subjected to igneous intrusion, metamorphism, Cretaceous and Tertiary uplift. Long-continued denudation, combined with recent glaciation and coastal submergence, has produced a very complicated pattern of relief.

In the west are the Green Mountains of Vermont (averaging more than 3500 ft), which divide southwards into the Taconic and Berkshire Uplands, between which the Housatonic River flows southwards to Long Island Sound. East of these eroded mountains spreads the broad Triassic lowland of the Connecticut valley, which, like its marginal uplands, trends from north to south. East again is another region of mountain and plateau culminating in the 6000-ft-high White Mountains of New Hampshire. Separating these highlands from the Atlantic is an ancient

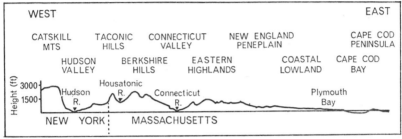

Fig. 52.—Generalised section across New England, lat. 42°5' N.

peneplain with a structure comparable with that of the Piedmont Plateau south-west of New York (see Figs. 52 and 54).

The present landscape of New England owes nearly as much to Pleistocene glaciation as to the nature of its solid rocks and the tectonic movements which they have experienced. In the north the ice-sheets stripped most of the soil from the uplands and, assisted by fluvio-glacial rivers, laid it down as moraines and assorted stony drift in the lowlands of the south and east. The greater part of Long Island, Martha's Vineyard, Nantucket Island, and the Cape Cod Peninsula (ending in a great hooked spit) are overlain with terminal moraines and outwash sands. The glaciation of New England also resulted in the diversion of many streams into ungraded channels punctuated with rapids and waterfalls; water has been ponded back into lakes and many inlets along the rocky coast of Maine have been scoured out.

CLIMATE AND NATURAL VEGETATION

New England has a cool temperate east coast marginal type of climate similar to that of the Maritime Provinces of Canada. Its winters are far more severe than those of old England, as the first, Puritan settlers were quick to discover, but, by way of compensation, its summers are much warmer. The precipitation, which includes heavy snowfalls, especially deep in the inland and upland areas, is well distributed, with a slight maximum in winter when the depressions with which most of the rain and snow are associated are most intense.

Climatic statistics for Boston are appended, for reference:

	J.	F.	M.	A.	M.	J.	Jy.	A.	S.	O.	N.	D.
Temperature (° F)	27	28	35	45	57	67	71	69	63	52	41	32
Precipitation (in.)	3·7	3·5	4·1	3·8	3·7	3·1	3·5	4·2	3·4	4·1	4·1	3·8

Mean Annual Temperature: 49° F; Mean Annual Range of Temperature: 44° F; Mean Annual Precipitation: 45 in.

Climate and soil have combined to produce a natural forest cover. In the north, mainly in the uplands, the trees belong to the coniferous and north-eastern hardwood family; in the south and reaching north in the Connecticut valley, they are chiefly southern hardwoods, with some pines and other conifers on very sandy soils.

THE ECONOMY

FORESTRY

Much of the forest, even in the interior, was ruthlessly cleared by the early settlers to make room for agriculture, but not all the timber was wasted. It came in useful for building houses and ships, and it provided fuel and charcoal for small iron smelteries, and bark for tanning leather. Three-quarters of New England is still clothed with forest, but the present growth is largely of a secondary kind, less valuable than the original. Some sawn timber is produced, especially in the north, and there are plywood and furniture works and other timber-using firms. But the manufacture of wood-pulp and paper, and the collection of finely flavoured maple-sugar tend to be more significant today than saw-milling. Among the paper-works are those of Holyoke, Pittsfield, and Fall River, all located at important water-power sites. The first-named leads all American cities in the production of fine paper, which, of course, depends not simply on wood-pulp, but on many other, imported, raw materials.

AGRICULTURE

Farming has never been easy in New England. There is a dearth of extensive lowlands, the growing season is only about 150 days even in the south, and barely 100 days in the north, and the soils—podsols in the north, acidic grey-brown earths in the south—are generally scrabbly and often so stony that many farmers say they can grow stones better than crops.

It is not surprising that many farms, particularly those in the more remote areas, have been abandoned in the last century as better farm lands have been opened up west of the Appalachians, and more profitable means of livelihood have suggested themselves in New England itself. Much agricultural land, in fact, is now held by part-timers and week-enders—by people who earn part of their living in other jobs, and by well-to-do city-workers who like to boast that they possess a country estate even if they use it for nothing more than recreation, including fishing and shooting.

Some existing farms suffer from soil erosion consequent upon timber-felling. On others, boulders interfere with the use of farm machinery, and mechanical stone-pickers are called into service. Nearly all the soils, whatever their depth and texture, require heavy manuring to keep them in good heart. But lowland farmers have the advantage of nearby in-dustrial markets, and therefore can do fairly well if they specialise in dairying, poultry-farming, truck-farming, and fruit-growing. Most holdings are small and highly capitalised and are often worked by non-English people, e.g. in the north by French-Canadians.

Seventy-five per cent. of the total cropland is in hay, and in Vermont

[Courtesy: U.S. Information Service.

FIG. 53.—Farm landscape, Vermont. This photograph shows the characteristic New England blend of well-kept village, rolling farmland, and wooded hill country.

and the three southern states milk is the chief saleable product. Some oats are grown in Vermont and a little maize, mostly cut green for silage, in Connecticut, but the cows are fed chiefly on grass and hay, supplemented by a few concentrates brought in from the Middle West.

The poultry industry is widespread, and the name "Rhode Island" is of world-wide renown among hen-keepers, but only in New Hampshire do poultry products bring in more cash than milk. Suburban small-holdings are particularly well favoured commercially for the disposal of eggs, chickens, and turkeys.

Truck-farming, of course, is even more closely tied to urban markets than dairying and poultry-raising. Large quantities of vegetables, *e.g.* carrots, tomatoes, celery, onions, and lettuce are carefully cultivated and sold fresh from the roadside or in the New England cities and in New York. Aroostook County, in eastern Maine, like the adjacent part of New Brunswick, specialises in the raising of potatoes, which do well on the local sandy loams, and can be profitably marketed in many north-eastern cities. Many are sold for seed purposes, and others are converted into starch. Cranberries are a speciality of the bog-soils of Cape Cod, and are much in demand, as turkey and cranberry sauce is a national dish, now eaten in city restaurants the year through. Blueberries, and in the south sweet corn, are important crops near the shores of Maine, and south-east Massachusetts is noted for its strawberries. Apples, pears, and peaches have a wide distribution in the south of New England, but there are fewer orchards than there were in 1920. Some tobacco is grown in the lower Connecticut valley.

The rural population of New England is very small. Less than 10% of the people of Rhode Island and Massachusetts live in the country, but in Vermont and Maine, where industry and trade are little developed, the figure is 65%.

FISHING INDUSTRIES

As in the Atlantic Provinces of Canada, fishing has long been a significant source of employment in New England, and several ports have whaling traditions as part of their heritage. Today, the region lands more fish than any other part of the United States except California, and Boston claims first place as a U.S. fishing port. Gloucester, the second fishing port in New England, is more exclusively devoted to this activity. Massachusetts as a whole accounts for about 60% of the total catch, Maine for about 35%.

Among the principal fish caught, haddock, herring, whiting, ocean perch, flounder, lobster, and other shellfish occupy high places. Some cod are still dried for export by methods similar to those practised in Newfoundland, but there are large freezing plants and packing stations at Boston and Gloucester, and frozen fillets, for consumption in the United States, are now the chief product. Oysters are collected from the sandy coasts of Connecticut, Rhode Island, and Cape Cod.

The reasons for the growth of important fishing industries in New England are obvious. They include: (a) the existence of shallow offshore banks, e.g. George's and Brown's; (b) the numerous harbours of the drowned coast; (c) the inhospitable nature of much of the land; (d) the long tradition of boat-building and sea-faring; (e) the existence of large urban markets within convenient reach. The industry on the whole is more modern than that of eastern Canada, and trawling is much more characteristic.

MANUFACTURING

For a long time, from the early days of domestic industry through into the modern period of factory industry, New England was the principal seat of manufacturing in the United States. Its workshops supplied the needs of thousands of immigrants as they streamed westwards to settle in the Central Plains, and even today, when its industrial momentum has slackened, it is an important manufacturing area. In fact, its southern lowlands support a greater proportion of people engaged in manufacturing than any other part of the United States.

The early advantages of New England as a manufacturing area may be summarised as follows:

1. It was one of the first parts of North America to be settled by Europeans, who found there a climate stimulating to both physical and mental effort.

2. The early immigrants who adhered to the Puritan virtues of hard work and thrift, were largely drawn from Britain. They took with them to the New World a tradition of domestic industry and inventive genius.

3. Small deposits of iron ore, a wealth of forest, and the settlers' own farmstock provided a number of essential raw materials, viz. metal, timber, charcoal for smelting, wool, and hides, before the Industrial Revolution.

4. Capital for financing early industries was acquired from the trading, fishing, and whaling activities of coastal towns like Boston.

5. With its many ungraded rivers, resulting both from glacial derangement and igneous intrusion, its abundant, well-distributed rainfall, and storage lakes, the region had considerable water power available for early factory industry. Also, the growth of textile

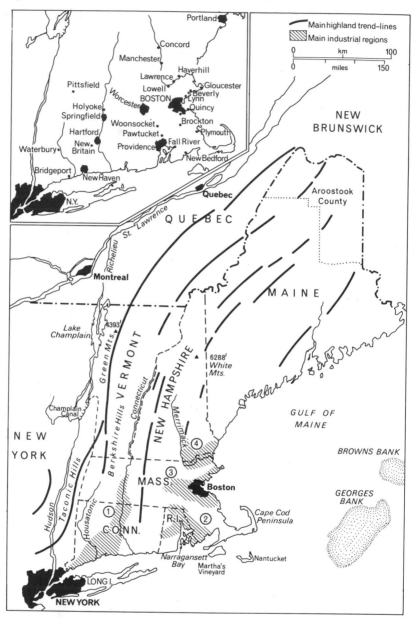

FIG. 54.—New England. General features and main manufacturing regions. *Inset:*
major cities and towns. The following industrial regions should be noted: 1.
South-west Connecticut and lower Connecticut valley; 2. Narragansett Bay;
3. Boston Bay; 4. Merrimack valley. The river and coastal locations of most
of the large settlements should be observed.

manufacturing was assisted by the softness of most of the water supplies.

6. Any prosperity the region might acquire could not depend, as in the South, upon the growing and transporting to Europe of crops different from those of the home country. Moreover, productive farm-land was very limited in extent, therefore there was every inducement to develop manufacturing industries to supply the expanding consumers' market in the United States.

Since the flood-tide of industrialism and commercialism set in, certain additional advantages have accrued:

7. The acquisition of an increasing volume of skilled labour and managerial enterprise.

8. The conversion of the more important water-power sites, in-cluding most of those on the Connecticut and Merrimack Rivers, into hydro-electric power-stations. (Many of the smaller power sites, like the upland farms, are now derelict.)

9. The development of communications by land and sea, which has enabled the region to expand its markets and widen the areas from which it can draw materials.

10. The phenomenal growth of the internal market, especially in the north-eastern part of the nation.

But New England suffers from certain serious drawbacks which have caused a contraction in some of its main industries, particularly those concerned with cotton textiles and leather:

1. A shortage of domestic raw materials, e.g. cotton and hides.

2. A lack of fuel and minerals (apart from small amounts of asbestos, graphite, and mica), e.g. coal, petroleum, and iron ore. Hence it has been difficult to develop heavy industry, and expensive to build factories remote from hydro-electric power sites and the coast.

3. The decline in the high value of its workers due to increased mechanisation, which has enabled other areas, e.g. the Middle West and the South, to compete successfully.

4. The out-of-date character of much of its long-used plant.

As might be expected, New England now concentrates on light in-dustries which require highly skilled labour but comparatively small quantities of raw material and fuel. The principal ones are electronics and the manufacture of small metal goods, finely woven cloth of wool and cotton, stylish footwear and high-quality paper. Most of the engineering works are situated in the south-west, *i.e.* in western Massachusetts and Connecticut, most of the textile and leather mills in the south-east, *i.e.* in south-eastern New Hampshire, eastern Massachusetts, and Rhode Island. There are few factories (apart from food-processing works, saw-mills, and pulp-mills) in Vermont and Maine.

Metal products include precision instruments, clocks and watches, typewriters, sewing machines, firearms, brass and bronze ware, and electrical apparatus, *i.e.* "Birmingham goods." Bridgeport, Springfield, New Britain, Hartford, New Haven, Holyoke, and Waterbury, all in the south-west, are important engineering centres. In the south-east, Worcester and Manchester make machine-tools, Fall River, firearms and cycles, Portland and Quincy, ships. Altogether, engineering industries now provide more employment than any other group of industries.

Textile factories lie in two main groups: (1) those in the Merrimack valley and in the immediate hinterland of Boston, *e.g.* at Lawrence, Lowell, Manchester, Concord, and Worcester; (2) those on and near the south coast, *e.g.* at Fall River and Providence, two large hydro-electric power centres on the great indentation of Narragansett Bay; and at New Bedford, Pawtucket, and Woonsocket.

The wool textile industry, which embraces the manufacture of both woollens and worsteds, is heavily dependent upon the import of raw material from Australia, Argentina, and other countries. It has never provided as much employment as the cotton industry, but has not declined to the same extent. The Southern States took the lead in cotton-manufacturing from New England in the 1920s, and now spin more yarn and weave far more cloth than the north-east. Among the factors which have favoured the South are the following: (*a*) easier access to raw material; (*b*) cheaper fuel costs, partly due to the lower cost of heating in a warmer area; (*c*) more modern machinery and better laid-out plants; (*d*) lower land values and taxation rates; (*e*) less-restrictive trade-union regulations governing such matters as hours of work and numbers of machines an individual can look after.

Man-made fibres, especially rayon, are now made in many former cotton factories, and textile machine works have a wide distribution.

The boot and shoe industry is concentrated within a few miles of Boston. Lynn and Beverly (mainly women's shoes), Haverhill and Brockton (chiefly men's), and Boston itself still turn out nearly a third of the nation's footwear, despite competition from New York and the Middle West, and New England continues to manufacture a large proportion of the machinery used in the American industry. Hides are imported from the western states and also from South America. The rubber used in the industry is either imported from south-east Asia or else purchased from synthetic producers in other parts of the United States.

THE TOURIST INDUSTRY

Of recent years, much propaganda has been issued to attract visitors to New England, and there has been a boom in the tourist industry, which has done much to offset losses in other activities. The region has much to recommend it to the holiday-maker: a historical background, a rich literary and cultural tradition, the sandy beaches of Cape Cod and other southern coasts, the varied upland scenery. Many tourists find recreation there not only in summer but also in the fall, when the maples are aflame with colour, and in winter when the snows of the Vermont and New Hampshire Highlands lie deep enough for winter sports. Moreover, the region is very accessible to the citizens of New York and other large settlements.

MAJOR CITIES

Most of the towns and cities of New England are no more than about 40 miles from the south and south-east coasts, where the gentle relief has facilitated the spread of communications, and there is easy access to imported raw materials and also to the coal of West Virginia and Pennsylvania, most of which reaches New England via New Jersey and Chesapeake Bay.

Portland is the largest settlement in Maine. It is situated on a coastal inlet not far from the Massachusetts border. It is a fishing port with shipbuilding and engineering industries, textile mills, shoe factories, and canning works. A railway to Montreal allows it to compete with Halifax and St John as a winter outlet for Canadian grain, as it is the nearest ice-free port to the St Lawrence valley.

Boston is very much larger. With a city population of nearly 650,000 (1970), and well over $2\frac{1}{2}$ million people in its total metropolitan area, it has long been the regional capital of New England as well as the main route focus, trading centre, and manufacturing city. It retains its well-established place as the principal wool and leather market of the United States, and has many factories dependent on these two materials, as well as clothing mills, engineering works, sugar refineries, and chocolate works.

Boston's deep, sheltered, tidal harbour, formed by the estuaries of two small rivers, the Charles and the Mystic, opens out into Boston Bay, which flanks the main transatlantic shipping route. As a port, however, it has largely given way to New York, which gained earlier, easier, and quicker access to the interior of the country. Its imports, largely of petroleum, coal, wood-pulp, wool, hides, and sugar, far exceed its exports, chiefly grain and manufactures, and it now tends to concentrate on coastal trade, New York being free to conduct most of New England's foreign trade. The coastal route between Boston and New York utilises a 12-mile canal cut through the neck of the Cape Cod Peninsula so that shipping may avoid the dangerous waters east of the sand-spit.

Chapter XV

NEW YORK
AND THE HUDSON–MOHAWK GAP

GENERAL CHARACTER OF THE REGION

In many respects the area which forms the subject of this chapter is not a geographical region. It includes the metropolitan area of New York, the most populous conurbation in the world; the great ⊢-shaped traffic-way of the Hudson valley and its arms, the Mohawk Gap and the Lake Champlain–Richelieu corridor; the plains on the south side of Lake Ontario and the St Lawrence; and a rugged outlier of the Canadian Shield known as the Adirondack Mountains. There is therefore no physical unity (*see* Fig. 57). On the other hand, almost the whole area is in some way tributary to New York City. How could one, for instance, discuss the Hudson–Mohawk lowland without reference to its outlet? And does not most of the value of the Adirondacks lie in their charm for New York's holiday-makers?

NEW YORK

THE NEW YORK METROPOLITAN AREA

The New York Consolidated Area, with a total population of nearly 15 millions, of which the city accounts for nearly 8 millions, is no longer confined to the state of New York. It has long included several cities in New Jersey, and has recently spread into Connecticut.

The nucleus of the city is Manhattan Island, a small part of the Appalachian Piedmont zone (*see* Chapter XVII) of ancient crystalline rocks. It measures about 13 miles by 2 miles, and is sandwiched between the lower Hudson River and East River, which joins the drowned mouth of the Hudson to Long Island Sound. On the north, the island is cut off from the mainland by the Harlem River, a link between East River and the Hudson (*see* Fig. 55). The site was occupied by fur-traders in the early years of the seventeenth century and bought by the Dutch from the Indians in the 1620s, when it was christened "New Amsterdam." The name "New York" was given to it by the British when they took possession of it in 1664.

From Manhattan Island, New York has expanded to the western end of Long Island (Queens and Brooklyn), to Staten Island (Richmond), across the Hudson to the New Jersey mainland, and north of the Harlem to Bronx and Yonkers. The boroughs of Manhattan, Brooklyn, Queens, Richmond, and Bronx are included in the City. Beyond, but well within

Fig. 55.—Site of New York. The shaded area indicates the main built-up portions of the city and its metropolitan area. The road bridge linking Richmond to Brooklyn is called the Verrazano Narrows Bridge. It has the longest span (4260 ft) of any suspension bridge in the world and is helping to reduce traffic congestion in Lower Manhattan.

the metropolitan area, are Yonkers, Jersey City (270,000), Bayonne, Newark (400,000), and Elizabeth.

Manhattan Island remains the heart of the city. Apart from the rectangular Central Park and a few other, smaller, open spaces, it is almost entirely built up. The southern end of the island is the main business and financial quarter, with skyscrapers like the Empire State Building and the even higher (1350 ft) World Trade Centre towering over canyon-like thoroughfares such as Wall Street. On the lower east side are Chinatown and Greenwich Village, the Latin quarter. To the north runs Broadway, the fabulous land of theatres, and the luxury shopping centre. West of Central Park stretches a high-class residential quarter and the buildings of Columbia University, while to the east, by contrast, are poorer blocks of tenements housing eastern Europeans and other foreign nationals. North of Central Park, in "uptown" New York descending to East and Harlem Rivers, runs the main negro quarter.

[Courtesy: U.S. Information Service.

FIG. 56.—New York: general view. In the centre are the skyscraper blocks of Manhattan, whose shores are washed by the Hudson and East Rivers. In the foreground is Queens (Long Island), in the background Jersey City and Hoboken. The Brooklyn and Manhattan bridge and the extensive wharfing facilities should be observed. Compare Fig. 55.

It will be observed that New York is a very cosmopolitan city. Since 1820, 60 million immigrants have entered the United States; the majority have disembarked at New York, and many have never gone beyond the city to live. The foreign-born population is still very large, and is indicated by such names as Little Italy, Little Greece, and Little Puerto Rico. The latter section of the city is now pressing upon the million negroes of Harlem. In Brooklyn about half the city's 2 million Jews have their homes: easily the greatest urban concentration of these people in the world.

THE PORT OF NEW YORK

On ·approaching New York by transatlantic liner, passengers are first brought into the Lower Bay between Sandy Hook on the New Jersey mainland and Rockaway Beach on Long Island. To the north, this outer harbour is restricted by the westward thrust of Coney Island, New York's nearest sea-shore playground. Beyond it, the ships' passengers are guided through the Narrows, a gap through a moraine bridged in 1964, to the almost landlocked Upper New York Bay. Ahead, their eyes are drawn to the massive figure of the Statue of Liberty on Bedloe's Island, renamed Liberty Island in 1960. To the north-west the skyscrapers of Manhattan reach up, their grandeur a symbol to the travellers of the material power of the country they are entering. On its way to its berth on the bank of the mile-wide Hudson, the ship keeps these mountains of steel and concrete on its starboard side.

New York's harbour is one of the most magnificent in the world. The water is ice-free at all seasons, and so deep that the largest liners can reach their piers independently of the tide. Though their range is only about 4 ft, the tides and river currents have a certain scouring action, and little dredging is required. Since the harbour is accessible at any time of the day or night, no docks have had to be excavated to accommodate ships. The total water frontage in the City alone is nearly 600 miles, and jetties and quays line almost all of it. There is additional wharfage on the margins of Kill van Kull, an opening on the west of the Upper Bay, and on Newark Bay, into which the passage leads.

New York and its satellite ports on the New Jersey side of the Hudson conduct over 35% by value of the total foreign commerce of the nation, and also have a big share in its coastal traffic, notably in petroleum and coal. Specialised equipment is always at hand for coping with cargo whether it comes in as imports by sea or ready for export by road (40%) or rail (60%). Among the chief landings are petroleum (crude and refined), paper and timber, raw sugar, tropical fruit, coffee, raw rubber, flax, raw silk, and specialised manufactures. Shipments include iron, steel and scrap, refined petroleum products, motor cars, wheat, and flour.

The port stands at one end of the busiest oceanic shipping lanes in the world: those of the north Atlantic. It also controls the lowest routeways across the Appalachians: via the Hudson–Champlain and Hudson–Mohawk gaps (see Fig. 57). The latter is particularly important. It was, however, little used until the latter part of the eighteenth century, when the powerful Iroquois confederacy, which held it, was finally broken. In 1825 the Erie Canal was opened, and the port of New York was much better able to tap the products of a hinterland which included the Great

Lakes and Ohio Basin, and the expanding Middle West. The shares in the long-distance trade of the nation held by Boston, Philadelphia, and Baltimore slowly dwindled despite all their attempts to overcome their geographical problems, as more and more trade reached New York along this easiest of trans-Appalachian crossings. When the New York Central Railroad and subsequent motor-roads were added to the canal and the canal itself was deepened to nearly 12 ft in 1918 (when it was re-named the New York State Barge Canal), New York leapt even farther ahead of its rivals.

MANUFACTURING AND OTHER ACTIVITIES OF NEW YORK

New York is the world's financial capital and the headquarters of most of the leading business firms of the United States, including the great manufacturing corporations. The city also conducts a considerable pro-portion of the internal trade of the country, including a quarter of the entire wholesale trade. Over a third of its people are engaged in tertiary occupations, including not only trade but also transport and various public services. But even larger numbers are engaged in manufacturing.

It is necessary to distinguish between the type of manufacturing carried on in New York itself and that undertaken in its satellites. The normal manufacturing unit in the city itself is the workshop or small factory. The typical products are those depending on "ingenuity of design, adapt-ability to changing styles and uses, initiative, promotional effort, and rapid distribution rather than upon low unit cost or mass production methods" (P. M. Stern in *Focus*, published by the American Geographical Society, June 1952). The largest single industry is the manufacture of clothing, especially women's, which is concentrated in a small area on the lower west side of Manhattan. The industry turns out about half the nation's apparel. Other activities employing large numbers include the printing and publishing of books, magazines, and periodicals, the pro-cessing of food, including the preparation of "Kosher" meat for the big Jewish population, and light engineering industries.

Heavy industries are more typical of Jersey City, Newark, Bayonne, and Elizabeth, where factory sites are cheaper than in New York, and where there is more direct rail communication with the hinterland, though examples are not entirely wanting on the East River and Brooklyn waterfronts. Among these heavy industries are oil-cracking, heavy engineering, including shipbuilding, the manufacture of chemicals, leather-tanning, sugar-refining, and the smelting of non-ferrous metals such as copper and zinc (the latter is worked at Franklin, New Jersey). North of Newark lie Paterson, with the United States main silk works and also rayon factories, and Passaic, with linen, woollen, and worsted mills.

The New York Metropolitan area as a whole accounts for about 10% of the nation's industrial products.

PROBLEMS OF NEW YORK

All very large cities have their problems. Among common ones are those relating to water-supplies, food supplies, housing, and traffic. In New York the last is probably the most serious.

The city is located on the edge of an area of considerable relief which receives a well-distributed precipitation. New York itself averages 40 in. a year, and the driest month brings nearly 3 in. The Catskill Mountains and other upstate catchment areas receive much more than this amount. Many of their rivers have been impounded to form reservoirs from which water can be piped to the city.

As a major port and route focus, it is not difficult for New York to obtain food, e.g. sugar-cane and tropical fruits from the West Indies and elsewhere, grain and meat from the continental interior. Near the city, and benefiting from their contiguity to this huge market as well as from their cool temperate, well-watered environment, most farmers concentrate on the production of milk, eggs, poultry, fresh vegetables, and fresh fruit. Among these farmers are some of the most intensive producers in the continent; their holdings, though mostly fairly small, are usually highly capitalised and heavily fertilised. Oats may be grown as a winter feed, and maize may be raised and cut green for silage, but most of the dairying and poultry-farming districts are under pasture. Truck-farms —very numerous on the sands of Long Island and New Jersey, but also found in the Hudson valley—yield large quantities of fresh tomatoes, asparagus, green beans, cabbages, potatoes, and sweet corn. There is much cultivation under glass, as there is round London and Paris.

The state of New York produces more apples than any other in the United States except Washington. Many apple orchards, and also peach-groves and vineyards, are found on the lacustrine soils bordering Lake Ontario, and also on the glacial deposits overlooking the moraine-blocked "finger lakes" south of the Mohawk corridor. In both these areas the presence of sloping ground and water mitigates frost damage.

As the population of New York grows, housing becomes more difficult and traffic congestion more acute. Urban areas are constantly encroaching on rural. New houses, for example, are now rising on the former potato patches and market-gardens of Long Island. Whites, especially, are moving out into the spreading suburbs, leaving negroes and Puerto Ricans to take over the central parts.

Transport problems are linked not only with the great size and expansion of New York but also with the growing tendency for people to take up residence in the suburbs while continuing to work in the city. The physical difficulties presented by the site of New York exacerbate the situation. Several bridges and tunnels have had to be built between Manhattan and surrounding districts, and numerous ferries have had to be brought into operation. When the downtown skyscraper office blocks disgorge their occupants at the end of each working day near chaos ensues on the roads and in the subway railway stations. Because of the inadequacy of car-parking space, growing pollution, and high land costs, many large corporations are now beginning to move their offices to sites beyond Manhattan, but a third of the country's office space remains there. To speed transport to and from the city, a number of express toll-roads have been constructed, but they have not relieved congestion in the city. These modern turnpikes are very fast, but of gentle gradient, and are equipped with four to eight traffic-lanes. One follows the Hudson—Mohawk corridor to Buffalo, a second joins New York to Philadelphia, and then follows the Pennsylvania Railroad to Pittsburgh, whence Chicago can be reached. A third will link New York and Boston.

Much long-distance, including transatlantic traffic, now enters New York by air. The very large La Guardia Airport, on the south side of East River 7 miles from the centre of Manhattan, is now used mostly for internal flights, the principal international services using the newer John F. Kennedy (formerly Idlewild) Airport, farther away from the nucleus of the city near the south side of Long Island.

THE HUDSON—MOHAWK VALLEY

PHYSICAL GEOGRAPHY

The Hudson—Champlain corridor forms a prominent part of the Great Appalachian Valley (see Chapter XVII). Its strata, though folded, are not very resistant, and have been eaten into by the Richelieu, leading north to Montreal, and even more by the Hudson, leading south to New York. Off Manhattan, the mile-wide Hudson is confined to a very steep-sided, partly cliffed trench. North of Yonkers, the river broadens temporarily to 3 miles, and the valley walls retire, but there is another constriction in latitude 41° 30' N., where the Hudson Highlands—a continuation of the Appalachian Blue Ridge—cross the river towards the Taconic Mountains of New England (see Fig. 57). Ten miles above Albany, at Cohoes, the Mohawk enters from the west, after following the eastern part of an old glacial overflow channel between the Catskills and the Adirondacks, which nowhere exceeds 500 ft in altitude. Along the Mohawk valley, the New York State Barge Canal conveys shipping to Lake Ontario and Lake Erie, and a canal link between the upper Hudson and Lake Champlain allows small amounts of traffic to reach Montreal. Far busier today are the roads and railways which thread these valleyways.

MAJOR CENTRES AND THEIR ECONOMY

The Hudson confluence area, and the broad Mohawk corridor between Albany and Buffalo, house well over 2 million people. Most live in

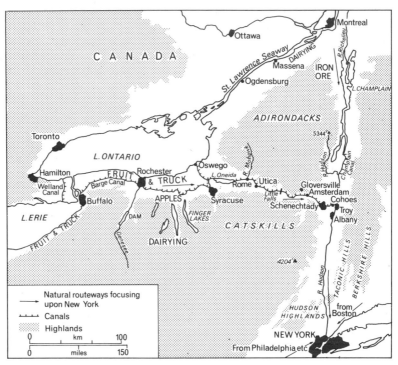

FIG. 57.—New York and the Hudson–Mohawk Gap. New York's command of both the Hudson–Mohawk and Hudson–Champlain routes should be noted. Ships approach New York via several Atlantic crossings and Panamá Canal routes.

industrial and trading cities which can easily tap the many raw materials and foodstuffs moving along the routeway to and from New York. Factories line the canal and the New York Central Railroad. Their products are generally such as demand considerable skill in manufacture: textiles and metal goods are especially important. Often there is a choice of power available to them: "hydro" from Niagara in the west, the Genesee River from the south, Little Falls on the Mohawk, Cohoes Falls on the Hudson; coal from Pennsylvania; petroleum from the refineries at Buffalo and Bayonne.

There are four significant settlements near the Hudson–Mohawk confluence: Albany, Troy, Cohoes, and Schenectady. Albany, the New York State capital, is nearly 150 miles from the submerged mouth of the Hudson, and at the tidal limit of the river. The river channel is 27 ft deep at low tide and many bulky goods reach the city by water. It ships some Prairie grain and flour, and receives wood-pulp from Canada. Its factories make a variety of goods, e.g. stoves, chemicals, and toys. Troy, which is smaller, and on the opposite bank of the Hudson, manufactures shirts and collars. Cohoes, at the actual Mohawk confluence, is one of the principal centres in the United States for the manufacture of knitted goods. Schenectady, on the navigable Mohawk and about as far from the confluence as Albany on the Hudson, is the headquarters of the great General Electric Company of the United States, which produces loco-motives, electric motors and dynamos, radio and television sets.

North-west of Schenectady is the carpet-making town of Amsterdam, on the Mohawk canal, and north-west again, beyond the river, is Glovers-ville, the "glove capital of the United States." Between the latter and Lake Oneida are Utica and Rome, and south of Lake Oneida is Syracuse. The first makes cotton and woollen textiles and hosiery, the second handles copper and brass. The industries of Syracuse, a larger settlement, with an important University, are more varied. Local salt deposits have encouraged the establishment of soda-ash chemical works. Other in-dustries include motor-engineering and the manufacture of typewriters, ready-made clothing, and shoes.

Rochester, half-way between Syracuse and Buffalo, where the Barge Canal approaches Lake Ontario, is the headquarters of the Eastman Kodak Company. With electricity derived both from the Genesee and Niagara Rivers, it makes photographic materials and optical goods, but much more: flour, men's clothing, footwear, electrical apparatus, and miscellaneous machines. Its population numbers 300,000, excluding suburbs.

Buffalo, with nearly half a million people, is the second most populous city in New York State. It benefits not only from Mohawk–Hudson communications but also from the Great Lakes waterway, and is an ob-vious transportation break-point, well located as a port, manufacturing city, and general trading centre. It ships Pennsylvanian coal to Canada and Prairie grain to New York. It collects iron ore from ports on Lake Superior and Lake Michigan, and with coking coal from Pennsylvania converts it into steel in its Lackawanna suburb. It has the most capacious flour-mills in the continent, and a wide range of additional industries: linseed oil-milling, timber-working, motor, aircraft, and locomotive engineering, oil-refining, shipbuilding, the manufacture of drugs and soap, rubber goods, and rayon.

Hydro-electricity derived from the power of the Niagara River serves not only Buffalo's needs but also those of many neighbouring electro-chemical and electro-metallurgical plants, pulp- and paper-mills, and a number of fruit-canning, fruit-juice bottling, and wine-making establishments in the Lake Ontario fruit-growing district.

THE ADIRONDACK MOUNTAINS AND THE ST LAWRENCE VALLEY

The Adirondacks, rising to more than 5000 ft, stand out as a thinly peopled island surrounded by the Hudson–Champlain lowland, St Lawrence valley and Mohawk corridor. Consisting chiefly of igneous and metamorphic rocks, the area is one which, in its rounded hills, U-shaped radial valleys, and glacial lakes, provides a good example of a thoroughly glaciated upland.

Agriculturally, it is a "negative" area, with a few dairy-farms at low levels only. Most of it is forested, and a number of pulp- and saw-mills are dependent on its timber. It has deposits of magnetite iron ore, but they are deep-seated and expensive to work. Perhaps its chief value is as a summer and winter resort for surrounding city-dwellers, for several good roads penetrate it.

To the north-west, the New York State boundary marches with that of Ontario for some distance along the broad St Lawrence River, which has recently been the scene of the St Lawrence Seaway project (see Chapter VII). Power supplies, generated as part of the international engineering programme, benefit New York equally with Ontario. Among enterprises which have profited are the aluminium-refining industry of Massena and the paper-milling industry of Ogdensburg. The fields surrounding these cities are mostly devoted to the raising of dairy-cattle, like those on the Canadian side of the river, and those in the Champlain lowland east of the Adirondacks.

Chapter XVI

THE ATLANTIC COAST PLAIN SOUTH OF NEW YORK

THE ATLANTIC COAST PLAIN AS A REGION

The Atlantic Coast Plain is a purely physical entity. Some unity is, however, given to it by the way in which its people, historically, have looked eastwards across the ocean to Europe. Offshore, the fisheries of the continental shelf have given some of its people a similar mode of life, even though they may live a thousand miles apart. Economically, however, there is in fact great diversity, much of which springs from climatic change. In the north the climate is of a cool temperate continental kind, very stimulating to hard physical and mental effort. Here, although there is much farming of an intensive type, the great majority of people live in large cities, especially Philadelphia, Baltimore, and Washington. South of the capital, "plantation crops", such as tobacco, and farther south still, cotton, become of major economic importance as the temperature rises and the growing season lengthens. Negroes form a more significant element in the population of the south, there are fewer large industries than in the north, and large towns have a very sporadic distribution. In this section, too, trans-Appalachian links are much weaker than they are farther north. Florida, with its almost tropical climate, is again distinctive: citrus fruit and winter vegetables, and the accommodation of winter tourists are the most prolific sources of income in this sub-region. It is also different from contiguous areas in that the proportion of negroes in its population is smaller (*see* Fig. 105).

PHYSICAL ASPECTS

PHYSICAL GEOGRAPHY

Between New York and Boston, the Atlantic Plain is simply represented by a number of morainic islands, *e.g.* Long Island, Martha's Vineyard, and Nantucket, and by the Cape Cod peninsula, all of which were referred to in Chapter· XIV. South of New York are the low-lying

New Jersey and Delmarva peninsulas (the latter comprising Delaware, eastern Maryland, and a very small part of Virginia), and their bounding estuaries, Delaware Bay and Chesapeake Bay (*see* Fig. 58). Beyond

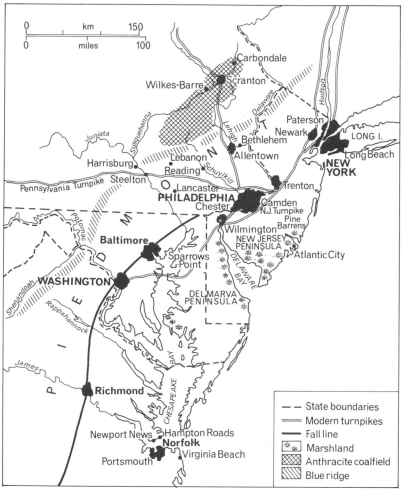

Fig. 58.—Northern part of the Atlantic coast plain and adjacent Appalachian region.

Washington, successively in the states of Virginia, North Carolina, South Carolina, and Georgia, the plain is a broad belt mostly more than 100 miles wide. In Florida it takes the form of a long, south-projecting peninsula which almost reaches latitude 25 degrees N. at its southern extremity.

The entire Atlantic Plain consists of young sediments (Cretaceous and more recent), which overlie the old crystalline rocks of the Piedmont Plateau, the ancient continental margin. It descends gently eastwards and is continued beneath the Atlantic as a continental shelf. Its surface is diversified by a number of low, infacing escarpments produced by the outcropping of fairly resistant sands and limestones, which are separated by bands of weaker clays. Two distinct longitudinal belts may be recognised over and above these minor variations in relief:

1. An outer belt, consisting of: (a) offshore bars such as Cape Hatteras, and a multiplicity of sand-spits and dunes; (b) a central depressed zone of marine marshes such as Dismal Swamp, Virginia, broad tidal waters such as Pamlico Sound off North Carolina, and long narrow lagoons such as Indian River off Florida; (c) a western band of very light, sandy soils.

2. An inner, more raised belt known as the Inner Coast Plain, whose topography is somewhat rougher.

Crossing the whole plain are many rivers, of which those in the north, e.g. the Delaware, Susquehanna, Potomac, and James, rise well inside the Appalachians and provide routes to and from the interior, while those further south, e.g. the Cape Fear, Santee, and Savannah have their sources on the eastern side of the mountains and traverse the plain without giving access to the interior. Waterfalls or rapids occur where the rivers leave the resistant rocks of the Piedmont for the softer strata of the coast plain or, as in the north, the continental shelf. Geographers have long recognised the existence of a "Fall Line" joining together these rapids, which mark the head of navigation on their respective rivers and also furnish power for industry. It is to be noted that in the north the Fall Line is virtually at sea-level, while in the south the Coast Plain may reach a height of 300 ft above sea-level. All the rivers have estuaries, but those in the south also have broad flood-plains.

CLIMATE AND NATURAL VEGETATION

As we saw in Chapter XII, the whole of the Atlantic Coast Plain has a well-distributed precipitation which generally exceeds 40 in. annually, but only the northern parts experience snow. January average temperatures vary much more than those of July. At New York, for example, the January average is 30° F, at Cape Hatteras 46°, at Miami 66°. The corresponding July averages are 75°, 78°, and 85°. More significant is the varying length of the growing season: 150 days in the north to upwards of 300 days in Florida. Annual temperature ranges decrease with latitude, from 45° in the north to less than 20° in the south. There is more risk of frost in the north, where only one crop a year can be grown, than in the south, where two may be feasible, though even the Florida peninsula occasionally suffers from a cold snap when "northers" sweep down across the continent.

The natural vegetation of the plain varies from northern broad-leaved species to the tropical mangroves and cypress swamps of southern Florida. Hardwoods are characteristic, but in sandy areas between the coastal swamps and the Inner Coast Plain pines are dominant: largely of the long-leaved, slash, or loblolly variety in the south.

THE ECONOMY

FORESTRY AND AGRICULTURE

Though much forest has been cut in the interests of agriculture and settlement, much remains. Many of the existing forests, however, are neglected, there is much cut-over land used for cattle-grazing rather than timber production; conversely, there are many bare and eroded areas, notably in the south, which would benefit from reafforestation. Hardwood timber is cut for furniture-making, and pines are felled for constructional purposes, and are widely used for pulp and paper production. The largest paper-mills are on the coast, e.g. at Georgetown, Charleston, Savannah, and Jacksonville. Some pines yield naval stores, i.e. resin (formerly used for caulking the seams of ships) and turpentine. Georgia is the leading state for "turpentine farming."

The types of farming characteristic of the Atlantic Plain vary with climate and accessibility to large urban markets, but they are also influenced by tradition and soil. The latter is rarely good, except along some of the alluvial valleys, where careful attention must be paid to drainage. Nearly all the soils are pedalfers and acidic in reaction, especially where the bedrock is not calcareous. They vary in colour from grey-brown in the north to red and yellow in the south. Many are sandy and hungry and require very heavy manuring to produce good crops. Others are swampy and peaty, with clay sub-soils. As high a proportion as one-sixth of New Jersey—especially well placed for the marketing of farm produce—is denied to agriculture owing to the coarse, gravelly character of the soil, and is occupied by "Pine Barrens."

In the north, from early colonial times, people of north European origin have always tilled the land carefully. Today, they concentrate on the rearing of cattle and poultry and the cultivation of fresh fruit and vegetables for local city markets. South of Washington, where summers are hot enough to be enervating, and where many of the early settlers were of gentlemanly origin and regarded manual work as a menial occupation, plantations, based on negro slave-labour, were soon established. Devoted at first primarily to rice, these plantations came to be producers of tobacco, and, south of Virginia, of cotton. Nowadays, these southern farms are largely run by tenant-farmers and share-croppers. Though some large estates remain, most of the holdings are small, under-capitalised, and under-mechanised, and farm incomes are commonly much less than they are in Delaware, Maryland, and New Jersey.

Throughout the coast plain, but most notably in the New Jersey and Delmarva peninsulas and in Florida, many farmers make a good living out of the supply of truck-farm produce to the north-eastern cities of New York, Philadelphia, Baltimore, and Washington. In the north, where the growing season is rather short, most of the market gardens are situated near the coastal margin where the incidence of frost is less than it is at some distance from the sea, and where easily worked, well-drained sandy soils or marls have the advantage of warming up quickly in spring. The purchase of fertilisers, however, entails heavy expenditure. Tomatoes, asparagus, sweet corn, and green beans are typical crops. The Camden district, which also yields apples, pears, and peaches, is especially productive. If the fresh market becomes glutted canning and freezing are undertaken, e.g. in Camden and Baltimore. Other activities in this northern truck-farming region include poultry-farming, which provides eggs, chickens and turkeys, and intensive milk production.

In Florida, fresh vegetables such as celery,* early potatoes, onions, peas, beans, tomatoes, radishes, and lettuce, may be sold in northern markets as early as January, when no other eastern producing region can compete. In Georgia and the Carolinas truck-farming is only patchy. But each of these states can in turn dominate the northern market for vegetables for two or three weeks in spring.

Tobacco is the great money crop of North Carolina, and is also important in South Carolina, and less so in southern Virginia and Georgia. It is mostly grown in small patches and dried in special barns on the producing farms (see Fig. 59). Cotton is most widely grown on the Inner Coast Plain of the Carolinas and Georgia, whence it spreads into south-

---

* Near Sanford, on the St John's River, in Seminole County (see Fig. 60) is the famous "Seminole Celery Delta," of about 30,000 acres, which enjoys the reputation of growing more celery than any other comparable area in the world. The district is especially well-irrigated, effectively drained, and very generously manured.

east Alabama, but hardly at all into the Florida peninsula. Maize and beans have long been the chief subsistence crops in the south.

Owing very largely to monocultural practices, much land south of Washington has become exhausted and eroded, and increasing attention is now being paid, as in the South generally, to agricultural diversification. Among crops, sweet potatoes, peanuts, and soybeans (the two latter returning nitrogen to the soil and yielding vegetable oil and cattle-feed)

[*Courtesy: U.S. Information Service.*

FIG. 59.—Drying tobacco, N. Carolina. The tobacco leaves hanging in the shed are being "flue-cured" by the new system of indoor heating, an improvement upon the older method of conveying heat by flues from wood-burners outside the shed. "Burley" tobacco, by contrast, is dried in the open, or "sun-cured."

have recently been more widely sown, and more attention has also been paid to the raising of cattle (for both beef and milk), and poultry. Much eroded land is now under pasture. Georgia and South Carolina have long been noted for their peaches and watermelons.

FISHING AND TOURISM

Coastal industries include fishing and tourism. The former, while widespread, is more important in the northern states than in New England, but diminishes greatly in significance south of North Carolina. Shad and alewife—relatives of the common herring—are caught inshore or in the lower courses of many rivers, but in all the states except Georgia menhaden is the chief catch. Off the sandy shores of New Jersey, but especially in the shallow coastal waters of Delaware and Chesapeake Bays, table-oysters are normally caught in greater quantities than in any other part of the world. Off Florida, turtles and sponges are sought, and there is much fishing for sport.

Tourist industries have developed in response to the recreational needs of city-dwellers. In summer such northern resorts as Atlantic City, Long Beach, and Virginia Beach are thronged with pleasure-seekers, while in the cooler months of the year Miami, Palm Beach, and other resorts in Florida attract large numbers of well-to-do people from the colder north. Many tourists also visit Washington, where they can gaze upon such buildings as the Capitol (where Congress meets), the White House (where the President lives) and Mount Vernon (the country home and burial-ground of George Washington), and visit many of the capital's fine museums and art galleries. Such memorials as those dedicated to Lincoln and Washington also draw many people.

INDUSTRIAL ACTIVITIES

Industrial activity is dominant only in the north of the coast plain, *i.e.* in such Fall Line cities as Philadelphia and Baltimore, which have the advantage of hydro-electric and some nuclear power, routes into the interior along which coal and petroleum can be transported, and shipping facilities enabling them to import iron ore and other materials.

South of Baltimore, factories are few and far between, the only clusters being in ports such as Richmond and Norfolk and in the principal Fall Line towns, viz. Richmond itself, Raleigh (North Carolina), Columbia (South Carolina), Augusta, Macon and Columbus (Georgia), and Montgomery (Alabama). In most of these towns, the chief industry is the manufacture of either tobacco (especially prominent in the first two), or of textiles (mainly cotton). Cotton-seed-oil milling and peanut-oil milling, and the manufacture of wood products, pulp and paper may also be carried on. Factory work is expanding in the south, but most of it is carried on west of the coast plain, *i.e.* in the Piedmont. Industries in the southern coast plain still mainly supply local needs, despite the impetus first given by the Civil War (1861–65), and the stimulus administered later by the coming of modern transport, the development of hydro-electricity and the increase in labour skills.

LARGE SETTLEMENTS

North of Florida, the major settlements in the region are all estuarine in their location, and command trans-Appalachian routes. Extending coastwise for 500 miles from Washington to Boston is an almost continuous belt of such settlements. This gigantic urban area, forming the "longest city in the world," was called "Megalopolis" by the geographer Jean Gottman. It houses more than 30 million people, and includes, in the region under study, a number of separate nuclei, of which the most populous and bustling are Philadelphia, Baltimore, and Washington. In time, doubtless, it will stretch further south and engulf Richmond, Newport News, and Norfolk. These smaller cities are already being tied to the countryside south of Washington by commuters' residences, and by a string of roadside cafés, drive-in cinemas, petrol-stations, factories, and shops, like those which at present link more closely Philadelphia and New York.

Philadelphia, until recently the third largest city in the United States, has now been overtaken by Los Angeles. Two million people live in the city itself, and nearly another three million in its satellites, especially in Camden, Chester and Wilmington. Its nucleus lies between the Delaware River, at the head of the estuary and the tidal limit, and the smaller Schuylkill River, which here hurries over its Fall Line.

As a port, Philadelphia, like Baltimore and Boston, is subservient to New York, to which it is connected by broad roads and railways as well as a shipping route. Successively, following the Susquehanna valley, an old turnpike road, canal, Pennsylvania Railroad, and modern express toll-road have put it into touch with the two Pennsylvanian coalfields, for which it acts as an outlet, and from which it derives much of the power for its extremely varied industries. Its imports, dominated by petroleum, greatly exceed its exports (of coal, grain, and manufactures), but it conducts much coastal trade.

Philadelphia's early industries of spinning and weaving, iron-smelting, wagon- and boat-building have grown into the large-scale manufacture of woollens and worsteds, hosiery, carpets, apparel, steel and machine-tools, locomotives (the firm of Baldwins is the largest in the world), motor cars, and ships. There is a very large oil-cracking plant, sugar refineries, and cigar-works.

Camden, opposite Philadelphia on the left bank of the Delaware, and *Chester,* below the metropolis, both have large shipyards (the Delaware as a whole normally builds more ships than any other river in the United

States). Camden also makes radio and television sets; refines copper brought thence originally from small deposits worked in New Jersey but now delivered from the Western States and from Chile and Peru; and has large vegetable canneries and some textile works. Chester also manufactures textiles. *Wilmington*, farther down river, is an important centre of chemical-manufacturing.

Trenton, situated on the Fall Line of the Delaware, where it makes a right-angled bend, is the most important of a number of industrial centres between Philadelphia and New York. Its principal industry is the manufacture of pottery and china, an activity originally dependent on local clays but now supported by kaolin, some of which is quarried in the Blue Ridge, the rest being imported. Across the Delaware from Trenton, at *Morrisville*, the U.S. Steel Corporation has recently built a huge, integrated steel plant,* supplied with iron to a slight extent from the Adirondacks and from the Cornwall mines (Pennsylvania), but mainly with ores imported from Chile, Venezuela, Liberia, and Labrador, with coal from west Pennsylvania and West Virginia, and with local limestone.

Baltimore stands near the head of the 180 mile-long Chesapeake Bay, and again on the Fall Line; it is a city about half as big as Philadelphia, but lacking important satellites. Its general trading and industrial character is not unlike that of its northern neighbour, but it is even less well placed, in comparison with New York, for direct trans-Appalachian communications. Its main railway, the Baltimore and Ohio Railroad, built as early as 1828 in reply to the challenge of the three-year-old Erie Canal, links it with Pittsburgh and the Middle West. From its harbour, formed by the short Patapsco River, grain, steel, and coal move out, petroleum, iron, and other ores in.

Baltimore stands out as the south-eastern buttress of North America's chief manufacturing region. It builds ships and aircraft, refines petroleum and sugar, manufactures chemicals including fertilisers, and produces cotton textiles and clothing. Its copper refinery has been overshadowed by the expansion of the Bethlehem Corporation's giant iron and steel works at Sparrows Point, just outside the city limits. This plant is comparable with the Morrisville works in Pennsylvania.

Washington, the third of the largest north-eastern cities, with a city population of 750,000 (70% negro) and a metropolitan population of more than two millions, is very different from Philadelphia and Baltimore. Its only significant industry, apart from government and tourism, is, as one might expect of a large capital city, that of printing and publishing.

* Known as Fairless Hills.

Washington is situated at the tidal limit and at the head of navigation of the Potomac River, which provides a route into the interior, but it is in no sense a port. A clean city, it was ingeniously planned and laid out by Charles l'Enfant, on the instructions of the new nation's first President, and is noted today for its tree-lined avenues, and its spacious, dignified appearance, befitting that of a seat of government. The District of Columbia, however, to which it is confined, is now no longer large enough to house all the government offices, its central location between the northern and southern states has become a very eccentric location since America spread to the Pacific, and it probably remains more vulnerable to attack than a more westerly site would be.

Richmond is the largest city in Virginia. It stands on the Fall Line of the James River, which provides access to the interior. The port, which deals mainly in raw tobacco and in tobacco manufactured in the city, has 25 ft of water. Minor industries are pulp-milling and sugar-refining. Close by there are very large chemical works.

Leading into the southern end of Chesapeake Bay are Hampton Roads, which support the coaling ports of *Norfolk* and *Newport News*, both outports of Baltimore. They ship West Virginian coal coastwise and overseas, and also handle tobacco, cotton, and timber. Newport News is also a naval base and has large shipyards, and Norfolk is a major centre of the U.S. peanut trade, and assembles motor vehicles. A new road bridge and tunnel, 17½ miles long, linking Norfolk with the southern tip of the Delmarva peninsula, was opened in 1964 and there is now a similar but shorter link across the narrower opening of Hampton Roads.

• None of the seaports of North Carolina, South Carolina, and Georgia is very large, and none serves a trans-Appalachian hinterland. The chief are *Savannah, Charleston,* and *Wilmington.* Their shallow estuaries are only kept open at considerable expense. All ship cotton, cotton-seed, and lumber, and import fertilisers and petroleum. Their traditional export trade is declining owing to the development of cotton-manufacturing and timber-working industries in their hinterlands.

THE FLORIDA PENINSULA

PHYSICAL GEOGRAPHY

The Florida peninsula, nearly 400 miles long, is one of the most distinctive parts of the Atlantic coast plain, as was suggested on p. 187. Physically, climatically, vegetationally, agriculturally, and recreationally it is of great interest.

The peninsula is everywhere low-lying, the maximum height being only a little more than 300 ft above sea-level; no point in the southern third reaches even 50 ft. It forms a slightly uplifted portion of a submarine platform of recent limestone which once joined it to the Bahamas and even to Yucatán. In the north the limestone is partially covered with sand, which locally increases its elevation. Along the coasts there are

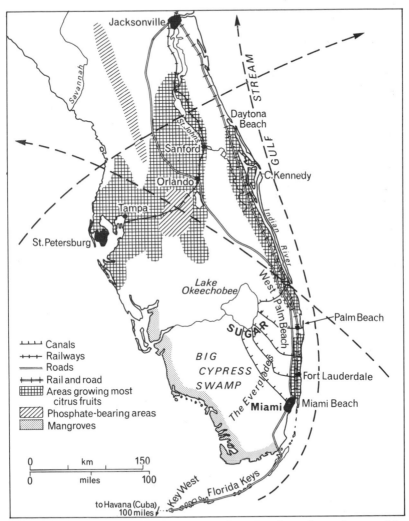

FIG. 60.—Florida: general features. The Florida panhandle, to the north-west of the Suwanee River, has not been included. The arrows show the general paths of the chief hurricane tracks.

sand-bars, spits, and lagoons, which are particularly marked on the east and south-west shores. In the south the waters, warmed by their low latitude and by the Gulf Stream as it emerges from the Gulf of Mexico,. carry a string of low coral islands known as the Florida keys (*see* Fig. 60).

Many parts of the limestone surface are pockmarked with solution hollows or sink-holes, and there is much underground drainage. In the south the very shallow Lake Okeechobee, draining naturally to the west, and artificially also to the south and east, is prominent. To the south,

[*Courtesy: U.S. Information Service.*

FIG. 61.—Everglades National Park, Florida. Park rangers are shown making their rounds in "swamp buggies," *i.e.* shallow-draught vessels specially adapted to the watery environment.

only a few feet above sea-level, and almost uninhabited, are the Everglades, and to the south-west the Big Cypress Swamp, margined by a broad belt of mangroves (*see* Fig. 61). These very low-lying swamplands consist mainly of black, salt-water muds from which many hygrophytic trees rise.

THE ECONOMY

Florida, as we have seen, is well known for its winter vegetables and its citrus fruits, which rival in importance those of California and those of the lower Río Grande valley in Texas. They benefit from the equable moist climate and the almost tropical temperatures. The citrus fruit harvest, largely gathered by migrant workers, normally lasts from November to March; some fruit is frozen or tinned before sale (mainly in northern markets), but 90% of the crop is made into fruit juice.

Florida pioneered the commercial production of oranges in the United States a century ago, but the "Big Freeze" of 1894–95 killed all the trees. Nowadays, cultivation is no longer practised in the north. It is restricted to a belt in the rolling country of the central part of the peninsula, where the danger of frost, especially in the case of groves planted on sloping ground near lakes, is less menacing than elsewhere. About half the American orange crop comes from Florida. Other citrus fruits are grapefruit (in which also the state leads the nation), lemons and limes, the latter grown mainly near the south-east coasts, along with a few pine-apples. The most progressive plantation managers give much thought and attention to scientific fertilising, chemical spraying, and overhead or well-irrigation (necessary during occasional periods of drought), and have oil-pots or coke-heaters or piles of firewood handy in the event of frost-warnings. But they can do little to prevent damage from hurricanes (which may also harm crops farther north along the Atlantic margins of the United States).

Other agricultural activities include the growing of grain and sugar-cane (mainly on the fertile peat muck soils occupying the south side of Lake Okeechobee), the cultivation of the tung-oil tree (in the north) and the development of cattle-raising. Most of the cattle are of Indian Brahma stock, and are partly nourished on citrus-fruit waste. They are mainly raised for beef except near the cities, where dairying is undertaken.

Florida has an important source of mineral fertiliser in its huge phos-phate deposits, easily worked by open-cast methods, chiefly in the west, inland from Tampa. The state produces over one-third of the world's supply and processes some of them, e.g. in Tampa, in plants which supply the Cotton Belt.

The main source of income nowadays is neither the production of truck-crops, nor citrus fruits, nor minerals, but the tourist trade. Even in January, the average temperature is 60° F, there are sandy beaches of great extent facing warm, shallow seas and there is good transport to the north by road, rail, and air. The newly-opened Disney World amuse-ment park in the inland Orlando area is attracting an additional number of visitors.

The greatest resort is *Miami*, which has grown phenomenally in the last forty years (*see* Fig. 62). In 1920 its population was only 42,000, in

1970, over 300,000, with nearly another million in its suburbs. It has become a retired home for many northern business men as well as one of the world's largest holiday centres. Its prosperity is shared by West Palm Beach, St Petersburg (on the west coast), and several smaller places like Daytona Beach. *Key West*, a small naval base and a centre of sponge and turtle-fishing at the western end of the Florida keys, is visited by many

[*Courtesy: Pan-American World Airways.*

FIG. 62.—Miami Beach, Florida. Note the many modern luxury-hotels, the surf-beaten sandy beach and lagoon, the strong sunlight, and the quasi-tropical palm trees.

tourists who wish to "get away from it all." Its former railway link with the peninsula was damaged so much by hurricanes and corrosive sea-water that it has now been replaced by a motor-road. The new rocket-base on the cuspate foreland of Cape Kennedy is attracting many scientists and less-informed sightseers.

The largest city in northern Florida is *Jacksonville* ("Jax"), 30 miles up the St John's River, which, with the Suwanee (Swanee), helps to drain the northern part of the peninsula. It exports phosphates, lumber, and naval stores obtained from the many pine-forests still remaining in Florida, and manufactures pulp, paper, and ships. Near by there is an important naval base.

Tampa, with its suburbs larger than Jacksonville and almost as populous as Miami, is the main phosphate port. It also manufactures cigars, chiefly from Cuban ("Havana") tobacco. It is joined to Jacksonville and the state capital, Tallahassee, by road and rail. A generation ago, a start was made on the construction of a waterway across the northern part of the peninsula from Jacksonville, but it was abandoned. It would have been useful, as the north-east of Florida is already in touch with New York via the "Atlantic Inland Waterway," and the north-west is linked to Texas by the "Intra-Coastal Canal," a similar, sheltered means of communication which carries much traffic. It is not surprising that the scheme has been recently resurrected.

Chapter XVII

THE APPALACHIANS SOUTH OF THE HUDSON-MOHAWK VALLEY

PHYSICAL ASPECTS

THE APPALACHIAN BARRIER

As we have seen, elements of the Appalachian Mountains are to be found in New England, the Maritime Provinces of Canada, and even in Newfoundland. South of the Hudson-Mohawk valley, however, the region is more compact, and more uniform in its characteristic north-east to south-west trend-lines.

At the close of the Carboniferous period the area now occupied by the Appalachians was subjected to orogenic movements from the east, which raised it up and folded and fractured many of its rocks. It was then peneplaned, and twice thereafter uplifted to give it a rejuvenated drainage system.

Though not particularly high—Mt Mitchell, in North Carolina, the loftiest summit, reaches only 6710 ft—the Appalachians, because of their intricate physiography, width (300 miles), and length (over 900 miles), presented a formidable barrier to the expansion of early settlers along the Atlantic margins of the United States, and for long confined them to the coast plain. It was fairly easy, however, to reach the Piedmont Plateau. Later frontiersmen, with much greater difficulty, found it possible, by making use of the valleys of some of the longer northern rivers, *e.g.* the Susquehanna, Potomac, and James, to make their way across the various ridges and valleys of the mountains west of the Piedmont. Then they were confronted by the steep, east-facing escarpments of the Appalachian plateaus. The hardiest of them subsequently passed through gaps in this "front" into the Ohio Basin. Others, turning south, down the valleys of the Tennessee headstreams, especially the Holston, located the Cumberland Gap, which led them into the basins of Kentucky and Tennessee.

Those pioneers who were persistent enough to make the complete trans-Appalachian journey had to cross in turn each of the four main longitudinal divisions of the Appalachian Mountains: (*a*) Piedmont

Plateau; (b) Blue Ridge; (c) Ridge and Valley Province; (d) Appalachian Plateau. The first two of these divisions consist mainly of Pre-Cambrian crystalline rocks, chiefly of igneous and metamorphic origin. The last two are composed in the main of Palaeozoic sedimentaries. Each will be examined in turn (see Figs. 63 and 64).

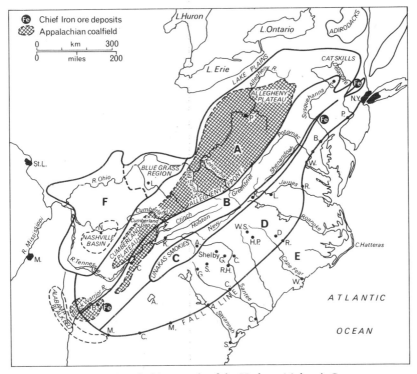

FIG. 63.—Appalachians south of the Hudson–Mohawk Gap.

A = Appalachian Plateau; B = Ridge and Valley Province; C = Blue Ridge; D = Piedmont; E = Atlantic Coast Plain; F = Interior Low Plateaus.

The thronging of textile- and tobacco-manufacturing towns on the Piedmont Plateau and on the Fall Line should be noted. The names of individual towns should be identified from an atlas map.

THE OLDER APPALACHIANS

The Older Appalachians consist of: (a) the Piedmont Plateau; (b) its high western edge, forming the loftiest part of the whole mountain system, and known by various names, of which the Blue Ridge is the chief. The denudation of this ancient land-mass provided the sediments out of which the more westerly parts of the Appalachians were built.

The Piedmont is a fairly broad plateau averaging about 50 miles wide in Maryland, and over 100 miles in the Carolinas and Georgia. It slopes gradually upwards from the Fall Line—its junction with the Atlantic Coast Plain—to about 1200 ft. It is lowest north of the Susquehanna, where its old crystalline rocks have been largely overlaid by Triassic deposits (as in the Connecticut valley of New England) to give a more gentle relief than farther south, where residual hills punctuate its surface. Rivers meander across the Piedmont in broad, shallow valleys until they are ready to leave it, when they race across the Fall Line in rapids *en route* to the Atlantic.

To the west, the Piedmont gives way to the igneous rocks of the high, smooth-surfaced Blue Ridge of Pennsylvania and Virginia, and the metamorphic rocks of the higher, more rugged Bald, Smoky, and Unaka Mountains of the North Carolina frontier. This mountain zone is only about 15 miles wide in Pennsylvania, but 100 miles wide in North Carolina, where the highest ground (exceeding 6000 ft) is found. In the north several rivers have carved through the Blue Ridge in gaps: they include the Delaware, Susquehanna, Potomac, and James. A few wind gaps, too, have been eroded through the barrier to provide ways now used by roads and railways. In the south the mountain fastnesses are more inviolate.

THE NEWER APPALACHIANS

The Newer Appalachians, west of the Blue Ridge and its associated highlands, comprise: (a) the great Appalachian Valley and the more westerly Ridge and Valley Province, an area of highly folded Palaeozoic strata; (b) the Appalachian Plateaus, a zone of almost horizontally bedded rocks, roughly of the same age.

The Great Appalachian Valley is a broad lowland occupied by a number of distinct river valleys, e.g. the Shenandoah in the north, the Tennessee and its Holston headstream in the south. The Ridge and Valley Province is composed of a close alternation of longitudinal ridges, mostly of resistant sandstone and dolomite, and of parallel valleys, chiefly of softer limestones and shales. The ridges, which are really remnants of the original Appalachian peneplain, are most numerous in the north, but they are well broken in places by transverse water and wind gaps. The drainage pattern is trellised.

West of the Ridge and Valley zone, as the section shows (Fig. 64), the eastern margin of the Appalachian Plateaus is represented by a scarp face, known in part as the Allegheny Front. Beyond this high, steep slope, the plateau sandstones, limestones, and shales have been dissected by dendritic rivers, most of which, e.g. the Monongahela, Kanawha, New,

Big Sandy, and Cumberland, drain into the Ohio, a tributary of the Mississippi. It should, however, be noted that the Susquehanna and Delaware flow eastwards from their sources in the Plateaus to the Atlantic.

The Appalachian Plateaus are known by different names in different parts: (*a*) the Catskills in the· north-east, overlooking the Hudson

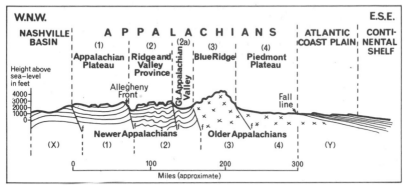

FIG. 64.—Section across Southern Appalachians.

X = Part of an eroded dome, composed mainly of Ordovician shales and limestone.

1 = Very gently warped sedimentaries, Carboniferous and more recent.

2 = Highly folded and faulted sedimentaries, Cambrian–Carboniferous, chiefly
built up by Hercynian earth movements of Permian period.

3, 4 = Mostly uplifted crystalline rocks, affected mainly by Caledonian orogeny in
Devonian period.

Y = Recent sediments, gently dipping seawards.

f = Main fault-lines.

valley from heights exceeding 4000 ft; (*b*) the Allegheny Plateau to the south-west, reaching 4000 ft in West Virginia; (*c*) the lower Cumberland Plateau of eastern Kentucky and Tennessee, south of the Cumberland River.

Among the strata of the Appalachian Plateaus are coal seams, which are best developed in south-western Pennsylvania, West Virginia, north-eastern Kentucky, and central Alabama. Collectively, these beds comprise the Appalachian Coalfield, which produces about 70% of the nation's coal. There are other coal deposits, mainly anthracitic, in the Ridge and Valley zone, chiefly in eastern Pennsylvania.

THE PLAINS WEST AND SOUTH OF THE APPALACHIANS

North of the Allegheny Plateau are the Lake Plains. Along the southern shores of Lake Erie they are very narrow, but along the corresponding shores of Lake Ontario they are quite broad. They are mainly of lacustrine origin, but in places carry glacial deposits, e.g. drumlins. It should be noted that the main mass of the Appalachians lay too far south to be overrun by the Pleistocene ice-sheets.

Westwards, the Appalachians gradually descend to the Central Plains of the United States. In Kentucky there is the famous Blue Grass basin of the eroded Lexington dome, and in Tennessee the analogous Nashville dome. These two physical basins, floored with limestones and shales, yield much richer grass and heavier crops than the less-fertile Appalachian Plateaus. South of Nashville, at Maury, phosphates are worked in quantity.

South of the Appalachians, in the northerly part of the transitional region between the Atlantic and Gulf Coast Plains, is the renowned "Black Belt" of western Georgia, central Alabama, and Mississippi, where the soils are dark-coloured and calcareous. They have long been well-cultivated, like the interior basins of Kentucky and Tennessee, and support a large negro population.

CLIMATE AND NATURAL VEGETATION

The climate of the Appalachian region is not dissimilar to that of the Atlantic Coast Plain as far south as Georgia, but the greater physiographic variety leads to many more micro-climates. For example, in the Ridge and Valley Province, rainfall is heavier and temperatures lower on the exposed ridges than in the sheltered valleys.

Speaking broadly, the northern part of the region has a cool temperate type of climate with a growing season of about 150 days, and temperatures varying from about 30° (January average) to 70° F (July average). In the south, where the climate may be described as warm temperate, the growing season extends to more than 200 days. January temperatures average about 45° F, July ones about 80° F, at low levels.

The rainfall is well distributed throughout the Appalachians, and rarely averages less than 35 in. a year. In general, it tends to increase southwards, and may be excessive at high levels, e.g. in the Great Smoky Mountains, where it tops 80 in. On many upland slopes the high intensity of the rainfall has contributed to soil leaching and, especially where the native forests have been removed, to accelerated soil erosion.

Considerable areas in the Appalachian region are still covered with a natural vegetation of temperate mixed forest. Except at high altitudes and in very sandy districts, deciduous trees, e.g. oak, beech, hickory, and chestnut, predominate. In the Piedmont, on some of the valley floors and slopes of the Ridge and Valley zone, and on parts of the Appalachian Plateaus, the primary forests have been greatly depleted, and on land once cultivated but now abandoned there may be simply secondary forests.

THE ECONOMY

FORESTRY AND TOURISM

The Blue Ridge province supplies some timber for railway sleepers, pit-props, barrel-making, furniture, pulp, and paper. In the south, where trees mature quickly, the importance of pulp and paper industries is growing, just as it is on the Atlantic coast plain.

Many forests, especially in the Appalachian Plateaus, are now under State control and carefully conserved by practices analogous to farming. Many upland farmers work part-time in these forests; other men have permanent, full-time jobs in saw-mills and wood-working factories. Notable is the production of pit-props for Appalachian coal-mines.

Neither climate nor natural vegetation have especially attracted tourists to the Appalachians, though the prospect of cool summer days at high altitudes may induce city-dwellers from the plains to visit the mountains in hot weather, and forests may enhance the mountain scenery. Most tourists, however, visit the Appalachians for the scenic features provided by the highlands rising sharply above the Piedmont. An indication of these is suggested by the setting aside of land in the Blue Ridge of Virginia and in the Great Smoky Mountains as National Parks. Near the second Park, and also fairly close to Mount Mitchell, is the resort town of Asheville. But it is the first Park which derives more benefit from its proximity to large cities, e.g. Washington, Baltimore, and Philadelphia. In the Ridge and Valley province notable beauty-spots include the Natural Bridge of Virginia (a limestone arch) and various karstic features, e.g. sink-holes and caverns. Popular among New Yorkers are the forested Catskills and the "finger lakes" country. In the Southern Appalachians the numerous lakes created by the Tennessee Valley Authority have introduced a new recreational element (see Fig. 68).

First-class roads lead into and traverse all these resort areas, and are especially well used in summer and during week-ends by people who are anxious to escape from city business-blocks and industrial pollution, if only for a short time.

AGRICULTURE

As might be expected in a region of diverse topography, soil, and climate, parts of which are accessible to nearby markets while others are remote, farming patterns and crops vary greatly. Broadly, the distinctions between north and south, and between ridge, plateau, and valley are fairly clear.

Most of the Piedmont of northern Virginia, western Maryland, southeastern Pennsylvania, and northern New Jersey consists of very gently undulating country of low relief. Its soils, mainly of Triassic sedentary origin, are fairly fertile, its farmers are hard working and knowledgeable, its communications are good, and urban markets near. Dairying is the dominant activity, though there are also poultry-farms, mixed farms (some of which produce tobacco and potatoes), apple-orchards, and truck-farms (marketing tomatoes, sweet corn, cabbages, etc.). Especially productive as an agricultural area is the intensively farmed Lancaster County bordering the Susquehanna River, where the classic "Pennsylvania Rotation" of winter wheat, hay (usually clover), maize, and either tobacco or potatoes is still followed. Most of the farms in this district are of less than 100 acres, but their soils are well-fertilised and conserved by their "Pennsylvanian Dutch" (actually "Deutsch" or German) owners. Milk is dispatched daily by rail or road to Philadelphia.

In the more southerly parts of the Piedmont farming generally follows the same pattern as on the inner side of the Coast Plain, with tobacco the dominant commercial crop in the north, cotton in the south. The characteristic clay loams are, on the whole, somewhat more fertile than the coastal soils, however, especially in districts well to the west of the Fall Line. Farming is less intensive and less scientific than in the north, and some of the ground has become exhausted and badly eroded. More diversified forms of agriculture are being adopted, however, and greater use is being made of fertilisers, derived, for example, from menhaden caught in the Atlantic, and from phosphates mined in Florida and Tennessee. Corn, the main subsistence crop, still occupies large acreages, but less is now being consumed as human food, and more is being fed to livestock, including dairy-cattle and poultry near the growing cities and towns. On the outer Piedmont, fruit-trees like the peaches of the Carolinas and Georgia are becoming more numerous, and sweet potatoes and peanuts are receiving more attention. But farm incomes remain rather low and there is too much population pressure on the land in some places.

Agriculture is often well developed in the Ridge and Valley zone, especially in the broader, more fertile and sheltered valleys. In the Shenandoah valley, for example, many dairy and beef cattle are tended, good crops of wheat and maize are obtained, and there are many productive apple-orchards on the valley sides. Dairy-farmers in the Susquehanna valley have a ready market for their milk in such industrial towns as Scranton and Harrisburg. In the southern part of the Ridge and Valley zone agriculture, for long very backward, has been revitalised by the example and encouragement of the Tennessee Valley Authority (*see below*, p. 212).

On most of the Appalachian ridges, and over wide areas of the Appalachian Plateaus, farming is unrewarding. Soils are often thin and sandy, the terrain often rough and sloping and communications are not always adequate. Some sheep-farming is practised where the uplands have been cleared of trees, and quite prolific apple-crops are obtained from the well-drained slopes of the northern section of the Blue Ridge. In some of the valleys cut in the Appalachian Plateaus, especially those in the north near Pittsburgh and the Lakes, fairly prosperous dairy-farms have been established, and sheep are grazed at higher levels for wool and lamb. But in the south much of the upland is impoverished, too much maize is grown without adequate support from rotation crops, many farms are seriously eroded, buildings are often dilapidated. Such conditions are typical of much of the hill country of West Virginia and Kentucky, where descendants of early, westward-trekking pioneers, who for some reason or other never travelled as far as the fertile Blue Grass plains, still live a very rough life, mainly as subsistence farmers. Here are the "agricultural slums" of the United States, where living-standards are much below the national average. Often referred to as "poor whites" or even "hillbillies," these ultra-conservative farmers continue to plant their corn and beans for subsistence, and to keep a few pigs (largely fed on forest-mast) and a few sheep and poultry. Outside their unpainted, crumbling, verandahed log-cabins, they may cultivate a small patch of fruit and vegetables. They may even now use scythes and sickles for harvesting. The nearest motor road or railway may be miles away, and they may be impelled to market whatever produce they have for sale, *e.g.* corn-whisky, berry-fruits, and hand-woven textiles by mule or pony. There is much malnutrition and inbreeding among such folk. Rural depopulation is now setting-in as the younger and more progressive members of the family migrate into the growing industrial towns below these upland farms.

MANUFACTURING ACTIVITIES

The greatest manufacturing area in the Appalachian region is in western Pennsylvania, where the coking and steam coals of the Pittsburgh region have stimulated industrial activity. This area will be discussed in the next chapter. Elsewhere, four areas stand out for the value of their manufactures: (1) eastern Pennsylvania; (2) central Alabama; (3) the Piedmont; (4) the Tennessee valley.

Eastern Pennsylvania is the oldest and most closely settled of the above industrial areas (*see* Fig. 58). It embraces both Piedmont and Appalachian Valley country. Already in the eighteenth century it was making iron goods from local ores, smelted with charcoal. The industry expanded as ways of using the local anthracite deposits were found, and during the 1840s there were more blast furnaces in the region than anywhere else in North America. The Civil War gave a fillip to the industry, but the rise of Pittsburgh in the 1860s dealt it a severe blow. By then, steel was taking the place of cast iron and wrought iron, west Pennsylvanian coke was produced more cheaply than the local anthracite, and the production of ore from Cornwall and other districts in eastern Pennsylvania, New Jersey, and New York was giving way to that from the more abundant, more easily worked haematite deposits near Lake Superior. The existing steelworks at Allentown and Bethlehem in the Lehigh valley, at Reading on the Schuylkill, at Steelton on the Susquehanna, and at Lebanon are now largely supported by the import of iron ore and the transport of coking coal from west Pennsylvania and West Virginia (cf. the steelworks at Sparrows Point and Morrisville).

Harrisburg, Lebanon, and nearby localities, using local anthracite, and the shale and limestone of the Lehigh valley, make larger quantities of cement than any other neighbourhood in the United States. Providing opportunities for female labour are the textile industries (woollen, cotton, silk, rayon, and nylon) of Scranton, Wilkes-Barre, Reading, Harrisburg, and other centres. Engineering industries include the manufacture of locomotives and mining machinery at Scranton, machinery and wire ropes at Wilkes-Barre, motor cars at Bethlehem, and miscellaneous hardware at Harrisburg and Steelton.

The anthracite deposits of eastern Pennsylvania occupy an area of about 5000 square miles located mainly between the Susquehanna and Delaware Rivers in the Appalachian Ridge and Valley province. The main producing area lies in the Lackawanna and Wyoming valleys between Carbondale and Wilkes-Barre, Scranton roughly marking the mid-point. Peak production (98 million tons) was reached in 1916; today, less than 10 million tons a year are raised. Besides providing some of the power used in local industries, anthracite is railed to Philadelphia and New York, whence some reaches New England for use in central-heating plants. As a fuel, however, it is very expensive to work and does not generally lend itself to cutting by machinery, as the seams in which it occurs are irregularly distributed, often thin and deep, badly faulted, and frequently

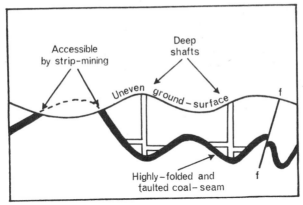

FIG. 65.—Typical mining conditions in Pennsylvanian anthracite field.

steeply inclined or contorted (*see* Fig. 65). It has met severe competition as a source of domestic and office heating from oil, natural gas, coal gas, coke, and electricity. Therefore, although it remains the chief source of anthracite in North America, eastern Pennsylvanian mines are gradually shutting down.

Central Alabama has become the seat of an iron and steel industry since 1880. Here, almost uniquely, deposits of haematite iron ore, excellent coking coal, and dolomitic limestone occur in extremely close proximity (*see* Fig. 66). Bessemer—which bears an honoured name in the history

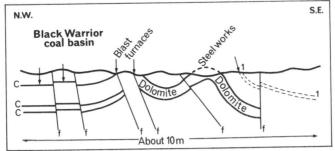

[*Adapted from Jones and Darkenwald.*

FIG. 66.—Section through Alabama coal- and iron-field.

C = Coal seams suitable for coking.
I = Iron ore beds (red phosphoric deposits).
f = Faults.

The arrows show mineral workings.

of the steel industry—is situated here, but the main works are at *Birmingham* (metropolitan population 740,000 in 1970), overlooking the southern end of the great Appalachian valley. Some of the steel turned out is made into rails and exported to Asia and Latin America, much is used in the construction of ferro-concrete buildings, which are becoming more numerous in southern cities, and some cast iron is used in the manufacture of pipes to carry natural gas and petroleum. The Birmingham industry, however, lacks a large market in that there are few important engineering industries in the surrounding district, therefore the amount of iron and steel produced is much smaller than that made in northern cities such as Pittsburgh and Cleveland.

The Alabama coalfield is for the most part situated in the southern part of the Appalachian Plateau province, though it spreads into the Appalachian valley zone. The main seam—easily worked by short shafts or even open-cast methods—is 4 ft thick. The Black Warrior River, and its continuation the Tombigbee, flowing into the Gulf of Mexico just east of Mobile, have been canalised, and some coal and steel are shipped to the coast by barge. The coalfield is also fairly well supplied with rail and road communications.

Unlike Alabama and the Ridge and Valley Province of Pennsylvania, the Piedmont has no coal or iron. Neither are other minerals, except for a little bauxite, manganese, and mica in Georgia, of importance. But there are supplies of water power (additional to those of the Fall Line), raw materials such as timber, tobacco, and cotton, a surplus rural population, and a gentle enough relief to allow of good communications, hence manufacturing has come to be of considerable, though sporadic importance in the last generation.

The largest city in the Piedmont is *Atlanta*, with a central city population of half a million in 1970, more than half negro. It is the political capital of Georgia, and the regional capital of a wide area in the south-east United States. It is the principal railway hub of the south-east, and its excellent communications have helped to make it an important seat of trade and industry. *Inter alia*, it is the headquarters of the Coca-Cola Company, it manufactures motor cars and aircraft, cotton and cotton-seed oil, agricultural machinery, and furniture.

Most of the industries carried on in the Piedmont cities resemble those of Atlanta, with the exception of motor and aircraft engineering, which are uncommon. The main concentration is in North Carolina, but manufacturing and trading cities are to be found in all the Piedmont States. Coal from West Virginia or Alabama, piped petroleum and gas, and nuclear electricity are in many places available for power purposes apart

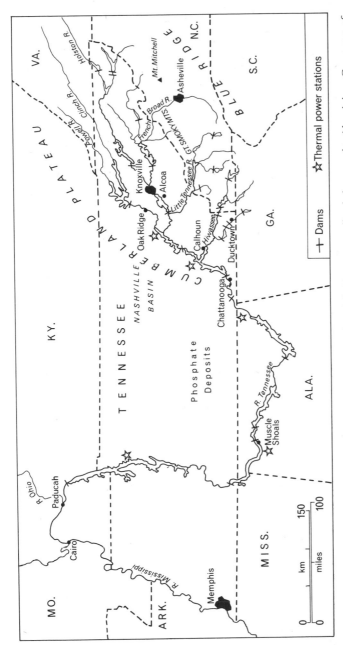

Fig. 67.—Tennessee Valley development. Most of the dams in the Little Tennessee valley belong to the Aluminium Company of America. Note that, despite the generous provision of hydro-electric power facilities, the agricultural and industrial development of the Tennessee Basin has now gone so far that several thermal-electric stations have had to be erected to ensure that power supplies remain adequate during peak demand periods.

from the more local supplies of hydro-electricity, and there is an expanding market with rising living-standards. Moreover, factory-work is attracting increasing numbers of redundant coal-miners, poor whites from upland farms and people from eroded farms in both the Piedmont and the Coast Plain.

Tobacco-processing, and especially the manufacture of cigarettes, are important at Durham and Winston-Salem (North Carolina), furniture and paper are made at High Point (North Carolina) and at many other places, and the extraction of oil from cotton-seed and peanuts is widespread. Aluminium is made at Badin (North Carolina). But the chief industries are concerned with textiles. Both Carolinas have many cotton and rayon factories, and even Georgia and Alabama now turn out more yarn than Massachusetts. Excluding Fall Line cities (see p. 193), cotton-towns include Gastonia and Charlotte (North Carolina), Spartanburg and Greenville (South Carolina), and Lynchburg (Virginia). Rayon is made at Rock Hill (South Carolina), Roanoke (Virginia), Charlotte and Asheville (North Carolina), nylon at Martinsville (Virginia) and other towns, and a Terylene plant has been erected at Shelby (North Carolina).

THE TENNESSEE VALLEY AUTHORITY

In 1933, during a period of world-wide economic depression, the Tennessee Valley Authority was inaugurated. The measures it was authorised to undertake by Act of Congress were both imaginative and revolutionary, and the area over which it was given a large measure of control was, most unusually, a geographical and not an administrative unit. Indeed, it transgressed the boundaries of seven different Appalachian states, and involved the whole of the Tennessee Basin, an area of 40,000 square miles, equal to the combined dimensions of Denmark, Netherlands, and Belgium (see Fig. 67). Its work has been so successful that it has become a model for other areas, e.g. the Damodar Valley in north-east India.

In 1933 the Tennessee Valley had a population of over 2 millions, one-eighth negro, most of the rest "poor whites." It was a region of depressed agriculture, of very badly eroded land, of low incomes and of little industry. The main river, choked with silt from ravished hillsides, and interrupted by rapids, was virtually unnavigable. Its uncontrolled course led to the periodical flooding of the better valley farmlands, and also contributed to the severity of the Mississippi floods lower down.

The Authority was granted the power to plan the complete social and economic rehabilitation of the valley and its people, and to pay special attention to flood control, navigation, and the generation of hydro-electricity.

What has it accomplished? In brief, by the building of about 30 dams on the main river and its tributaries, it has ensured all-the-year-round navigation; it has rendered the danger of floods negligible; made it possible to generate 10 million kw of electricity; encouraged the building of factories; reduced the incidence of "vitamin deficiency diseases" such as hookworm; initiated widespread soil-conservation measures; and, through its provision of reservoirs and the landscaping of their margins, has made it worth while for tourists to take holidays in the region. By 1957, the *per capita* income of the valley had grown from less than a half to two-thirds of the national average. At least partially through its example, the material standards of the entire South have undergone improvement during the last twenty years.

By 1935 the first dam had been completed. Since then, through the construction of further dams not only on the Tennessee itself but also on the Clinch, Holston, French Broad, Little Tennessee, Hiwasee, and other headstreams and tributaries, virtually the whole of the river system has been harnessed (*see* Fig. 68). Each dam is equipped with locks, and a 9-ft channel has been provided for navigation throughout a 625-mile stretch from Knoxville to Paducah, where the Tennessee joins the Ohio not far from the latter's confluence with the Mississippi. Goods carried on the river include many from the Middle West and the mid-interior and even from the Gulf Coast, *e.g.* coal, petroleum, maize, steel, machinery, and motor cars.

Below the dams, power plants have been built. From them, and also from a number of supplementary thermal-electric and nuclear power plants, electricity is conducted to farm, factory and town. Before the Tennessee Valley Authority began its work only 4% of the farms in the river-basin had electricity; the figure is now nearly 100%. The demand for power is still growing and further nuclear power stations are under construction or planned.

Already, in 1933, there was a not very efficient power plant at Muscle Shoals, where the United States operated two large nitrate plants to provide material for high explosives. More armaments are now being made in the region, but much besides. The region's rock phosphate deposits are being developed and are now converted into fertilisers at Muscle Shoals and elsewhere with the help of sulphuric acid produced at the Ducktown smelter, which handles copper from the mountains of eastern Tennessee. In the Chattanooga district bauxite deposits are worked, and aluminium refineries have been built at Alcoa and Listerhill.

At Oak Ridge, near Knoxville the Government runs an important atomic energy plant. At Calhoun, on the Hiwasee River, Bowaters have recently set up large paper mills, fed with pulp from new pine forests established on eroded hillsides. There are small iron blast furnaces at Rockwood, and Knoxville has a steel furnace.

Chattanooga and *Knoxville* are the largest settlements. The former is a large trading centre which manufactures malleable and cast iron, and has a chromium smelter. Knoxville manufacturers textiles, furniture, pottery,

[Courtesy: U.S. Information Service.

Fig. 68.—Norris Dam, Knoxville, Tennessee. This is one of the numerous T.V.A. multi-purpose dams. The use made of the lake by tourists should be observed.

zinc products (a little zinc is mined in the Appalachian mountains), and hardware. Some of its craftsmen polish marble quarried in the vicinity. The University of Tennessee is situated at Knoxville.

The provision of electricity for industrial purposes has caused a migration from land to factory, and so permitted a growth in the size of the average farm in the Basin. But agriculture has been even better assisted by the Authority's recommendations on soil erosion, and their implementation. Brushwood barriers have been erected across gullies, and steep slopes have been planted with forests. Among the trees established are black walnut, yielding nuts, black locust, providing timber for fence-posts and railway sleepers, honey locust, whose pods provide a cattle-feed, and various fruit-trees. Some of the more gently eroded slopes have been either put down to grass (thereby allowing an extension of animal industries) or else sown with close cover crops such as lespedeza, an Oriental legume which fixes nitrogen in the soil. Strip-cropping, terracing, and contour-ploughing are now common. A farm bureau extension service has been inaugurated, and recommendations are given regarding crop rotations and the proper use of fertilisers and insecticides.

By adopting these various soil-conservation measures—which have now become common practice in other eroded areas—the Tennessee Valley Authority has done much to prevent the silting-up of its new reservoirs and to reduce the risk of floods. Most of the basin's rainfall—which averages over 50 in. yearly—is of high intensity, but the prevention of further soil erosion, and the regulation of the river's régime by dam construction, is proving very effective in reducing the rate of run-off from the border catchment areas.

Chapter XVIII

THE NORTHERN INDUSTRIAL INTERIOR

EXTENT OF THE REGION AND ITS RELATION TO THE MIDDLE WEST

THE Northern Industrial Interior of the United States, as it may be called, is an amorphous region roughly delimited by the Mississippi on the west, the lower and middle Ohio on the south, the Allegheny Front on the east, and the Great Lakes on the north. It embodies the western portion of the great north-east manufacturing region of the country and also the Upper Lakes region in so far as it contributes to the industrial production of the whole area. West of the Mississippi, parts of central Iowa, together with the districts centred upon Kansas City and Omaha, may be regarded as outliers of the main region.

Thus demarcated, the Northern Industrial Interior may be roughly equated with the area known to the Americans as the "Middle West," to which, however, must be added western Pennsylvania, part of West Virginia, and the northern and eastern margins of Kentucky. Even with this appendage, the Middle West is more than an amalgam of industrial centres. It has mines and manufacturing plants, true, but it also possesses prosperous farmlands, for it embraces the Corn Belt of the United States, much of the interior Wheat Belt, and large parts of the Hay and Dairying Zone. It has a very well-balanced economy in which neither city nor country is dominant. In many ways it is at once an epitome of the nation and its core region. Formerly well known for their isolationist views, its very mixed people, feeling little affected by either Atlantic or Pacific affairs, still remain self-reliant, optimistic, rather brash, and vitally interested in the material rewards of work. They are apt to turn their eyes inwards to their own country, in which they take much pride, rather than outwards to foreign lands, even those from which they spring. They have produced for themselves a remarkably uniform cultural landscape: the farms, laid out in chequerboard fashion, vary little in shape or mode of operation; the cities—though differing, like the farms, in size—all look pretty much alike, their buildings—houses, hotels, factories, cinemas, but not, with but few exceptions, theatres—grouped together in a regular grid-iron pattern, their "Main Street" dominating social life.

In this chapter the focus of attention will be the Middle West city as an industrial unit, but it will be necessary also to pay attention to mining activities, especially the production of coal, petroleum, and iron, without which any geographical discussion of industrial patterns becomes purposeless.

HISTORICAL DEVELOPMENT

The more easterly, naturally well-wooded parts of the region were occupied in the later years of the eighteenth century by settlers filtering into the Ohio Basin and the fertile lowlands of Kentucky after crossing the Appalachian barrier during the course of their westward expansion. A few Frenchmen, entering the area via the Great Lakes, had preceded them, but only as fur-traders or missionaries. The land occupied by the newcomers was laid out in regular sections like the Canadian Prairies at a later date, and adapted for farming. Gradually, in the early decades of the nineteenth century, settlers took up land beyond the eastern hardwood forest zone, i.e. in the tall-grass Prairies, and slowly began to colonise land west of the Mississippi.

While most of the pioneers acquired land for farming purposes, others came forward as traders. These latter took up quarters in places which appeared to be well suited to act as supply-centres, e.g. river-crossings, lake margins, and where rapids interrupted river navigation. Such places quickly progressed from pioneering outposts into commercial cities, most of which developed industrially as the surrounding farm population grew. They began to make goods the landsmen needed and also to process their products for general consumption. As roads and railways replaced the early trails, and largely superseded the rivers as routeways, the markets for processed products were expanded. Manufacturers, more and more diversifying their output, took advantage of the abundant mineral deposits of the region, and certain cities, better situated than the rest as nodal centres, or more strategically located with respect to coal and iron supplies, swelled into giant metropoles. Concurrently, as the rural population grew and the fertile soils came to be more intensively farmed, many smaller market towns came into being, most of them equipped with at least one factory, e.g. a meat-packing plant, a corn-mill, a boot and shoe making establishment, a vegetable cannery, or an agricultural machine factory.

Today, the region is one of several large cities, and a very large number of towns, each separated from its fellows by croplands and pastures, most of which are well-farmed. The pattern of settlement tends to become more open going westwards, away from the most valuable coal deposits, and towards progressively drier areas.

THE ECONOMY

COAL, PETROLEUM, AND MINOR MINERALS

Coalfields. The Northern Industrial Interior is richer in coal than any other part of the United States (*see* Fig. 50). There are two large coal-fields and one less important one:

1. *The Appalachian Coalfield* contains an estimated 90% of the total known reserves of high-grade coal in the country, and produces over two-thirds of the present national output of coal of all kinds. It is based on the virtually horizontal strata of the Appalachian Plateaus, and extends about 850 miles from north to south, but its continuity is broken in south-east Tennessee and northern Alabama, where rivers, deeply incised in the plateau, have removed the mineral deposits. Particularly notable mining areas have developed in western Pennsylvania and West Virginia, the former extending into eastern Ohio, the northern part of West Virginia, and the extreme north-west prong of Maryland, the latter into western Virginia and eastern Kentucky. (The Central Alabama section of this great Appalachian Coalfield was discussed in Chapter XVII.)

2. *The Eastern Interior Coalfield* extends from Illinois southwards into western Kentucky and eastwards into south-west Indiana. It produces chiefly soft and smoky bituminous coal of medium grade, of lower calorific value and higher sulphur content than most of the Appalachian coal. In terms of output, however, this field is second in importance in the United States to the Appalachian field, and although its product is unsuitable for metallurgical coke, it is of considerable value as a general domestic and industrial fuel to cities such as Chicago, St Louis, and Louisville, and some is railed westwards. Mining is easily carried on by strip-methods or by short shafts, as the coal outcrops on the edges of an extensive shallow basin and is generally overlain by nothing more than a thin cover of glacial drift. The chief seam is 6 ft thick.

3. *The Western Interior Coalfield* is of less importance; it is located west of the Mississippi, chiefly in Iowa, Kansas, and Missouri, and yields a rather poor coal, chiefly used in the manufacturing cities of Des Moines, Kansas City and Omaha.

The Utilisation and Movement of Coal in western Pennsylvania and West Virginia. The coalfield of western Pennsylvania and adjacent areas is separated from the Eastern Interior field by the Cincinnati anticline, which runs from Toledo, through Cincinnati, into the Nashville Dome (*see* Chapter XVII). Its high-grade coal-seams, yielding excellent coking, steam, and domestic fuels, are only very slightly folded, and are advan-tageously exposed on the sides of both shallow synclines and anticlines, especially in districts where rivers, *e.g.* the Monongahela, Allegheny, and Youghiogheny (all headwaters of the Ohio), have cut through them. The main seam—producing about half the total output—is the Pittsburgh Bed, sandwiched between massive limestones (above) and sandstones and shales (below) (*see* Fig. 69). Over a wide area, the Pittsburgh Bed is virtually horizontal; it is about 6 ft thick throughout and is rarely more than 100 yards below ground-level. It is very economically worked by drifts cut into the valley sides, or by surface stripping, or by excavating short vertical shafts. Coal-cutting machinery can be used with maximum efficiency, therefore the output of coal per worker is very high.

West Pennsylvanian coal is in great demand in the industrial cities located on and close to the coalfield, *e.g.* Pittsburgh, but it is also railed and shipped westwards to such large Lake cities as Chicago and Cleveland, and eastwards to Atlantic ports, *e.g.* New York, Philadelphia, and Baltimore, whence a proportion reaches New England. Some is shipped across the Great Lakes into Canada, chiefly from Toledo, and there is a small export to Europe, but the large market formerly provided by the railways has now been lost, since most American locomotives are now burning diesel oil.

West Virginia and Kentucky have now surpassed West Pennsylvania as coal producers, following a century of Pennsylvanian dominance. Each turns out about a quarter of the bituminous coal mined annually in the U.S., Pennsylvania producing a sixth. As in Pennsylvania, the coal worked in West Virginia and Kentucky is of high grade; much is capable of conversion into excellent metallurgical coke, the seams are almost horizontal and again of good thickness. The principal producing areas are once more valley tracts, notably, in this case, those eroded by the New, Kanawha and Big Sandy Rivers. The Pocahontas district, in the Big Sandy valley is a particularly prominent mining area. The industry has become highly mechanised and much of the coal is obtained by strip-mining. Fewer colliers are now needed and there is much unemployment and distress.

Manufacturing is less prominent in West Virginia than in Pennsylvania. Much coking coal is supplied to steel-making cities on the shores of the Great Lakes and large amounts are shipped down the Ohio by barge, or are sent to tidewater ports on Hampton Roads, *e.g.* Newport News and Norfolk, for coastwise movement and export to Europe. In this connection it is significant that the headwaters of the New and Big Sandy Rivers approach closely to those of the James and Roanoke, flowing eastwards to the Atlantic. Just as Appalachian valleys farther north have been utilised for the construction of such coal-bearing railways as the Pennsylvania line, terminating at Philadelphia, and the Baltimore and Ohio

Railroad, so these southern valley-ways have been brought into commercial use by the laying-down of the Chesapeake and Ohio Railroad,
leading to Richmond and Newport News, and the Norfolk and Western
track, and the Virginian Railroad, both serving Norfolk.

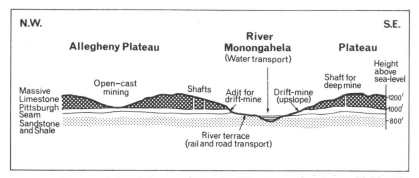

FIG. 69.—Characteristic mining conditions in West Pennsylvanian coalfield. This
section is drawn across the Monongahela valley near Pittsburg. Conditions are
similar in West Virginia, and bear some resemblance to those in South Wales.
The valleys are crowded with collieries, communications and industrial plants,
and houses climb up the hillsides, but the higher parts of the plateau show much
less evidence of man's activities.

Petroleum deposits. To one Colonel Drake goes the honour of drilling
the first oil-well ever put down in North America. The site was at
Titusville, Pennsylvania, 80 miles north of Pittsburgh, the date 1859. Oil
was struck at 69 ft. Thousands of wells, many of which now go down for
well over a mile, have since then been drilled in North America, but only
after the invention of the internal combustion engine and the introduction of the motor car to our civilisation has the market for oil expanded
greatly. Now the demand is almost insatiable.

In the region under study there are wide expanses of sedimentary rocks
containing petroleum, but the present total productive capacity is only
fractional compared with that of the newer Gulf Coast, Mid-Continent, and Californian fields. Most of the States embraced in the Northern
Industrial Interior have refineries, which are especially numerous in the
Chicago district, but a leading proportion of their industrial oil is brought
by pipeline from such western States as Texas and Oklahoma.

Four oilfields may be recognised:

1. *The Appalachian Oilfield,* currently contributing less than 2% of the
total United States output. This field occupies a fairly narrow sedimentary
belt extending through western Pennsylvania, into West Virginia, eastern
Ohio and eastern Kentucky. The producing area in western Pennsylvania
reached its maximum output in 1900, but it still yields a little very

high-grade oil by periodic pumping. The product is easily refined and is valuable as a lubricant; it also contains a very high percentage of gasoline. This area has also been an important source of natural gas since 1880; this fuel continues to furnish power for both domestic and factory premises, and is especially useful in the glass, pottery, and cement industries of the Pittsburgh district.

2. *The Illinois field*, extending into south-west Indiana and western Kentucky. The oil, chiefly refined in Chicago, is more variable in its character than that of Pennsylvania. Though at present obtained in larger quantities than Appalachian oil, the actual output is diminishing.

3. *The Lima–Indiana field*, located in north-west Ohio and the adjacent parts of Indiana. This field, too, is now past its prime. Its oil is of high grade, but is less pure than that of Pennsylvania.

4. *The Michigan field*, newer in development than the others, but yielding only small and waning quantities of fuel from a wide scatter of wells.

Miscellaneous minerals. Next to coal, iron ore is the most valuable mineral worked in the Northern Industrial Interior, which, in fact, yields 80% of the total output of the United States, for many years the greatest producing country in the world. But iron ore is so important as to merit special treatment (see the next section).

The richest and oldest deposits of copper in the United States are worked in a basaltic lava occupying part of the Keeweenaw Peninsula on the southern shores of Lake Superior. Even the Indians worked this deposit of pure metal, and white people first broached it in the 1840s, but as a producing area this district was long since overtaken by Western Cordilleran mines. To reach the ore now necessitates very deep shafts. It is reduced near the mines by coal carried up-Lake.

Another mineral of economic consequence which contributes to the diversification of industry is salt, which is obtained from workings in Ohio and Michigan, and in smaller amounts in West Virginia. Chemical industries, based in part on these deposits, are fairly widespread. The Great Kanawha valley, in West Virginia, has one of the largest: it turns out caustic soda, sulphuric acid, chlorine, ethylene, synthetic rubber, raw nylon, and other articles, many of which, however, depend rather on coal and petroleum as raw materials than upon salt.

THE IRON AND STEEL INDUSTRY

Iron-mining and transportation. Having first come into production in the 1840s, the Upper Lakes region of the United States has been the nation's leading producer of iron ore since the 1880s. The deposits (non-phosphoric, high-grade haematite) are easily worked, normally by quarrying, and are nowhere more than 100 miles from navigable water.

But after more than a century of exploitation, their iron content, once averaging 70%, has declined in the last decade to 50%. Attention is now being given to the working of a lower-grade ore (taconite), containing 25–30% metal, which occurs at lower levels in the same area, in even greater quantities than the haematite. The big steel corporations have already invested large sums in this new project, which, however, involves not only deep-mining, but also the "beneficiation" of the ore, i.e. its

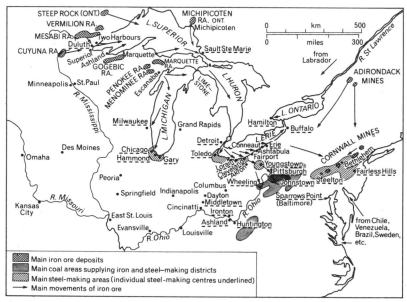

FIG. 70.—Iron and steel industry of north-east U.S.A. and adjacent parts of Canada.

crushing and concentration into pellets containing 60% iron, to reduce the cost of transport. For this purpose, large and expensive concentration plants have to be erected.

The Upper Lakes iron deposits are located in a number of "ranges" in the Pre-Cambrian rocks of the Shield (see Fig. 70). Four areas are particularly noteworthy:

1. *The Mesabi Range*, Minnesota. This single area by itself has produced over half the ore already worked in the whole region, and today yields nearly three-quarters of the entire annual output. The deposits occur in vast, thick, horizontal masses covered only with scanty glacial material, an over-burden which is very speedily and cheaply removed by mechanical grabs, which, however, have to cease their operations when the hard winter freezes the ground.

2. *The Vermilion Range*, Minnesota, 10 miles north of the Mesabi Range, and believed to contain more ore than remains in the latter.

3. *The Cuyuna Range*, also in Minnesota, south-west of Mesabi. Here the ores are associated with manganese.

4. *The Ranges between Lake Superior and Lake Michigan*, which include the Marquette, Menominee, and Penokee Ranges in Michigan, and the Gogebic Range in Wisconsin. The ores in this area are somewhat more

[*Courtesy: U.S. Information Service.*

FIG. 71.—Loading iron ore, Superior, Wisconsin. This ore will be taken by special lake-carrier to Buffalo.

deep-seated than those in the other ranges, and most of the metal is secured by sinking vertical shafts rather than by terrace-quarrying. But ore is obtainable from these ranges the year through, the average metal content is no lower, and important markets and to some extent even navigable water are nearer.

From the various iron ranges, ore is directly loaded into rail-cars, and transported down-grade to conveniently situated Lake ports, where it is transferred into specially constructed carriers for shipment to the large iron and steel manufacturing cities on the Lakes, *e.g.* Chicago and Cleveland, or else to smaller receiving ports from which it may be taken by rail to inland centres such as Pittsburgh. Some ore is also exported to lakeside iron and steel works in Ontario, notably Hamilton.

All the ore ports are situated on deep water, and most are sited at the mouths of small rivers. The chief of the dispatching ports is Duluth, at the head of Lake Superior, well equipped and conveniently located to ship ore from the Mesabi Range, and also from the Cuyuna and Vermilion Ranges. Additional to it are Superior (see Fig. 71), and Two Harbours, the trade of which is declining with the growing exhaustion of the richest ores of the Mesabi Range. Ashland dispatches most of the ore from the Penokee–Gogebic deposits, while Marquette handles the bulk of the Marquette iron, Escanaba most of the Menominee supply.

Receiving centres include South Chicago and Gary, on Lake Michigan, Detroit between Lakes Huron and Erie, Cleveland, Buffalo, Erie, Toledo, and Lorain on Lake Erie, all of which have their own blast-furnaces and steel works; Ashtabula, Conneaut, and Fairport, each on Lake Erie, and each railing ore to Pittsburgh, Youngstown, and other inland steel centres. Since shipping on the Great Lakes is halted between December and April, owing to winter freezing, ore has to be stockpiled at the ports or manufacturing plants to check seasonal hold-ups in production.

The main producing centres. The manufacture of iron and steel is far more important in the Northern Industrial Interior than in any other part of the United States. The plants belong to three principal areas: (1) the Pittsburgh region; (2) the Lake Erie–Detroit region; (3) the Chicago region. There are additional steelworks at Duluth and in and near the West Virginian–Kentucky coal-mining area. All depend fundamentally on the ores of the Upper Lakes, the coking coals of the Appalachian Coalfield, and the limestone strata of the western shores of Lake Huron, various islands in Lake Erie, and the Appalachian mountains. All of them also use varying quantities of scrap, and small amounts of carbon, manganese, chromium, tungsten, nickel, and other metals drawn from diverse, and often distant sources. Many plants are integrated, *i.e.* they possess their own coke-ovens (yielding, as by-products, coal-gas for heating and lighting, ammonia, benzol, coal-tar, etc.), and their own blast-furnaces (producing pig-iron) as well as steelworks (turning out steel ingots, plates, castings, rails, tubes, etc.). Most of the steel is made in open-hearth furnaces, which can use scrap; increasing quantities are handled in electric furnaces, decreasing amounts in Bessemer converters.

The Pittsburgh steel region. Iron was already being manufactured in Pittsburgh as early as 1790, to help satisfy the needs of frontiersmen. Charcoal was then used for smelting local ores, but in the first half of the nineteenth century manufacturers turned to the excellent coking coals of the district, *e.g.* those of Connellsville, and by 1850 the approaching exhaustion of west Pennsylvanian ores led to the growing use of Upper Lakes deposits. When the first "Soo" Canal was made in 1855, between Lake Superior and Lake Huron, a fillip was given to the use of these supplies, and by the 1870s Pittsburgh, by then the main centre of the American iron industry, was dependent chiefly upon iron ore from the ranges near Lake Superior.

The Pittsburgh region, which includes Youngstown (Ohio), Wheeling (West Virginia), Johnstown (Pennsylvania), and a number of smaller satellites, has one-third of the total United States steel capacity. For ease of access to both west Pennsylvanian coal and Upper Lakes iron, most of the steel plants have been built on river-terraces in rather narrow valleys, consequently there is little room available for large-scale expansion.

The Lake-shore steel region. Just as west Pennsylvania and adjacent areas fully established their iron and steel industry later than east Pennsylvania (*see* Chapter XVII), so the steel-making centres on the Lakes began to grow after west Pennsylvania had reached its prime. In fact, the heyday of the Lakes district did not come until after the First World War. Many cities are now engaged in the industry, viz. (*a*) those of the Calumet district, including South Chicago, Gary, Hammond, Indiana Harbour, and the Milwaukee outlier; (*b*) those of the Lake Erie shore, including Cleveland, Buffalo, Toledo, Lorain, and Erie; (*c*) Detroit; (*d*) Duluth. All draw their ore principally from ports in Minnesota, Michigan, and Wisconsin, to which they are directly accessible by water, though they are also well placed to receive new supplies from Labrador (*see* Chapter V) via the St Lawrence Seaway; and all obtain their coking coal from Pennsylvania and West Virginia, which reaches them chiefly by down-grade rail transport.

Outlying centres of the steel industry. Though the two regions just discussed account normally for two-thirds of the steel produced in the United States, the contribution made by more southerly towns in the Industrial Interior should not be overlooked. The West Virginia–Kentucky border country lacks a Pittsburgh, a Gary or a Cleveland, but it has nevertheless a few significant steel-making centres on the River Ohio, notably Ironton (Ohio), Huntington (West Virginia), and Ashland (Kentucky). None of these, however, has a situation as advantageous from the point of view of iron-ore supplies as those of the Lake-shore cities or those of the Pittsburgh area.

MISCELLANEOUS MANUFACTURES

The chief markets for the steel-producing firms in the Northern Industrial Interior are to be found in the hundreds of engineering works supported by the Middle West. Apart from such examples as the motor-car manufacturers of Detroit, who take steel made in that city, many of the engineering firms are not located in steel-making cities, but are well scattered; indeed, there is scarcely a manufacturing town without at least one. In such an important farming region as the Middle West the production of agricultural machinery is a widespread occupation. Cities such as Chicago, Springfield, and Peoria have such important works that Illinois has come to contribute about 50% of all the nation's farm implements; neighbouring states account for another 30%. The industry is expanding as farm mechanisation is still advancing.

Other engineering industries include the somewhat more concentrated activities of motor-car production, the manufacture of equipment for mines and railways, of wire-fencing, tin-plate for canning, structural steel for building, wire-mesh for highway construction, the fabrication of pipes for carrying petroleum, water, and gas, and the building of aircraft, ships, and marine engines.

To such steel-using industries as the above may be added, among engineering activities, the manufacture of aluminium ware, carried on in the Ohio valley, near Pittsburgh. Aluminium ingots are received from a variety of sources, e.g. smelters along the Kentucky–West Virginian border, Massena (New York), Badin (North Carolina) and Alcoa (Tennessee). Electrical apparatus is also made in Pittsburgh and other centres, e.g. Cincinnati and Milwaukee.

Several industries besides the manufacture of farm machinery are closely associated with the agricultural pursuits of the Middle West. They include:

1. Corn-milling, concentrated at such cities as Chicago, Minneapolis, Buffalo, St Louis, Kansas City, Duluth, i.e. at focal points in or near the maize and wheat lands and also in or close to large consuming areas.

2. Meat-packing, carried on in places connected with stock-raising and maize-growing, e.g. Chicago, Kansas City, Omaha, St Louis, St Paul, Cincinnati, Indianapolis, Des Moines.

3. The boot and shoe industry, employing many people in St Louis, south-east Wisconsin, southern Ohio and Illinois, collectively producing more footwear today than New England, the historic home of the industry.

4. Vegetable canning, making headway in several localities, especially in the eastern part of the Corn Belt and in Wisconsin, where vegetable-growing is widely undertaken.

Other prominent industries which provide work for many people in the Northern Industrial Interior include the manufacture of furniture, based on the eastern hardwood and Upper Lakes pine forests, and particularly significant at the Grand Rapids water-power site, Michigan; and the production of glass and chemicals, which is a salient feature of the industrial complexion of the Pittsburgh area, the Kanawha valley, St

Louis, and many of the Lake cities, *e.g.* Chicago, Detroit, and Cleveland.

The manifold industrial activities of the Middle West benefit from the presence within the region of abundant power supplies, now being extended by the building of nuclear electricity stations, a wide range of foodstuffs and raw materials, a plentiful supply of skilled labour and managerial enterprise, a wealthy internal market, a close communications mesh, and efficient transport links to the east coast of the United States. As compared with the Atlantic parts of the nation, the Northern Industrial Interior also has the advantages, generally speaking, of possessing more level ground and cheaper land for factory-building.

THE CITIES

THE MAJOR LAKE CITIES

Occupying high places among the leading industrial and commercial cities of the region under study are Chicago and Milwaukee, on the western shore of Lake Michigan, Detroit between Lakes Huron and Erie, Cleveland and its neighbours along the southern margin of Lake Erie,

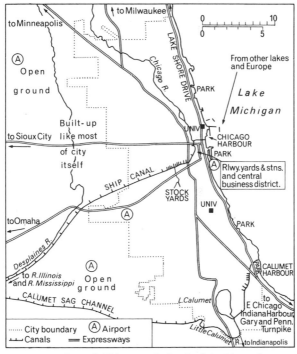

FIG. 72.—Site of Chicago. Only the lakeside parks are shown. There are several others.

and—less significant because of its smaller, more infertile immediate hinterland—Duluth, at the western end of Lake Superior.

Chicago. Among all the major cities, Chicago stands out as the most populous in the whole of North America, with the exception of New York. Yet it housed barely 100 people in 1830, and less than 5000 in

[*Courtesy: U.S. Information Service.*

FIG. 73.—Chicago: general view. In this panoramic view of a city landscape in North America the "downtown" section is marked by numerous sky-scrapers, a common feature. Part of Lake Michigan has been reclaimed and made into parkland. Compare Fig. 72.

1850. In 1852, however, it was joined to New York by rail, and since then—despite the disastrous fire of 1871—it has grown phenomenally. In 1970 it had nearly 3½ million people, and close upon 7 million were living in its metropolitan area. It ranks as one of the most cosmopolitan cities in the New World, yet is in many ways one of the most truly American. 20% of Chicago's total population is of negro descent, and there are large groups of Irish, German, Czech, Polish, and Italian origin, many of whom, as in New York, inhabit their own quarters in the city. Expansion is still going on, and Chicago now stretches along the Lake front for 15 miles; part of the former bed of Lake Michigan has been reclaimed for the construction of railway yards and also parkland (see Fig. 72). Almost as many skyscrapers (a style of architecture pioneered by the Chicagoans) as there are in Manhattan overlook the Lake and the problem of traffic congestion again appears to be virtually insoluble despite a developing underground railway system (see Fig. 73).

Known often as the "Windy City," on account of the frequent breezes which sweep across it both from the Lake and from the western plains, Chicago is at once the capital of the Middle West, the greatest railway centre in the world, the headquarters of nation-wide mail-order firms, the seat of 10,000 factories, the largest wholesale and retail trade centre of the interior, a busy and growing sea-port, a focus of air routes, the chief cultural and recreational city in central North America, and one of the world's principal conference centres. Carl Sandburg epitomised it thus:

> Hog butcher for the World,
> Tool Maker, Stacker of Wheat,
> Player with Railroads and the Nation's Freight Handler;
> Stormy, husky, brawling,
> City of the Big Shoulders.*

Chicago was originally chosen by the French as a small fur-trading post where the small river Chicago offered a sheltered harbour and led by an easy portage (a former glacial overflow channel) to the navigable Illinois tributary of the Mississippi. Its early settlers moved in via the Lakes, its later ones mainly by rail. Today they may enter by air or express roadway. The portage route is now followed by a 12-ft-deep sanitary and ship canal, and an improved channel also leads into the Calumet district of south Chicago, where the city has a second harbour into which move large quantities of bulky commodities, e.g. iron ore, coal, timber, and grain. Many goods, however, and most of Chicago's manufactures, are transported by rail or road. Since neither railways nor roads can cross the central United States any farther north, Chicago has become the terminus of 40% of the nation's rail mileage, and a great hub of highways, all discharging freight and passengers into the congested city.

In Chicago's factories and other industrial plants goods are produced with a value equal to one-half of all the manufactures of New England. Among them are iron and steel and refined oil (mainly from the heavy industrial region of Gary and Indiana), locomotives, agricultural and electrical machinery, paints, varnishes and soap, furniture, leather, clothing, books and newspapers. The city's stockyards, closed in 1970, were the largest in the world. The city ranks first as a wheat and maize market.

Milwaukee. Ninety miles north of Chicago, and possessing a good harbour at the mouth of another small river, stands Milwaukee, with a

* Quoted in *Chicagoland*, pub. by Chicago Ass. of Commerce and Industry.

city population in 1970 of nearly ¾ million. It ranks as a miniature Chicago. Another early fur-trading station, it has become the chief Lake port, manufacturing city, and commercial centre of Wisconsin. It receives, largely by Lake carrier, coal and timber, and it exports wheat. It is now enlarging its harbour, like Chicago, Cleveland, and other Lake cities in the United States and Canada, to deal with the increasing volume of water-borne trade the St Lawrence Seaway is bringing. The principal industries of Milwaukee and its satellites are flour-milling, brewing (a reminder that the city is largely a German settlement), meat-packing, and the manufacture of leather, clothing, electrical apparatus, and motor-vehicles.

Detroit. Like Chicago and Milwaukee, Detroit began as a fur-trading establishment. It has a metropolitan population of 4 millions and is the largest city in Michigan and the fifth largest in the country. On the River Detroit, where the Great Lakes route can be crossed by bridge, it exports many American products to Canada and is served by many Lake carriers. But it is its development as the "Motor City" which has occasioned its rapid growth. It is the headquarters of the Ford, Chrysler, and General Motors Corporations, and manufactures half of all the motor-vehicles made in the United States. It owes something to the local hardwood forests, which early provided material for carriage-building, to its position with respect to coal and iron supplies, and to its accessibility to the vast American market, but it probably owes just as much to the fact that it was in this city that Henry Ford pioneered mass-production methods, leading to the modern assembly line. Many industries are now carried on in Detroit which are ancillary to motor-engineering, *e.g.* glass, paint, rubber, non-ferrous metals. There are other quite distinct manufactures, too: meat-packing, flour-milling and the chemical industry.

Like New York and Chicago, Detroit has a black "ghetto" just outside its central business district. Two-thirds of its entire central area are taken over by motor-cars either in the form of freeways and other carriageways or parking-lots.

Akron, in Ohio, south of Lake Erie, manufactures most of the tyres fitted to Detroit motor cars. It is the greatest rubber-manufacturing city in the country, and handles both natural and synthetic materials.

CLEVELAND AND THE SMALLER LAKE ERIE CITIES

Cleveland (metropolitan population 1970, 2 millions) is by far the most populous of the Lake Erie iron and steel centres. It is situated at the mouth of the small Cuyahoga river. Its harbour, in part natural, in part artificial, is equipped to import limestone and also Upper Lakes and Labrador iron ore. Besides making iron and steel, the city assembles motor cars and

produces men's clothing. Oil refineries, based on Ohio supplies of petroleum, but by no means confined to them, provide materials for an increasing range of chemical products, e.g. paints, synthetic fibres, plastics,
and detergents, which are now being made on a big scale in a number of
plants spreading beyond Cleveland along the lake margins.

Erie and *Toledo* share in Cleveland's prosperity as steel-making centres.
The former, which is Pennsylvania's principal Lake port, also builds ships
and constructs marine engines. The latter, at the western end of Lake
Erie, at the entry of the Maumee River, is a great coaling port, formerly
dependent upon a canal link with Cincinnati but now receiving most of
its supplies by rail. It has important oil refineries, a large new natural gas
plant, glass works, and it manufactures much transport equipment.

For Buffalo, at the eastern end of Lake Erie, *see* p. 185.

Duluth. Duluth occupies an unusual site at the head of the Great Lakes
shipping route, where the small St Louis River provides a harbour
accessible by a canal cut through an almost enclosing sand-spit.. It handles
Prairie grain, Upper Lakes timber and iron, and has important wood-
working and iron-working industries. Its elevators dispatch wheat, its
docks ship iron ore.

THE MAJOR RIVER CITIES

In the Northern Industrial Interior river-based cities are as numerous as
Lakeside ones. They include major settlements on navigable waterways
such as Minneapolis–St Paul and St Louis on the Mississippi, Kansas City
and Omaha on the Missouri, Pittsburgh, Cincinnati, Louisville, and
Evansville on the Ohio, and a number of other cities on less-important
rivers, e.g. Indianapolis, Dayton, Columbus, and Des Moines.

Mississippi cities. The main settlements on the Mississippi are the twin-
cities of Minneapolis–St Paul, St Louis and East St Louis. All are marginally
located with respect to the Northern Industrial quadrilateral.

Minneapolis–St Paul, separated by the river, but alike in Minnesota, are
located at the head of a 9-ft navigable channel, where the Falls of St
Anthony bar further effective movement upstream. These falls, the
lowest on the river's upper course, have been harnessed to provide power
for a variety of industries, which are also supported by coal drawn chiefly
from the interior coalfields and a nuclear power station. The milling of
corn and wheat ranks first, at least in Minneapolis. Others include linseed-
oil crushing, meat-packing, engineering, clothing and footwear, printing
and publishing and the manufacture of plastics. In 1970, Minneapolis-
St Paul had a combined metropolitan population of nearly 2 millions.

St Louis, with a similar metropolitan population, is the largest city in
Missouri. It faces the highly industrialised satellite of East St Louis from its

terrace above the Mississippi flood-plain 20 miles below the Missouri confluence. It was at St Louis that pioneers, having moved down the Ohio valley, made their early crossing of the great north-south river. Established in 1823 as a French fur-trading port, it quickly became important as the starting-point for the down-river movement of large Mississippi steamers, many of which were built and launched there. Railways following the old water-routes—now mainly used by fleets of 3000-ton steel barges—converged upon this established trading city and enabled it to maintain its reputation as the chief commercial centre of a wide area, covering the southern part of the industrial and agricultural interior. It remains a very busy agricultural market, especially for livestock. It also serves the lead-, zinc-, and bauxite-mining districts of the Ozarks and their margins. Using chiefly Eastern Interior coal and petroleum piped from the west in its factories, the twin-city turns out large quantities of meat products, leather and footwear, women's clothing, motor cars, railway rolling-stock, aircraft components, books, newspapers, and magazines, glass and chemicals, flour, and alumina. No one industry is dominant like the steel industry of Cleveland, the motor industry of Detroit, the flour-milling industry of Minneapolis.

Missouri cities. Standing on the River Missouri are two important outliers of the Northern Industrial Interior: Kansas City and Omaha. Both form twin-cities, like the cities just examined on the Mississippi. Opposite Kansas City, Missouri, is the smaller Kansas City, Kansas, while facing Omaha, Nebraska, is Council Bluffs, Iowa. These cities lie close to the junction of grain-lands (to the east) and stock-raising lands (to the west). Both pairs are important railway foci with interests in meat-packing, grain storage, flour-milling, and the manufacture of farm machinery. Kansas City also has creameries, motor-car assembly plants and aircraft factories and is the principal United States market for winter wheat. With $1\frac{1}{4}$ million people in its metropolitan area in 1970, it lies close to the confluence of the Kansas and the Missouri. For some time during its formative period it occupied the place from which the pioneer trails (Oregon and Santa Fé) left the Missouri for the Platte and Arkansas Rivers and the west (*see* Fig. 89). Hence, like Pittsburgh and St Louis before it, it served as an outfitting or refitting place for west-moving migrants.

Ohio cities. Moving down the River Ohio, one approaches in turn the cities of Pittsburgh, Cincinnati, Louisville, and Evansville. As populous industrial centres, their importance declines as their distance from Pennsylvanian coal increases.

Pittsburgh (metropolitan population, 1970, almost $2\frac{1}{2}$ millions), one of the most strategically located cities in the whole country, lies at the confluence of two of the headwaters of the Ohio (the Allegheny and the Monongahela, leading respectively to the Susquehanna and Potomac gaps through the Appalachians), and is only 10 miles below the junction of a third (the Youghiogheny). It was established as a French fort (Duquesne) in the early 1750s, was renamed Fort Pitt in 1758 after its capture by the British, and finally became Pittsburgh (or Pittsburg). During the nineteenth century, it grew as both a commercial and manufacturing centre. It became a hub of railways as it was already a meeting-place of waterways, and quickly developed into North America's great "Steel City," at the same time, inevitably, becoming its "Smoky City." Coal transported into the city along the Ohio head-streams, and neighbouring supplies of petroleum and natural gas (the latter particularly cheap and capable of maintaining high and constant temperatures) have enabled Pittsburgh and its immediate district to take up other industries, including the manufacture of glass (for which the fine sands of the upper Ohio valley are valuable), optical goods, lamp bulbs, electrical equipment, "Westinghouse" air-brakes, aluminium goods, pottery (including clay refractories for the steel industry), cement, chemicals, and clothing. Like most regional capitals, small and large, it processes several foodstuffs, and has a number of printing and publishing works.

Sited initially on flat valley-terraces above its rejuvenated rivers, Pittsburgh has spread upwards on to the Allegheny Plateau, but its rail-ways and larger factories still throng the lower ground. Though still smoky, industrial pollution has been reduced by clean air measures, undertaken earlier than in most cities.

Cincinnati (metropolitan population, 1970, over 1¼ millions) stands down-river, at a marked northerly bend of the Ohio; it was already large in 1850. It was founded in 1819 at a point where one of the pioneer trails left the Ohio for St Louis and the west and where an easy connection could be made (by canal) with the Great Lakes. It also lay at a river-crossing. Now it acts as a rail focus and river port. The oldest of the meat-packing centres, it has also made a name as a producer of machine-tools, agricultural machinery, motor lorries, clothing and soap, radio and television sets.

From Pittsburgh to Cairo, where it joins the Mississippi, the Ohio functions as a busy navigable waterway. Like the parent river, it has a 9-ft channel, along which, at much lower rates than the railways charge, barges transport upstream bulky commodities such as petroleum, Gulf Coast chemicals, wheat, corn and soybeans and, downstream, coal, iron and steel. From time to time, however, especially when heavy spring rains coincide with the thawing of deep winter snows, the river overspills its banks and damages property in Cincinnati and Louisville. *Louisville* was an early trans-shipment point at falls on the Ohio (now by-passed by a canal and navigable locks, and harnessed to provide hydro-electricity). It is an important centre of the Kentucky tobacco industry and processes much leaf. It is also a notable hardwood market and supports many planing mills and furniture works. Distilleries, footwear factories, synthetic rubber and paint works are located there, and motor-vehicle bodies are made. Its close association with the "Blue Grass" country is shown by the fact that Louisville is the scene of the annual Kentucky Derby.

Evansville is a small edition of Louisville at a bridge-point on the lower Ohio. Furniture factories, breweries, machine-shops, and motor-car body works all provide employment.

OTHER SETTLEMENTS

Among settlements other than those located on the Lake shores and on the major rivers of the Northern Industrial Interior are the following:

Indianapolis, a metropolitan city of a million people, the largest settlement, railway focus and capital of Indiana. Its industries are mostly typical of the region: they include meat-packing, corn-milling, the fabrication of farm machinery, motor cars, railway equipment, hosiery, and drugs.

Dayton, making cash registers for sale all over the world, and also aircraft.

Columbus, capital of Ohio, an important engineering city of nearly half a million people, turning out large quantities of mining equipment.

Des Moines, in central Iowa, an agricultural trading city of some consequence, noted for its meat-packing and flour-milling plants, its creameries, clothing works, and chemical factories.

Chapter XIX

THE NORTHERN AGRICULTURAL INTERIOR

MAJOR CHARACTERISTICS

THE boundaries of the Northern Agricultural Interior do not accord with those of the corresponding industrial region, although the numerous manufacturing centres described in the last chapter are really no more than islands in an ocean of farmland. The eastern frontier extends no farther than the western margin of the Appalachian Plateaus, but the western frontier reaches many miles beyond the Mississippi, as far, in fact, as the Great Western Plains, while the southern frontier trespasses beyond the line of the lower Missouri–lower Ohio to the northern edge of the Ozark Mountains and the Cotton Belt (*see* Chapter XX). On the whole, therefore, the areal extent of the Northern Agricultural Interior is greater than that of the Northern Industrial Interior. Its boundaries are set, not by a decline in the volume of industrial production, but by physiographic considerations and crop limits.

Patterns of agriculture being largely set by relief, climate, and soil, a study of the region's physical geography may well precede that of its agricultural activities.

Apart from small areas drained northwards, chiefly to the Great Lakes, the whole of the Northern Agricultural Interior is tributary to the Mississippi River, which rises in the small Lake Itasca (Minnesota) and flows southwards into and through the Cotton Belt. The region is one of plain, developed mainly over only slightly dipping strata of later Palaeozoic, Mesozoic, and Tertiary rocks, earlier beds (Ordovician and Silurian) being exposed only in the Lexington and Nashville Domes in the south-east and in the Shield area of the Upper Lakes country (pre-Cambrian). Its topography is for the most part gently undulating, and scenically not very interesting, but the following features, the first three of which are shown on Fig. 85, lend it variety.

1. The east-facing escarpments of the Côteau de Missouri and allied but less marked *cuestas* farther south, which act as an acceptable physiographic frontier for the Western Plains, on their eastern side.

2. The north-facing escarpment of Pine Ridge, on the northern border of Nebraska, succeeded southwards by the Sand Hills, an area of sand-dunes and lake-filled hollows.

3. The deep trenches dug by rivers entering this region from the Western Plains, *e.g.* the Platte and the Kansas.

4. The physical basins of Lexington and Nashville, produced by the erosion of Palaeozoic domes at the ends of a geological anticline.

5. The glacial erosional features and glacial deposits in the northern part of the region. The former are notable in the Upper Lakes district, the latter farther south, but, generally speaking, not equator-wards of the Missouri–Ohio line. In south-west Wisconsin there is a "Driftless Area" which escaped the Pleistocene glaciation; this is a dissected plateau region of poor, light sandy soil and some "badland" topography, though where the underlying rock is limestone more fertile clay loams have developed, with a few sink-holes.

Just south of the area dominated by erosional forms, *e.g.* in northern Ohio, Indiana, and Illinois, there is a tract of rather rough ground covered by recent drift, but farther south are level "Till plains," only sporadically ridged by eskers, drumlins, and terminal moraines. In the west there is some loess.

6. The Red River Plain of northern Dakota, an area of lacustrine deposits similar in origin and character to those of Canada's Manitoba lowland (*see* Chapter IX).

The Till plains, like the Red River plain, are extraordinarily fertile, whether, as in the east, they are covered by grey brown earths, or, as in the west, by Prairie soils and chernozems, and they form some of the finest farmland in the continent.

CLIMATE AND NATURAL VEGETATION

The whole of the region has a temperate continental type of climate, with hot summers (averaging 68°–80° F according to latitude) and cold winters (except in the far south). Winter frost, while restricting farm operations, is not entirely harmful: it reduces soil leaching and checks the incidence of pests and diseases. The rainfall, largely of a frontal type, is well distributed in the east, while the spring or summer maximum of western areas, induced by convectional storms, benefits most crops. Broadly speaking, the mean annual precipitation, much of which, especially in the east, is in the form of winter snow, decreases westwards from about 40 in. in eastern Ohio to 20 in. on about the 100th meridian. The growing season varies from about 200 days in the south to 120 days in the north. The amount of sunshine received is often more than half of the potential for the latitude, a factor which assists the ripening of crops. Also, the frequent weather changes the region experiences encourage the expenditure of human energy in both mental and physical work. Unfortunately, tornadoes may be destructive in the west, and heat waves prostrating in the east.

The appended climatic statistics may prove helpful:

Cincinnati (east)	J.	F.	M.	A.	M.	J.	Jy.	A.	S.	O.	N.	D.
Temperature (° F) .	33	34	44	54	65	74	78	76	69	58	45	36
Precipitation (in.) .	3·5	2·9	4·0	3·1	3·6	3·7	3·4	3·3	2·6	2·5	2·9	3·1

Mean Annual Temperature: 56° F; Mean Annual Range of Temperature: 45° F; Mean Annual Precipitation: 38·6 in.

Omaha (west)	J.	F.	M.	A.	M.	J.	Jy.	A.	S.	O.	N.	D.
Temperature (° F) .	22	25	37	51	63	72	77	75	66	55	39	27
Precipitation (in.) .	0·7	0·9	1·3	2·8	4·1	4·7	4·0	3·2	3·0	2·3	1·1	0·9

Mean Annual Temperature: 51° F; Mean Annual Range of Temperature: 55° F; Mean Annual Precipitation: 29·0 in.

The more northerly and easterly parts of the region (east of the Red River valley) were naturally covered by coniferous forests (notable in the Upper Lakes section) or by mixed forests, in which deciduous hardwoods predominated. Southwards and westwards, however, due in the main to a less effective rainfall, Prairie grassland was characteristic: tall grasses in the more humid east and central parts, shorter grasses on the western margins, with trees generally confined to the watercourses. Owing to the expansion of cultivation and settlement, little of the natural woodland remains, except in the less-fertile parts of Minnesota, northern Wisconsin, and northern Michigan, though farmers in the east and north may have small wood-lots, and Prairie farmsteads are often sheltered by a windbreak of planted trees.

AGRICULTURAL SUB-REGIONS

Owing mainly to climatic variations, but, at least locally, to differences in soils and physiography, the Northern Agricultural Interior is not without agricultural diversity. As we have seen, summer temperatures decline going northwards, the growing season shortens, and the winters become more severe and more protracted, therefore maize (which the Americans always refer to as "corn"), though ripening satisfactorily over wide areas, does not do so in the north, and the sowing of wheat, which may be safely undertaken at the approach of winter in the south, must be delayed until spring in the north. Moreover, since aridity increases with longitude, a crop such as maize, which takes up more water than wheat, is usually displaced by the latter as the Great Plains are approached. On the eastern shores of Lake Michigan and on the southern margins of Lake Erie, much land has been put under orchard-fruits because of the climatic amelioration produced by these large bodies of water. Near some of the major cities, *e.g.* Chicago, dairy-farming has been stimulated by the presence of large urban markets, while in the east, near the Canadian border, the cool, humid climate and the rough topography have for different reasons favoured this type of land-use.

In the light of such considerations as these, the region under study may be divided into a number of agricultural sections (*see* Fig. 49), each dominated by a particular farming programme. The following will be examined in turn: (*a*) The Corn Belt; (*b*) the Winter Wheat Region; (*c*) the Spring Wheat Region; (*d*) the Hay and Dairying Zone; (*e*) the Lumbering and Dairying Region; (*f*) the General Farming Region; (*g*) the Fruit-growing Districts.

It should be noted that none of the above areas has rigid boundaries. Weather fluctuations, variations in the intensity of demand for particular products, improvements in agricultural techniques, and the progress of agricultural research may all cause boundaries to shrink or expand from time to time.

THE CORN BELT

The states of Iowa, Illinois, Indiana, and Ohio form the heart of the Corn Belt, but maize is also the dominant crop of eastern Nebraska and the adjacent parts of South Dakota, Minnesota, and Missouri (*see* Fig. 74). The Corn Belt produces half the entire corn crop of the United States, which in all amounts to nearly 50% of the world's total. It also grows large quantities of oats, hay, soya (or soy) beans, wheat, vegetables, and other crops. The bulk of the farmer's income, however, is derived, not from the sale of corn or other crops, but from the marketing of livestock and their produce. The area is, in fact, the most important agricultural one in the country: almost the only cultivated American plants not raised are citrus fruits, rice, and cotton, and all the domestic animals have their place in the farm economy. Most holdings are highly capitalised and mechanised, the output per man is much greater than the national average (though crop yields are normally below those of western Europe), and farm incomes are generally higher, especially in Iowa and Illinois, than in any other part of the Union except California. Most farms are worked on a family basis and few hired men are employed. Their average size—which is growing with the advance of mechanisation—is now about 320 acres, *i.e.* half a section (of 640 acres, or 1 square mile).

In Iowa, Indiana, and Illinois corn usually occupies more than 40% of the year's cropland, in Ohio and Missouri over 30% . Planting normally begins at the end of April, or early in May, when the last killing frosts are expected to be over. In the growing season, of at least 150 days, high daytime temperatures (averaging about 70°–80° F) and warm nights (not much below 55° F) are desirable, especially after the early stages of growth. For adequate ripening, a mean summer (June–August) temperature of 66° F is needed. Sun and showers assist maturation, and it is most helpful if over 4 in. of rain fall in July, when the plant's water requirements are high. Little corn is grown where the mean annual rainfall is less than 20

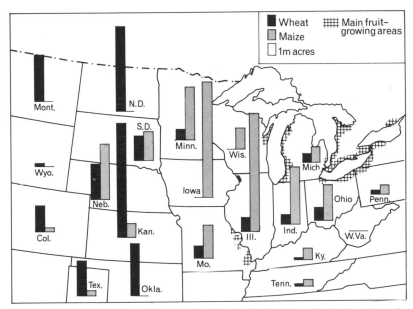

FIG. 74.—Wheat, maize, and fruit production in the Northern Agricultural Interior and adjacent areas. The height of the columns is proportional to the average acreages of wheat and maize harvested, 1968–70.

in. yearly, or where at least 8 inches do not fall in the three summer months. The crop can be grown under a variety of edaphic conditions, but the rich, dark-brown Prairie soils of Iowa, northern Missouri, and Illinois undoubtedly benefit the crop, as do the grey-brown, more leached forest earths of Indiana and Ohio. Though Corn Belt soils are among the richest in North America, their initial fertility has now vanished, and increasing sums are being spent on fertilisers, especially nitrogenous types. Livestock husbandry, associated with corn-growing, also provides manure, and the adoption of suitable crop rotations helps to keep the land in good heart. There is comparatively little badly eroded land (*see* Fig. 76).

The limits of the Corn Belt are set chiefly by the climatic needs of the dominant crop, and by the extent of competition from other types of land-use, which may be more profitable in border areas. In the north the summer isotherm of 70° sets a rough boundary; in the south, beyond the limits of Pleistocene glaciation, more pedalferic soils, unsuitable topography (in the Ozarks), and competition from tobacco and soft winter wheat cause the Corn Belt to give·way to a "General Farming" region; westwards, hot, drying summer winds and the existence of the Sand-hills of Nebraska are detrimental to corn-growing; and eastwards, in the Appalachian Plateaus of eastern Ohio and Pennsylvania, dairying becomes more profitable.

It should be noted that: (*a*) corn requires only about one-twelfth as much seed per acre as wheat, and yields much more heavily, therefore it will generally be grown in preference to it if conditions allow; (*b*) the cultivation of hybrid corn, which was first successfully undertaken in the 1930s, has not only increased corn yields considerably (by 40% throughout the United States as a whole), and so encouraged more variety in crop production, but has also permitted an extension of the Corn Belt to the north, west, and south, as this new variety of maize is resistant to drought, cold, and disease. Ninety-five per cent of the United States corn is now of the hybrid type.

Generally speaking, less than 1% of the corn produced in the Corn Belt is exported, and no more than 15% is used as a human foodstuff (*e.g.* as meal for cakes, boiled meal, or "corn on the cob"), or is converted into alcohol, starch, glucose, and cooking fat. The great bulk of the crop is consumed by animals, especially swine and cattle, and 70% of the total never leaves the farm on which it is harvested.

Livestock industries in the Corn Belt. Most of the maize grown in the Corn Belt is said to be "marketed on the hoof," since it is fed to hogs, cattle, and sheep, whose products bring the farmer most of his earnings. Corn is a great fattener, largely because it contains more oil than other cereals. It is used not only to build up the flesh of animals bred in the Corn Belt itself but also to nourish cattle and sheep brought in from the drier Western plains for finishing.

Half the swine in the United States spend all their lives in the Corn Belt, alternatively called the "Hog Belt." They are then sent by lorry ("truck" in the United States) or rail-car to various meat-packing stations within and just outside the region for slaughter and the preparation of pork, bacon, sausages, lard, etc. They are fed in various ways. They may be turned into fields of standing ripe corn, across which temporary wire fences are erected: a practice known as "hogging down corn," which economises in labour, reduces the cost of harvesting, and ensures that all parts of the plant are eaten and the fields manured; they may be given shelled corn, or corn on the cob, or corn which falls from the troughs when cattle are feeding; they may be offered silage, made by chopping up and preserving maize, fresh and moist, in the tower-like silos which are so prominent in the Corn Belt landscape; or they may, in dairying districts, be fed partially on skimmed milk. Like poultry, but unlike cattle, they require little pasture.

Most Corn Belt cattle are kept in beef herds, though in many areas in the north and east, where the summers are cool and large cities numerous, dairy herds are frequent. Many other Corn Belt farmers keep a few dairy cows (and also poultry) and sell milk (and eggs and chickens) locally.

Cattle are normally fed on grass during much of their early life, but subsequently they feed on a mixture of grain (corn, oats, or wheat), hay, and some concentrates, e.g. molasses, cottonseed meal, soybean meal, flaxseed meal. Corn is the dominant item in the rations used for fattening. Some cattle are now entirely raised in buildings (like poultry), where they demand less attention, and can be fed more scientifically, so that more farmland is available for crops, which bring the farmer more profit than grass. Like swine, beef cattle are slaughtered and their carcases sent to the great meat-packing centres, where they are converted into meat (especially steaks) and also various by-products, e.g. fertilisers (bone-meal) and buttons.

Sheep have never been as numerous in the Corn Belt as cattle and pigs. Some farmers, however, keep a small flock to raise lambs, sold in autumn, and to obtain a wool-clip. A few buy lambs born in the dry west, e.g. on the Rocky Mountain pastures, and fatten them for the American meat market on corn, oats, and hay. Far less lamb, however, is consumed in the United States than beef, pork, or bacon.

As in other agriculturally advanced areas, horses are declining in numbers with the advance of farm mechanisation.

Minor crops of the Corn Belt. In the Corn Belt the main crop is usually rotated with soybeans, small grains (e.g. spring oats in the cooler north and north-west, winter wheat in the south and south-west), and grasses (most commonly timothy in the damper east, alfalfa in the drier west— see Fig. 75).

Soybeans are raised partly as an animal feed, eaten in the form of meal or cake, partly as a human food in soup, pastry, or sweets. First grown on a small scale in the early nineteenth century, soybeans have become much more widely grown since 1945, when a world shortage of fats and oils made itself felt. They supply nitrogen to the soil and often do better on poor land than corn. They have displaced small grains and rotation grasses on some farms, and now occupy more than 10% of the area occupied by corn itself in the Corn Belt. Their cultivation is concentrated in southern Minnesota, Iowa, north-east Missouri, Illinois, Indiana, and the western half of Ohio, but they are also grown outside the Corn Belt, *e.g.* on the Middle Atlantic Plain, the borderlands of Kansas and Missouri, and the Mississippi valley between St Louis and Vicksburg.

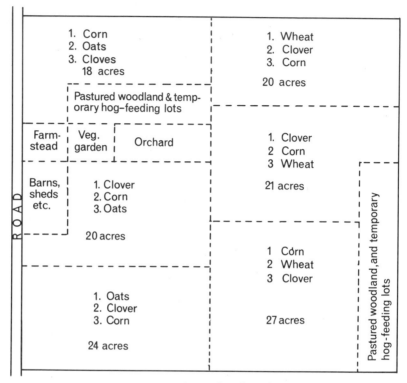

FIG. 75.—Rotations which may be adopted on a small Mid-West farm.

The winter wheat grown in the Corn Belt (generally sown in late September) is of two kinds: soft winter wheat, nurtured in the damper east, *e.g.* in southern Illinois, southern Michigan, and Ohio, and hard wheat, harvested in the drier west. Most is of the hard variety and is widespread west of the 95th meridian. It begins to displace corn as the dominant cereal in the western borders of Iowa and Missouri, where it is rotated with alfalfa, oats, and corn (to the north) and with alfalfa and grain sorghums (in the south).

Oats, the third of the important Corn Belt cereals, capable of ripening at lower temperatures than even wheat, do not range as far south as corn, but, paradoxically, are not very widespread north of corn-growing areas.

They are generally sown earlier than maize, and often serve as a nurse crop for clover, with which they are often drilled in rotation with corn. In acreage, oats are the second crop to corn in Iowa and northern Illinois.

Permanent pasture is not very widespread in the Corn Belt, but alfalfa and clover are valued plants, not only for their feeding qualities but also because they restore nitrogen to the soil. Alfalfa, a deep-rooted grass, is favoured in the west, where there may be a shortage of water for shallow-rooted grasses and where soils are less acid than in the moister east. It may provide several cuttings a year.

Most Corn Belt farmers grow potatoes and other vegetables, e.g. peas, green beans, and tomatoes for their own use, and many maintain small orchards, producing apples and small berry fruits, and more rarely plums, peaches, pears, and cherries. Fur-ranching is carried on in places.

THE WINTER WHEAT REGION

As we have seen above, winter wheat is widely cultivated in various parts of the Corn Belt, especially in the south, but it takes precedence over corn only to the south-west of the Corn Belt, where a rough quadrilateral, spreading somewhat from all four borders of Kansas, may be designated the "Winter Wheat Region." This area is separated from the Spring Wheat Region by a westerly extension of the Corn Belt, where a decreasing and more variable rainfall limits both the acreage and the yield of maize. As in the cooler Spring Wheat Belt, wheat is frequently the only crop on many Winter Wheat farms, and monocultural techniques, which involve the extravagant practice of fallowing, are often characteristic. In the east the mean annual rainfall is about 30 in., and wheat-growing is often combined with corn-growing and cattle-fattening, but in the west, where the rainfall may average less than 20 in., farms are larger, there is more pasture, and sorghums rather than corn may be grown for winter fodder. The western boundary of the region fluctuates considerably, but often lies well within the Western Plains (see Chapter XXII). Throughout, farming practices are much less intensive than in the Corn Belt.

In Kansas over 60% of the cropland is under wheat, its only serious rivals being corn and soybeans in the more humid north-east, sorghums in the south-west, and alfalfa in the Flint Hills. Irrigation-farming is spreading along the river valleys, e.g. alongside the Arkansas River, where sugar-beet, potatoes, beans, and orchard-fruits are grown in addition to wheat, corn, and alfalfa, but many of these artificially watered crops belong rather to the Western Plains than to the Winter Wheat Region. Similar types of farming are characteristic of Nebraska, where the tall grasses of the Sand Hills encourage cattle-grazing, the North Platte River is tapped for irrigation, and the corn–hog economy of the Corn Belt is not uncommon in the east.

Kansas produces approximately one-sixth of the U.S. wheat crop, and there is normally some export, mainly through Gulf ports. The usual harvest month is July, when many "custom Operators" hire out machines, equipped for both day and night reaping. Some casual labourers are often called into service at such a time: they may, during the harvest season, gradually migrate from Texas (where winter wheat is also grown), through Oklahoma, into Kansas and Nebraska, then into the Dakotas, as the ripening season advances, and end up in the Canadian Prairies.

The sale of cattle, many of which are owned by wheat-farmers, may bring as much money to the Winter Wheat Region as the marketing of wheat. Many western range cattle are finished in eastern Kansas and Nebraska, on special feed lots, as in Iowa and other Corn Belt states, and Kansas City is one of the chief meat-packing centres in the country.

THE SPRING WHEAT REGION

This region, lying to the north-west of the Corn Belt, has a shorter growing season than the Winter Wheat Region (120–140 days, compared with 150–200) and a much harder winter. Hence sowing is delayed until the winter snow has melted and the danger of severe frost, it is hoped, is at an end, *i.e.* until April or early May. Thanks to the lower evaporation rates experienced in this more northerly area, the wheat of the Dakotas, north-east Montana, and western Minnesota can be grown with a rather lower precipitation than is essential in the Winter Wheat Region, consequently spring wheat tends to range farther west than winter wheat. It is fortunate, however, that two-thirds of the annual rainfall normally comes in the warmer half of the year, *i.e.* when the crop is in the ground. Westwards, beyond the 15-in. annual isohyet, extensive livestock grazing generally replaces extensive grain cultivation in both the Spring Wheat and Winter Wheat Regions.

As a rule, the Spring Wheat Region produces less than a quarter of the nation's wheat crop. North Dakota is the leading State. Much spring wheat is milled at such cities as Minneapolis, Duluth, and Chicago, and there is a very large export via the Great Lakes and Atlantic ports as the grain, like that from the Canadian Prairies, is hard, rich in protein, and excellent for bread-making. Farms are comparable in size with those of the Winter Wheat Region and average at least one section (640 acres). Production is more assured in the more humid east—an area of rich, black chernozem soils—than in the more arid west, where fertile chestnut soils predominate. Both these soils, and also the localised lacustrine soils of the Red River valley, the heart of the region, have an excellent structure, but owing to the practice of extensive farming, the average yields rarely exceed 20 bushels per acre.

The physical and cultural environment of the U.S. Spring Wheat Region resembles that of the Canadian Prairies, which adjoin the area. Relief, climate, natural vegetation, and soils are similar. The farms are

[Courtesy: U.S. Information Service.

Fig. 76.—Strip-planted farm, east central Ohio. Here, as in most of the Corn Belt, scientific agricultural methods, including soil conservation practices, are employed.

again extensive in size and methods and there is a high degree of mechanisation. Similar subsidiary crops are grown, e.g., flax, barley, hay, and oats. The farm-buildings, painted a dull red, with their surrounding windbreaks, are alike, and one again notices wind-pumps and grain elevators reaching upwards. The fields are sectioned in the same way, and individual farms are connected similarly by long, straight roads. As in Manitoba, so also in the American portion of the Red River valley and in the more populous, damper parts of the region, mixed farming, with subsidiary dairying, is gaining ground at the expense of wheat with fallow.

Drought is the great enemy of the spring wheat farmer in the Dakotas. To conserve moisture, and also soil, many farmers, both here and in the Winter Wheat Region, have now adopted contour-ploughing methods (see Fig. 76), and have planted rows of trees as shelter belts. They make a habit of sowing more drought-resistant crops (barley in the north, sorghums in the south), and they have begun trash-farming, i.e. the custom of leaving the stubble in the harvest fields and working the refuse into the soil.

THE HAY AND DAIRYING ZONE

East of the Spring Wheat Region, there is usually less sunshine and increasing amounts of rain and cloud. The thin, leached soils of the Shield, recently eroded by ice-sheets, enter the scene in Minnesota and continue into northern Wisconsin. Under these conditions, dairying, supported by pasture and small quantities of oats, becomes more profitable than grain cultivation. It is too cool to ripen corn, though a little is sown and cut for silage. Some 80–90% of the cropland is normally in feed crops, especially hay, which, like oats and green corn benefits from the well-distributed rainfall. In contrast to the elevators of the Spring Wheat Region, silos are typical of the cultural landscape, as are winter cattle-sheds and basement hay-barns, creameries, and cheese factories. Most of the farmers are of north European stock, accustomed to dairying in their homelands: they include Swedes, Germans, Dutch, Poles, and Swiss.

Wisconsin, Minnesota, and Michigan support one-fifth of all the dairy cattle in the United States. Roughly 80% of all Wisconsin farms are devoted to dairying, and similar figures are reached in many parts of Minnesota and Michigan. Most of the cattle are of the Holstein breed, of Danish origin, but Jerseys and Guernseys yield more butterfat and are therefore often preferred in districts concentrating more on the production of butter than on milk and cheese. Wisconsin, the chief dairy state, accounts for about half the cheese made in the United States, and also produces large amounts of butter, condensed milk, and dairy milk. There is a very big demand for the latter in Chicago, where this northern dairy zone passes into the Corn Belt. Minnesota leads Wisconsin as a butter-producer.

A typical farm in this region averages about 160 acres. On it, the occupier (usually the owner) keeps about 10–20 head of cattle, a few pigs (fed mainly on skimmed milk from the creameries and whey from the cheese factories), and a flock of poultry. The sale of milk, eggs, and meat is the chief commercial enterprise.

Vegetable-growing is common in the immediate hinterlands of Chicago and Milwaukee, where beans and peas are grown (largely for canning), and also potatoes, sweet corn, and tomatoes. In south-west Wisconsin cigar-tobacco is a significant subsidiary crop.

THE LUMBERING AND DAIRYING REGION

The extreme north-eastern and north-central parts of Minnesota, northern Wisconsin, and northern Michigan form the main Laurentian

Shield region of the United States, whose major resource, as we saw in Chapter XVIII, is iron ore. It is a dissected, glaciated, lake-strewn area, overlooked by cloudy skies. It has a short growing season, heavy winter snows, and highly podsolised, thin soils. Formerly covered with forests of white pine and a few deciduous species, it is now a "cut-over" land from which much of the original forest was removed in the last quarter of the nineteenth century and the early years of the present one by New England foresters working westwards, cutting as they went, but not replanting. Forest rehabilitation is now making some progress, and there is still some lumbering and pulp-making.

Where the soils are deep enough, pasture, hay, and a few root crops are grown in forest-clearings, and a number of dairy farms, much less prosperous than those farther south, have been established. A few small settlements are supplied with milk, but much of the liquid is converted into butter and cheese in the absence of large markets for fresh milk. To increase their food-supply and their income, the farmers often combine their work with forestry, fishing and catering for lakeside tourists.

THE GENERAL FARMING REGION

Transitional between the Corn Belt and the Cotton Belt is an area where, over quite extensive tracts, no one crop nor animal industry is dominant. Some writers, including Dr. O. E. Baker, of the U.S. Dept. of Agriculture, who first formulated the agricultural regions of the central United States, have called it the Corn and Winter Wheat Belt, and have pointed out that while these crops are important, the harvests they yield, especially in the case of maize, are normally lower than those in the Corn Belt because: (a) the soils are more pedalferic and eroded; (b) the area never benefited from glacial deposition. There is also more woodland here than in the Corn Belt.

The two most prosperous parts of this region are the Kentucky Blue Grass country and the Nashville Basin of Tennessee. In both these subregions tobacco, wheat, and corn are grown, and many cattle, hogs, and sheep are raised. Tobacco is the chief commercial crop. It is favoured in both Tennessee and Kentucky by the humid, sub-tropical climate, and the existence of phosphatic limestone soils. It may be rotated with hay, wheat, and corn. On the gently rolling, rich, Blue Grass pastures many racehorses are grazed. On the whole, the value of crops sold and the value of livestock and animal products sold is in nice balance.

FRUIT-GROWING

As we have seen (p. 245), many Middle West farms grow a few orchard-fruits round their farm buildings, chiefly for their own consumption. But there are also certain specialised fruit-growing districts, shown on Fig. 74:

1. The southern margins of Lake Erie, between the manufacturing cities, where grapes, threatened by the expansion of chemical and other works, are particularly notable.

2. The eastern side of Lake Michigan, devoted in the south chiefly to grapes, peaches, and small fruits, in the north mainly to apples, pears, and cherries.

3. The Dore peninsula, Wisconsin, on the western side of Lake Michigan, where cranberries, strawberries, cherries, and apples do well.

4. The Mississippi valley of southern Illinois and eastern Missouri, noted for apples and peaches.

Along the lake margins the fruit-belt is up to 20 miles wide. The soils are mostly favourable, warm, sandy loams, and urban markets, *e.g.* Cleveland and Chicago, are readily accessible. But the climatic factor is the most important. In spring the cold waters and shore ice of Lakes Erie and Michigan combine to chill the dominant west and north winds, which therefore reach the eastern and southern margins as cool air masses. The low temperatures they bring delay budding until the likelihood of frost is over. In autumn the reverse happens: lake waters remain warmer than the surrounding land areas, and winds crossing the Lakes are therefore heated by their passage, consequently the onset of autumn frost is usually retarded until October, when the fruit is safely gathered in.

Chapter XX

THE SOUTHERN INTERIOR

THE SOUTHERN INTERIOR, THE COTTON BELT, AND THE SOUTH

South of the corn and winter wheat lands of the central United States is an area in which cotton has long been the dominant crop. Hence the name "Cotton Belt" bestowed upon it by most agriculturalists and geographers. But it must be noted that the Cotton Belt extends beyond the Southern Interior. It overlaps the Southern Appalachians and spreads eastwards into the Piedmont and Atlantic Plain on the one side (*see* Chapters XVI and XVII), while on the other it trespasses into the High Plains of Texas and Oklahoma (*see* Chapter XXII).

Another term we shall use in this chapter is "the South," which is sometimes defined as the cultural and economic region south of a line joining Oklahoma City, Cairo, and Washington, a boundary roughly marching with the Mason–Dixon line of the Civil War period.* As compared with the North, this human region has a climate warm enough to have encouraged the early development of plantation agriculture based on negro slave-labour and adapted to the production of cotton and other subtropical crops. Farming has never become as intensive as it has in the North, mechanisation has proceeded much less far, and farm incomes and therefore living standards have remained persistently lower. Manufacturing engages fewer people, and rural settlement tends to remain more common than urban. Educational standards are lower and the pace of life is slacker. The Southerners' attitude has always been conservative, the Northerners' progressive. But the South has recently begun to change: farming has become more diversified and the use of machinery has spread; urban life has begun to expand at the expense of rural; the volume of industrial production is growing, and living standards are more closely approaching those common in the North. But the negroes—freed from slavery a century ago—are only now gaining their place in the community as equal partners with the whites, their former masters.

---

* Mason and Dixon were two surveyors who first charted the border between Pennsylvania and Maryland. To the north, slave emancipation laws were put into effect soon after 1800, but to the south, slavery was regarded with less distaste. Maryland did not, however, join the Southern Confederacy during the Civil War.

PHYSICAL ASPECTS

PHYSIOGRAPHY

Physiographically more varied than it appears to be on a map, the Southern Interior may be divided into the following sections: (a) the Ozark–Ouachita Highlands: (b) the sedimentary plains; (c) the Mississippi flood-plain.

The Ozark–Ouachita Highlands consist mainly of Palaeozoic rocks which rise above the general level of the Central Lowlands of North America like an island in a sea of less-resistant and newer sediments. They are bordered on the north and south by the Missouri and Red Rivers respectively, and are slashed through by the valley of the Arkansas River. In detail, they resemble the Appalachians in rocks and structure, and, like them, bear on their western and southern flanks coalfields and oilfields. They take the form of a large dome, creased and eroded into the following sub-regions: (a) the Ouachita Uplands, reaching nearly 3000 ft, marked by parallel and folded ridges and valleys; (b) the Boston Mountains, highly dissected and rugged, but of less disturbed strata; (c) the Ozark Plateau, a peneplaned dome characterised by rejuvenated drainage; (d) the deep, broad, through valley of the River Arkansas, dividing (a) from (b) and (c). (See Fig. 81.)

West of these Interior Highlands is a portion of the unglaciated, horizontally bedded Central Lowlands of North America, corresponding roughly with the interior low plateaus east of the Mississippi in which the Lexington and Nashville basins have been carved. On either side of the Mississippi flood-plain are large portions of the Gulf Coast Plain of the United States, bordered on the north-west by the Black Prairies of Texas, on the north-east by the similar Black Belt of Alabama. The Gulf Coast Plain, like the Atlantic Plain of the continent, is floored with Cretaceous and younger sediments, mostly of a sandy nature. The two "Black Belts" are the most fertile areas, their underlying rock being limestone.

A narrowing embayment of the Gulf Plain extends northwards for 500 miles to Cairo, at the confluence of the Mississippi and Ohio, but its deposits are largely masked by a broad spread of fertile alluvium (up to 70 miles wide) laid down by the river. Bordering the existing flood-plain are bluffs which are partially covered with loess. The lower Mississippi (the portion below Cairo) makes its slow but irresistible way southwards for nearly 1400 miles to its bird's foot delta on the Gulf margin with such an imperceptible gradient as to justify its selection as the classic example of a large, senile river. Its course is marked by exaggerated and abandoned meanders, ox-bow lakes, and high levees, the latter reinforced by State and Federal authorities as a precaution against floods.

THE MISSISSIPPI FLOODS

The Upper Mississippi contributes little more than 20% of the water contained in the river at Cairo because it drains an area of cold winters which reduce the run-off, and also passes through several lakes which smooth out the flow and relieve the river of a large part of its suspended silt. The Missouri, for all its length of nearly 2500 miles, brings in even less water, most of it arriving in the fulness of summer, following the early summer rains and mountain snow-melt, but, as its name "Great Muddy" implies, it furnishes large quantities of solid matter. The Ohio contributes almost 60% of the water. Its régime is marked by a spring maximum, a summer minimum. When, as happened in 1927 and again in 1937, heavy rains in the Ohio Basin coincide with the rapid snow-melt of an early spring, the Ohio may rise with abnormal speed and join a swollen Mississippi, whose period of maximum flow above Cairo is generally in April. Under these circumstances very serious floods are likely lower down. During the last two decades more stringent methods have been adopted to reduce the extent and severity of inundation. The construction of dams on both the Missouri and its headwaters and on the Tennessee, a tributary of the Ohio, is helping to control the run-off; and the provision of "slipways," i.e. emergency flood-ways, and the straightening of the Mississippi by dredging operations proved effective until 1973, when millions of acres were again inundated, and 20,000 people made homeless.

CLIMATE NATURAL VEGETATION, AND SOILS

The Southern Interior has a temperate climate not unlike that of the Northern Interior except that both winter and summer temperatures are somewhat higher, and the growing season lasts at least 200 days. Almost everywhere July temperatures average at least 80° F, while January means vary from about 40° to 50° F, according to latitude. Cold spells occasionally sweep down from the north and may bring squalls and hailstorms and perhaps unseasonable frost, but the influx of warm, moist air masses from the Gulf is more characteristic. As in the Northern Interior, the rainfall is well distributed in the east, where it may exceed 50 in. annually, but again it declines steadily westwards to about 20 in., and becomes increasingly concentrated in spring and summer. The precipitation also decreases slightly from south to north. Over three-quarters of the whole area has a mean annual rainfall of at least 40 in. Most of the rain is frontal in type, but in summer, when depressions are less intense and less numerous, convectional rains are common. Locally, and spasmodically, rainfall amounts are supplemented by tornadoes, which are associated with very small but intense "lows," and which generally travel from south-west to north-east.

The accompanying figures for Vicksburg, in the south-central part of the region, illustrate some of the above features:

	J.	F.	M.	A.	M.	J.	Jy.	A.	S.	O.	N.	D.
Temperature (° F) .	47	51	58	65	73	79	80	80	75	65	56	49
Precipitation (in.) .	5·2	4·8	5·5	5·0	4·3	4·0	4·6	3·4	3·3	2·6	4·3	5·0

Mean Annual Temperature: 65° F; Mean Annual Range of Temperature: 33° F; Mean Annual Precipitation: 52·0 in.

The natural vegetation of the Southern Interior, like that of the Northern Interior, changes from hardwood forest in the east to tall grassland in the west. East of the Mississippi, there are still fair amounts of the original oak-chestnut forests, containing some yellow poplar, while west of the river there remains some oak–hickory woodland, with occasional ashes, elms, and elders. The Mississippi bottoms, where not cultivated, carry swamp cypress and other moisture-loving species, while in certain areas of sandy soil there are forests of southern pine, less extensively developed, however, than on the Atlantic and Gulf coastlands. The Black Belts of Alabama and Texas bear natural tall grassland.

Primary soils vary with climate and natural vegetation, and are only locally much affected by the parent rock. On the whole, they are much more leached and altogether less fertile than the soils of the Northern Interior. They commonly belong to the pedalferic group, they are usually red or yellow and they need heavy manuring for continuous cropping, but they are often deep and loamy. In the Ozarks grey-brown podsols, best left under grass, are typical, though in some valley-tracts better soils, developed on limestone, appear. The best soils in the whole region are: (a) the recent alluvia of the Mississippi, Arkansas, and Red River flood-plains; (b) the dark, limy, Prairie soils of Alabama and Texas; (c) the fine textured loess, most marked in a belt 15–40 miles wide on the eastern side of the lower Mississippi valley.

COTTON

THE SOUTHERN INTERIOR AS A COTTON-PRODUCING REGION

Cotton has long been the most valuable cash-crop of the Southern Interior, as of the south Atlantic plain and Piedmont region north of Florida, and over wide areas it remains dominant, though no longer perhaps meriting the title, "King Cotton." It has been grown in the American south since the seventeenth century, but did not become of very great consequence until the invention, in 1793, of an improved gin for separating the fibre from the seeds. The crop did not spread into Texas, at the western end of the Cotton Belt, until the following century.

Climatically, the Cotton Belt is a very favourable area for the production of large amounts of cotton. The plant is a sub-tropical one requiring at least 200 days free from killing frost. The "200 frost-free day" line marks the approximate northern limit of cotton cultivation in the United States; this line also corresponds closely with the summer (June–August) isotherm of 77° F, and the 43° F January isotherm. Very occasionally, a late spring frost to which Texas, in particular, is susceptible destroys part of the crop, which may therefore have to be resown or replaced by other seeds. Conversely, bolls which ripen late may from time to time be lost through the incidence of a killing frost in early autumn. During the growing season fairly warm nights, as well as hot days, are beneficial, but in July or August a fall in temperature may assist, rather than impede, maturation.

In the main, cotton cannot be grown successfully in an area with a mean annual rainfall of less than 20 in., except with irrigation, therefore the 20-in. isohyet marks the approximate western boundary of the Cotton Belt. But in parts of the High Plains of Texas and Oklahoma it is in fact sown in areas with an average rainfall of only 17 in. annually, though artificial means of supplying extra water are sometimes available. Here yields are commonly less than elsewhere in the Belt.

The heavy autumnal rains of most of the Gulf coast, and the occurrence of swamp-lands backed by sandy, pine-forested soils along both the Gulf and Atlantic margins of the United States, have prevented the extension of the Cotton Belt to the south-east coast of the country (see Fig. 77).

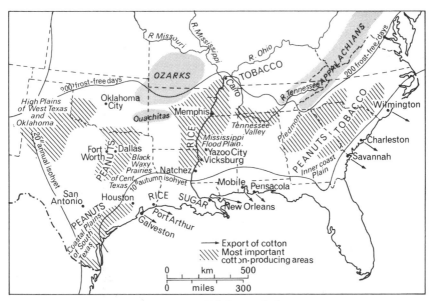

FIG. 77.—Old Cotton Belt.

The customary alternation of summer sunshine and shower within the Southern Interior makes for a good cotton crop. Too wet a spring may cause too many unwanted weeds to flourish, and lead the seed to rot; too wet an autumn may cause the bolls to be mud-splashed, and difficult to gather, and may encourage the growth of pests.

Cotton is an exhaustive crop, and quickly removes both potash and

[*Courtesy: U.S. Information Service.*]

FIG. 78.—Cotton-picking by hand in the Mississippi flood-plain. Cotton is still largely hand-picked, especially in the "Old South," where negroes are valued farm-workers.

phosphates from the soil. Consequently, the monocultural practices associated with the old plantation system, and even with the present widespread share-cropping and cash-tenancy systems (*see* p. 260) have led to much soil exhaustion and erosion within the Cotton Belt. During the early years excessive erosion was limited by the large acreages of woodland in the Belt, but the spread of cultivation has greatly reduced these, and a highly intensive rainfall, especially when falling on sloping ground, has accelerated the loss of soil, multiplied the amounts carried into the Mississippi, and contributed to farm abandonment and river floods. Fertilisers are now generally applied to the soils of the Cotton Belt, which is favourably located with regard to the phosphates of Florida and Tennessee. Potash is brought in from Searles Lake, California, nitrates from Chile. Ammonium sulphate, basic slag, fish offals, refuse from slaughter-houses, residues from cattle-cake are among the other manures used: most are made in the American South or border areas.

The labour required to produce cotton has generally been plentiful

[*Courtesy: U.S. Information Service.*

FIG. 79.—Mechanical cotton-picking. Mechanical cotton-picking is gradually replacing manual methods. Most of the new machines, like the one shown here, are operated by white men, and use suction devices.

enough and cheap enough in the United States (*see* Fig. 78). At first it was virtually all negro slave-labour imported from the West Indies or West Africa. Now it includes white labour as well, especially in the newer, more westerly cotton-growing areas, where nearly all the workers are non-coloured. The various farm operations—deep-ploughing and harrowing in winter, ridging and fertilising in early spring, sowing in March or April, weeding or "chopping" and insecticidal spraying in the growing season, picking from late August to November, ginning and baling in late autumn and early winter—all demand much non-seasonal labour. But increasingly, on the larger, more prosperous, and more progressive farms (mostly in the west), labour is being saved by mechanisation. Large amounts of cotton are now sown and picked by machine, and insecticidal spraying by aircraft is not uncommon (*see* Fig. 79).

THE WESTWARD SHIFT OF COTTON-GROWING

The "Cotton Belt" of the United States today is much more broken up than it was half a century or even a generation ago (*see* Fig. 77). Over half the total crop now comes from Texas (which normally has twice the output of Mississippi and Arkansas, two of the leading states in the older part of the Belt), Oklahoma, New Mexico, Arizona (chiefly the Salt River valley), and California (mainly the San Joaquin valley) (*see* Fig. 80).

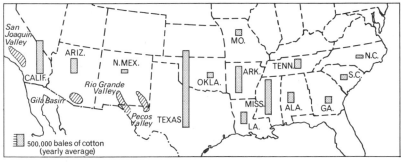

FIG. 80.—Production of cotton in the U.S.A. Columns are proportional in height to average cotton production, 1968–70. Shading represents important cotton-growing areas west of Texas.

None of these states belong to the "Old South," at one time the only important cotton-growing area in the country. Within Texas and Oklahoma, three districts, as shown in Fig. 77, stand out for their cotton-production: (1) the High Plains of north-west Texas and an adjacent area in south-west Oklahoma; (2) the coastal plain of southern Texas; (3) the Black Waxy Prairies north of (2). Farther east, four areas remain of more significance than others: (1) the Mississippi flood-plain and adjacent loess-lands, especially those parts in eastern Arkansas, western Mississippi, and Tennessee; (2) the Inner Coast Plain of the Carolinas and Georgia, where the soils are loamy rather than sandy (*see* Chapter XVI); (3) the Middle Tennessee valley in northern Alabama; (4) the Piedmont Plateau of the Carolinas and Georgia (*see* Chapter XVII).

Most U.S. cotton is of the medium-stapled Upland variety, but in the Mississippi valley, Texas, and more westerly states "Long Stapled Upland," with an average fibre length of $1\frac{1}{8}$–$1\frac{3}{8}$ in., is grown in considerable amounts. The very fine, silky Sea-island cotton, grown in the West Indies and to some extent in a few small islands off the coasts of Georgia and the Carolinas, has a staple of between $1\frac{1}{2}$ and $2\frac{1}{2}$ in., but was largely destroyed in the eastern United States by the boll weevil (*see below*).

The centre of gravity of the cotton-growing industry has shifted west-wards in recent years, because:

1. The exhaustion and erosion of soils in the "Old South," and the break-up of the plantation system east of the Mississippi, has induced more ambitious farmers to practise cotton-cultivation in the newer, richer soils of the under-occupied west.

2. The ravages of a pest known as the boll weevil, now largely curbed by spraying, have been far more serious in the damper east, where the insect breeds in natural woodland, than in the drier west and the frostier north-west, where the natural vegetation is grassland. The weevil—a small beetle which may attack and destroy the cotton-boll before it has a chance to open—first entered Texas from Mexico in 1892, advanced to the Mississippi by 1907, and to the Atlantic coast by 1920. The damage it caused, especially in the east, induced Lancashire cotton-manufacturers to look elsewhere for a source of raw cotton in the early 'twenties, and led to an expansion of cotton-growing in Africa as well as Texas.

3. The recent measures adopted by the Federal Government to sup-port the price of cotton, related as they are to the costs of production in the less-efficient east, are encouraging more western farmers to plant cotton, as their costs are lower, generally because more capital is avail-able for mechanisation and less money is required for fertilising.

COTTON PRODUCTS AND MARKETS

The cotton-boll yields two principal products: fibre, the basis of the world's cotton textile industry, and seed, crushed for oil at numerous mills within and near the Cotton Belt, and used as a cooking-fat, and also in the manufacture of margarine, soap, candles, and lubricating oil. The residue is made into oil-cake, a cattle feed and a fertiliser. The hulls of the seed have some value as a feeding-stuff and as a raw material in the paper in-dustry. Attached to the seed after ginning are a large number of very short fibres known as linters: these are used for the manufacture of wad-ding, cotton-felt and gun-cotton, celluloid and photographic films, and rayon. The stalks and roots need not be wasted: the former may be used to make feed and paper, and they also form a ready fertiliser, the latter may be burnt as fuel, or again used to fertilise the soil; the roots also have some medicinal value.

Much cotton fibre goes to mills, either in the Southern States (*see* Chapter XVII) or in New England (*see* Chapter XIV), or in Philadelphia and the Hudson–Mohawk corridor towns. A proportion, varying with the harvest and with world demand, is exported, chiefly to Japan and western Europe. Ports engaged in these shipments include Houston and Galveston (serving Texas, mainly), New Orleans (the main outlet of the Mississippi flood-plain), and Savannah (handling part of the Piedmont and Atlantic crop). Less-important distributing centres include Port Arthur, Mobile, Pensacola, Charleston, and Wilmington.

THE PRESENT ECONOMIC AND SOCIAL CHARACTER OF THE COTTON BELT

As has been mentioned above, cotton remains the chief cash-crop of the Cotton Belt as a whole, and, in fact, remains the chief crop sold off farms in the entire Union. But the nation's production has shrunk from 60% of the world's supply in 1916 to less than 40% in 1950 and to less than a quarter today. Within the Cotton Belt, less than 10% of the total area is now under cotton, a reduction of 50% in less than a generation. The adoption of more efficient methods of production, however, has not caused a very marked decline in the absolute weight of fibre which is baled each year, and the United States, despite its efforts to restrict acreages, has been building-up large cotton surpluses during the last several years.

About 30% of the population of the Cotton Belt is of negro origin. Many of these coloured people, and many "poor whites" too, have a very low income, and suffer from undernourishment, deficiency diseases, and a high mortality rate. Their homes are poorly built and ill-furnished, and often lack electricity and modern sanitation. The relationships between such people and the landowners give them little chance to improve their lot. Many are share-croppers, who receive land, seed, fertilisers, and implements from the landlord, and in return pay him up to half the value of their cash-crop; others are share-tenants, who pay a smaller proportion of their harvest, but provide their own seed, implements, etc. Often they can only afford to grow, besides cotton, a patch of maize and a plot of vegetables, mainly beans; they may possess, in addition to a working animal, only a few pigs and chickens.

The "Old South" has been described as "a miserable panorama of unpainted shacks, rain-gullied fields, straggling fences, rattle-trap Fords, dirt, poverty, disease, drudgery, and monotony." Today, this statement has become inapplicable to a number of areas within the eastern part of the Cotton Belt. Indeed, during the last twenty years or so certain fundamental and far-reaching trends have become evident which, if not entirely reversing this picture, are certainly modifying it. Only a lack of capital is retarding more widespread progress. These trends include:

1. A fluctuating but discernible reduction in cotton acreages, and a decrease in monocultural production.

2. Improved methods of producing cotton, in particular an advance in farm mechanisation, which has reduced the demand for labour, an increase in the expenditure on fertilisers, and the incorporation of cotton in rotation systems.

3. A decline in the farm tenancy system, including a marked decline in the number of share-croppers and share-tenants, and a growth in the number of owner-occupiers, brought about, in part, by a rise in the number of negroes migrating into the industrial cities of the north and of poor whites into southern factories.

4. A reduction in the number, and therefore a growth in the average size, of individual farms, which encourages the advance of mechanisation, and raises farm incomes.

5. An extension of soil conservation measures, following the example set by the Tennessee Valley Authority, e.g. the addition to the farm programme of dairy cattle, clover, and other leguminous crops, the adoption of carefully planned rotations, contour-ploughing and strip-cropping, the development of tree-fruit crops and the reafforestation of denuded hill-slopes.

6. An improvement of crop yields made possible by the above measures.

7. An increasing amount of rural electrification and an extension of piped water supplies.

8. A decrease in the rural population and a corresponding increase in the urban, now proceeding at a faster rate than in any other major part of the United States.

9. An amelioration in both health and educational standards.

As Wilbur Zelinsky wrote, referring to the "Changing South":*

"The various North–South differentials are being chipped away, unevenly to be sure, but unmistakably. The South has too long been a paradoxical land of poverty in the midst of potential plenty. . . . It will not be many years before we shall have to stop calling the South poor. . . . Both farming and industry are becoming varied, balanced, and profitable as they have never been before."

* *Focus*, Vol. II, No. 2, 1951.

OTHER ASPECTS OF THE ECONOMY

FARM DIVERSIFICATION

As in the southern part of the Atlantic Plain and the Piedmont zone, agricultural diversification is now rapidly progressing in the Southern Interior, and is destroying the reality of the Cotton Belt as a one-cash-crop region. Diversification springs from many sources, of which the following are some:

1. The losses suffered by farmers from boll-weevil infestation.
2. The competition cotton has to face from rayon, nylon, and other new fibres, which tend to reduce world prices and demand.
3. The advance of cotton-growing in areas where it can be produced more cheaply, e.g. India and Brazil.
4. The growth of population in the South, and the improvement in living standards, which are increasing the local markets for foodstuffs.
5. The realisation that it pays to diversify in order to safeguard the soil from undue erosion, and to reduce the farmers' dependence upon the price of a single crop.

Hence, the acreages under cotton have been curtailed, and even corn, the staple grain, is now less widely grown than formerly, and has been largely replaced by the heavier-yielding hybrid variety. Grain sorghums are becoming common in the drier parts of Texas and Oklahoma. In many areas a transition is being made from a cotton economy to one based on pasture and livestock, as the soil-building advantages of animal husbandry are coming to be more appreciated. Most cattle are of the beef type and incorporate a tropical Brahman strain, but a growing number of selected dairy-herds are being established despite a general lack of good feeding grasses and a hot climate which makes cattle more prone to disease. Many fodder crops are now widespread in the Southern Interior, e.g. peanuts and soybeans (which also yield oil), velvet beans, cowpeas, lespedeza, and kudzu. Cotton today is often grown in a three-year rotation with hay and grain or a nitrogenous crop such as peanuts and soybeans.

Here and there, the broiler industry and the production of eggs have made almost unbelievable progress. In the alluvial valley of the Mississippi, especially in Arkansas, with the help of well-irrigation as well as river-water, rice is advancing. Sweet potatoes—a human food as well as a cattle feedstuff—are raised on many farms, any surplus being converted into starch. The growing of vegetables and fruits is receiving more attention in some districts, though less than on the Gulf and Atlantic margins.

Agricultural diversification is not only contributing to a rise in farm standards in the South but is also helping to give the people the kind of nutritional standards which have been common for some time on the mixed farms of Texas.

MINERAL WEALTH

The Southern Interior is less important as a mineralised region than the Northern Interior. The total coal production, for example, amounts to no more than about 6 million tons a year. The chief mines are in the southern part of the Western Interior field, in southern Missouri and Oklahoma, and there are scattered deposits of lignite farther south, and small amounts of semi-anthracitic coal in the Ouachitas. The quality of coal is generally poor, and there are few important industrial markets, but the output would certainly be increased if it were not for the competition of petroleum and natural gas, which the Southern Interior produces in much greater abundance than its northern counterpart. Indeed, the great "Mid-Continent" oilfield is rivalled in the United States only by the Gulf Coast field. It occupies large areas in northern Texas and Oklahoma, and there are many wells also in New Mexico, southern Arkansas, northern Louisiana, Mississippi and Kansas. The oil-pools and natural gas supplies occur in domes of Carboniferous sandstone and occupy a similar position with respect to the Ozarks as the much less important Appalachian field with respect to the eastern mountains.

Near and within the Ozarks lie other important minerals, though the iron worked in the St Francis Mountains of the north-eastern Ozarks is in very small supply compared with the huge quantities located in the Upper Lakes region. South-east Missouri is the chief single source of lead and cobalt in the United States, while the Tri-State district of south-west Missouri–Kansas–Oklahoma is outstanding for zinc, and also produces lead. In both areas the metals are obtained by deep-mining. Silver is a relatively unimportant by-product of lead and zinc reduction. Joplin is the chief commercial centre for the Tri-State mines, and makes white lead and paint. The Ozarks also produce barite, used in the preparation of sludge to protect the bits used in oil-drilling, and also in the nation's chemical, glass, paint, and synthetic-rubber industries.

The district south-west of Little Rock (Arkansas) produces over 90% of the national output of bauxite, the main raw material of the aluminium industry. Alumina is made at Hurricane Creek, near the deposits, and there is an electrolytic refining plant at Jones Mills, to the south-west (see Fig. 81). At Rockdale, in Texas, at some remove from the ore supplies, the first alumina-smelting works in the United States to use electricity based on local lignites has been established.

MANUFACTURING

Despite the abundance of petroleum, natural gas, and coal in the Southern Interior, manufacturing industries have never employed more than a small fraction of the population. In the South as a whole it is the Piedmont and the Gulf coast which are industrially important, not the Interior. Of course, cotton-ginning, cotton-seed milling, and the preparation of foodstuffs are of some significance, and reference has been made to metal-working industries, but there are virtually no industrial towns of any magnitude except on the margins. The population of the Southern Interior has for too long concentrated on rural activities, capital investment has been lacking, and both available labour supplies and markets have been much smaller than in the North. Yet changes are coming, as they have already come in agriculture. Pulp and paper mills are active at Little Rock and other places, mainly in Arkansas; fertilisers and other chemicals are being manufactured at Memphis, Helena, Yazoo City, and other localities; and a steel industry has been established at Lone Star, in north-eastern Texas, on the basis of local iron-ore deposits. Fruit and vegetable canneries are growing more numerous, and the harnessing of such rivers as the Arkansas, White, and Ouachita in the Interior Highlands, should stimulate further developments as living-standards and the purchasing power of the people rise.

MAJOR URBAN CENTRES

MISSISSIPPI CITIES

The only significant cities in the Southern Interior stand on the Mississippi, apart from a few western cities such as Tulsa, Oklahoma City, Dallas, San Antonio and Fort Worth.

Memphis, the largest city on the Mississippi between St Louis and New Orleans, both marginal to our region, is a settlement of 600,000 people built on a bluff at the eastern edge of the flood-plain where the river can be bridged by both road and rail. It is reputed to be the largest cotton market in the United States, and ships much raw material downstream for export. It is a great furniture-manufacturing city and has a number of other industries, mostly producing consumer goods. *Vicksburg,* lower down, is a miniature Memphis, commanding a railway crossing. It occupies a similar site to Memphis, and is another river-port. *Cairo,* at the confluence of the Ohio, is remarkably small for a town located at the junction of two major rivers, but its site is liable to inundation.

Ever since the first steam-boat was launched on the Mississippi in 1811, these places, like St Louis upstream, have had water-borne traffic. But the volume of trade carried along the river reached its zenith in the 1840s, and began to decline in the late 1850s as railways spread. Water transport remains cheaper, however, than rail carriage, and though movement is slow on the winding Mississippi, many barge-fleets even now carry bulky, non-perishable commodities such as bauxite, cotton, petroleum, and also some grain (downstream) and sugar (upstream).

WESTERN CITIES

Close to the western margin of the Southern Interior are several cities which act—like Omaha and Kansas City and to a less extent Sioux Falls and Sioux City in the Northern Interior—as commercial centres, not only for the western part of the region under study but also for the drier Western Plains beyond. Such are Oklahoma City, Fort Worth, Dallas, and San Antonio, all of which are linked together by road and rail. Each is a collecting centre for cattle, grain, and cotton. All have cotton-seed crushing works, meat-packing plants, and grain mills, and all have grown phenomenally owing to the development of oil-refining and associated petro-chemical industries.

Dallas ("Big D" to its inhabitants) had a metropolitan population of 1½ million in 1970 and ranked as the fastest growing of the twenty largest cities in the U.S. It has acquired a large number of industries besides the above, *e.g.* the manufacture of agricultural, ginning, oil-field and air-space machinery, the making of harness and saddlery, the assembly of motor-cars and the tailoring of apparel. It is the headquarters of many small, independent oil companies and a marked route focus. *San Antonio*, an old, historic Spanish settlement and now a winter resort, is also noted for its clothing industry, and has grown into a modern commercial city of 850,000. Near *Fort Worth*, a nearby rival of Dallas, though with little more than half its population (*cf.* Bradford and Leeds in Yorkshire), the aircraft industry, taking advantage of western space, good ground communications, and excellent flying weather, has gained a foothold. *Oklahoma City*, a centrally placed state capital on the Canadian River (an important tributary of the Arkansas) is a very notable trading city, while *Tulsa*, on the Arkansas itself, is the great business centre of the Oklahoma petroleum industry, a city, like Fort Worth and Dallas, of oil corporations and refineries, set in the midst of the vast oil-producing area of the Mid-Continent. Close by the new port of Catoosa is developing as a result of the recent provision of a nine-foot deep waterway along the Arkansas River almost as far up as Tulsa. (Some of the dams built on this river to improve navigation are also assisting flood control and are being used to support hydro-electricity stations.)

THE OZARKS

A few references have already been made to this ancient land-mass of the Southern Interior, but since its physique and economic character are so distinctive, it calls for some separate treatment (*see* Fig. 81).

Agriculturally, the Ozarks, on the whole, form a "negative" region quite apart from the Cotton Belt, on the margin of which it lies. Its people, largely drawn from similar highland areas in Kentucky and Tennessee, are

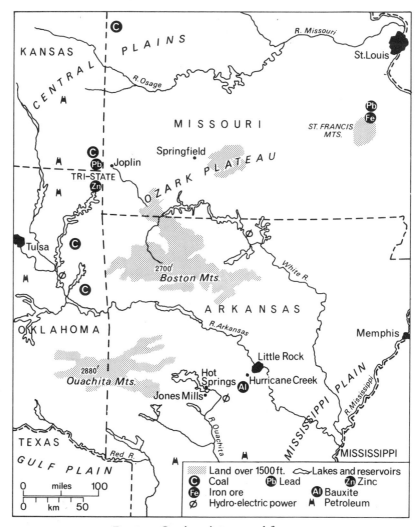

FIG. 81.—Ozark region: general features.

somewhat backward in their outlook. They grow corn in the remoter valleys, pasture cattle and sheep on uplands cleared of the native broadleaved forests, and rear pigs on forest-mast. Much of their land is badly eroded. There is a steady flow of people out of the Ozarks into the Corn Belt and other, naturally more favoured parts of the nation. One-fifth of the area remains under forest, and some timber is cut for fuel, pit-props, railway sleepers, and furniture.

Apart from the districts where metals are worked, the most productive parts of the Ozark–Ouachita massif lie in the broader valleys, notably that of the Arkansas, where large commercial crops of red apples, strawberries, peaches, and grapes, apricots, and vegetables are grown. There is also some cash-farming on the Springfield Plateau, where a little cotton is cultivated.

Despite the poverty of communications, some tourists are drawn to the Ozarks, as the region represents the most scenically varied area in the United States between the Rockies and the Appalachians. The most popular resort is Hot Springs, at the eastern end of the Ouachitas, where thermal waters are an attraction.

Chapter XXI

THE GULF COASTLANDS

THE NATURAL BACKGROUND

FOR a number of reasons, the humid, sub-tropical coastlands of the Mexican Gulf are not particularly well suited to either close human settlement or to agricultural production. The region, like the Atlantic margins south of New York, consists essentially of a low-lying plain of recent marine sediments threaded by narrow bands of river alluvium. Extending seawards from this belt of unconsolidated sands, clays, and gravels is the great and growing delta of the Mississippi, the main drainage-line.

Neither offshore bars, sand-spits, enclosed lagoons, coastal swamp, nor inland areas of hungry, sandy soils encourage continuous farming and habitation. Nor do the heavy autumnal rains, reinforced by hurricanes; the yellow, leached soils east of the Mississippi; the loblolly, long-leaf and slash-pine forests of the sandy tracts; nor the river-swamp forests with their prolific vegetation of marsh cypress, tupelo, and gum trees, delicately draped with drooping Spanish moss.

The region, however, has the advantage of warm winters and hot summers, a growing season of at least nine months and in many parts virtually twelve, a broadly adequate yearly rainfall, varying from 60 in. in the east to 20 in. close to the Mexican border, and a Prairie vegetation, with good soils, in southern Texas and western Louisiana. Even parts of the natural swamp-lands, when satisfactorily drained, as in parts of Louisiana, yield fertile "black muck" soils, eminently suited to the cultivation of rice and sugar-cane.

Regional climatic variations, affecting land utilisation, are suggested by the following figures:

Mobile	J.	F.	M.	A.	M.	J.	Jy.	A.	S.	O.	N.	D.
Temperature (° F) .	51	54	60	66	73	79	80	80	77	68	58	52
Precipitation (in.) .	4·7	5·2	6·4	4·9	4·4	5·4	7·0	7·1	5·3	3·5	3·7	4·9

Mean Annual Temperature: 67° F; Mean Annual Range of Temperature: 29° F; Mean Annual Precipitation: 62·5 in.

New Orleans	J.	F.	M.	A.	M.	J.	Jy.	A.	S.	O.	N.	D.
Temperature (° F) .	54	57	63	69	75	80	82	81	78	69	61	55
Precipitation (in.) .	4·5	4·3	4·6	4·5	4·1	5·4	6·5	5·7	4·5	3·2	3·8	4·5

Mean Annual Temperature: 68° F; Mean Annual Range of Temperature: 28° F; Mean Annual Precipitation: 55·6 in.

Galveston	J.	F.	M.	A.	M.	J.	Jy.	A.	S.	O.	N.	D.
Temperature (° F) .	54	56	63	70	76	82	84	83	80	73	63	57
Precipitation (in.) .	3·4	3·0	2·9	3·1	3·4	4·2	4·0	4·7	5·7	4·3	3·9	3·7

Mean Annual Temperature: 70° F; Mean Annual Range of Temperature: 30° F; Mean Annual Precipitation: 46·3 in.

AGRICULTURAL SUB-REGIONS

As was explained in the last chapter, the Gulf Coastlands are unsuited to cotton cultivation except in the far west, where the crop generally requires irrigation. Crops better adapted in the main to the Gulf environment are early vegetables and fruit, sugar-cane and rice. The importance of the tung-tree should also be noted. It was introduced from China in 1905, but has only produced commercial quantities of oil since 1924. The oil dries even more rapidly than linseed, and is therefore highly valued in the paint and varnish industry. Much is also used in the manufacture of linoleum. The crop is susceptible to frost, therefore trees are most successfully planted on gently sloping terrain. The tung belt extends from eastern Texas into Florida, southern Mississippi being the main producer. Other crops, besides those mentioned, include sorghums and flax, both grown in the dry west, largely for fodder but also for the oils they contain. Corn and most other crops important farther north are little grown.

Reference to Fig. 82 will show that four agricultural sub-regions may be recognised:

1. *The coastlands east of the Mississippi delta.* Agriculture is not very important here, but vegetables and fruit, grown for the northern market, do well in the warm, light, sandy soils backing the coastal swamps, and some cattle are raised, chiefly for meat, in the pinewood clearings and on the "cut-over" lands.

2. *The Louisiana coastlands near and in the Mississippi delta tract.* Here is the only significant sugar-cane-growing area in the United States outside Hawaii. The climate is marginal: just hot enough, but not free from frost every year. The yield is rather low, and diseases are inclined to be troublesome. Moreover, the industry, though well organised, is dependent upon high tariffs, a few, large modern mills, and casual labour from Mexico. Consequently, the amount raised is not great, and the conterminous United States must import 90% of her needs (chiefly from Hawaii and the West Indies). Molasses form an important by-product of the mills: they are used for fattening cattle and preparing industrial alcohol. The crushed canes are used for making fibre-board when not burnt as fuel in the mills.

3. *The humid eastern part of the Texas coastlands and the adjacent parts of Louisiana.* Here is the nation's Rice Bowl, rivalled only by the Mississippi bottoms in Arkansas. In contrast with Monsoon Asia, relatively

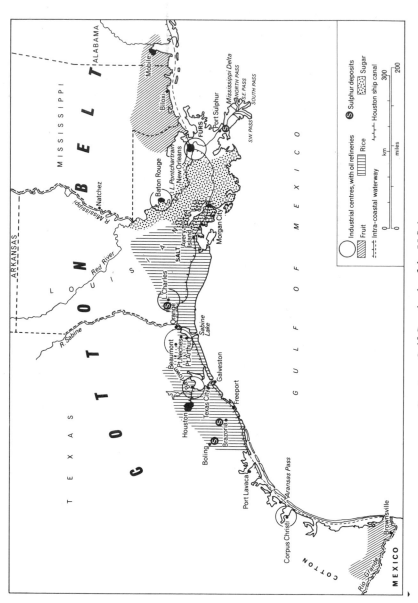

Fig. 82.—Gulf Coastlands of the U.S.A.

little labour is required in this rice-producing area owing to the large amount of machinery used, not only for ploughing but also for drilling and reaping. Even combines have a place there. The soil is deep, the sub-soil impermeable, but water pumped from shallow wells and led into the fields from rivers and bayous is needed to supplement the rain-fall. Negroes grow much of the crop. Since even their consumption of rice is very limited, it is possible after a bumper harvest to export small quantities.

4. *South-west Texas.* On the Corpus Christi Plain and in the lower Río Grande valley bordering Mexico, cotton, needing some irrigation, is cultivated in a highly mechanised way. Cattle are widely distributed, and in fact are kept in varying numbers throughout the Gulf coastlands. In the Texas section, in particular, good strains, well suited to the almost tropical environment, have been produced by crossing imported Brah-mans with the native long-horned variety. These breeds are relatively immune to tick-fever.

The lower Río Grande valley is notable as one of the principal areas in the country for the production of truck-crops, and in some respects rivals Florida and California. Many vegetables and a few fruits can be harvested even in January, so that, although the area is far from north-eastern markets, it can successfully compete with longer-established areas. The southern market is also growing, and already more grapefruit are grown than in California, though oranges are less important. Other fruits include water-melons. Among vegetables are green beans, cabbages, carrots, onions, spinach, lettuce, and tomatoes. Many of these crops are canned or frozen prior to sale. The waters of the Río Grande River have been used for many years by both Texas and Mexico to water their crops, but only recently have large, joint multi-purpose dams been built to control supplies. The Falcon Dam, near Laredo, incorporating two small hydro-electric power-plants, and the Mesilla Dam are notable.

Truck-farming is not, as we have seen, confined to Texas, although it is better developed there than elsewhere along the Gulf coast. North-west of Lake Pontchartrain in Louisiana, for example, there is an important strawberry district.

OTHER ASPECTS OF THE ECONOMY

FUR-TRAPPING AND FISHING

These two occupations engage fewer people than agriculture. It is, nevertheless, a surprising fact that, Alaska apart, Louisiana ranks as the chief fur-trapping state in the Union. The salt-marsh lands of southern Louisiana provide a home for musk-rat, in particular, but also for otter, mink, skunk, raccoon, and other animals, all of whose furs are taken in winter, largely by French-speaking trappers, and sold in New Orleans.

Fishing is a little less important than it is along other U.S. coasts, but several places, especially in Mississippi and Florida, are well known for their shellfish, including oysters, and many small fishing-ports in Texas and Louisiana are noted for their shrimps. Red snapper, mullet, menhaden, grouper, and other warm-water fish are also caught. Pensacola (Florida), Biloxi (Mississippi), Morgan City (Louisiana), and Aransas Pass (Texas) are notable fishing-ports.

MINERAL WEALTH

It is the wealth of the Gulf coastlands in petroleum and natural gas which is mainly responsible for the importance of the region in the present economy of the nation. The Gulf Coast Oilfield is one of the greatest in the world, its only rival in North America being the Mid-Continent field referred to in Chapter XX. It extends eastwards from Texas into Louisiana, and since the salt-domes which bear the deposits were first broached in 1901, thousands of wells, up to 4 miles in depth, have been dug behind the coastal marshes and lagoons, and even in the swamplands themselves. Recently, drilling has been taking place from island-platforms set up offshore, as the deposits are continued in the continental shelf. There has been some conflict between the Federal Government and the States over the rights to these offshore oil reserves, but a Supreme Court ruling in 1960 allowed the claims of Texas to her undersea resources for a distance of 9 nautical miles, at the same time limiting the claims of Louisiana to the deposits within only 3 miles of the low-water mark. The latter state thereby lost her royalties from over 1500 wells already drilled beyond the 3-mile limit.

Texas, which also has a share in the Mid-Continent field, produces over one-third of the nation's oil: 1250 million barrels in 1970, compared, for example, with 125 million for the whole of the northern interior of the U.S.A. Louisiana occupies second place as an American producer. Both states also produce more natural gas than any others in the country.

Most of the Gulf Coast petroleum is very heavy and best suited to the production of fuel oil. Much is now being used for industrial purposes along the Gulf Coast, especially in Texas, but there are large shipments by tanker to Atlantic destinations, and also a number of oil and gas pipe-lines along which the products of the wells are moved internally.

Among other important minerals produced in the Gulf Coast region are sulphur, salt, and magnesium. The United States produces 60% of the world's native sulphur (excluding that obtained from pyrites), and its supplies are drawn, for the most part, from the Boling and Brazoria districts of Texas, and from the neighbourhood of Port Sulphur in Louisiana. They are obtained from the cap-rock overlying the huge rock salt domes of the coastal region, and are normally extracted by the Frasch process, *i.e.* they are melted in the ground by pumping hot water into it, and brought to the surface by air pressure. Afterwards, the sulphur is solidified in huge vats. Salt, of course, is another important raw material drawn from the salt domes. At Avery Island hill, Louisiana, is the largest salt-mine in the world. Magnesium—the very light metal used in the manufacture of engines fitted to aircraft and motor vehicles—is extracted electrolytically from magnesium chloride obtained from sea-water at Freeport, Texas.

INDUSTRIAL DEVELOPMENT

The Gulf coastlands, especially the parts between Corpus Christi and Mobile, with concentrations at Houston, Beaumont and Port Arthur, New Orleans and Baton Rouge, are now taking their place as one of the nation's important industrial regions. Especially significant are those industries which use petroleum and natural gas as fuels and raw materials, and those which depend upon the treatment of metals, which are easily brought into this coastal region by ship. Cotton-manufacturing is as yet undeveloped despite the existence of large, nearby supplies of raw material and ready access to overseas markets.

Oil refineries, as would be expected, are numerous in both Texas and Louisiana. A very large one is located at Baton Rouge, and there are others, of varying capacities, at Lake Charles and New Orleans (Louisiana), and at Houston, Galveston, Baytown, the Sabine Lake ports of Port Arthur and Beaumont, and Corpus Christi (all in Texas). Some of these refineries are up-to-date cracking plants, where simple refining gives place to the subjection of heavy petroleum products to tremendous heat and pressure, thereby breaking them down into a greater range of by-products.

Arising from the oil-refining and cracking industries there is a vast range of chemical industries, now being steadily developed in a growing number of Gulf ports and cities. They include the raw nylon industry, established at Orange, the manufacture of synthetic rubber, *e.g.* at Port Neches, Baton Rouge, and Baytown, the motor-tyre industry, the preparation of fertilisers, insecticides, paints and detergents, solvents, industrial alcohol and explosives, and the production of plastics.

The regional sulphur and salt deposits have also contributed to the growth of the chemical industry, as sulphuric acid and common salt are among the chief raw materials used. Paper is made from sulphide pulp at Orange and in a number of mills lining the Houston Ship Canal, and sulphur is also required for the vulcanisation of rubber. Lime is produced from coastal shell deposits, and large amounts of chlorine and caustic soda are turned out. The power for most of these industries is electricity derived from natural gas.

Metal industries involve principally the use of bauxite, iron, tin, and zinc. From sources of supply near Little Rock, Arkansas, Jamaica, and the Guianas, alumina is made in large quantities at Mobile and Baton Rouge, and at various places on the Texan coast. Refineries have been established at New Orleans and Port Lavaca, while on Corpus Christi Bay a fully integrated plant has recently been established. (The new development at Rockdale, 50 miles north-east of Austin, was referred to in Chapter XX.) Most parts of the world which support aluminium refineries, e.g. Canada, Washington (United States), and Norway, depend upon very large and cheap amounts of hydro-electric power, but in the Gulf coastlands the source of power is natural gas or even lignite.

Steel mills have been erected at Houston. They depend chiefly upon the use of iron and steel scrap, with some haematite from eastern Texas. Part of the output is used in the shipyards of Beaumont, Mobile, and New Orleans. At Texas City the only tin-smelter in the United States was erected at the outbreak of the Second World War. It is fed by concentrates imported chiefly from Bolivia, and uses natural gas as a fuel. Zinc is refined at Corpus Christi.

The above industries and others, such as the canning of fruit and vegetables and fish, and the scattered working of lumber and pulp are benefiting from the relative cheapness of land, low taxation rates, and the ease with which waste products can be disposed of. There is also a growth in the purchasing power of the southern market to be taken into account. But most of the manufactured products still leave the region for other destinations in more populous parts of the United States or abroad. Of considerable value is the Intra-Coastal Waterway, linking Brownsville on the Mexican border to north-west Florida, and providing a sheltered route for the carriage of bulk commodities, e.g. petroleum and sulphur. Its construction was facilitated by the use of natural lagoons protected from the open waters of the Gulf by coastal sand-bars (see Fig. 82).

MAJOR URBAN CENTRES

All the major urban settlements in the Gulf coastlands are ports, therefore they benefit from both sea and land communications, along which marketable products and industrial materials can be moved.

New Orleans is the oldest important city, situated, as might be expected, close to the outlet of North America's greatest drainage basin, that of the Mississippi–Missouri. It was founded by the French in 1718 as an outlet for their fur-trade, but underwent a period of Spanish rule (1762–1803) before being incorporated into the United States following the Louisiana purchase. There remains much French and Spanish colonial architecture, French and Spanish traditions are maintained in restaurant food and in music, and many of the inhabitants ("Creoles") are proud of their mixed Spanish and French descent. For these reasons it is a city unlike others in North America, and attracts many discriminating tourists.

One hundred and ten miles from the open waters of the Gulf, New Orleans occupies a narrow neck of land between the widely meandering Mississippi, from which it is protected by levees, and Lake Pontchartrain, an arm of the sea which serves as an inland harbour and also acts as an escape-route for some of the Mississippi flood-water. Below the city, a dredged and deepened river channel runs 90 miles to the "Head of the Passes" before breaking up into the three chief distributaries (or "Passes") of the bird's-foot delta. This channel has recently been replaced as the main shipping route by a new 36 ft deep waterway leading east-south-east from the city to Eloi Bay and Breton Sound, and bringing the port 40 miles nearer the sea. Above New Orleans, a deep, wide channel pro-

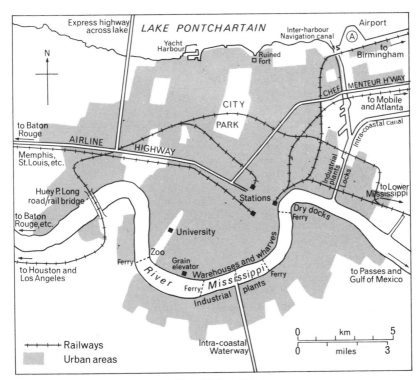

FIG. 83.—Site of New Orleans.

vides a line of movement for goods leaving and entering the port, but
much traffic is now carried by the railways which link the city with
Atlanta, Birmingham, Chicago, Texas, and California. Bridges built
across both the wide Mississippi and the extensive waters of Lake Pont-
chartain reduce the congestion on the roads and railways entering the city
from east and west (see Fig. 83).

Until the present century the only large city on the Gulf coast, New
Orleans remains the chief foreign port of the Southern States. Its exports

[Courtesy: U.S. Information Service.

Fig. 84.—Houston Ship Canal. The turning-basin, wharves, warehouses and oil
storage facilities should be noted. Houston is on the right.

include cotton, grain and flour, lumber, refined petroleum, tobacco, farm
machinery, and vehicles, drawn from a very extensive hinterland. Among
imports, mainly originating in the West Indies and Latin America, and
including many products which reach it via the Panamá Canal, are crude
petroleum, sugar, coffee, sisal, nitrates, bananas, bauxite, and jute. The
city has industrial plants for the refining of raw sugar and petroleum, the
milling of rice and cotton-seeds, and the manufacture of fertilisers and
furniture. There are also shipyards. The population in 1970 numbered
a million, including those in the metropolitan area.

Baton Rouge, farther up the Mississippi, is a great oil-port and oil-refining centre which also imports bauxite, and manufactures alumina. It is accessible to ocean tankers, and ships much refined oil up-river. Some of this material may be taken as far as Minneapolis, Pittsburgh, Knoxville, and Chicago by barge.

Mobile is another port, the chief one in Alabama, with the best natural harbour on the entire Gulf coast. It serves as an outlet for the state's cotton-growing and lumbering industries and is accessible by water, rail, and road to the Central Alabama coalfields. It has a number of important industries: shipbuilding, the manufacture of cement (using lime derived from sea-shells), alumina (from imported bauxite), pulp and paper (from southern pines and hardwoods.)

Pensacola, at the end of the Floridan panhandle, deals in lumber, naval stores, cotton, and phosphates. It manufactures fertilisers and serves the country also as an air base, fishing port, and winter resort.

Galveston and *Houston*, are the two great ports of Texas, linked together by a Ship Canal, 34 ft deep and 58 miles long (*see* Fig. 84). Galveston has an almost wholly artificial harbour built on the inner sheltered side of a reinforced offshore sandbar; its sea-wall affords some protection from an occasional rampaging hurricane, though the city was severely damaged in 1961. It imports a number of bulky commodities, notably petroleum, sulphur, tin, and sisal, and exports, chiefly by coastal ship, cotton, petroleum, wheat, and sulphur. Houston, a city which has recently outstripped New Orleans in population and now houses 2 million people, is joined to Galveston, its outport, by the Houston Ship Canal, along which, in the last 20 years, many large oil refineries, chemical plants, and cement works, as well as the city's manganese and steel plant, have been erected. Other factories, *e.g.* meat-packing, engineering, and cotton-seed milling plants, line Houston's five trunk railways. As a port, Houston handles in some years more tonnage than any other city in the country except New York, and although the bulk of its trade is still coastwise and dominated by oil and petroleum products, it has recently been taking over from New Orleans some of the latter's imports of coffee, jute, bananas, and newsprint. It has long exported cotton and grain from the Texan prairies. It gains added importance as the headquarters of both major oil corporations and the U.S. air-space research programme.

Chapter XXII

THE WESTERN PLAINS

PHYSICAL ASPECTS

BOUNDARIES

No consensus of opinion exists on the extent of the Western or Great Plains of the United States. The western boundary, marching with the outer bulwarks of the Rocky Mountains, is reasonably clear, and fairly obvious on the ground. But the eastern frontier is more blurred: it is much more of a transitional zone between the steadily rising ground of this region and the lower levels of the crop belts examined in Chapters XIX–XXI. Physically, there are only partial breaks in the landscape, produced, for example, by the Cretaceous escarpment of the Missouri Coteau in the north, and other, less-marked *cuestas* farther south. Climatically, the region is very much drier than the land to the east, but it is questionable whether the 20-in. or 15-in. isohyet would form the better boundary. Pedalogically and vegetationally, it is also possible to distinguish the Western from the Interior Plains, for the former are characterised by brown soils in which the alkaline layer approaches to within at least 2 ft of the surface and by short-grass Prairie, while the latter carry darker soils, with a deeper alkaline layer and a surface cover of tall-grass Prairie. Agriculturally, there is less to differentiate the two plains regions, for while the west is, generally speaking, better suited to grazing, the east to cultivation, the economic boundary is one which fluctuates with the year's actual rainfall and with the price of grain.

This eastern frontier has been called a "dead line" or a "distress line," without any precise attempt at definition, on the grounds that cultivated plants are more likely to die than to live in the west, while unsuccessful attempts at continuous cultivation have resulted in nothing better than farm abandonment and widespread indebtedness. A refuge has sometimes been found by defining the Great Plains as those parts of the central plains of the United States which lie west of the 100 degrees W. longitude line, but some writers have substituted the 98th meridian. Certainly the frontier cannot be equated with any administrative boundary, for—whichever criterion is adopted, and each produces a different result—the boundary, even if zonal and not linear, passes roughly through the middle of most of the states concerned (*see* Fig. 85).

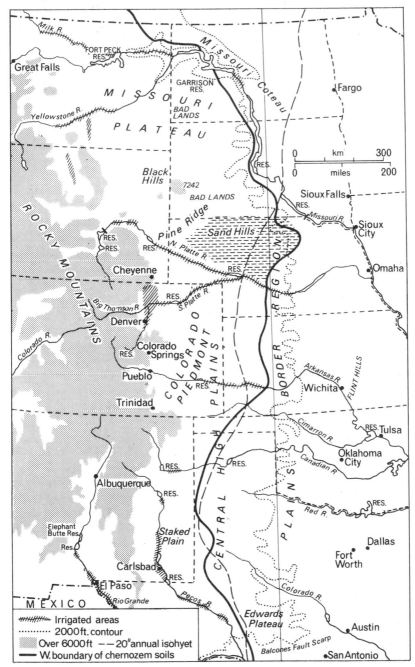

FIG. 85.—Western Plains of the U.S.A.

GENERAL PHYSICAL CHARACTER

However delimited, the Western Plains average about 400 miles in breadth, and on the whole form an area of plateau, rather than plain country, like the Great Plains of Canada, of which they are a continuation. From a height of about 2000 ft on their eastern side, they rise unevenly westwards to the 5000–6000-ft high foothills of the Rocky Mountains. Their rocks derive mainly from the denudation of the Rockies; for the most part, they dip very gently eastwards in slightly synclinal fashion, but present sharply upturned edges in the west. In many places they are overlain by superficial deposits, consisting of unconsolidated sands, gravels and muds of residual origin, with morainic deposits in the northern and eastern parts of the Missouri Plateau, i.e. in the area north and east of the Missouri River. In the "Badlands" of South Dakota, rising from the Missouri Plateau, flat beds of soft sandstone and clay have been gullied by rain and wind into an intricate mass of steep-sided, fantastically etched *mesas*, often preserved by their gravelly caps, while in the Sand Hills of Nebraska, south of the Pine Ridge escarpment, which marks the southern margin of the Missouri Plateau, there are broad expanses of drifted sands covered with tall-grass vegetation.

South of the Nebraskan Pine Ridge, three physical divisions, each trending north–south, may be recognised:

1. The Plains Border Region in the east, bordered on the west by a low escarpment often called the "Break of Plains."

2. The Central High Plains, of higher average elevation, enclosing in northern Texas and New Mexico, the level, unaccidented Staked Plains (Llano Estacado), with their numerous sink-holes, and in the south of Texas, the Edwards Plateau, resting on resistant Cretaceous limestones and presenting the high edge of the Balcones fault scarp to the Gulf Plain.

3. A Piedmont zone, best developed in Colorado, of markedly eroded land-forms, including *mesas*.

Across the Great Plains meander numerous tributaries of the Missouri and Mississippi, usually in trenches carved deeply below the general land surface. The Missouri itself traverses the region, and is joined by the Milk, Yellowstone, North and South Platte, and other rivers. Striking for the Mississippi are the Arkansas, Cimarron, Canadian, and Red Rivers. Farther south, the Texan Colorado and other watercourses make their way independently to the Gulf of Mexico, while the Pecos, draining a large part of the Piedmont zone, flows into the Río Grande on the Mexican border.

The greatest elevations of the Western Plains are to be found in the South Dakota–Wyoming frontier country, where a great forested dome of granite and schist, known as the Black Hills, thrusts its way skywards to heights of more than 7000 ft.

CLIMATE AND VEGETATION

The Western Plains, reaching as they do from Canada to Mexico, have many climates, differing mainly in temperature conditions, but throughout, seasonal temperature ranges are extreme, and the low precipitation shows a distinct spring or summer maximum.

In the most northerly areas, January temperatures average only 0° F, but the thermometer rises to nearly 70° F in July. On occasion, winter temperatures may fall to −50° F, while in summer 100° F may be experienced. Southwards, the temperatures rise to January norms of 50° F, July norms of almost 90° F, and the growing season lengthens from rather more than 100 days on the Canadian frontier to more than 200 days on the Mexican border.

Precipitation generally declines northwards on the same meridian, but since evaporation rates also fall, the agricultural value of the rainfall does not diminish. Unfortunately the rainfall is not only marginal from the farmer's point of view but it is also extremely fickle, and runs of dry years often bring serious economic consequences. Most of the precipitation is brought about by the convergence of warm, moist Gulf air (moving more often to the north-east than to the north-west) and colder, drier Polar continental air, but the summer rainfall is augmented by convectional downpours.

As in Alberta, the periodic arrival of a warm *chinook* wind in the northern plains helps to mitigate the severity of the long winters, and may be valuable in hastening snow-melt in spring, so allowing stock to be put outside earlier than might be expected.

The following climatic data for Denver (the "Mile High City" at 5300 ft), though not truly representative, may prove helpful:

	J.	F.	M.	A.	M.	J.	Jy.	A.	S.	O.	N.	D.
Temperature (° F) .	30	32	39	47	57	67	72	71	62	51	39	32
Precipitation (in.) .	0·4	0·5	1·0	2·1	2·4	1·4	1·8	1·4	1·0	1·0	0·6	0·7

Mean Annual Temperature: 50° F; Mean Annual Range of Temperature: 42° F; Mean Annual Precipitation: 14·3 in.

References have already been made to the natural vegetation of the Western Plains as a whole (short-grass Prairie) and to that of the Nebraskan Sand Hills (tall-grass) and Black Hills (forest) in particular. Here it is only necessary to add that in the driest parts (normally those farthest west) grass grows merely in sporadic tufts, *i.e.* in the form of bunch-grass, and that the river valleys generally carry deciduous forest. As the valleys are generally deeply sunk, the early pioneers who followed them into the Western Highlands gained an erroneous impression of the Great Plains as an area well-wooded and humid, an impression also received by modern railway travellers.

THE ECONOMY

THE HISTORY OF SETTLEMENT

In relation to the western spread of population in North America, the semi-arid, grassy Western Plains are revealed as part of the broad zone of transit between the desirable, wooded east and the moist, fertile Pacific valleys and coastlands. The absence of trees from all but the valleyways of this region denied most of the migrants a material to which they had been accustomed for building houses, fencing land, and making fuel, while the restricted supplies of surface water deterred stockmen, and the scanty rainfall discouraged cultivators. The bison-hunting Plains Indians also presented a threat to agricultural occupance, and many were the clashes between "Cowboys" and "Indians" in the nineteenth century. Texas became a cattle-ranching area early on (in the 1830s), and gradually the range extended northwards, but not until after 1868, when the first through railway was made and most of the native buffalo were slaughtered, did much settlement take place in the north. After the Indians had finally been driven westwards or destroyed by whites armed with Colt revolvers, new problems arose owing to the conflict between cattlemen and grain-farmers. The latter tended to advance towards the Rocky Mountain foothills in wet years and to retire in dry, the ranchers all the time competing with them for ground, and sometimes harrying them.

Today, the more arid western parts are generally left to the stockmen, the more humid eastern parts to the spring-wheat farmer in the north, the winter-wheat cultivator in the centre, and the cotton-grower in the south. Between these groups there remains a "no man's land," occasionally tilled, often carrying only cattle and sheep.

Most of the Western Plains are now divided into fields marked off by barbed-wire fences. Wind-pumps and oil-pumps capable of drawing water from deep wells are a common sight. The original stock of Longhorn cattle, descended from animals first taken into Mexico by the Spaniards, has been improved, and more drought-resistant varieties of wheat and other crops have been brought in. Law and order have also entered the Western Plains. The "Western" tradition remains, but no longer can one see, except on film, the cattle-rustler, the Indian with his bow and arrow, the sheriff with his brace of revolvers. The "Wild West" has departed from North America, and lives on only in print and celluloid.

STOCK-REARING

In such a "short-grass Prairie" region as the Western Plains, with its low and highly variable rainfall, grazing is a more satisfactory and secure form of land occupance than cultivation. Extensive beef-cattle ranching is, in fact, the chief and most widespread occupation. Land-holdings are usually large, and may run up to 10,000 acres, especially in areas of poor pasture. The Whiteface breed is dominant in many parts: a cross between the English Hereford (also found in large numbers, especially in the cooler north) and the native Longhorn. In the south many native cattle are now being crossed with Indian Brahman animals to produce types more suited to a hot environment and less prone to disease than pure-bred European stock.

Texas normally carries more cattle than any other state in the Union, and only Iowa outranks Nebraska and Kansas. Indeed, some of the best cattle-country in the west is to be found in the Sand Hills of Nebraska and in the long, bluestem pastures of the Flint Hills of Kansas.

In the south, notably in Texas, it may be warm enough for cattle to remain outdoors all the year, but in the north it is generally necessary to grow hay for winter feeding. Some cattle are sent eastwards into the Corn Belt for fattening, but there is a growing tendency to finish them in the rearing states, where natural grass feed is supplemented by alfalfa, sorghums, corn, cotton-seed cake, sugar-beet pulp and tops, if and where available.

Sheep bring in less money than cattle, but in Kansas and Nebraska, in particular, there is a fairly large output of lambs, and Texas and Montana have a useful wool-clip. Usually, however, sheep are relegated to the driest and roughest pastures, e.g. those in the Rocky Mountain foothills, whence, to avoid the heat and to escape from the sun-scorched grass of the Plains, they may be taken in summer to the alpine pastures in the mountains themselves (a form of transhumance). Like cattle, they require winter shedding in the north.

Goats, especially the Angora variety, which yield mohair, are a speciality of the Edwards Plateau, where they are grazed alongside sheep, largely on sub-tropical chaparral, in which cedar bushes, scrub oak, prickly pear and yucca thrive.

Horses are far less numerous than they were before the ranges were enclosed, but are still required by cowboys for rounding-up and driving herds. They are also common at "dude ranches" where tourists play at being horsemen.

Cattle, sheep, and goats are not always tended in complete isolation. In the better-watered east at least the first two may well be combined with the growing of wheat, alfalfa, and sorghums, and in irrigated districts, *e.g.* near Denver, dairying may be practised. Whatever systems are used, the stockman is often faced with inclement weather. Droughts, winter blizzards, which may bring heavy snowfalls, violent summer hailstorms and torrential rainstorms, and tornadoes (or "twisters") may all cause losses.

CULTIVATION

Dominant along the eastern margins of the Western Plains, cultivation in years of good rainfall and high crop prices may encroach on the western grazing lands. The spring and summer rainfall maxima assist the grain

[*Courtesy: U.S. Dept. of Agriculture.*

FIG. 86.—Drought-stricken area in Texas. Cattle are shown grazing on grain-sorghum stubble, following a poor crop.

and cotton farmer, and the soils, though they become lighter in the west as their organic content declines, all have a good structure and a high mineral content. Drought is the great enemy, and may well bring disaster in its train.

To overcome the problem of a low mean annual rainfall, dry-farming has been practised since the 1880s. It involves deep-ploughing followed by the production (by repeated harrowing) of a pulverised surface layer of soil which acts as a mulch and thereby reduces evaporation. Although a fair crop of wheat may well be obtained in this way at least one year in two or three, the practice leads to excessive wind erosion during dry periods and has resulted in the removal from cultivation of considerable areas of the Western Plains.

Wheat, whether dry-farmed or not, is the principal grain-crop of the Great Plains. It is spring-sown in the north (the Dakotas and Montana), winter-sown farther south. One can, in fact, regard the Western Plains wheat lands as low-yielding extensions of the Spring Wheat and Winter Wheat Regions of the Agricultural Interior. In parts of southern Nebraska, Kansas, western Oklahoma, eastern Colorado, and Texas grain sorghums are now being widely grown, especially as a cattle-feed, while —as we saw in Chapter XX—cotton-growing activities are expanding on the High Plains of Texas and Oklahoma. Large cotton-farms are now encroaching upon the Staked Plains and Edwards Plateau. In such areas deep-well irrigation is often resorted to in order to eke out the meagre rainfall.

IRRIGATION

At least 90% of the western half of the United States requires artificial watering for intensive agricultural productivity. Within this area lie the Western Plains, where, as we have seen, the rainfall is agriculturally marginal. Irrigation facilities are not yet widely available, but they are spreading, notably on riparian land. Unfortunately, large works are often needed for complete success, since so many of the river valleys are deeply trenched, but well-irrigation may be employed profitably, as in Nebraska, for example, where over half a million acres are thus watered.

Some years ago a Missouri Valley Authority was set up, but, because of the great size of the area covered by it, and the administrative problems involved, it has up to now been less effective in its operations than the Tennessee Valley Authority (*see* Chapter XVII). To assist navigation and flood control, and to provide hydro-electric power as well as water for irrigation, the large Fort Peck Dam—the world's largest earth-filled dam— has been completed, and other extensive reservoirs, *e.g.* the Garrison, have been constructed lower down. Smaller schemes have been initiated on various Missouri tributaries, *e.g.* the Milk, Yellowstone, North and South Platte, and altogether over 100 projects have been put forward for the proper control of the great river and its affluents, and for the economic well-being of its basin. Other schemes, in part accomplished, relate to Mississippi tributaries, *e.g.* the Arkansas and Canadian, and dams have already been made on the River Pecos. One of the most interesting undertakings, and forming part of the work of the Missouri Valley Authority, is the Colorado–Big Thompson project, which has provided water for parts of the Colorado Great Plains north of Denver by diverting the Big

Thompson eastwards through a 13-mile tunnel under the Rockies (Fig. 85).

Crops at present irrigated include corn and cotton (where it is warm enough), wheat, sugar-beet and potatoes (both produced in large quantities in Colorado), alfalfa (a most useful hay crop), and miscellaneous fruits and vegetables.

THE "DUST BOWL"

The notorious "Dust Bowl," which suffered from the worst ravages of wind erosion in the drought years of the 1930s, in particular the period 1934–36, covers parts of western Kansas and also, but to a less extent, western Nebraska, north-west Oklahoma, and the Texan panhandle. It resulted largely from the spread of wheat cultivators into the semi-arid, western parts of the Great Plains after the First World War, when grain was fetching high prices and the region under study appeared to be moist enough to produce good crops. Unhappily the years of good rain were succeeded by several years of sub-normal precipitation, and it became apparent not only that monocultural methods of grain-cultivation were deleterious to the soil but also that the natural grassland was overstocked with cattle. The land lost its green cover and then its precious cover of top-soil, which the winds blew into the rivers, overcharging them with silt. Some of the dust was even carried as far as the Atlantic coast, where city skies were darkened by the migrating farms of Kansas.

Though much soil has gone for ever, and many landholdings have been abandoned, soil conservation measures have restored at least parts of the badly eroded land, and when a further run of dry years hit the Western Plains in the 'fifties, its effects were far less serious than they were twenty years earlier.

The following are among the practices adopted by Plains farmers for checking undue soil erosion and for maintaining the land in good heart:

1. The replacement of row-crops like wheat with grass.

2. The partial abandonment of dry-farming techniques, and the adoption of trash-farming methods, as in the Spring Wheat Belt.

3. The adoption of contour-ploughing and strip-cropping practices; the latter involving an alternation of plants holding moisture and binding the soil (e.g. grass) and crops with less compact root systems (e.g. grain).

4. The development and use of more drought-resistant wheat strains, and the substitution of rotations (e.g. wheat with sorghums and grass) for fallowing.

5. The planting of improved pasture-grasses and the raising of special feed-crops by irrigation.

6. The combination of arable and animal-farming, and the spread of mixed farming.

7. The planting of trees round the croplands as windbreaks to check long-distance soil movement and also to protect the ground in the neighbourhood against frost-heaving by ensuring that snow lies more evenly on the fields.

MINERAL WEALTH

Though the Mid-Continent Oilfield extends westwards into the Great Plains, its centre of gravity lies farther east, as we saw in Chapter XX. Considerable quantities of petroleum are raised outside the Mid-Continent field, especially in Wyoming, but also in Colorado, northern Montana, and Nebraska. Natural gas is also produced in the first three of these states. All these states have small refineries where gasoline and other oil products are made available for local use, but only in Texas is there a close mesh of pipelines. Low-grade coals and near-surface lignites are of wide distribution, but owing to competition from petroleum and natural gas, they are little worked, except in the Rocky Mountain foothill zone of Colorado.

Certain non-metallic minerals of value to the chemical industry are worked in the Western Plains. They include gypsum, of which there are extensive reserves in Texas, and potash. The latter—very notable for the part it plays in the manufacture of potassic fertilisers—is worked at Carlsbad, New Mexico, in greater amounts than anywhere else in the world except Saskatchewan. (Carlsbad is also the site of the tremendous Caverns, containing several miles of passageways cut by underground rivers, as well as the largest room in the world.)

One particular metal-mining district calls for comment. This is the Black Hills, a source of gold, silver, and beryllium, the latter mostly used, allied with copper, in the manufacture of springs for electrical devices, as the combined metal has great tensile strength and durability. Gold has long been the most valuable mineral of this area, the well-known Homestake mine being the largest single source of the metal in the United States.

POPULATION DENSITY AND DISTRIBUTION

As we have seen, the Western Plains do not present the Americans with their finest living-space. Belonging more to the west than the east, they are somewhat removed from the mainstream of the nation's life. They have a problematical climate which hinders the development of intensive farming, and their mineral endowment has proved insufficient to stimulate industrial activity.

The average population density is only about five persons per square mile. Numbers thin out markedly west of the Crop Belts studied in Chapters XIX–XXI. There are few urban settlements of any great size, and much of the region's trade is controlled by cities east of the region itself, e.g. Fargo, Sioux Falls, Sioux City, Omaha, Kansas City, Wichita, Oklahoma City, Fort Worth, Dallas, Austin, San Antonio, all collecting centres for cattle, most of which also possess grain-mills and, in the south, cotton interests.

At the foot of the Rockies there is a line of cities, too, which, like the above, are linked together by a north–south railway. They are gateways to the west, and command gaps through the Rocky Mountains leading to the Pacific coast. The largest, *Denver* (metropolitan population $1\frac{1}{4}$ million in 1970) is an old gold- and silver-mining centre with meat-packing industries. It is situated in the best-developed irrigation district in the Western Plains, where the South Platte River leaves the Rocky Mountain front. It makes machinery for both mining and sugar-refining activities and serves Rocky Mountain miners as well as Plains farmers. It is of some attraction to tourists, but more notable as a recreational centre is *Colorado Springs*, farther south. *Pueblo* is a foothill town of a different character: a busy metal-smelting centre with glass works and the largest iron and steel plant in the west. The coking coals of Trinidad, near at hand, and the ore deposits of Colorado, Wyoming, and Utah, though limited in quantity, have made it possible for the steel industry to operate successfully. *Great Falls* (Montana) and *Cheyenne* (Wyoming) are two other foothill cities, trading communities and mountain gateways of rather less industrial significance, though the former has a copper refinery.

Chapter XXIII

THE ROCKY MOUNTAINS

STRUCTURE AND RELIEF

The Rocky Mountains of the United States are a structural continuation of those of Canada. They divide the Great Plains from the intermontane plateaus of the Western Cordillera, as in Canada, but south of the 49th parallel they are broader (almost 200 miles across) and higher (with summits exceeding 14,000 ft), they enclose larger basins and are geologically more complex. They contrast even more with the Appalachians than with the Canadian Rockies: they are more than twice as high, their landforms are much less rounded, and they are of far more recent origin.

The U.S. Rocky Mountains were folded and faulted from the east towards the end of the Mesozoic era, when the "Laramide Revolution," a precursor of the alpine earth movements which built up most of the world's young fold mountains, took place. There was a further period of orogeny during Tertiary times. These repeated mountain-building forces tore open the stratified rocks in many parts of the present mountain region, and—assisted by subsequent denudation, which included Pleistocene glaciation—laid bare the underlying crystalline rocks dating from Pre-Cambrian times, *e.g.* in the Uinta, Big Horn, and Colorado Front Ranges, where ancient granites and schists are flanked today by sedimentaries. Volcanic activity and igneous intrusion have further complicated the structural pattern, and have also contributed to the concentration and exposure of economically valuable minerals.

Physically, the U.S. Rocky Mountains may be most satisfactorily divided into two areas: (1) the Northern and Central Rockies, mostly in Montana, Idaho and northern Wyoming; (2) the Southern Rockies, dominant in Colorado (*see* Fig. 87).

The ranges, basins, and valleys of the Northern and Central Rockies trend mainly from north-west to south-east. Structurally, the focal area may be regarded as the Yellowstone National Park, whence various ranges run northwards, leading in the east to the overthrust Lewis Range, while others run southwards. In Montana, especially, the mountains show clear signs of recent heavy glaciation: horned peaks, U-shaped valleys containing shrunken glaciers, hanging valleys, cirques, etc. Dissecting the area today are numerous swiftly flowing rivers, including some

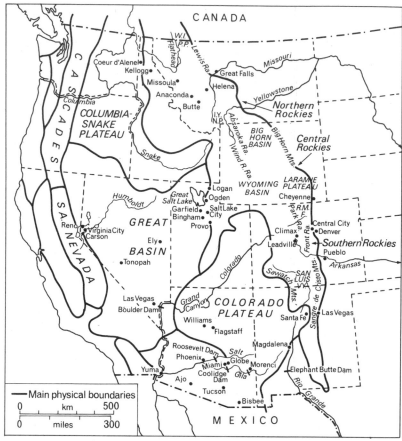

FIG. 87.—Rocky Mountains and Interior Plateaus and Basins of western U.S.A.
W.I.P.P. = Waterton–International Peace Park.
Y.N.P. = Yellowstone National Park.
R.M.P. = Rocky Mountain National Park.

of the headwaters of both the Columbia and the Missouri, *e.g.* the Flathead, which occupies the southern part of Canada's Rocky Mountain
Trench. Eastwards, beyond the main ranges, in the latitude of Helena,
are outliers known as the Big Belt and Little Belt Mountains, while in the
west, chiefly in Idaho, there is a great mass of tangled mountain country
guarding narrow valleys draining to the River Snake.

The Central Rockies, in Wyoming, are notable for the two large basins
they enclose: (1) the Big Horn Basin, bordered by the Big Horn Mountains on the east, the Wind River Range on the south-west, and the
Absaroka Range on the north-west; (2) the Wyoming Basin, hemmed in

on the south by the Uintas and on the west by a northerly projection of Utah's Wasatch Mountains. This basin, which leads eastwards to the Laramie Plateau, a part of the Western Plains, and southwards to the Colorado Plateau, divides the Central Rockies from the Southern Rockies.

The latter consist essentially of a double line of north–south ranges separated by high valley basins. On the east is the Colorado Front Range and its southern extension the Sangre de Cristo Mountains, on the west the Park Range, succeeded southwards by the more westerly Sawatch and San Juan Mountains. The enclosing basins are known as "Parks": North, Middle, and South. The latter gives way to the San Luis valley, traversed by the headstreams of the Río Grande. In Colorado, over 30 mountain summits top 14,000 ft. They include Mt Elbert, Long's Peak, and Pike's Peak (*see* Frontispiece).

Passing into New Mexico, the Rocky Mountains lose height. They are represented by what may be called the Trans-Pecos Highlands, which enclose most of the longitudinal valley of the upper Río Grande, descending to the Mexican border at El Paso.

THE ECONOMY

HUMAN GEOGRAPHY

Settlements are few and far between in the Rocky Mountains, but the region presents many features of interest and wonder to a transient population of tourists, and ever since "prairie schooners" moved into the area from the east in 1859, bravely displaying their banners, "Pike's Peak or Bust," many places have attracted the attention of miners and prospectors. However, the great height of the mountains, the frequency of steep slopes, and the engineering problems attending the provision of communications, have deterred long-term sedentary colonists. Summer pasturage is available in many parts, and the mountain forests bear useful timber, but cultivated ground is normally restricted to small, often high valleys through which railways and highways have been pressed, *e.g.* the upper valleys of the Flathead and the North and South Platte Rivers, the Río Grande valley, and parts of the Big Horn Basin.

Indicative of the low population density of the Rocky Mountains as a whole, and the scattered nature of its resources, is the lack of any major cities. *Butte*, the commercial hub of the Montana mining region and a minor food-processing centre, is the largest settlement, but has a population of well below 50,000. *Helena*, a significant railway town on the North Pacific Railway, is located in one of Montana's irrigated areas, while *Santa Fé* and *Las Vegas* are well-known tourist centres in New Mexico. The main trading places serving the Rocky Mountains actually lie beyond them, the two most notable being Denver (*see* p. 288) and Salt Lake City (*see* p. 309).

MINING

Fortune-hunters and miners are the only people who have ever been induced to seek the Rocky Mountains in large numbers. The first and greatest influx came in 1859 and 1860, when, ten years after the "rush" to California, gold was discovered in the creeks and gulches of the Colorado Front Range. Many of the adventurers and their hangers-on, however, disappointed in their efforts to "get rich quick," soon withdrew, as the region offered so little apart from mineral wealth. Today, individual prospectors have been almost entirely ousted by large mining corporations, many of which have interests in other parts of the world.

For the past hundred years, mining and metal-smelting have been the economic mainstay of the Rocky Mountains. But since mining is an extractive industry, communities dependent upon it are very unstable, and the region is liberally sprinkled with "ghost towns" and abandoned mine-workings. Central City, west of Denver, for example, had its heyday in the 'sixties and 'seventies, then its prosperity ebbed. Having lost its *raison d'être* with the closure of the surrounding mine-workings, it slowly fell into ruin and decay, and survives today only because it caters for a handful of summer visitors.

Many non-ferrous metals, *e.g.* gold, silver, copper, lead, and zinc, have been worked in the Rocky Mountains at various times. To them may be added such ferro-alloys as molybdenum, vanadium, tungsten, chromium, and manganese. Power-producing minerals, including petroleum, coal, oil-shales, and uranium, exist, mostly in scattered basins, and recently phosphates have been extensively mined in Idaho, western Wyoming, and western Montana, as a source of fertilisers. Supporting the mines are concentrators, smelteries, and a few refineries, largely dependent upon the provision of hydro-electric power. Most of the refineries, however, *e.g.* those in New Jersey, are very distant from the mines.

Colorado no longer possesses its abundant mine-workings of the nineteenth century, but a few localities have maintained their importance for a long time, and new ones have entered the lists during the present century. Leadville, once a leading gold- and silver-mining centre, and a larger town than it is today, is noted for its zinc; its neighbourhood still produces small amounts of gold and silver, and also lead and copper, and fractional quantities of iron, manganese, and bismuth. To the north, at 11,000 ft, is the great Climax mine, the world's principal source of molybdenum; this metal, when alloyed with steel, is used in the manufacture of certain machine-tools, and also in the motor-car and aircraft industries.

Some tungsten is obtained as a by-product of the recovery of molybdenum. Vanadium, a metal with similar properties and uses, and uranium are also produced in Colorado. The chief smelters are at Leadville, Denver, and Pueblo.

Butte is the heart of the Montana mining area, but the principal smelter (one of the world's largest) is located at Anaconda, 20 miles farther west. Copper has been worked in this district since 1880. The ore, which occurs in veins in the local granite rocks, is associated with gold, silver, lead, and zinc, which are separated out at the Anaconda smelter. The copper itself is concentrated to a 95% pure form in Anaconda, and is mostly refined at Great Falls, Montana, where hydro-electric power is available. Other Montana products include manganese, chromium, cobalt, and sulphuric acid.

The chief mines in Idaho are on the western margin of the Northern Rockies at Cœur d'Alène, which produces a quarter of the United States' lead (less, however, than south-east Missouri), and 90% of Idaho's silver and zinc. A little gold is obtained as a by-product of the smelting of these ores, which is undertaken at Kellogg, near Cœur d'Alène.

New Mexico and Wyoming lag behind the other three Rocky Mountain states as metal producers, but the former works zinc at Magdalena and elsewhere and also uranium. Both states have large reserves of petroleum and natural gas. The latter, chiefly in its Big Horn and Wyoming Basins, produces more petroleum than any other Rocky Mountain state. Colorado is another important source of this mineral, and Montana's production is growing. The total output is analogous to that of Canada, but much of it comes from the Great Plains portions of the states concerned. Coal, used largely in regional smelters, is worked in a number of intermont basins in Montana, Wyoming, and Colorado. It varies in quality from lignite to anthracite, but suffers from the competition of petroleum and natural gas. In western Wyoming, extending into Utah and Colorado, are the vast oil shales of the Green River formation, one of the greatest oil reserves in the world. Like the Athabaskan tar-sands in Alberta (p. 123), this source of oil is mainly an insurance for the future because the present cost of obtaining oil from it is much dearer than the cost of obtaining it from oil-wells.

FORESTRY

Large areas in the Rocky Mountains are sufficiently rainy and warm to carry a forest cover. In Montana forests of lodgepole pine, larch, and other conifers range from about 5000 to 10,000 ft, in Wyoming and Colorado sugar-pine, yellow pine, and cedar are common above about 6000 ft. with fir and spruce higher up, while at comparatively low levels in the drier New Mexico there is much juniper and sweet-smelling piñon woodland. Most of the Rocky Mountain forests are in the possession of the Federal Government, which takes care to preserve them while allowing controlled cutting. The timber obtained is, in fact, very limited, partly because much of it is small and at high altitudes, but partly because tidal water is distant, and large markets are remote and difficult of access. The main lumbering centres are in Montana and Idaho, where the precipitation is, in part, heavier and the growth richer, but some trees are felled elsewhere for use in mine-workings (*e.g.* as pit-props), on the railways (*e.g.* as sleepers), for building and fuel. Missoula, Montana, is one of the chief saw-milling centres.

CLIMATE AND AGRICULTURE

As we have seen, the middle and some of the higher slopes of the Rockies are damp enough for forest growth, but it should be noted that, for the most part, only the Pacific slopes are well watered, and even these receive less rain than the Canadian Rockies because they are farther from the maritime air of the Pacific Ocean. The mean annual rainfall rarely exceeds 30 in. Many of the intermont basins receive only 5–10 in. yearly, and carry only bunch-grass and a few low bushes. In New Mexico there is an overall deficiency in rainfall amounts.

Temperatures, of course, decline with altitude, and the higher mountain summits are covered with perpetual snow, below which there is often room for a narrow zone of alpine pasture, profitable for summer sheep-grazing.

The amount of land suited by relief, soil, and climate to cultivation is clearly very limited, but dry-farming methods and the use of irrigation water permit the growing of crops in restricted valley bottoms. The most usual crops are sugar-beet, cereals, vegetables (especially potatoes), and fruit. Alfalfa is grown in many of the northern and central valleys for feeding dairy cattle, whose products are marketed in mining centres. Irrigation facilities are being extended: notable dams are the Elephant Butte Dam on the Río Grande in New Mexico and the Hungry Horse Dam on the Flathead River in Montana.

The ranching of cattle and sheep is far more widespread in the Rocky Mountain zone than the cultivation of crops. Ever since the Spaniards utilised the San Luis valley for this purpose in the seventeenth century, the basin pastures have been given over to grazing. Sheep are generally more numerous than cattle owing to the rough topography and the poor quality of most of the pasture. They are generally subject to transhumance, being taken up to the alpine pastures in May, as soon as the snows have melted, and being brought down again in October. Cattle may be given the same treatment. In the Wyoming Basin the outdoor grazing period lasts longer than in most areas owing to the influence of the *chinook* wind, but all the animals kept in the region must either be stall-fed in winter or else sold in autumn to farmers and meat-packers on the Western Plains or in the Corn Belt. Irrigated valley-tracts produce some of the feed required for winter consumption.

THE TOURIST INDUSTRY

As in Canada, the Rocky Mountains furnish some of the most spectacular scenery in the continent. Unfortunately for the government bodies and individuals who set out to attract tourists, the region is remote from large centres of population, and therefore draws fewer visitors than either the Appalachians or the Sierra Nevada.

The railways sponsored the first resorts, but the chief scenic attractions are now most often reached by roads, which enter and thread the most popular districts. The Federal Government has encouraged visitors by setting aside areas of outstanding beauty and interest as National Parks, an example followed by the various state authorities, which have added State Parks. These areas have their own hotels and motels, and may also offer fishing grounds, dude ranches (*see* p. 283), winter ski-runs, and sports programmes.

Three Parks are particularly well-known: (1) the Glacier National Park, in Montana, a continuation of Canada's Park, called, in its entirety, the Waterton–Glacier International Peace Park; (2) the Yellowstone National Park, in north-west Wyoming; (3) the Rocky Mountain National Park, in Colorado, north-west of Denver.

As its name implies, the higher parts of the Glacier Park are still glaciated. Indeed, 70 small glaciers are located there. A number of lakes, including cirque lakes, overlooked by snow-capped peaks and mountain forests, prove a popular tourist attraction to people on either side of the international frontier.

The Yellowstone National Park is quite different, for its distinctive character is due, in the main, not to glaciation, but to vulcanicity. The oldest of the National Parks (opened in 1872), it is well known for its examples of extinct volcanoes, mud volcanoes, lava flows, geysers, and hot springs. "Old Faithful," one of the most spectacular geysers, hurls into the air a spout of superheated water, 120–150 ft high every 63 minutes on average, while the smaller "Minute Man" erupts a few feet every few minutes. Other wonders include the magnificent Yellowstone Waterfall, over 300 ft high, the extensive Yellowstone Lake, many canyons, and numerous small but picturesque, forest-rimmed lakes. Beaver, bison, moose, and bear may be observed in their natural surroundings in this large Park, and some of the headwaters of both the Missouri and the Snake may be inspected.

The Rocky Mountain National Park contains Long's Peak and many other exciting features untouched by the hand of man, *e.g.* canyons and glaciated valleys.

In the south of the Rocky Mountain region tourists are drawn to many parts of New Mexico, especially to Santa Fé and Las Vegas, by their combination of Spanish, Mexican, and Indian life and architecture. The area is one of sunshine and blue skies, the latter sometimes dappled with fleecy cumulus, but rarely darkened by rain clouds. In the neighbourhood—a sign that man is not always, or even principally, a holidaymaker —the first of the world's atomic bombs was tested.

RAILWAY GEOGRAPHY

Engineers always find it difficult to drive railways through high, mountainous terrain, because they have to consider the high cost of making cuttings, tunnels, and bridges. The problem is exacerbated when the area has not been properly surveyed in its entirety, and when adequate supplies of labour have to be recruited from distant sources. Such was the case with the Rocky Mountains. Fortunately, early pioneers such as Lewis and Clark, who crossed the Montana Rockies in 1803–6, Lieutenant Pike and his successors Major Long and John Frémont, who examined the Colorado Mountains between 1806 and 1853, and various pathfinding fur-traders and mineral prospectors, had already blazed several trails, including the Oregon, California, and Santa Fé, which had come to be used by the Stage Coach and Pony Express (*see* Fig. 89). It was to a considerable extent these already-trodden routes that the railway companies decided to utilise for their tracks.

Seven main lines now cross the Rockies in the United States, the more northerly routes traversing a number of fairly wide, low passes, the southern lines skirting the southern margins of the highest mountain areas, and the central tracks striking through the more formidable barrier of the Colorado Front Range (*see* Fig. 101).

Through Montana, the North Pacific and Great Northern lines give access from Duluth, Chicago, Milwaukee, and St Paul to Spokane and Seattle, the former following a more southerly track, and passing through Helena (Montana) at the approach to the Rockies, or alternatively through Butte. The Union Pacific Railroad, from Omaha to Sacramento and San Francisco, enters the Rockies at Cheyenne (Wyoming), climbs through the Evans Pass (8240 ft) to attain the Wyoming Basin, and reaches its destination via the Great Salt Lake. The Denver and Río Grande Railroad links the Great Plains with Salt Lake City and passes *en route* through the 6-mile Moffat Tunnel, an alternative route utilising the Royal Gorge of the Arkansas River west of Pueblo and passing through Leadville between the Sawatch and Colorado Front Range. Farther south, the Santa Fé Railroad, originating at Chicago, makes its way south-westwards through Kansas City, and rounds the southern margins of the high Rockies *en route* to Albuquerque (New Mexico). It misses Santa Fé itself, and eventually reaches Los Angeles. The latter is also the terminus of the South Pacific line from New Orleans, which roughly follows the margin of the Mexican border after leaving San Antonio (Texas). Among important places served by this railway are El Paso and Tucson. San Antonio, El Paso, and Tucson all control lines running southwards to Mexico City.

Many highroads also traverse the mountains from east to west and provide additional means of transport, much used by tourists, between the High Plains and the Pacific coastlands, especially California. Though capable of negotiating steeper gradients, roads, like railways, are influenced by relief and, in choosing the best lines of route, engineers again take advantage of river valleys and mountain passes. The world's longest road tunnel cuts through the Colorado Front Range west of Denver to supersede an earlier, more sinuous, high level route over a mountain pass.

Chapter XXIV

THE INTERMONTANE PLATEAUS AND BASINS OF THE WESTERN HIGHLANDS

PHYSICAL ASPECTS

GENERAL CHARACTERISTICS

Between the Rocky Mountains and the Pacific Mountains of the United States lies a group of intermont basins and plateaus which together form a region of considerable physical diversity. Land-forms run from deep river canyons to upraised block mountains, and from salt-flats and lakes to lava plateaus. Owing to variations in latitude, altitude, and exposure, climates range widely, but the whole region suffers from marked aridity, and agriculturally is suited only to grazing or dry-farming in its natural state. Therefore the overall population density is low. There are, however, marked nuclei in certain mineralised districts and in irrigated valleys.

Broadly speaking, the area may be said to interpose a wide barrier between the populous Pacific coastlands and valleys on the one side, and the fairly well-settled Central Plains on the other, a barrier which is, of course, reinforced by the marginal Rocky Mountains. As regards human occupance, the region under review bears some comparison with the Western Plains examined in Chapter XXII.

STRUCTURE AND PHYSIOGRAPHY

Structurally, the region may be divided into three entities:

1. The Snake–Columbia Plateau and the adjacent Snake River Plain in the north, a sub-region which is examined in detail in Chapter XXV.
2. The Great Basin in the centre, parts of which extend into California, the subject of Chapter XXVI.
3. The Colorado Plateau and the Gila Basin in the south (*see* Fig. 87).

The Great Basin, mostly between 3000 and 7000 ft in elevation, forms the main part of the so-called "Basin and Range Province," a large area of tilted, block-faulted, and often slightly folded ranges and depressions extending into the south-western portion of the Colorado Plateau. The ranges are generally short, they usually trend from north to south, and they commonly show evidence of Tertiary warping as well as vertical uplift.

The accompanying basins occupy downwarped areas filled with material derived mainly from the denudation of the flanking ranges (*see* Fig. 94).

The sub-region contains several inland drainage basins, descending, by intermittent streams, either to shallow *playas* (depressions only rarely water-filled) or to salt-lakes. Some of the latter, known as *salinas*, are only small and semi-permanent, but some are large and are recognisable by such names as Great Salt Lake, Carson, Pyramid, and Humboldt lakes. The three latter are almost all that is left of the extensive Pleistocene Lake Lahontan, while Great Salt Lake is a remnant of the even vaster Pleistocene Lake Bonneville. Great Salt Lake is still shrinking, owing to the deviation from it (for irrigation purposes) of feeders from the

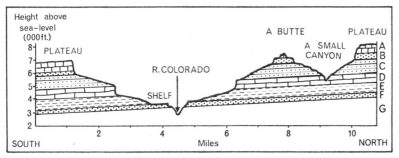

FIG. 88.—Geological Section across Grand Canyon, Colorado River.

Carboniferous series:
    A, light grey limestone;
    B, grey sandstone;
    C, alternating red shales and red sandstones;
    D, blue-grey limestone with red staining.

Cambrian series:
    E, greenish shales;
    F, coarse sandstone.

G = Archaean granites and gneiss.

Wasatch Mountains. Its maximum depth is now only about 18 ft. Its water is extremely salty, and its shores are white with salt incrustations.

The Humboldt is the longest river in the Great Basin. It flows westwards for 500 miles through Nevada into the saline Humboldt Lake.

The northern part of the Colorado Plateau, ranging from 5000 to 10,000 ft in height, is hemmed in by the Uintas, Wasatch, central Arizona Highlands, and Rockies. The southern part, including the Gila Basin in south-west Arizona, has a topography—of basins and ranges—approximating closely to that of the Great Basin. The bulk of the sub-region consists of horizontal beds of sedimentary rocks, upstanding in places as *mesas* and buttes, in others deeply incised with broad canyons, of which the 65-mile-long Marble Canyon and the 125-mile-long Grand Canyon, both carved by the Colorado, are the most notable examples. The latter is 10–12 miles in width and up to 6000 ft in depth. Through it races the powerfully eroding Colorado, which descends 1500 ft in its course. The top four-fifths or more of the Grand Canyon have been trenched through sedimentary strata, whose varying resistances to weathering and erosion have produced a "cliff and bench" cross-profile (see Fig. 88). The river is now cutting down through the basal granites and metamorphic rocks. In canyons such as this and in various arroyos (smaller gorges which carry rivers only spasmodically), the colours of the rocks have been wonderfully preserved by the aridity of the climate. The desert climate has also contributed to the restricted width of these spectacular land-forms, since normal weathering agents have had little opportunity of wearing back the valley sides.

CLIMATE AND NATURAL VEGETATION

The region under study suffers greatly from aridity. It is shielded from oceanic influences by the Pacific Mountains, and only rarely does Gulf maritime air penetrate beyond the Rockies. Generally speaking, the mean annual rainfall, except in the basin ranges, does not greatly exceed 10 in., and in the far south-west of the region averages only 3 in. In the north there is a slight tendency for a winter or spring maximum, when westerly influences are strongest, while in the south a late summer or early autumn maximum is common owing to the prevalence of convectional storms at those times.

As in most other parts of North America, seasonal temperature ranges are extreme. In the south-west, at low levels, average temperatures may well exceed 90° F in July, making this area the hottest, as well as the driest, in Anglo-America. Owing to the frequent absence of cloud, diurnal as well as seasonal temperature ranges tend to be excessive throughout the region, and in many parts 80% of the possible sunshine is received. The length of the growing season—100 days on the Columbia Plateau, 300 days in Arizona—is everywhere adequate for cultivation, except at high levels, but the actual acreage under crops is very severely limited by slope and aridity.

The following climatic statistics for Salt Lake City, in the eastern part of the Great Basin, and for Yuma, in south-west Arizona, illustrate some of these climatic conditions:

Salt Lake City	J.	F.	M.	A.	M.	J.	Jy.	A.	S.	O.	N.	D.
Temperature (° F) .	29	33	41	50	58	68	76	75	65	52	40	32
Precipitation (in.) .	1·4	1·5	2·1	2·1	2·0	0·8	0·5	0·8	0·9	1·5	1·4	1·4

Mean Annual Temperature: 52° F; Mean Annual Range of Temperature: 47° F; Mean Annual Precipitation: 16·4 in.

Yuma	J.	F.	M.	A.	M.	J.	Jy.	A.	S.	O.	N.	D.
Temperature (° F) .	55	59	65	70	77	85	91	90	84	72	61	56
Precipitation (in.) .	0·4	0·5	0·4	0·1	0	0	0·1	0·5	0·2	0·2	0·3	0·4

Mean Annual Temperature: 72° F; Mean Annual Range of Temperature: 36° F; Mean Annual Precipitation: 3·1 in.

The slopes of the marginal mountains—Cascades and Sierra Nevada in the west, Rockies and Wasatch in the east—are moist enough to support light forests, chiefly of conifers: western yellow pine and higher Douglas and white firs, lodgepole, and sugar pines. Elsewhere, at altitudes of about 4000–6000 ft, on the ridges, there may be enough precipitation to nourish open piñon and juniper woodland, with some pine and oak, but at low levels throughout the region bunch-grass, sage-brush, and scrub are characteristic, with cottonwood and willow along watercourses. Yucca, cacti, tall creosote bush, mesquite grass, and, in the salt plains and *salinas*, greasewood (tolerant of salt) are typical of the "great American desert" of the southern areas (*see* Figs. 4 and 47).

HUMAN GEOGRAPHY

INDIAN POPULATION

In parts of the intermontane region native Indians, adhering to many of their pre-European habits of living, still survive in considerable numbers, both on reservations and outside. Indeed, it is only in the desert tracts of New Mexico and Arizona, generally on land unattractive to recent white immigrants, that Indian settlements are at all numerous in the United States. Here live, among other Indian groups, the Hopi and the Navajo, Christianised by the Spaniards, but otherwise living largely as they did when first encountered by white people, and not yet assimilated with the white Americans. The Spaniards called the Hopi "Pueblo" (village) Indians, because they dwelt in settled communities, in flat-roofed houses of stone and sun-dried mud, often perched (for defensive purposes) on *buttes* or *mesas*, and built in an early skyscraper style, the upper storeys, often containing outdoor workrooms and balconies, reached by ladders. Only one such skyscraper village remains inhabited, but the Hopi continue to live gregariously.

Today, most of the Hopi and Navajos wear dress which is indistinguishable from that of Europeans. Some of them may work in white settlements and all send their children to school, but they remain for the most part somewhat backward cultivators or herders, and continue to practise—largely, it must be admitted, for the benefit of tourists—their traditional arts and crafts, including weaving, basketry, pottery, and jewellery-making. Again, to please visitors who contribute to their upkeep, they occasionally don their colourful native costumes and perform tribal dances. At Indian markets, *e.g.* at Santa Fé, they sell their farm produce and handicrafts, and buy beans, coffee, flour, calico, and other commodities.

Usually by continuing rather primitive means, the desert Hopi grow maize, beans, squash, chillies, and other crops, which are generally planted in occasionally flooded river bottoms. The more pastoral, more nomadic Navajos, most of whom live in scattered, dome-shaped huts or *hogans*, graze sheep, goats, donkeys, and cattle, which they originally acquired from Spanish immigrants. Their reservation covers about 16 million acres, and extends from north-eastern Arizona into the adjacent parts of New Mexico and Utah. Over-grazing, to some extent a result of a growing population, has led to soil erosion and rural pressure on the land, though the population density does not exceed three persons per square mile.

THE SPREAD OF COMMUNICATIONS AND WHITE SETTLE-MENT

The first white people to infiltrate into this area were Spaniards, who, in small numbers, began to move northwards from Mexico in the late sixteenth century and succeeded in establishing a number of scattered mission stations and trading posts in what we now know as New Mexico and Arizona. It was more than two centuries later when the first pioneers of north European descent entered the region from the east, as we saw in Chapter XXIII, where reference was made to three major trails, precursors of the modern transcontinental railways: (1) the Santa Fé trail, which began near the present Kansas City, and was later extended into the southern part of this region via the Gila valley *en route* to San Diego (California), with an alternative northern route from Santa Fé to Los Angeles; (2) the Oregon trail, which also stemmed from Kansas City, crossed the Rockies by the South Pass (Wyoming), and ultimately reached Fort Vancouver, near Portland (Oregon) after threading an intricate system of valleys, including the Snake and Columbia; (3) the California trail, greatly used by the forty-niners *en route* to Sacramento (California) and San Francisco, which crossed the Great Basin via the Humboldt River (*see* Fig. 89).

The first permanent agricultural settlers in the Great Basin were the Mormons, who followed the Oregon trail under Brigham Young in 1847 to escape from persecution in the Middle West, and who started farming in the "Garden of Utah" almost at once. Very quickly, the Salt Lake Oasis sprang to life as a resting and equipping centre for the "forty-niners" and later prospectors searching for mineral wealth in California and elsewhere. Other cultivators and graziers, seeking to take advantage of the (limited) markets provided by the growing mining population of the intermontane plateaus, followed in the wake of the Mormons. These frontier valley-farmers and their successors, as well as the more successful miners, became active supporters of the railways and irrigation works which today form the most obvious items in the cultural environment of the arid West.

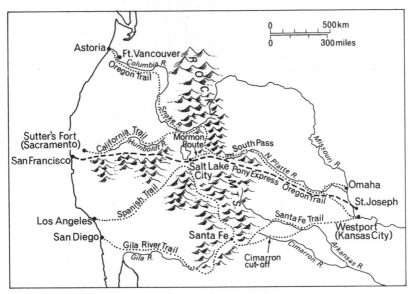

FIG. 89.—Early routes across western U.S.A.

Natural conditions of climate and physiography limit the density of population in the region under study, but in places where valuable mineral deposits and fertile valley-tracts are found, and where communications and modern irrigation facilities have been installed, local densities are now growing markedly. Between 1950 and 1960, for example, the population of Nevada and Arizona rose by over 70%, compared with increases of only about 10% for many eastern states. The total population of Nevada, however, was only 489,000 in 1970, the average density, 4·4. Arizona and Utah, with more extensive irrigation facilities, had densities of 15·5 and 12·4 per sq. ml., respectively.

THE ECONOMY

MINING

As in the Rocky Mountain zone, where ores have been similarly concentrated in areas of intense folding, faulting, and igneous activity, mineral wealth has for long been the economic mainstay of many localities in the intermontane plateaus and basins, but, again, little industrial activity has resulted, partly owing to the lack of generous quantities of coal, petroleum and iron ore, partly to the limited nature of the local market, and partly to the thin spread of communications and the distance from seaboard contacts.

Each of the principal states included in the region under review—Nevada, Utah, and Arizona—has a group of mining colonies, but also, like the Rocky Mountain region, a number of ghost towns. Mining continues to be the principal economic activity in Nevada, but Virginia City, site of the fabulous Comstock lode, which at first was famed for its gold and later for its silver, is now much less active than it was in the nineteenth century. The most productive mines in Nevada today are in and near Ely (Fig. 87), where large amounts of copper, silver, gold, and lead are extracted. There are gold-mines at Carlin, in north central Nevada, and others in western Nevada at Tonopah. Mercury is worked on the Oregon border, and elsewhere small quantities of iron, lead, and zinc, but since the state has no coal-mines and no petroleum or natural gas wells, it cannot support a steel industry, and its only smelters are the copper works near Ely and a magnesium plant at Henderson, near Boulder Dam.

Utah's minerals are better exploited, and its smelters and refineries are more numerous, for this state has a larger population, there are coal-mines in the Wasatch Range, and Salt Lake City operates a big oil re-finery. Utah boasts one of the foremost mining areas in North America. It lies within about 30 miles of Salt Lake City on the south side of Great Salt Lake, where Bingham is the chief centre. Copper, lead, zinc, gold, and silver are all produced in quantity, largely by open-cast methods. At Garfield, north of Bingham, there is a large smelter and refinery which chiefly turns out copper, but also other metals, e.g. molybdenum, cobalt, and tungsten. West of Bingham there is a smaller lead refinery. At Geneva, near Provo, an important steel plant—dependent chiefly on iron-ore deposits worked in south-western Utah and on smaller manganese deposits mined elsewhere in the state—has been erected. In south-eastern Utah, as in western Colorado, uranium and vanadium are extracted at several localities, and uranium concentrators have been built both here and in the state capital. Utah's principal non-metallic minerals are potash, salt, and phosphates, all owing their origin to the desiccation of former lakes. Salt Lake City, Garfield, and Geneva all possess fertiliser and other chemical works, though much sodium chloride is sold direct to western livestock farmers.

Arizona's gross yield of copper is greater than that of Utah. Mines proliferate in the southern highlands, notable centres being Bisbee, Ajo,

Globe-Miami, Casa Grande and Morenci, all of which possess smelters which extract gold, silver, and molybdenum as well as copper. The state has few important lead- and zinc-mines, but she possesses some of the most productive manganese deposits in North America, the main mining areas being in the west. In the north-east, over against Colorado and Utah, she shares the uranium wealth of those states.

AGRICULTURE

As has already been noted, agriculture does not hold a very important place in the economy of most parts of the intermontane plateaus and basins. The greater part of the terrain is suited only to extensive livestock grazing, and away from valley-tracts the problem of water, as well as that of satisfactory pasture, is often acute. Cultivation is almost entirely confined to relatively small areas of fairly low-lying, irrigable ground, where slopes are gentle and markets near and accessible. Few crops are marketed beyond the region itself owing to competition from areas with greater natural advantages for cultivation, and with better access to large urban markets.

Pastoral farming, introduced into the region by early Spanish migrants, is now carried on by both Indian and white people. Year-round grazing may be carried on throughout the region, but transhumance is widely practised, especially in the hot, dry south. Because of the general poverty of the natural vegetation, which may restrict the cattle population to one animal per 100 acres, many beasts are railed east, and to some extent west, for fattening purposes. Increased amounts of winter feed, however, are now being grown in irrigated plots within the area, and the value of beef production is being slowly raised. Horses are widely employed for herding and driving cattle, as most of the ranches are very large.

Sheep are well adapted to the natural conditions, but they are grazed in smaller numbers than heretofore. This is surprising because, unlike cattle, they can find nutrition in short-shrub country, and they can range higher, especially during the period of summer transhumance. Many, however, have been badly affected recently, especially in Nevada, by the spread of *Halogeton glomeratus*, a poisonous plant, and the production of both wool and meat has fallen.

CROPS AND IRRIGATION FACILITIES

No more than 3% of the entire region is under field crops, for reasons which have already been made clear. The chief irrigated crops in more northerly areas tend to be sugar-beet, potatoes, and alfalfa, the latter a valuable adjunct to the native herbage, while in the south fair acreages are devoted to cotton. Though altitudes are generally too high for citrus fruits, most irrigated areas have some orchards, and vegetable plots are common.

Among the many scattered irrigated districts, dependent upon small or large, local, regional, or federal projects, three are of outstanding importance: (1) the Salt Lake Oasis, or Garden of Utah; (2) the Salt River valley in Arizona; (3) the Reno Oasis and neighbouring districts in western Nevada.

The Salt Lake Oasis, in Utah, lies in the main between the foot of the western slopes of the Wasatch and the Great Salt Lake. It supports three-quarters of the population of the State, including the occupants of such towns as Salt Lake City, Ogden, Logan, and Provo. The annual precipitation averages little more than 10 in., but increases eastwards up the Wasatch, to support a large number of snow-fed streams whose waters are tapped for irrigation. Cereals like wheat and barley may be dry-farmed, the spring rainfall maximum favouring growth, but most of the high-value crops, e.g. sugar-beet and alfalfa, beans, tomatoes, potatoes and other vegetables, and fruit, including the vine, peaches, and apricots, require irrigation. The finest soils, especially rich in phosphates and potash, are those of the middle delta lands of the former Lake Bonneville, which are closer than the upper delta soils and more open and less saline than the lower delta lands, which are largely reserved for cattle. Most of the farm-holdings are small, and a majority of their owners live in villages rather than in dispersed buildings, a legacy of the days when life was more insecure and when fear of the Indians was more general. Sugar refineries, dairies, and fruit and vegetable canneries are fairly widespread in this part of Utah; Salt Lake City has important meat-packing plants, and Ogden has flour-mills.

The Federal Bureau of Reclamation began its work in the Salt River valley, where the large Roosevelt Dam, begun in 1902 and completed in 1911, and the smaller Gila and Coolidge Dams have been built for irrigation purposes. Today the area, which includes many of the tributary valleys of the Gila, as well as a portion of the main river basin, is dominated by the cultivation of high-quality cotton. The mean annual rainfall of only about 8 in. is inadequate in itself for cultivation of any kind, and, despite the extensive use of well-water as well as surface-water, there seems little prospect at present of a large increase in crop production, though attempts are being made by Arizona, against fierce Californian opposition, to command extended quantities of Colorado River supplies, at present only of value in small riparian areas, including the Yuma irrigation district near the Mexican border. On the level, alluvial plains of the Phœnix district the cotton crop yields heavily, but the market is distant and labour is not always plentiful, even with the addition of temporary Mexican and Indian workers. Also, there has lately been some deterioration in the fertility of the soil owing to a growth in the proportion of fine clay brought to it along irrigation channels, Besides cotton, other crops are grown in the Salt River and adjacent oases. They include cereals, alfalfa (of which eight crops a year may be harvested), fruits such as cantaloupes, figs, dates, and a little citrus, including grapefruit, and a variety of vegetables, e.g. lettuce and carrots. The long growing season (300 days) permits many of these crops, but not cotton, to be raised in winter.

In western Nevada there is a group of small oases in the vicinity of Reno. They are supplied with water from such rivers as the Truckee, Carson, and Humboldt, none of which, however, has a very large volume. Dairying is of less importance than in the irrigated tracts of Utah and Arizona, but similar crops are raised as in the Salt Lake Oasis.

It should be noted that, as far as irrigation is concerned, the waters of the River Colorado chiefly benefit the Imperial Valley in southern California, even though such major works as the Boulder Dam, opened in 1933 as the first multi-purpose dam in North America, lie within the area under study. Dams such as the Grand Coulee, on the Columbia River, will be described in the next chapter.

THE TOURIST INDUSTRY

The intermontane plateaus and basins present many features of interest to the tourist, and, as speedy transport facilities by road, rail, and air have developed, several areas have begun to proclaim their virtues to the outsider. All advertise the advantages of their climate; abundant sunshine, low rainfall, low humidity, clear, unpolluted air. All point to their varied scenic attractions: Arizona, for example, can boast of its Grand Canyon, its Petrified Forest, its Painted Desert, and its large Meteor Crater, its giant saguaro cactus plants and its smiling oases. Both this State and New Mexico make much of their surviving Indian life and the architecture of the early Spanish missions. Such a place as Reno, in Nevada, is favoured in many minds by the extreme liberality of its gambling laws, and in others by the ease with which grounds for divorce may be obtained. Recently, gigantic man-made engineering works such as the Boulder Dam and the newer Glen Canyon Dam, impounding Lake Powell (southern Utah) have proved a draw to many people and the resort town of Las Vegas (Nevada) has become very popular (see Fig. 90).

Each state acts in some measure as a passage-way between the populous east and the attractive Pacific coastlands, especially California, and many travellers find it worth while to halt for a few days in Utah, Nevada, New Mexico, or Arizona before pressing on to their goal.

FIG. 90.—Boulder Dam, Colorado River. Water gushes from the outlet
valves in the canyon wall. Behind the 726 ft high dam is Lake Mead.
A large mesa forms the back-drop of this desert landscape.

Southern Arizona and New Mexico, with their relatively warm winter
climates, attract many visitors from November to April, while more
northerly areas cater mainly for summer tourists.

MANUFACTURING INDUSTRIES

The intermontane plateaus and basins lack a significant manufacturing
region, and the manufacturing town, so typical of the eastern United
States, is non-existent. Such industries as are carried on are designed in
the main to satisfy purely local needs for consumer goods.

Apart from the smelting of base metals, the only important heavy industry is the manufacture of steel, which is carried on at the Geneva Mills near Provo, on the eastern shore of Utah Lake, 35 miles south of Salt Lake City. Part of the finished product is sold in Washington, Oregon, and California.

More widespread industries include the canning, preserving, and drying of fruit and vegetables, common to all irrigated districts; and sugar-refining, more important in Utah than elsewhere. Ogden and Salt Lake City have flour-mills, and the latter has large meat-packing plants. Suitably located places, e.g. Flagstaff and Williams in Arizona, use upland pine-trees in their saw-mills, while the manufacture of fence-posts from lower juniper, piñon, and oak forests is fairly widely distributed. Recently, the construction of aircraft and electronic equipment has gained a foothold in Arizona, which has the advantage of a comparatively invulnerable situation; and parts of Nevada, where empty spaces abound, are currently being used for the testing of nuclear bombs and missiles.

LARGE SETTLEMENTS

Salt Lake City, for long the largest city between the Rocky Mountains and the Pacific coast region, is the chief northern metropolis in the region. It acts as the main commercial city of the Utah oasis and neighbouring mining centres, and is the world headquarters of the expanding Mormon Church. A city of broad, tree-lined avenues, it is located on the small River Jordan, 10 miles east of the Great Salt Lake at the foot of the Wasatch. It has lately become an important focal point, not so much of roads and railways as of western airways, and it accommodates many aircraft from Portland, San Francisco, Los Angeles, and Chicago. Its industries include oil-refining, metal smelting, engineering, and the manufacture of chemicals. *Ogden*, its near neighbour, on a delta of the former Lake Bonneville, benefits from its situation on the main transcontinental railway of the Union Pacific system, which, immediately west of the city, crosses the shallow Great Salt Lake on a great causeway.

Phœnix, the largest settlement in Arizona (metropolitan population, 1970, nearly a million) has, in recent years, overtaken Salt Lake City in size. It is the principal commercial city of the large Salt River oasis. Aircraft components are made there, and, like Salt Lake City, it has a large passenger airport. The chief tourist centre in Arizona is *Tucson*, well located in a mountain-rimmed basin, with a wealth of curious desert plants and a number of interesting Indian settlements in its neighbourhood. Like Phœnix, it attracts more tourists in winter than in the excessively hot summer. *Reno*, in Nevada, is a gap town, commanding a route through the Truckee or Donner Pass (Sierra Nevada) into California, from which it draws many visitors. It has agricultural business interests.

Chapter XXV

THE NORTH-WEST : WASHINGTON, OREGON, AND THE SNAKE RIVER PLAIN OF IDAHO

PHYSICAL ASPECTS

GENERAL CHARACTERISTICS

Excluding the remote Alaska, the north-west of the United States is occupied by the states of Washington, Oregon, and Idaho. Most of the latter's panhandle and south-eastern tracts are taken up by the Northern Rockies, discussed in Chapter XXIII. The rest comprises, in the main, the Snake River Plain, linked with Washington and Oregon, not only by rail and road but also by the river itself. The Snake is the chief tributary of the Columbia, which for much of its course forms the boundary between the two western states. The whole region, therefore, is to some extent united by the River Columbia and its affluents. It must, however, be noted that the western parts of Washington and Oregon form a distinctive Pacific realm of mountains, valleys, and forests, while the rest of the region falls into the broad system of interior plateaus and basins of which the British Columbian Plateau (Chapter XI) and the Great Basin and Colorado Plateau (Chapter XXIV) are other elements.

White people were rather slow to penetrate this region, remote as it is from Atlantic America, and it was not until after 1800 that it was reached by the overland route. From that time until the 1840s, it was very much a "no man's land," partially inhabited by Indian hunters and fishers, and more sporadically by fur-trappers and traders in the service of rival Canadian and American companies. The first agricultural settlers, having entered the region via the Oregon trail, began to take up land in about 1840. Less than a decade later, by the Oregon Treaty, the 49th parallel was accepted by both Britain and the United States as the U.S.–Canadian frontier, and more American citizens were free to move in. Many were drawn from the Middle West, which by then had ceased to be a pioneer farming area. Immigration quickened with the completion of the North Pacific Railroad (1883) and the Great Northern line (1893) to Puget Sound, and lumbering began to assume real importance after 1900. During the first twenty years of the present century many of the newcomers came from Scandinavia, Germany, Finland, Switzerland, and the Netherlands, as well as from more settled parts of the United States, and their experience has proved of great value in the development of the dairying, fishing, and bulb-growing industries.

Economically, the Indian element in the population is of little account nowadays, though a number of the able-bodied men take up seasonal work in the food canneries, fruit-orchards, and saw-mills of the area.

PHYSICAL DIVISIONS

As we observed in the last section, the region may be divided into two parts: (1) a Pacific zone; (2) an interior zone (*see* Fig. 91).

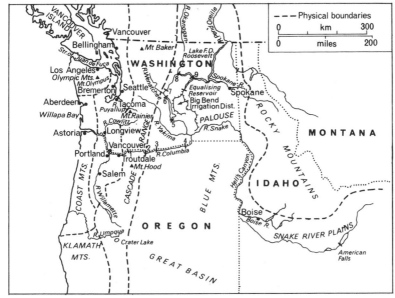

FIG. 91.—Washington, Oregon, and Snake River Plain of Idaho. The dams on the Columbia River are numbered thus:

1. Bonneville; 2. Dalles; 3. John Day; 4. McNary; 5. Priest Rapids; 6. Rock Island; 7. Rocky Beach; 8. Chief Joseph; 9. Grand Coulee.

As in British Columbia, the Pacific zone consists of a number of longitudinal divisions, here running from north to south:

1. *The Coast Ranges*, extending northwards across the Strait of Juan de Fuca into Vancouver Island, and southwards into California. In few places does the altitude of these folded and upfaulted mountains exceed 4000 ft, but in the north-west of Washington Mt Olympus reaches 8000 ft. Numerous transverse rivers, of which the most notable, of course, is the Columbia, cross the Coast Ranges *en route* to the Pacific.

2. *The central depression*, consisting of: (*a*) the Puget Sound trough, an island-strewn waterway broadened and deepened by Pleistocene glaciation, and forming the southern end of Canada's "Inside Passage"; (*b*) the Puget Sound Lowland, consisting largely of sands and gravels, with some alluvium near the Sound, and a number of low hills of glacial and fluvioglacial deposits farther away; (*c*) the Cowlitz valley, leading southwards to the Columbia River; (*d*) the Willamette valley, a wide, fertile alluvial plain, tributary to the Columbia, and to some extent continued southwards by the middle course of the Umpqua valley.

This central depression, which may be compared with the Central Valley of California, is closed in on the south by the deeply dissected plateau of the Klamath Mountains, which Oregon shares with northern California.

3. *The Cascade Range*, a broad, elevated upland, more broken in Washington than in Oregon, which gives way northwards to the Coast Ranges of British Columbia, and southwards to the Sierra Nevada of California. Above the roughly accordant summits of the Cascade Mountains rise a number of high volcanic cones, especially obvious on the western side. They include Mt Baker (10,827 ft), Mt Rainier (14,408 ft), and Mt Hood (11,245 ft). The Cascades were heavily glaciated in the Ice Age, as the depth of some of their northern valleys indicates, and a few shrunken glaciers remain.

Quite distinct from the Pacific zone of the north-western United States, is the plateau country east of the Cascades. Most of this belongs to the Snake–Columbia drainage system, but in the south of the Oregon Plateau there is an area of inland drainage properly belonging to the Great Basin. The greater part of the region consists of a vast lava plateau, akin to that of the north-west Deccan in India. It is an area of horizontally disposed lava beds, derived from fissure eruptions, which in places cover the older rocks with a mantle a mile in thickness. Only in a few areas, *e.g.* in the Blue Mountains, do pre-existing rocks rise above the lava overlay, though a few volcanic cones—the product of subsequent more violent eruptions—may do so.

The Rivers Columbia and Snake thread their way through the lava plateau. The former, whose course bears a remarkable resemblance to that of the Fraser in Canada, rises in the same country, similarly utilises the Rocky Mountain Trench in its upper course, and breaks through the Selkirk Mountains. It then flows southwards through the Arrow Lakes before crossing the frontier just beyond Trail. In latitude 48 degrees N. it turns westwards and, after receiving the Okanogan tributary, makes a right-angled bend before flowing south again, in a gorge, to the Oregon border. In this section it is joined by the Yakima on the right bank, the

Snake on the left. Finally, it resumes its westerly track and, probably as an antecedent river, cuts through the Cascades in a great gorge. Just beyond Portland, the Willamette enters, and at Longview the Cowlitz. Beyond is the estuary, flanked by the Coast Range.

The Snake rises in the Yellowstone National Park. While much of its valley, notably in southern Idaho, is broad, it is markedly canyon-like along the divide between Idaho and Oregon, where one section, 40 miles in length, exceeds 7000 ft in depth. Known as Hell's Canyon, this stretch is deeper than the Grand Canyon of the Colorado, but is reached only by a pack-animal trail.

The north-west has many scenic attractions, several of which are much more accessible to tourists than Hell's Canyon. Included among them are the Mt Rainier and Mt Olympus National Parks, both of which offer winter sports as well as summer recreation. Crater Lake National Park, in Oregon, provides the classic example of the circular, deep kind of lake which often collects in the crater of an extinct volcano. From an island in this lake rises a small volcanic cone.

CLIMATE

In a region like the north-western United States great climatic diversity is to be expected from the variety of relief features, the most prominent of which are aligned at right angles to the direction of the dominant moist Pacific airstreams (cf. British Columbia). Orographic as well as frontal influences are characteristic of the Pacific zone, but beyond the Cascades there is a marked rain-shadow area.

The Pacific zone has a north-west European type of climate, with a precipitation, including heavy winter snows, exceeding 60 in. in the Coast Range and on the western flanks of the Cascades, and a total of over 140 in. on Mt Olympus. The central depression, which lies in the rain-shadow of the Coast Range, has a mean annual rainfall which may not exceed 35 in., while in southern Oregon and on the north-east margin of the Olympic peninsula the yearly total falls to less than 20 in. Throughout this Pacific zone, there is a well-marked winter maximum in the precipitation, and in the Cowlitz and Willamette valleys there is a short but distinct summer drought: a presage of the Mediterranean climate of the Central Valley of California.

East of the Cascades, a dry, continental type of climate prevails. Most of the Columbia Plateau has less than 10 in. annually, and south-eastern Oregon is even drier. But eastwards, in the Palouse (eastern Washington), the precipitation increases somewhat and may reach 25 in. yearly on the Idaho border.

Temperature ranges are rather low in coastal areas, and the winters are far milder than in corresponding latitudes in New England. The central depression and inland plateau areas show greater extremes.

Many of the above climatic features are illustrated by the following statistics for Salem (in the Willamette valley), and Boise (in the Snake River Plains):

Salem	J.	F.	M.	A.	M.	J.	Jy.	A.	S.	O.	N.	D.
Temperature (° F) .	41	43	46	51	56	61	66	66	61	54	47	42
Precipitation (in.) .	5·8	5·3	4·7	2·8	2·2	1·3	0·4	0·4	1·6	3·1	5·6	6·2

Mean Annual Temperature: 53° F; Mean Annual Range of Temperature: 26° F; Mean Annual Precipitation: 39·6 in.

Boise	J.	F.	M.	A.	M.	J.	Jy.	A.	S.	O.	N.	D.
Temperature (° F) .	29	34	42	50	58	66	73	72	62	50	40	32
Precipitation (in.) .	1·7	1·6	1·3	1·2	1·4	0·9	0·2	0·2	0·5	1·2	1·3	1·5

Mean Annual Temperature: 51° F; Mean Annual Range of Temperature: 44° F; Mean Annual Precipitation: 13·1 in.

THE ECONOMY

FORESTRY

Though much of the interior of the region under study is naturally covered only with sage-brush and a few other shrubby plants, or (in the Palouse) with bunch-grass, most of the coastlands, and all but the dry eastern slopes of the Cascades, bear very rich, dense coniferous forests. The giant Douglas fir is the dominant species: one tree alone furnishes a very large amount of timber, and there are many close stands. In some areas the Douglas fir is mixed with western red cedar, hemlock, Oregon pine, or Sitka spruce, all commercially valuable types. In the higher Cascades smaller firs appear, while in some of the sheltered valleys of south-western Washington the first of California's redwoods make their appearance, as well as yellow and white pine. The eastern slopes of the Cascades carry light forests of yellow pine, often mixed with rather weak specimens of other coniferous species, e.g. Douglas firs.

The forests of Washington and Oregon furnish about one-third of all the lumber produced in the United States, the Douglas fir accounting for about 60% of all the saw-mill timber. The forests were not greatly exploited until the present century, when the value of reafforestation was beginning to be recognised, hence there has been much less depletion than in the north-eastern United States. But the present industry owes much to the work of immigrants from Maine and other older lumber-producing areas.

Already by 1910 the region had surpassed the Great Lakes region as a source of lumber, and by 1930 it was producing more than the Southern States, its only rival today for softwood timber. Oregon normally produces more than Washington. Each state has its saw-milling centres, the largest on or close to ice-free, tidal water, and accessible to large supplies of hydro-electric power, *e.g.* Portland and Longview on the Columbia River, Seattle and Tacoma on Puget Sound. As in British Columbia, the number of saw-mills greatly exceeds the number of pulp and paper mills (here, by nearly 20 to 1). Much of the wood production (whether in the shape of logs, sawn timber, laths, shingles, plywood, or other forms) is railed or shipped (via the Panamá Canal) to markets in the timberless plains or in the densely populated north-eastern section of the country, but some is also sold abroad, *e.g.* in Latin America, Australia, Japan, Hawaii, and even western Europe.

AGRICULTURE IN THE PACIFIC ZONE

Just as the Pacific Mountains are noted for their timber products, so the broad depression extending from Puget Sound to the Klamath Mountains is noted for its agricultural output, particularly for its dairy supplies, fruit, and vegetables.

The farmers of the Puget Sound lowland—once covered with big stands of Douglas fir—and the Cowlitz valley, like their fellow men in north-western Europe, take advantage of a fairly cool, rainy climate to pasture cattle and/or poultry, to grow oats and other fodder crops, and to raise deciduous fruits, *e.g.* raspberries, strawberries, blackberries, and loganberries, and garden truck, *e.g.* cabbages, peas, beans, tomatoes, and potatoes. A few of their products, *e.g.* Carnation milk and canned peas, are railed east, but most are sold in the Puget Sound ports and other north-western cities. In the Puyallup valley, under the stimulus of Dutch immigrants, an important daffodil-bulb industry has been established, and other small areas specialise in the growing of Easter lilies and tulips, largely for eastern markets.

The Willamette lowland, about 125 miles long and 20 miles wide, is somewhat drier, and its alluvial soils are very rich. It was originally an area, not of close forest, but of parkland, and for a period was utilised for extensive wheat-cultivation. Farming nowadays is much more varied, and the average size of the holdings, though still exceeding that of the Puget Sound lowland, is only moderate. Dairying is again important, and oats, barley, and hay are grown for fodder. Beans, peas, lettuce, and other vegetables take up more ground than wheat. Large acreages are under orchard-fruits, *e.g.* plums (for drying as prunes) and peaches (in the south), apples, pears, cherries, filbert-nuts, and walnuts. Many fruit-farmers use irrigation water in summer to supplement the meagre rainfall at that season. They may send their products to places like Salem, for canning, before they are marketed.

Lowlands occur only patchily along the coastlands of Washington and

Oregon. Some dairy-farming is undertaken on land cleared of its native forest, and such products as Cheshire-type cheese are prepared.

AGRICULTURE AND IRRIGATION IN THE INTERIOR

East of the Cascades, there are three principal types of land-use: (1) extensive ranching, especially of cattle, on the natural vegetation of the lava plateau: (2) extensive arable-farming in the Palouse, and in north-eastern Oregon, where wheat and seed-peas are notable crops; (3) intensive irrigation-farming in (a) the "apple valleys" of the Columbia Plateau, (b) the new Great Bend section of the Columbia Plateau. (c) the Snake River Plain in Idaho.

The Palouse is a large area in eastern Washington and western Idaho which derives its name from a small north-bank tributary of the Snake. It is a maturely dissected, rolling plateau rising north-eastwards from about 1200 to 2800 ft, and has a mean annual rainfall varying in the same direction from about 12 to 22 in. Winters are cloudy and cold, and heavy snows may delay ploughing, but summers are hot, dry, and sunny. Normal processes of water and wind erosion have reduced most of the underlying lava to a fertile, silty loam, bearing, in places, a fine, porous overmantle of loess, which lends itself to easy cultivation. Large crops of winter wheat are grown, and some barley and peas, but the adoption of dry-farming techniques in response to the small precipitation has led to a noticeable decrease in the amount of ground-water, and to an acceleration in the rate of erosion. Some farmers have begun contour ploughing, and there is a growing trend towards rotation systems (involving, for instance, the planting of alfalfa and sugar-beet), trash-cultivation, and the seeding of selected trees, shrubs, and grasses on the steeper slopes. Most of the Palouse wheat is milled at Spokane, an important railway and woodworking centre, which is served by hydro-electricity generated from the Spokane river.

As in British Columbia, many plateau valleys, receiving only 8–10 in. of rain annually, are served by irrigation, and there is an intensive crop production, though acreages are restricted to areas of fairly gentle slope and comparatively modest elevation. Such valleys as the Yakima, Wenatchee, and Okanogan, between the Cascades and River Columbia, watered by snow-fed streams rising in the high Cascades, and possessed of natural shelter, good air drainage, an abundance of sunshine, and rich volcanic soils, have about 60% of their cultivated land under fruit-trees, notably apples, but including also pears, peaches, plums, cherries, and apricots. The apple crop accounts for about a quarter of the total national production. The bulk of the produce is marketed by co-operative methods, and may be sold fresh, canned, or frozen. Other crops of these irrigated valleys include potatoes, sugar-beet, alfalfa (for cattle and sheep), vegetables, especially peas and tomatoes, and hops.

Along the Snake River Plains of Idaho there are many other irrigated farms, supported by dams such as the large one at American Falls, and others lower down, e.g. near Boise. As a result, Idaho potatoes have become as well known in the United States as those of Maine. Other irrigated crops, covering in all nearly 4 million acres, include sugar-beet, cereals and alfalfa, fruit and vegetables. Some farmers concentrate on the raising of dairy cattle, others on lamb production.

Undoubtedly the most ambitious irrigation project in the north-west, however, is the one associated with the Grand Coulee Dam on the River Columbia, a multi-purpose scheme devised by the Federal Bureau of Reclamation which is opening up to intensive cultivation over a million

[Courtesy: U.S. Information Service.

Fig. 92.—Grand Coulee Dam, River Columbia. A large herd of sheep is being led across the dam from the neighbouring pastures. The electricity transmission lines from the associated power-house should be noted.

acres of the Great Bend country (*see* Fig. 92). In its natural state the Grand Coulee was a virtually dry gorge, 200 miles long and about 400 ft deep, which had been carved by the Columbia River during the Pleistocene period when its normal outlet was dammed by ice, but which was later abandoned. The dam built at the entrance to the gorge was completed in 1940, when it ranked as the largest man-made structure in the world: 4173 ft long, 550 ft high, and 500 ft thick at its base. It has impounded the 150-mile-long Lake Roosevelt, extending northwards to the Canadian border, whose water, lifted 630 ft by pump into the Grand Coulee, itself converted into a great "equalising" reservoir, can now be fed by canal into a large expanse of fertile land south of the river, an area which is gradually being taken up by irrigation farmers, and put under a variety of crops, *e.g.* sugar-beet, alfalfa, very high yield wheat, apples, peaches, beans, peas, and potatoes. Previously, most of this land was under sage-brush, or, sporadically, dry-farmed wheat.

FISHING INDUSTRIES

River and sea fisheries, utilised by many coastal and valley Indian tribes before white people entered the north-west, have been greatly developed during the last 100 years. Washington leads Oregon in its annual catch, but lags far behind British Columbia. Salmon are caught in the Columbia River and in Puget Sound, by both nets and traps. Some are sold fresh, but most are canned and marketed through Seattle throughout North America and in many oversea countries as well. Despite conservation measures, however, and the provision of fish-ladders at dam sites, the Columbia River salmon have suffered from industrial pollution and dam construction.

"Deep-sea" fish, caught off the shores of Washington and Oregon, include halibut, tuna, herring, and oysters. The latter are best known on Willapa Bay. Halibut have assumed first place among the various catches. They are generally sold in the freshly frozen form, most being distributed by Seattle. The extraction of halibut-liver oil is an important ancillary occupation.

Among the scatter of fishing ports in Washington and Oregon, many of which also have canneries, special mention may be made of Seattle, Astoria (at the mouth of the Columbia), Aberdeen (at the head of a river estuary farther north), Port Angeles (on Juan de Fuca Strait), and Bellingham (near the seaward entry to Puget Sound).

POWER SUPPLIES AND MANUFACTURING INDUSTRIES

In Portland, and in the Puget Sound cities, in particular, manufacturing industries have been quick to develop during the present century, with the growing demand for industrial products in the west, and with the provision of increased power supplies. Mineral wealth is not very notable, even in the interior plateau, but there is a small output of coal from northern Washington, notably the Bellingham district, and petroleum may be obtained fairly readily from either California (by tanker) or Vancouver (by pipeline).

Hydro-electricity provides the region with most of its power requirements. Indeed, with upwards of 200 plants, this area now produces more hydro-electric power than any other part of the United States, not excluding the Tennessee Basin. There are stations on many rivers, including the Snake, Willamette, and Spokane, but it is along the Columbia that the most spectacular developments have taken place. This great river is second only to the Mississippi in the United States in its annual discharge, which amounts to 240 milliards, i.e. 32 cubic metres per second. It descends 1300 ft in its course through the United States, and it drains one-seventh of the nation's continental area, besides having a long, powerful upper course in Canada. Fed by Canadian ice-fields and mountain snows, its régime is much more regular than that of most large rivers, e.g. the Nile and Colorado, and the Federal Government has now taken advantage of this fact by initiating, in co-operation with the Canadian Government, the comprehensive development of all its resources.

The first dam to be built on the Columbia River was the Bonneville, 50 miles above Portland, where the river crosses the Cascades in its great gorge. This dam, a "run of the river" structure, with little water-storage capacity, incorporates a ship lock through which oceanic vessels may pass to Dalles, 188 miles upstream, though in practice nearly all dock at Portland. Close to the dam is a hydro-electric power-station, serving Portland and other cities. Later came the Grand Coulee Dam, with two hydro-electric power plants generating nearly 2 million kW, and several other works, designed partly to control the river's discharge, partly to supplement power supplies: they include the Dalles, John Day (with a 2000 MW station), McNary, Priest Rapids, Rock Island, Rocky Reach and Chief Joseph Dams. The Dalles and Chief Joseph power plants should eventually generate 1750 MW each. The construction of additional dams, impounding large lakes, is now proceeding on the Columbia and its tributaries (see Fig. 39). They include the Duncan, Arrow and Mica Dams, all in Canada, but benefiting the U.S. The last-named, scheduled for completion in 1973, will have a 2000 MW electricity plant attached to it.

Over a third of the total electricity supplies are consumed by the aluminium-refining industry, mainly a war-time development, and much of the remainder is taken by the wood-working industries. Most of the alumina used in the north-west is railed thence from the Gulf Coast and other southern plants to refineries at Vancouver, opposite Portland, Longview, on the lower Columbia, Troutdale, just below the Bonneville Dam on the Oregon side of the Columbia, Tacoma, Bellingham, Wenatchee, the Dalles, and Spokane. Much of the refined aluminium is taken by the aircraft industries of Seattle and Los Angeles.

Shipbuilding is another north-western industry which greatly expanded as a result of the nation's war-time needs, though Puget Sound and the lower Columbia were already making ships in 1918. It is supported, in part, by the small steel mills of Vancouver (Washington) and Seattle. There is a large U.S. Navy yard at Bremerton, on Puget Sound.

Portland and Seattle have become important wool-clothing centres, specialising in sportswear. They use both American and Australian wool in their factories, some of which draw supplies of yarn and cloth from a number of small mills in the Willamette valley.

Food industries are widespread. They include the canning of fish, fruit and vegetables, berry fruits and peas, the production of condensed milk (especially in the Puget Sound lowland), and the milling of flour (notably in Tacoma, Seattle, Portland and Spokane). Tacoma, Seattle, and Portland depend in part on imported grain to supply their mills.

MAJOR CITIES

Washington and Oregon are among those U.S. states which are characterised by a rapidly expanding population. Both have more than doubled their numbers in the last 40 years. Idaho, by comparison, has raised its population by only 50%. In 1960 Washington had about 3,400,000 people, Oregon 2,100,000, Idaho 710,000. The two largest cities in these states are Seattle (metropolitan population, 1970, 1,380,000) and Portland (995,000). Both are great industrial cities as well as commercial ports.

Seattle is situated on a very large, deep, landlocked harbour between Puget Sound and the small freshwater Lake Washington, which are linked together by a ship canal. The business area lies near the water, the better residential properties climb the hillslopes above. Three transcontinental railways converge on Seattle: the Great Northern; North Pacific; and Chicago, Milwaukee, St Paul, and Pacific. It is also a focus of highways and has a large civil airport (as well as military airfields) for trans-Pacific flights.

Seattle sends fishing vessels into Alaskan waters and is well-located to conduct more trade with Alaska than any other U.S. port. It sends the 49th State mining machinery, manufactures of many kinds, foodstuffs, and general stores, and imports salmon and other commodities from her. To other countries, *e.g.* Japan, accessible by Great Circle route, it ships timber, pulp, paper, wheat, and fruit, and to lands such as Australia it dispatches tinned salmon. Its industries bear some resemblance to those of Los Angeles (*see* Chapter XXVI). They include the manufacture of furniture (for which some hardwoods are imported), wool clothing and aircraft, flour-milling, fish- and fruit-canning, oil-refining, shipbuilding, motor and aircraft engineering, and the fabrication of "iron chinks," *i.e.* machines for cutting up salmon preparatory to canning. The small steel industry is based chiefly on the use of scrap metal.

Portland, 120 miles up the Columbia River, and close to the confluence of the Willamette, is the normal terminus of oceanic ships serving Oregon. Vessels may, however, proceed farther up the river, as we have seen, and 7-ft barges can reach the confluence of the Yakima, over 300 miles from the Pacific, or ply up the Snake. There is room above Portland for two important railways and two well-graded highways along the banks of the river. Portland also acts as a focus of north–south communications, including railways from Los Angeles and San Francisco as well as lines from the Puget Sound ports.

Its industries, supported, like those of Seattle, by hydro-electric-power developments, efficient transport, and overseas access, are not unlike those of the Washington metropolis. They include wood-working, clothing, steel rolling, motor engineering, shipbuilding, flour-milling, and meat-packing. As a commercial city, it owes much to its regional setting and its position re communications, and it is more of a regional capital than Seattle, less of an oceanic port. Its main exports are wheat and timber.

Tacoma, the third largest city in the area under review, is less of a commercial city, more of an industrial centre, than either of the other two major settlements. Situated where the Puyallup valley enters Puget Sound, very near the head of navigation of the latter channel, it has a commodious, sheltered harbour into which move some of the bulky commodities used in its metal refineries, *e.g.* alumina and Latin American copper. It also treats Idaho copper and lead, and extracts some gold and silver. It has saw-mills, paper works, furniture factories, and electro-chemical works.

Chapter XXVI

CALIFORNIA

GENERAL CHARACTER OF CALIFORNIA AS A REGION

California, sometimes called the "Golden State" because of its air of prosperity, is third in size among the States of the Union, following Alaska and Texas. More than any other except Florida, it has sufficient unity for us to consider it as a regional entity, even though, in the north, it shares the Klamath Mountains with Oregon, and, like the latter, incorporates a portion of the Great Basin, while in the south-east it abuts, like Arizona and Mexico, on the lower Colorado River and embraces a large area of desert terrain, including the Mojave Desert and Death Valley, which also properly belongs to the intermontane plateau and basin country. All these peripheral areas, however, are thinly peopled, and serve only to accentuate the oneness of the remaining parts of the State, different though they may be in structure, relief, vegetation, land-use, etc.

The essential California, fronting the Pacific and physically separated from the rest of the State by mountain barriers, notably the Sierra Nevada and the San Bernardino Mountains, is distinguished by the following features, among others:

1. An extremely prosperous, intensive agricultural character, based on fruit, but devoted also to the growing of such diverse crops as cotton, rice, and truck vegetables, and the raising of livestock. Though surpassed by some states in cultivated acreages, the cash farm income of California exceeds that of any other.

2. A remarkable blend of well-developed forest, mineral, and oceanic resources, as well as agricultural wealth.

3. Some of the most diverse and most spectacular scenery within the United States, a powerful magnet for tourists.

4. A Mediterranean climatic régime, the detailed nature of which varies very widely with relief and latitude, though it is almost everywhere marked by summer drought and abundant sunshine, attractive to both residents and visitors.

5. A high degree of urban development. Eighty per cent of the Californians live in cities, of which Los Angeles and San Francisco are not only the largest in the State but also the most populous in the western half of Anglo-America.

322

6. A rapid and continued growth in the total population, which has increased more than fourfold in the last 40 years. In 1920, when the State held nearly 3½ million people, eight states in the Union were more populous; at the 1960 census, with 15¼ million, only New York was in front, and by 1964 it could claim to have an even larger population than New York. By 1930 Missouri, Michigan, and Massachusetts had been overtaken, by 1940 Texas, and in the next decade Illinois, Ohio, and Pennsylvania. The development of the State's varied resources has kept pace with this demographic rise, and average living standards are among the highest in the world. Included in the population is the largest minority of Japanese and Chinese people in the nation, though little Oriental immigration has been permitted since 1930. Both groups engage in market-gardening, fishing, and petty urban trade, and in Los Angeles and San Francisco tend to live in their own quarters.

PHYSICAL ASPECTS

PHYSICAL UNITS

Reference to Fig. 93 will show that California consists of several highly distinctive physical units, which may be roughly matched by those of Washington and Oregon. They include:

1. *The Coast Ranges*, culminating in the Klamath Mountains in the far north, and leading southwards into the peninsula of Lower California (Mexico). These coastal mountains, rising from a concordant coast, and in places forming bold headlands, are both folded and faulted structures, completely broken through only in the centre, where the Golden Gate and San Francisco harbour have been opened out as a result of the sinking of a fault-valley area. Elsewhere, a few transverse streams course down the Coast Ranges to the Pacific, and there is a considerable development of longitudinal valleys, *e.g.* the Santa Clara, and Salinas, especially south of Golden Gate. Off southern California there is a number of rocky islands, while on the mainland the San Gabriel and San Bernardino Mountains, forming a dissected, tilted, block-mountain zone akin to the higher, broader Sierra Nevada, strike inland to leave an undulating lowland on which Los Angeles has reared itself.

2. *The Central Valley*, a synclinal depression akin to the central depression of the Pacific north-west, 400 miles long and with a maximum width of 50 miles, closed in on the north by Mt Shasta and the Klamaths, on the south by the Tehachapi Mountains. Into this depression, the Sacramento, rising near the volcanic cone of Mt Shasta (14,162 ft) and the San Joaquin, springing from the Sierra Nevada, have poured thick layers of alluvium. They converge before entering San Francisco Bay in a marshy delta. In

FIG. 93.—Regions and surface features of California.

the south of the Central Valley there is the Lake Tulare inland drainage basin, an area of rather alkaline soils divided from the San Joaquin valley by an alluvial fan.

3. *The Sierra Nevada*, a massive block of volcanic, metamorphic, and

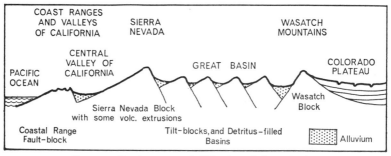

FIG. 94.—Section across California and Great Basin.

sedimentary rocks, uplifted along fault-lines and tilted so that the eastern face is very steep, the western face more gentle (*see* Fig. 94). Running parallel to the Central Valley, these mountains are about 400 miles long and 50–80 miles wide. On the western, rainy side they have been deeply trenched by river valleys, many of which, like the summit area, reveal evidence of Pleistocene glaciation. Both U-shaped and hanging valleys are common, and cirques, some of which interlock to produce arêtes, are numerous. Among other features are: (i) block-faulted lakes, *e.g.* Tahoe (the largest), Owens, and Mono; (ii) Mount Whitney (14,495 ft), the highest summit in the United States outside Alaska, and twelve other peaks reaching 14,000 ft; (iii) Mount Lassen, the only active volcano in the country; (iv) the Yosemite canyon and waterfalls, and the even deeper King's Canyon, 8000 ft deep.

CLIMATE AND NATURAL VEGETATION

California is no less varied climatically and vegetationally than physio-graphically, and the statement made above (p. 322), that the State has a Mediterranean type of climate, must be both amplified and modified, for the 10 degrees of latitude covered by California (32 degrees to 42 degrees N.), and the amount of exposure to and shelter from oceanic influences, introduce many complicating factors, some of which are illustrated by the following data for San Francisco (on the central part of the coast), Sacramento (in the Central Valley), and San Diego (on the southern coast):

San Francisco	J.	F.	M.	A.	M.	J.	Jy.	A.	S.	O.	N.	D.
Temperature (° F) .	49	51	53	54	56	57	57	58	60	59	56	51
Precipitation (in.) .	4·8	3·6	3·1	1·0	0·7	0·1	0·0	0·0	0·3	1·0	2·4	4·6

Mean Annual Temperature: 55° F; Mean Annual Range of Temperature: 11° F; Mean Annual Precipitation: 22·2 in.

Sacramento	J.	F.	M.	A.	M.	J.	Jy.	A.	S.	O.	N.	D.
Temperature (° F) .	46	50	54	58	63	69	73	72	69	62	53	46
Precipitation (in.) .	3·8	2·9	3·0	1·6	0·8	0·1	0·0	0·0	0·2	0·9	2·1	4·0

Mean Annual Temperature: 57° F; Mean Annual Range of Temperature: 27° F; Mean Annual Precipitation: 19·4 in.

San Diego	J.	F.	M.	A.	M.	J.	Jy.	A.	S.	O.	N.	D.
Temperature (° F) .	54	55	57	58	61	64	67	68	67	63	59	56
Precipitation (in.) .	1·8	1·9	1·5	0·6	0·3	0·1	0·1	0·1	0·1	0·4	0·9	1·8

Mean Annual Temperature: 61° F; Mean Annual Range of Temperature: 14° F; Mean Annual Precipitation: 9·6 in.

The following facts emerge from a study of the above figures:

1. The Central Valley is drier and more extreme in its climate than the coastlands in the same latitude, since the Coast Ranges sever it from maritime airstreams.

2. The mean annual precipitation declines southwards, as cyclonic storms become less frequent and less intense, even in winter.

3. The south is very dry.

4. Coastal temperatures in summer are lower than might be expected, considering California's latitude, owing partly to the dominance of north winds, partly to the effect of the cool Californian current. The latter is also responsible for the large number of foggy days in coastal areas, and accounts, along with industrial pollution and motor car exhaust gases for the "smog" from which Los Angeles suffers for about 60 days each year. It will be noted that San Francisco enjoys its highest temperatures in September, when the interior has lost enough of its summer heat to enfeeble the indraught of Pacific air.

Climatic details not revealed by the figures quoted include the following:

1. The very heavy precipitation, largely orographic in character, of the Sierra Nevada, the wettest part of California. These mountains may have a winter snowfall of over 400 in. in some years (the greatest in the country) and, despite the provision of snow-sheds, transport across passes like the Donner (west of Reno) is frequently halted. The Sierra Nevada enjoy some summer rain, especially on the windward side.

2. The very low precipitation of the interior rain-shadow areas, especially the Mojave Desert, Salton Sink, and Colorado valley, where the rainfall is extremely episodic and torrential in character and averages less than 5 in. yearly. In this same region, as in all desert areas, diurnal temperature ranges are excessive. One of the highest shade temperatures ever recorded anywhere—134° F—was measured in 1913 in Death Valley, 280 ft below sea-level, well fitted, by its very high mountain rims, to trap summer heat.

3. The fairly heavy precipitation of the Coast Ranges, generally exceeding 40 in. north of Golden Gate.

4. The long growing season enjoyed by the more low-lying parts of the State. The southern coast and the Salton Sea depression experience a frost-free period virtually twelve months long.

Mainly in response to the varying amounts of rainfall received in different parts of California, several regions of natural vegetation may be identified:

1. The redwood, yellow pine, and Douglas fir forests of the northern parts of the Coast Ranges.

2. The evergreen trees and shrubs (chaparral) of the southern parts of the Coast Ranges.

3. The giant sequoia and other forests of the Sierra Nevada, including yellow pine, Douglas fir, lodgepole and sugar pine, thinning out with ascent, and finally giving way to alpine flora.

4. The prairie and scattered oaks of the Central Valley, degenerating to bunch-grass in the drier south.

5. The thorny cactus, sage-brush, and desert vegetation of the Mojave, Sonora, and other very arid areas.

The Californian redwoods and especially the sequoias, often called the "big trees," probably include the largest and oldest plants in the world, individual specimens having a height of over 300 ft, a diameter of over 30 ft, and an age of 5000 years. The chaparral—the truly Mediterranean vegetation—consists chiefly of small, leathery-leaved and thickly barked trees, often equipped with knotty trunks and wide-spreading root-systems, well adapted to withstand summer drought. Interspersed with these gnarled trees are bulbous and tuberous plants, and many succulents.

HUMAN AND ECONOMIC GEOGRAPHY

HISTORICAL GEOGRAPHY

Like Washington and Oregon, California, being a Pacific state, is one of the newer parts of the country as far as north-west Europeans are concerned, but, unlike the other two, its recent history was preceded by a period of Spanish influence. Claimed by Spain in the sixteenth century, following several exploratory journeys from Mexico, various mission-stations were erected in the eighteenth, especially in the south, and coastal bases were established to ease communications with the Spanish settlement at Manila, in the Philippine Islands. Few Spanish colonists were, however, induced to settle in California, and they never pushed much beyond San Francisco. The present multiplicity of Spanish place-names, in fact, over-emphasises the part played by southern Europeans in the development of the State. Even in 1860, after a considerable influx of northern stocks from the east, the total population of California was less than 400,000.

The main history of California dates from 1849, when gold was discovered in the Sierra Nevada only a few months after the United States had acquired the territory from Mexico. Since then, four stimuli have produced a periodic quickening in the rate of immigration:

1. The completion of transcontinental railways: Union Pacific to San Francisco (1869), South Pacific to Los Angeles and Oakland (1881),

and Santa Fé to Los Angeles (1885), all of which induced farmers to come in and apply irrigation to the art of fruit-growing.

2. The establishment of the petroleum and motion-picture industries in the last quarter of the nineteenth century, followed by the introduction of the motor car and the modern highway which encouraged the industrial development of the State.

3. The development of the Western Plains "Dust Bowl," which led many ruined families to seek their fortunes in a more prosperous State.

4. The needs of the nation and its allies in the Second World War, which led to the introduction of many new industries and gave new life to several old ones.

Hand in hand with the growth of mining, farming, and manufacturing has gone the development of the marine fisheries of California, and the growing popularity of the region as a tourist and residential area offering a virtually unrivalled range of scenery and climate. The State is now almost fully mature economically, but there is no diminution in the number of people flocking into it.

AGRICULTURE

Since the days when the "forty-niners" and the first batch of Chinese and Japanese immigrants began to move into California, the agricultural pattern has changed considerably, and even now is not static. The early Spanish colonists of southern California were mainly cattle ranchers. Many of their estates were broken up in the 1860s, partly owing to severe droughts, partly to the acquisition of the territory by the United States. Some of the gold-seekers of the north, disappointed in their efforts to acquire easy wealth, moved southwards to acquire land, while others began wheat-growing in the Central Valley, and for a period were able to sell their produce to people in the eastern states. Barley, grown mainly as a feed for draft animals, also became important. But in the 1880s much land began to be put "under the ditch," and came to be used increasingly for the growth of irrigated fruit and vegetable crops.

Today, three areas are particularly noted for irrigation farming: (1) the Central Valley; (2) the Los Angeles lowland; (3) the Imperial and Coachella Valleys in the Salton Sink basin. Ranching is now of importance only on the rough hill pastures of the Coast Ranges, and in the semi-desert country of southern California, including the drier parts of the San Joaquin valley, where sheep, as well as cattle, are grazed. Wheat, and to a lesser extent barley, have been largely crowded out by fruit and vegetables, and by a number of even newer crops, e.g. rice, cotton, and the Mexican guayule, a resinous rubber substitute introduced into the Salinas and San Joaquin valleys from Mexico.

As has already been mentioned (p. 322), California is now the most prosperous agricultural state in the country. With few exceptions, the richest farming counties in the United States are all to be found in California, the richest of all being Los Angeles County, which alone produces crops of more value than all the farm products of New Hampshire, Vermont, West Virginia, or Nevada. Seventy-five per cent of all the crops grown in the State, however, come from the Central Valley, where holdings, as elsewhere, are mostly only of moderate size, but are very highly capitalised. The crop of highest value today is cotton, the yield of which is three times the national average, but California leads all other states in the production of barley, many truck crops, e.g. lettuce and cantaloupes, and several fruits, e.g. grapes, peaches, apricots, and plums. It also grows all the United States' olives, lemons, and figs, and more sugar-beet than either Colorado or Idaho, the other two main producers of this crop.

The main reasons for California's high agricultural productivity are:

1. The Mediterranean climate assists both the growing and drying of many commercially valuable crops.

2. The wide latitudinal range of the State permits the raising of a great diversity of crops, including both temperate and tropical varieties, and also lengthens the harvest season.

3. Irrigation facilities have been more widely provided than in any other state (two-thirds of the cropland is irrigated).

4. Most of the soils, including the alluvium of the Central Valley, are highly productive.

5. The people of the United States as a whole, with their high living standards, provide a large internal market for quality produce.

6. The internal transport system, including not only railways and roads but also special equipment such as the refrigeration car (invented in 1868), is well developed.

7. A number of excellent ports, e.g. San Francisco and San Pedro (serving Los Angeles), are available for export purposes.

8. The development of co-operative marketing methods has reduced costs and ensured high quality, and the products are packed both efficiently and attractively.

9. Markets have been widened by canning, freezing, and bottling processes.

10. There has been little difficulty in recruiting labour, and the employment of residential workers may be easily supplemented by transient labour from Mexico.

FISHING AND FORESTRY

The fact that California in most years lands fish of more value than any other state in the Union is often overlooked. With its long coastline and fair number of harbours, the State is, in fact, one of sea-farers as well as landsmen. San Diego, San Pedro, and San Francisco all have large fleets, including well-equipped refrigeration vessels ranging as far as Peru, Hawaii, and Alaska. Their catches include tuna, anchovy, mackerel, rockfish, sole, sardine, salmon, and crab, many of which appear to be encouraged in their breeding habits by cool Pacific currents. Fish canneries are numerous in California: they include those of Monterey, besides those of San Francisco Bay, Los Angeles, and San Diego.

Timber-cutting and saw-milling are very important in the northern Coast Ranges and on the western slopes of the Sierra Nevada, the most richly timbered areas. In fact, California comes second only to Oregon as a wood-producing state, its output far exceeding that of British Columbia. The most productive area is in the middle zone of the Sierra Nevada, between about 2000 and 5000 ft, where loggers—working chiefly in summer owing to the heavy winter snows—cut timber not only for the State's fruit-packing industry but also for a variety of other purposes, including the paper industries of the San Francisco Bay area. The dimensions of the forests are carefully guarded in the interests of soil conservation, irrigation water supplies, and recreational activities.

MINERALS AND POWER SUPPLIES

Since 1849, California has been a gold-producing state. Despite the vicissitudes of the mining industry, it remains one of the leading gold-producing states in the Union. The chief workings are located in the Klamath Mountains and in the northern foothills of the Sierra Nevada. Other significant minerals include mercury (from the south-central part of the Coast Range), borax (from Death Valley), potash (from Searles Lake, a remnant of a former inland sea south of Death Valley), tungsten (near the Fresno smelter), iron ore (from an open-pit mine at Eagle Mountain, 150 miles east of Los Angeles), chromium (south-central Coast Range), sulphur (Sierra Nevada), salt, asbestos, silver, and lead. Although California leads all other states in the country as a producer of tungsten and mercury, the total mineral production, excluding petroleum, is not very large, and a notable absentee from the list of mineral products is coal.

Indeed, were it not for the very substantial quantities of petroleum and natural gas raised in the south-west of California, the mineral basis of California's manufacturing industries would be very slender. Only Texas

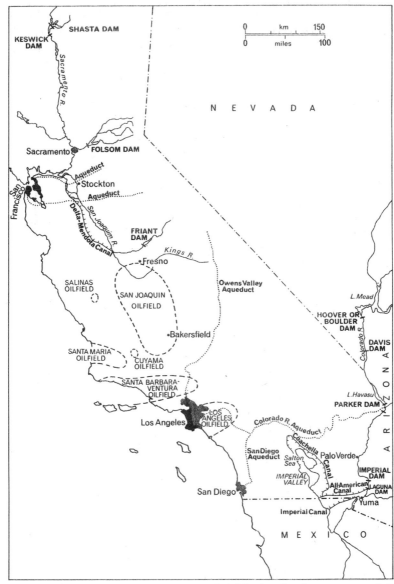

FIG. 95.—Water and petroleum resources of California. Of all the numerous irrigation canals in the Central Valley, only the Delta–Mendota Canal is shown.

and, in recent years, Louisiana, however, drill more petroleum than California, whose production totalled 372 million barrels in 1970 (two-sevenths of the enormous Texan output). The oil industry began in the late 1870s, but it was 50 years before the boom came, to make California independent of other U.S. supplies. A number of fields occur: (a) Los Angeles, where Wilmington is prominent; (b) Santa Barbara—Ventura, and Santa Maria, other coastal areas farther west, where some offshore drilling is undertaken: (c) the small valley fields of Cuyama and Salinas; (d) the large San Joaquin field, centred on Bakersfield (see Fig. 95). There are several refineries at Los Angeles and Bakersfield, and refineries and cracking plants have also been built on San Francisco Bay (especially at Richmond). Supplies of natural gas are limited and some is moved by pipeline to Los Angeles (from western Texas) and to San Francisco (from New Mexico).

Hydro-electric power supplies augment the power derived from petroleum and natural gas in California's industry. The largest plant is situated at Boulder (or Hoover) Dam, on the Colorado, which produces about 1·8 million kw. Other important sites, of more recent construction, include: Shasta Dam, on the Sacramento, generating 375,000 kw; the Keswick Dam, lower down; the large Trinity Dam, on a tributary of the Klamath River; and dams (e.g. the Fulsom) on the Feather and American Rivers, both left-bank tributaries of the Sacramento (see Fig. 95). All these northern projects are well placed to supply the industrial needs of the San Francisco Bay area, and to permit farm electrification in the Central Valley, while the Boulder and other plants on the Colorado satisfy most of the requirements of the Los Angeles Metropolitan Area.

MANUFACTURING

While gold and agricultural opportunities brought most immigrants into California in the nineteenth century, industrial and commercial activities have proved the main magnets during the past 60 years. Today, following a period of wartime and post-war expansion, the value of manufactured products exceeds that of farm and mineral products, and metropolitan Los Angeles and the San Francisco Bay area are among the first ten industrial centres in the United States.

Certain industries, of course, stem directly from primary occupations, e.g. the canning of fish, fruit and vegetables (seasonal occupations), saw-milling and furniture-making, meat-packing, the manufacture of oilfield equipment, oil-refining and resultant chemical industries, cotton-ginning and the processing of cotton-seed oil, the refining of sugar-beet and the preparation of wine. Even the iron and steel industry, established at Fontana, 50 miles east of Los Angeles, during the Second World War, partly to lessen the strain on American railways and also to help the West's engineering industries, is dependent upon iron ore from Eagle Mountain and upon local supplies of limestone and scrap, though the coal required has to be brought from Utah, over 500 miles away.

Another group of industries involves the processing of imported commodities, and has therefore become well established in the marine conurbations of San Francisco and Los Angeles. Into these cities are brought, largely from tropical lands, articles such as cacao, coffee, copra, cane-sugar, spices, rubber, vegetable fibres, and hardwood timber, each of which is turned into a secondary product.

Other manufactures include those which were either first established in this comparatively non-vulnerable area during the Second World War or which greatly expanded during that period with the rise of military needs and the growth of the expanding western market. Such are: (1) the very large aircraft industries of Los Angeles and San Diego, which have the extensive, empty spaces of the Mojave Desert on their doorstep as testing laboratories, spaces which are now also used for testing rockets and guided missiles; (2) the motor car industries of Oakland and Los Angeles, the latter now second only to Detroit as an automobile engineering centre; (3) the derivative manufacture of motor car tyres in Los Angeles, which itself, sometimes thronged with as many as 3 million vehicles on a single day, presents a by no means modest local market; (4) the shipbuilding industries of the Bay, San Pedro, and San Diego districts; (5) the manufacture of clothing, especially sportswear (more important in Los Angeles than in San Francisco), the electronics industry (dominant in the Bay area), and the manufacture of ceramics and photographic equipment (most notable in Los Angeles).

The latter industry is a reminder of the fact that one of the oldest industries in California is the production of motion-pictures, long centred in Hollywood (Los Angeles), which still has some right to call itself the "film capital of the world," though not even all California's studios are now located there, and Japan and India both claim to produce more films than the United States. The industry greatly benefited in its pioneer period, when "shooting" was done out of doors, from the dry, sunny climate of southern California, and from the wide range of scenery—mountain and plain, forest and desert, city and country—available within a narrow radius of Los Angeles.

THE REGIONS OF CALIFORNIA

California is such a large State, and possesses such abundant regional variety, that for purposes of further study it is advisable to divide it up into sub-regions. For reasons that should be apparent from what has already been written, the following suggest themselves as suitable units: (a) the Coast Ranges and valleys; (b) the San Francisco Bay area; (c) the Los Angeles area; (d) the San Diego district; (e) the Central Valley; (f) the Salton Sink basin; (g) the Sierra Nevada; (h) the desert periphery.

THE COAST RANGES AND VALLEYS

North of San Francisco, as we have seen, most of the Coast Ranges and valleys are well watered and therefore well timbered. Lumbering industries have been established at places like Eureka, dairying is undertaken in some of the valleys cleared of trees, and many small fishing ports have been built up. But there are no large settlements, and the only longitudinal railway (from San Francisco) terminates at Eureka.

South of San Francisco, forest gives way to chaparral as the rainfall becomes lighter and the period of drought longer, and farming, other than ranching, becomes more dependent upon irrigation. Particularly important agricultural areas are the Santa Clara valley, just south of San Francisco Bay, and the Salinas valley farther south. The former produces more prunes than any other part of North America. These fruits are dried either by the sun or by mechanical means. Other important crops include apricots (dried wholly in the sun), almonds, apples, pears, walnuts grapes, flowers, and vegetables, e.g. tomatoes and broccoli. Unfortunately, the lower part of the Santa Clara valley is being increasingly used to accommodate the overspill population of the Bay, just as the citrus groves of the Los Angeles area and the truck-farms of Long Island (New York) are being reduced in acreage by the outward spread of urbanism. The Salinas valley is especially noted for its carrots and lettuce (irrigated mainly by wells), and to a lesser extent for its strawberries, beans, alfalfa, and beef cattle.

At various places along the coast south of San Francisco there are tourist centres with good beaches, and a number of small fishing ports such as Monterey. Oil-wells proliferate in the Santa Maria and Santa Barbara districts, and some offshore drilling is also undertaken.

THE SAN FRANCISCO BAY AREA

This sub-region, centrally placed on the Pacific side of California, accessible by rail and road from the east, and by ship from the west, via the Golden Gate channel, forms a very prominent residential, commercial, and industrial conurbation dominated by the peninsular city of San Francisco, but including, on the east side, such large settlements as Oakland, Richmond, Berkeley, and Alameda (see Fig. 96). In 1970 the population of the San Francisco–Oakland conurbation was nearly 3 millions.

Despite the destructive earthquake of 1906 and the fires which followed it, San Francisco was the largest city in California during most of the early years of the present century. It has fallen behind Los Angeles in part because of its somewhat cramped, hilly, though beautiful, site, rather

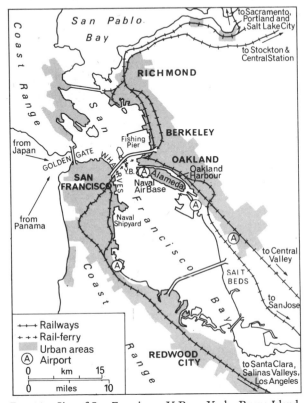

FIG. 96.—Site of San Francisco. Y.B. = Yerba Buena Island.
Note the peninsular site of this large Pacific city, and the way in which the problem of access has been largely solved by the Golden Gate and Oakland Bridges.

difficult of access from the continental interior, partly perhaps because of its cooler climate and fears of another earthquake along the line of the shifting San Andreas fault and in large measure owing to the lack of petroleum in the neighbourhood. Links to the north by the Golden Gate bridge (the longest single-span suspension bridge in the world at the time of its construction) and across the Bay by the San Francisco–Oakland bridge (8 miles long) did something to rectify the disadvantages of the city's location (*see* Fig. 97). More recently, a modern freeway system has cut swathes through the city and the Bay area authorities are now building a "Rapid Transit System" for speedy urban movement by rail.

Most of the main industries of San Francisco have already been mentioned. They include three which are more important here than in Los

[*Courtesy: U.S. Information Service.*

FIG. 97.—San Francisco: general view. Note the peninsular site of the city, the Golden Gate Bridge, the thinly-wooded Coast Range, the many wharves facing San Francisco Bay, and the San Francisco end of the Oakland Bridge. Compare Fig. 96.

Angeles: food-canning, shipbuilding and repairing, and the manufacture of electronic apparatus, Among others are: flour-milling, meat-packing, the processing of imported cacao, coffee, copra, and cane-sugar, and the fabrication of tin-plate, glass, and paper containers to serve these food industries. Chemicals, munitions, leather, clothing, cement, pottery, and motor cars are also made in the metropolitan area, and there is a small steel plant, a helicopter plant, and a productive oil-cracking plant. The largest factories and the heaviest industries are chiefly located along the Bay shores and close to the railways, where the land is level and reasonably cheap, and the disposal of industrial waste is easy.

As a port, San Francisco serves principally the Central Valley of California, to which it is connected by a network of roads and railways, but it also taps some of the trade of the Mountain States. It benefits from a deep, sheltered harbour on either side of the Oakland bridge, and its docks and wharves are capable of accommodating large numbers of ships. Its exports include fruit, timber, fish, refined petroleum, cotton, rice, and barley, as well as some of its own manufactures. Among imports are tea and silk (from Japan), sugar (from Hawaii and the Philippines), pineapples (from Hawaii), and much other tropical produce from south-east Asia, the Western Pacific, and Latin America, e.g. copra, bananas, coffee, spices, and rubber. It imports some newsprint for its printing and publishing works, crude petroleum, wool, and a number of metallic ores, including tin and copper. Normally, the port conducts more foreign trade than Los Angeles, and, like the latter, derives some benefit from the Panamá Canal, through which some of its ships pass *en route* for destinations in eastern America and Europe. Again like Los Angeles, San Francisco is a very cosmopolitan city, with a Chinatown (a great tourist attraction), an Italian section, and quarters occupied by Jews, Negroes, Filipinos, Japanese, and Mexicans.

THE LOS ANGELES AREA

Los Angeles—50 miles across—is probably the most extensive urban area in the world. The actual city population, of 3 million, makes it the third largest city in the country, but if the total population (nearly 7 millions) of its extensive metropolitan area is taken into account it almost outrivals Chicago. It sprawls much more than San Francisco, and has, indeed, been referred to as "nineteen suburbs in search of a metropolis." It occupies an undulating coastal lowland and has no natural harbour.

It has nearly twice as many factory employees as the San Francisco Bay area. Nearly one-fifth of them are engaged in the aircraft industry. Many are engaged in automobile works and in film and television studios. Some find work in factories turning out motor car tyres, oilfield equipment, clothing, furniture, ceramics and steel, in oil refineries and food-processing establishments. Manufacturing plants are less concentrated alongside railways and deep water than they are in San Francisco, because there are more roads and pipeline facilities, and level or near-level building sites are more abundant.

The port of Los Angeles–Long Beach conducts as much coastal trade as San Francisco, less purely foreign trade. Imports include rubber, coffee, lumber, paper, copra, metals, and vegetable fibres; exports include petroleum, fruit, cotton, films, motor tyres, canned fish, oranges, borax, and steel.

Both Los Angeles and San Francisco are very much concerned about water supplies for domestic and industrial purposes, since the Central Valley and southern California require so much of the State's water for irrigation facilities. Up to now, San Francisco has drawn much of its supply through a 170-mile aqueduct from the Yosemite National Park, while Los Angeles has depended upon the Owens River (Sierra Nevada) and Colorado River (see Fig. 95). On the latter, 150 miles below Hoover (Boulder) Dam, stands the Parker Dam, impounding Lake Hivasu, whence a 242-mile aqueduct, equipped with pumping stations and siphons, carries water to the southern metropolis. Los Angeles is now contemplating the large-scale distillation of sea-water, and even the feasibility of an 1100-mile pipeline from the Columbia River. The demographic and industrial growth of Los Angeles is also threatened with a shortage of electric power, despite the harnessing of the Colorado at several places and the construction of nuclear power plants.

Round Los Angeles, and menaced by its urban growth, are the most widespread citrus groves in California, and some of the State's most productive truck-farms. Three-quarters of California's oranges grow here, and many of its lemons, peaches, avocados, almonds, walnuts, grapes, and olives. Lettuce, tomatoes, celery, carrots, and early potatoes are also important, and there are dairy-farms close to the city. The mean annual rainfall is about 15 in., and irrigation facilities—wells, ditches, and sprinklers—are required for successful cultivation. Some orchards are beginning to suffer from salt-accumulation in the soil owing to over-generous applications of irrigation water without adequate drainage, and growers must safeguard their plots against occasional frost by providing them with smudge-pots or mechanical air-mixers. From time to time, the "Santa Ana," a hot, dry wind descending from the nearby mountains like the *chinook* or a European *föhn*, threatens the crops, and shelter belts of trees have been planted in places.

THE SAN DIEGO DISTRICT

San Diego and the surrounding district is in many respects a miniature of the Los Angeles Basin, but the climate in even drier and frost is altogether absent. Early vegetables and citrus fruits again flourish, and the city of San Diego bears some resemblance to Los Angeles. Its population, of well over half a million, is largely engaged in fishing and shipping, in aircraft construction, and in the tourist traffic, the latter dominant in winter. It has a large natural harbour which is used in part by the United States as a naval base. It is the southern terminus of California's Pacific

Coast Highway and is located close enough to the Mexican border to attract many Latin Americans. Near by, at Torrance, there is a large synthetic rubber plant.

THE CENTRAL VALLEY

The Central Valley is the most extensive and most level plain in the entire Pacific region of North America, and during the present century has become the largest fruit-growing area in the United States, as well as a major producer of rice, cotton, sugar-beet, and barley.

While certain of its crops, e.g. cereals and cool temperate fruits, may be grown in the northern parts without irrigation, artificial supplies of water are essential for most fruit crops, and in the southern section irrigation is required for nearly all crops, since the mean annual rainfall of the Central Valley, over 30 in. in the most northerly part of the Sacramento valley, declines to less than 10 in. in the southern part of the San Joaquin plain and the Tulare Lake Basin.

Prior to the 1930s, some of the irrigation water was provided by storage reservoirs on side-streams of the San Joaquin, but the bulk was drawn from wells, which are still numerous but of increasing depth, especially away from the watercourses. As agriculture expanded and intensified during this century, it became more and more evident that a comprehensive surface irrigation scheme would have to be adopted if the productivity of the land was to be maintained. Also, some of the fields in the deltaic area near San Francisco Bay had begun to suffer from salt-water encroachment, and it was desirable to reduce this form of land deterioration. Hence, in the early 1930s the well-known Central Valley Project was initiated, with the subsidiary aim of expanding the hydro-electric power supplies of the State, controlling the winter floods to which the lower Sacramento and San Joaquin were subject, and improving the navigational facilities of the lower Sacramento.

Three points need to be mentioned here: (*a*) about two-thirds of California's total rainfall is received by the northern half of the State, but two-thirds of the people live in the south; (*b*) the western slopes of the Sierra Nevada are much wetter and higher than the eastern slopes of the Coast Ranges; (*c*) the Central Valley descends southwards to the deltaic area, then ascends towards the southern part of the Central Valley. Hence the major water supplies had to be provided by damming back the upper Sacramento and as many of its left-bank tributaries as possible, and canals and pumping stations had to be installed farther south to conduct water on to the San Joaquin valley farms. To supplement and extend these supplies—based in the event upon the Shasta, Keswick, Fulsom, Oroville and other Dams (*see above*, p. 332)—it was decided to erect an independent irrigation system in the southern part of the Central Valley by building, on the upper San Joaquin, the Friant Dam and associated Madera and Friant–Kern Canals. In the deltaic region the Delta Cross Channel was dug, to eliminate the salinity resulting from sea-water pouring into the San Joaquin when the river was low (*i.e.* in late summer), and to help carry Sacramento River water across the delta to a further canal (Delta–Mendota) which could transport it into the San Joaquin valley. The Contra-Costa Canal was also built in the deltaic area to provide for the supply of domestic, irrigation, and industrial water in the Suisan Bay area, an inland extension of the San Francisco Bay area. Now the canal system is being extended beyond the San Joaquin valley over the Tehachapi Highlands to Riverside, east of Los Angeles.

Among the many fruits grown in the Central Valley are grapes, particularly important in the San Joaquin valley, and furnishing table dessert, raisins and wine; other deciduous fruits and nuts, *e.g.* peaches, apricots, figs, almonds, and walnuts; olives; and some citrus fruits, notably oranges.

Irrigated cotton-growing has expanded greatly during the last 30 years, and is especially important in the San Joaquin valley. The main variety is a fairly long-stapled one of high quality, and is in most places handled at every stage by machinery. Rice is cultivated on some of the wet clay soils of the Sacramento lowland. It is often seeded by aircraft, and always reaped by machine. It is generally rotated with ladino clover (a feed crop, subsidiary in the valley to alfalfa), beans, and wheat (nowadays a less abundant crop than barley). Sugar-beet is grown more extensively in California than in any other State in the country. Most of it is raised in the Sacramento valley, in the same areas as barley and clover, but it also finds a place in the delta, where, however, such vegetables as asparagus, beans, tomatoes, lettuce, and potatoes—mainly produced for the Bay markets—cover bigger acreages. Linseed and castor seed are minor crops.

Cattle and sheep are pastured chiefly on the drier margins of the Central Valley. In summer they may be taken up into the high pastures of the Sierra Nevada, as the valley fields furnish little feed during the dry season.

Numerous small food-processing plants have been built in the Central Valley. They include sugar-refineries, cotton-gins, cotton-seed oil works, flour-mills, meat-packing centres (which obtain some of their animals from the Mountain States), vineries, fruit and vegetable canneries, raisin-drying yards. Some agricultural machinery is made, but far less than in the Middle West.

Most of the Valley towns are agricultural business centres with food-processing works. They include Sacramento, the State capital and port; Stockton, which, by means of its recently improved deep-water channel, can ship fruit, etc., to San Francisco and beyond; and Fresno, the chief market in the San Joaquin valley, especially noted for its raisins.

THE SALTON SINK BASIN

In southern California, east of the Coast Ranges, lies a structural, faulted depression forming an alluvial lowland, once part of the Colorado delta, now separated from it by a low alluvial ridge. It is divided by the shrinking Salton Sea (345 ft below sea-level) into two areas of intensive cultivation: the Imperial Valley, south of the lake (*see* Fig. 98), and the Coachella Valley, north of it.

The mean annual rainfall is only about 3 in., but it is now possible for farmers to take advantage of a year-long growing season, marked by July temperatures exceeding 90° F, and January ones of over 50° F, to cultivate both temperate and tropical crops, owing to the harnessing of the Colorado and the laying down of irrigation channels.

The Colorado, 1450 miles long, and with a drainage basin of nearly 250,000 square miles, is one of the great rivers of North America. Largely fed by the melting snows of the Central Rockies, two-thirds of its course is devoted mainly to the erosion of those tremendous canyons which were described in Chapter XXIV. But the lower section of the river, including an 80-mile stretch in Mexico, runs through a flattish, alluvial region, well adapted for cultivation provided irrigation facilities are available. Unfortunately, the river's régime is extremely irregular, and it carries down to the Gulf of California almost as much silt as water.

Arizona and California, and to a less extent Nevada, all make demands upon Colorado water, and Mexico is also interested. Within each state the farmers' claims are contested by those of city-dwellers, who require water for domestic and industrial purposes. Hence the development, during the present century, of multi-purpose dams, hydro-electric power-stations, water-supply aqueducts, irrigation channels, and works designed to regulate the river and control its floods. Apart from power-stations built in the upper part of the basin, shackles have been placed on the main river at various places below the Grand Canyon. The greatest is Boulder Dam, opened in 1933 and ranking as the highest dam in the world (726 ft). It impounds the 115-mile long Lake Mead, now suffering from silting, despite the provision of settling basins, but capable of storing nearly two years' run-off (*see* Fig. 90). Other dams, subsidiary to Boulder, and lower down, include the Davis, Parker, and Imperial Dams.

Below the Parker Dam is the relatively unimportant, 80-year-old, Palo Verde Irrigation District, and below the Imperial Dam is the smaller, newer, Yuma Irrigation District, largely developed on the Arizona side of the river. More significant than either of these areas is the Imperial

Valley, first irrigated (shortly after 1900) by the Imperial Canal, tapping the Colorado near Yuma, and giving north-west Mexico the prior water-rights. In the 1930s and '40s the wholly Californian "All-American" Canal (80 miles long) and tributary Coachella Branch Canal (130 miles long) were led off from the Colorado to augment and extend the irrigation facilities of the Salton Sink area (see Fig. 95).

[Courtesy: U.S. Information Service.

FIG. 98.—An irrigated farm in the Imperial Valley, California. Fruits and vegetables are the main crops of these beautifully laid-out fields.

In both the Imperial Valley Irrigation District and the smaller Coachella Valley Irrigation District prosperous farmers, with the periodic assistance of migrant Mexicans, grow almost the only dates found in the United States; they produce a wide variety of high-value truck crops, including crisp-head lettuce (which dominates the entire American market from December to March), carrots, cabbages, tomatoes, and peas; grapes, figs, and cantaloupes; long-stapled cotton, flax, and alfalfa. The latter is cut about six times a year and fed to livestock. The irrigated fields have not yet suffered greatly from the deposition of fine silt (making the soil impermeable), owing to the provision of desilting works behind the Colorado dams, but there is some alkaline infestation.

THE SIERRA NEVADA

Towering above the Central Valley are the high, forested Sierra Nevada, forming one of the greatest climatic and human divides in the continent. The mountains are of some economic value for timber, grazing, and mining, and they provide much of California's water supply, but they are thinly peopled and only in a few places crossed by rail and road. The migrant population of tourists may, especially in summer, exceed the resident population, notably in the Lassen Volcano, Sequoia, General Grant, King's Canyon, and Yosemite National Parks, with their giant trees, deep canyons, waterfalls, lakes, glaciated topography, wild life, and sports facilities, including fishing and winter ski-ing. All the Parks are accessible by motor road and are linked together by the "Pacific Coast Trail." Their approximate sites are marked on Fig. 93.

THE DESERT PERIPHERY

As has been already explained (p. 322), California includes part of the West's Basin and Range Province, an area of inland drainage, salt lakes and flats, tilt-blocks, and xerophytic vegetation, well developed in the south-east and north-east. It is remarkable that Mt Whitney, the highest mountain in the country outside Alaska, and Death Valley, the lowest depression in the continent, should be less than 100 miles apart.

This desert fringe, in the lee of the Sierra Nevada and other mountains, is much less important to California than any other part of her terrain. It is thinly peopled, poorly served by communications, and is generally suited only to the poorest grazing. It does, however, attract a few tourists and, as has been mentioned, it can—by virtue of its emptiness, its spaciousness, and the clarity of its atmosphere—be used for military testing purposes.

Chapter XXVII

ALASKA

THE GEOGRAPHICAL FRAMEWORK

GENERAL GEOGRAPHICAL AND POLITICAL ASPECTS

Alaska, a large appendage of the United States in the extreme north-western segment of North America, covers an area of nearly 600,000 square miles, equal to about one-fifth that of the continental United States. Almost three times as big as France, and more than twice the size of Texas, it dwarfs all other states in the Union, to which it was admitted as recently as 1959. It is the first area to acquire statehood since Arizona was granted it in 1912, and the first outside the otherwise contiguous territory of the United States.

Only the 56 miles of Bering Strait separate Alaska from Soviet territory. It is not surprising, therefore, that the earliest foreigners to enter the region since it first acquired its population of Indians, Eskimos, and Aleuts, should have been Russians, who visited it for the first time, under Vitus Bering (himself a Dane) in 1741. Thereafter, Alaska lay under Russian sovereignty for over a century, but did little to reward its rulers. A settlement of fur-trappers and traders was established on Kodiak Island in 1784, and another, twenty years later, at Sitka, which became the seat of Tsarist government. Seals appeared to be the only valuable resource, but scarcely paid for the food the colonists had to import from Siberia. The territory was remote from Moscow and Petrograd, and when the seal population showed signs of becoming depleted Russia was not loth to sell out to the United States in 1867. Seward, the American Secretary of State who negotiated the purchase, spent $7,200,000 on what his vilifiers called "Seward's Folly," "Seward's Ice-chest," "Walrussia," "Playground of the Polar Bear," and other derogatory names.

For many years the new government did little more than the old to develop Alaska. But near the turn of the century came rumours of gold. A "rush" set in to Klondike, Yukon, near the Alaskan border in 1897, and fortune-hunters began to use the Alaskan panhandle as a mode of approach to the diggings. In 1898 a minor rush set in towards Nome on the Bering Sea, and later panners moved into the Yukon and Tanana valleys in Alaska. Gradually, other minerals began to attract attention, salmon-fishing developed, and a serious start was made with agriculture in the

344

1930s. The Second World War emphasised the strategic location of the territory *vis-à-vis* Japan and the Soviet Union, and the United States has spent considerable sums of money on defensive works, *e.g.*, the Alaska Highway and the air bases near Fairbanks, Anchorage, and Nome, and in the Aleutian Islands.

Though still a thinly peopled frontier land, whose wealth up to now has come chiefly from gold, copper, fish, and furs, Alaska is not nearly such a bad country as it is often painted. It is by no means entirely the land of snow, ice, and blizzards pictured by popular writers. Less than one-third of it lies within the Arctic Circle. Many of its harbours are continuously ice-free. It has large resources of oil, coal, timber, and water power, and far more agricultural and grazing land than has yet been utilised. It lies on the Great Circle route from Washington (District of Columbia) to Tokyo. As an indication of its potential importance, it is sufficient at this stage to note that 80% of its population is now white, the rest evenly divided between Eskimos and Indians. From 33,000 in 1880, numbers grew to 302,000 in 1970, an increase of 34% over the 1960 figure. Most live in the south, near the Pacific shores.

More capital is available for Alaska's development now that the territory is a state (the 49th). Unfortunately, its resources on the whole are not unlike those of other Pacific areas in the continent, but are less accessible. It is significant that the degree of economic advance gradually declines going north from California to this area.

The capital of Alaska is Juneau, an early settlement, with a present population of only about 13,500. It is now greatly outranked in population by the better-placed port of Anchorage (120,000), and has also been overtaken by Fairbanks (50,000), the main inland focus.

PHYSICAL GEOGRAPHY

Structurally, Alaska forms the northern part of the American Cordillera. Like British Columbia and Yukon, it consists essentially of a central plateau, trenched by rivers, bounded by high mountain ranges. The main relief features trend chiefly from east to west beyond the panhandle (*see* Fig. 99).

The Pacific Mountains, which represent a continuation of the offshore islands and Coast Ranges of British Columbia, thread the length of the panhandle before dividing into two main groups west of longtitude 140 degrees W.; (*a*) the St Elias Mountains (Mt Logan, Canada, 19,850 ft, Mt St Elias, Alaska, 18,000 ft), sweeping northwards round Prince William Sound and then turning south-west in the Kenai Peninsula and Kodiak Island; (*b*) the Wrangell and Alaska Range (Mt McKinley, the highest peak in North America, 20,320 ft), curving farther north to enclose Cook

Inlet and the Susitna Basin before running out to sea in the Alaska Peninsula and offshore Aleutian Islands.

North of the Pacific Mountains are the basins of the roughly parallel Yukon and Kuskokwim rivers, each terminating in an extensive delta in the lake-strewn, marshy Bering Sea lowland.

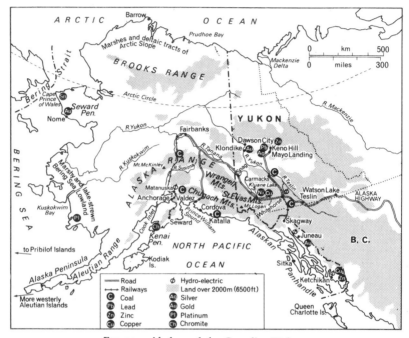

FIG. 99.—Alaska and the Canadian Yukon.

Beyond the Arctic Circle, Alaska is dominated by the Brooks Range (exceeding 8000 ft), a structural extension of the Rocky and Mackenzie Mountains.

The Pacific ranges nourish small icefields and glaciers, some of which descend almost to sea-level. The largest glaciers are those in the St Elias Range, where the piedmont Malaspina Glacier is prominent.

CLIMATE

Alaska is no more uniform climatically than structurally. Broadly speaking, the mean annual precipitation, much of which in the interior and north is composed of snow, declines northwards from the Pacific coast, where it averages over 80 in., to the Arctic shores, where it may not amount to more than 5 in. The panhandle—drenched by both frontal and orographic rain—shows a very well-marked winter maximum, the in-

terior a summer maximum. The Aleutian Islands, with a lower total rainfall than the southern mainland, benefit from a more even seasonal distribution.

The mean annual temperature, of course, is lowest in Arctic Alaska,
where it may average less than 20 degrees F. The winters, though not as
protracted, are almost as cold in the interior, but are 40°–50°F warmer on
the panhandle shores, where maritime influences, enhanced by a northerly
arm of the North Pacific Drift, are strongest. The summers are warm
both in the panhandle and in the centre, but are only cool in and north of
Brooks Range. The mean annual range of temperature is very extreme in
the interior, fairly equable on the Pacific coast.

The following climatic statistics, referring to typical localities in the
various regions of Alaska, are instructive:

	Mean monthly temp. (° F)		Mean annual range of temp. (° F)	Mean monthly rainfall (in.)		Mean annual rainfall (in.)
	Jan.	July		Jan.	July	
Juneau (Panhandle) .	28	58	30	11·4	3·5	90·9
Fairbanks (Interior) .	−12	63	75	0·3	2·0	10·9
Point Barrow (Arctic)	−19	40	58	0·3	1·1	5·6
Dutch Harbour (Aleutians)	32	51	19	5·4	2·3	62·8

THE ECONOMY

WATER POWER AND FORESTRY OCCUPATIONS

Most of Alaska is garmented only with tundra or very light forest owing
to the short duration of the growing season, but there is good coniferous
forest in most of the central and coastal valleys and on the lower slopes of
the Pacific mountains. The maritime forests are almost as rich as those of
the British Columbian coastlands, and there are fine stands of hemlock,
Sitka spruce, and western red cedar.

Alaska is rich in potential water power, especially in the panhandle,
but the region is much more distant from markets than the timberlands
of British Columbia, Washington, Oregon, and northern California.
Therefore, only small amounts of hydro-electricity have been developed,
and relatively few saw-mills and pulp-mills have yet been erected. Some
of the timber is used in the manufacture of salmon-cases, and a little Sitka
spruce is shipped southwards into the Pacific coastlands of Washington
and California, where it is of value to the aircraft industry and there is
some export to Japan. The scattered, small-tree forests of the inland
valleys supply modest amounts of timber and fuel for local purposes.

Fur-trapping, the oldest of Alaska's industries, remains of some consequence. The main catches are fox, musk-rat, and mink. Among the most
interesting animals are the famous brown bears of Kodiak Island, the
largest carnivores in the world, and the equally renowned fur seals of
the Pribilof Islands (three-quarters of the world's total), which are now
protected in government-owned herds, though some hunting is permitted.
A number of fur-ranches have been established.

FISHING

The fisheries of Alaska furnish the region's principal source of wealth
nowadays. Alaskan waters are particularly noted for salmon, of which
Alaska catches even more than British Columbia. Some are caught on the
Yukon and other rivers, but most are netted in coastal waters before they

[Courtesy: U.S. Information Service.
Fig. 100.—Ketchikan, Alaska. This scene is typical of the Alaskan panhandle, with
its fishing-harbours, thickly-forested mountain slopes, and long winding fiords.
Ketchikan supports a pulp-mill as well as a fishing fleet, and has a population of
about 7,000.

begin their annual run upstream. Both fishing and canning operations are
seasonal in character, and attract many transients, white and Indian, to
Alaskan coasts. The first cannery was established in 1878. Now almost
every inlet of any size and depth has at least one. Juneau, Sitka, Cordova,

Anchorage, and Ketchikan are among towns which engage in the industry, but there are also packing-stations on the south side of the Kenai Peninsula, on Kodiak Island, and at the head of Kuskokwim Bay (*see* Fig. 100).

Herring, halibut, cod, crabs (a speciality of Kodiak) and shrimps are other fish which live in the shallow seas off Alaska. Some are caught by fishermen operating from panhandle ports, but lack of capital and fresh-fish markets limit their catches. Ships from Prince Rupert (British Columbia) and Puget Sound also take part in these fisheries.

MINING

During the present century considerable amounts of many different ores and metals have been shipped out of Alaska to Puget Sound ports, but most of them have been minerals of high value in relation to the cost of transport, *e.g.* gold, platinum, silver. New deposits are still being located, as the careful geological survey of the country proceeds.

Gold was the first mineral to attract outsiders, *c.* 1900, though one or two discoveries had been made before then. It has been located in several places and is still worked round Juneau, Nome, and elsewhere. The principal seats of operation, however, are the Yukon and Tanana valleys, where power-driven dredges recover placer-gold from river-gravels.

Copper, obtained from the historic Kennicott mines at the foot of the Wrangell Mountains before 1938, when the economically valuable ores were exhausted, used to be Alaska's second chief mineral. Less is secured today, though deposits are known to exist in several localities, especially in the Wrangell and Chugach Mountains.

Coal is widely distributed and there are vast reserves in the interior. But most of it is sub-bituminous and lignitic, and the present market is very restricted. The best grades come from the Matanuska valley, about 25 miles from the sea: they chiefly serve the Alaskan railroad. A little anthracite is worked with difficulty in the Katalla field, 25 miles east of Cordova, and there are small mines near the Anchorage–Fairbanks railway on the north side of the Alaskan Range, especially in the Nenana or Healy River field, 75 miles from Fairbanks, where a high-grade lignite is worked. The main market is Fairbanks, but the metal industry in the vicinity takes some.

Petroleum and natural gas show phenomenal promise. Strikes were made near Cook Inlet in 1956 and both on- and off-shore wells are now numerous; several short pipe-lines have been laid down and ready markets found in Anchorage and other Pacific towns and a gas liquefaction plant has been built at Kenai. Far larger deposits of both oil and gas have been more recently located on the Arctic shore following the initial find of petroleum in 1968 at Prudhoe Bay, 150 miles east of Barrow. British, American and other international oil companies have all been attracted to this remote area whose vast resources of oil and gas have increased U.S. proven reserves by at least 30% and, though production costs will be very high, should in time greatly reduce her dependence on imports from politically less stable areas. A successful traverse of the Arctic sea-route along the northern shores of Canada in 1969 by S.S. *Manhattan*, a tanker equipped with an ice-breaking prow, showed the feasibility of shipping the oil in this way to the eastern U.S., but economists believe that movement by pipe-line would be cheaper. Hence the decision to build a line across Alaska to the deep, warm-water port of Valdez and Canada's suggestion of an alternative route through the Mackenzie valley to Edmonton. These pipe-line projects pose environmental problems; there are fears of the harm that could result from another earthquake of the severity which virtually wiped out Valdez and Seward and caused serious damage in Anchorage in 1964, and it is widely acknowledged that the engineering problems presented by a permafrost area will not be easily resolved.

Among other Alaskan minerals are the following: (*a*) platinum, worked in the hills south of the Kuskokwim delta; (*b*) tin, mined north of Nome, near Cape Prince of Wales; (*c*) copper, silver, zinc, and lead, worked on a small scale on the mainland coast opposite Ketchikan, but mainly produced as by-products of gold-mining; (*d*) chromite, obtained from the southern end of the Kenai Peninsula; (*e*) iron, found at the head of the Alaska Peninsula and south of Juneau.

AGRICULTURE

Little has yet been done to develop the agricultural potentialities of Alaska. There are several obstacles: a short growing season, except in the panhandle; a rugged relief in areas which may be suitable climatically; a low rainfall in the central basins, where the physiography is more favourable; a lack of sunshine and an excessive rainfall in lowland pockets near the otherwise satisfactory south coast; generally podsolised soils and ground which suffers from summer water-logging; inadequate communications and remoteness from any but small markets. It is not, perhaps, astonishing that 90% of the food eaten in Alaska still comes from outside.

Three areas of existing farmland stand out:

1. *The Matanuska valley*, a district producing, for fodder or local consumption in ports, mines, and military camps, dairy produce, hay, wheat, rye, oats, barley, potatoes, and hardy vegetables. In this area the growing season lasts about 110–120 days, more than 18 hours of daylight are available in summer, the mean annual rainfall totals about 15 in., soils are fairly

good, and the situation offers shelter from the worst weather. A few farmers began operations there in 1910, but few colonists moved in before 1935, when the Federal Relief Administration of the United States chose the area as the best place in Alaska for the resettlement of families ruined by the contemporary agricultural depression.

2. *The Kenai Peninsula*, a similar region, with, however, a cooler, rainier, and windier climate. The principal market is Anchorage.

3. *The Fairbanks district*, in the interior, with less favourable natural conditions: a growing season of only about 90 days, and a lower mean annual rainfall (little more than 10 in.).

Areas of good grass exist in the Alaskan Peninsula, Kodiak and adjacent islands, and in the Aleutians, and small numbers of cattle and sheep are pastured. But the heavy summer rains make hay-making for indoor winter feeding a hazardous occupation.

Reindeer were introduced to the Alaskan Eskimos in 1891, and at first multiplied rapidly. Though used for food and clothing, their numbers have recently greatly decreased, and though the State could probably support 4 million of these animals, there is as yet no evidence that a large commercial reindeer-meat industry will be developed.

MINOR INDUSTRIES AND TRADE RELATIONS

Little manufacturing is carried on in Alaska except for fish-processing, small-scale metal-smelting, a limited amount of saw-milling, boat-building, machine-shop work, printing and publishing. Among deterrents are the restricted labour supply and the absence of large, conveniently placed markets. Power supplies are not wanting. There is, in particular, a wealth of potential water power. Three important hydro stations have been erected: (a) at Juneau, to supply the capital; (b) at Ketchikan, to feed local saw- and pulp-mills; (c) near Palmer, north of Anchorage, where the newly built Eklutna Dam furnishes power for Anchorage, the Matanuska valley, and the modern pulp-mills of Seward. Plans have been made to divert the flow of the upper Yukon in Canada to the Pacific coast and to use its power for a new aluminium reduction plant to be built near Taiya, but Canada, having recently constructed its own plant at Kitimat and believing that a time may come when she will herself require the power latent in the river, has refused to sanction the scheme.

The more adventurous type of tourist is being drawn nowadays to Alaska, which he may reach by Alaska Highway, sea, or air. The Mount McKinley National Park is among the areas he seeks, but there are many others of spectacular grandeur, and many districts provide excellent opportunities for fishing and shooting and the study of wild life.

Nearly all the trade of Alaska is in the hands of U.S. merchants, and virtually all of it is conducted by sea, the main trading port in the United States being Seattle, those in Alaska including Anchorage, easily the largest city (pop. nearly 50,000), Ketchikan, and Juneau. Fish-products, furs, gold, and other metals are exported, food, machinery, petroleum, and general stores imported. The total volume of trade is very small.

COMMUNICATIONS

One of the keys to the future development of Alaska is the provision of a more adequate system of communications. The State, as we have seen, is not without resources, but these are widely scattered and markets are distant.

Existing communications have been developed mainly in response to the needs of miners and strategists. The state is naturally favoured by three long, navigable rivers: the Yukon, open for the three summer months as far as Whitehorse, Yukon, over 2000 miles from its mouth; the Tanana tributary, navigable to Fairbanks; and the Kuskokwim, available for 650 miles. Unfortunately, the shallow delta of the Yukon limits the size of vessels which can use it. In winter much use is made of overland dog-sledges and reindeer-sledges, which find it easy at that season to travel along the frozen waterways.

Coastal shipping is widely used, as most of the Alaskan settlements are ports. Most of the Pacific coast is ice-free throughout the year, but a few sheltered inlets, e.g. Cook Inlet, freeze up briefly. The Bering Sea, however, is open only four months, the Arctic coast for barely one.

Modern landways include two railways and a number of well separated roads. To serve the miners at Klondike, a panhandle railway was built from Skagway (now virtually a "ghost" town, since the line is little used now) to Whitehorse via the White Pass (2888 ft), and a second, longer track (measuring 500 miles) was laid down by the U.S. Government from Seward to Fairbanks. The latter serves Anchorage and Matanuska, and utilises en route the Susitna and Nenana valleys, as well as gaps through both the coastal and Alaskan ranges. Among motor-roads are:

1. The Alaska Highway, of which one-fifth of the 1500-odd miles was built in Alaskan territory. This road, constructed by American engineers in 1942, when Japan was threatening an attack on North America via the Aleutian Islands, has its origin at the railhead town of Dawson Creek, British Columbia, and its terminus at Fairbanks. It remains the only direct land link between the continental United States and Alaska.

2. The Richardson Highway, built in 1910 between Valdez (on Prince William Sound) and Fairbanks.

3. A road joining Seward to Anchorage and the Matanuska valley and extending, as the Glenn Highway, north-eastwards to the Alaska Highway.

4. A small number of additional roads focusing upon Fairbanks, including a new winter road for ferrying oilfield equipment to Prudhoe Bay.

To a remote country of indifferent ground transport such as Alaska, air services are particularly valuable. They carry passengers and also light but expensive freight. All the main settlements, including Juneau, Anchorage, Fairbanks, Kodiak, and Nome, have large modern airfields, and there are many smaller ones. Since 1957, Anchorage has been a halt on the Scandinavian Airlines route from Copenhagen to Tokyo via the north Polar Basin.

THE NATURAL REGIONS OF ALASKA

On the basis of physiography and climate, Alaska may be divided into the following natural regions: (a) the Pacific coastlands and mountains, including the panhandle; (b) the central basins, together with the Bering Sea lowlands; (c) the Arctic plains; (d) the Aleutian Islands.

The Pacific region is one of rugged mountains, lofty ice-fields, deeply cut valleys, fiords, and protective skerry guard. It is the most populous of Alaska's regions, owing to its relatively easy accessibility, its mild winter climate, its profitable fisheries, and its forests.

The Central Plateau region, threaded by the lower course of the Yukon and by the Kuskokwim and other rivers, is of much gentler relief, and consists in the main of flat-topped highlands and broad valleys. The climate is much more extreme than that of the Pacific area, and the precipitation is only about one-fifth as heavy, but there are extensive tracts, not as yet greatly used, available for cultivation and grazing. About two-thirds of the region consists of open woodland dotted with white and black spruce, white birch, balsam poplar, black cottonwood, aspen, and tamarack. Timber-working industries, at present in their infancy, as well as agriculture, could well be expanded.

The Arctic plains form a physical extension of the Canadian tundra. Here, in an area cut by the 70th parallel, the relief is low and rolling, variety being provided by streams flowing north from Brooks Range. Increasingly in this tundra environment the Eskimo population, traditionally caribou hunters and polar fishers, are trading furs for clothing and food at modern stores, e.g. at Barrow. In conjunction with Canada, the U.S. Government has established here part of the strategic Distant Early

Warning (DEW) Line system: a string of radar stations designed to warn the two allies of the approach of long-range Russian bombers across the Arctic. The new "radomes," housing the radar equipment, outwardly resemble large Eskimo igloos and are in part manned by native people. A wider outlet for the manual skills of the Eskimos is being provided by the international oil companies now operating on the north coast.

The Aleutian Archipelago extends westwards from the Alaskan Peninsula for nearly 1200 miles, and reaches within 600 miles of Kamchatka (U.S.S.R.). The islands are often shrouded in fogs born near the junction of the cold Bering and warm Japanese currents, and are frequently whipped by gales and lashed by heavy seas. In many places grass grows better than trees owing to the powerful winds. About 20 of the islands, including Attu and Unalaska, are large, the rest very small. Most are mountainous, even volcanic, and few are inhabited. The aboriginal Aleuts, now numbering less than 1000, appear to be dying out. They are mostly hunters of seal and walrus. Like the Indians of the continental mainland, they are wards of the American Government. Their largest native village stands on Unalaska, close to the modern naval base of Dutch Harbour.

STUDY QUESTIONS

1. Make a study of the physical geography of the shorelines of the United States.

2. Referring to specific examples in the United States, discuss the problem of soil erosion and describe the steps which are being taken to reduce it.

3. Illustrate from the United States the various types of agriculture which may give the farmer a surplus of cattle products.

4. Analyse, with reference to different parts of the United States, the conditions under which the truck-farming and dairying industries have developed.

5. Give a reasoned account of the distribution of wheat cultivation in the United States.

6. To what extent are the major industrial regions of the United States located on coalfields and oilfields?

7. To what extent is it true to say that the principal differences in the geography of the United States are to be found between north and south rather than between east and west? Where would you draw the boundary lines between these major areas?

8. For what reasons is the eastern half of the United States more populous than the western?

9. Account for the decline of the cotton textile industry in New England and its expansion in the Piedmont Plateau.

10. How far has the existence and growth of New York affected the geography of the north-eastern United States?

11. Discuss the problems common to large cities, and illustrate your answer with reference to New York, Chicago, and Los Angeles. What steps would you take to ease these problems?

12. Compare and contrast the agricultural production of Florida and California.

13. Divide the Appalachian Mountains into physical regions and draw contrasts between them. Which of them has the greatest economic advantages?

14. How far is the Middle West a distinctive geographical region?

15. Define the Corn Belt of the United States in terms of physical geography.

16. Give a reasoned account of the distribution of the steel industry of the United States.

17. Discuss the industrial and commercial activities of those cities in the United States which are situated on the shores of the Great Lakes.

18. Detail the factors which have led to the break-up of the American Cotton Belt as an area of virtually continuous cotton cultivation.

19. Account for the increasing industrial importance of the "South" in the United States.

20. Make a geographical study of the agricultural and industrial activities of Texas.

21. Why are there few large cities in the United States between longitude 100 degrees W. and the Pacific coastlands?

22. Examine the roles of the Rocky Mountains and the Sierra Nevada as geographical barriers.

23. Locate three large multi-purpose dams in the United States, and estimate the benefits their construction is conferring upon the people of the areas in which they are located.

24. Make a comparative study of: (a) Seattle and Portland (Oregon); (b) San Francisco and Los Angeles; (c) Chicago and St Louis; (d) Houston and New Orleans; (e) Philadelphia and Baltimore.

25. Discuss the importance of each of the following cities as industrial centres: Minneapolis–St Paul, Kansas City, Pittsburgh, Detroit, Tacoma, Atlanta.

26. Why do you think California has come to be the most populous State in the Union?

27. In what respects is Alaska unlike the major part of the United States? What geographical features does it possess which make it valuable to the United States?

PART FOUR

ANGLO-AMERICA

Chapter XXVIII

COMMUNICATIONS AND FOREIGN TRADE

GENERAL CONSIDERATIONS

Both the United States and Canada are of continental proportions, the one a little smaller than Europe, the other a little larger. Both have well-developed communications by rail, motor highway, and air, like Europe, but long-distance traffic is more common in North America than in Europe owing to the multiplicity of international frontiers in the latter.

Canada, of course, though more extensive than its neighbour, has fewer railway lines and fewer roads, as almost the whole of the north is unsettled. In the United States there are no "negative areas" of wide extent, but owing to their relief and low population densities, the Appalachians and Ozarks have fewer lines of route than other eastern areas, and the whole of the western half, except for the Pacific zone, is much less generously served by transportation facilities than the densely thronged eastern, and especially north-eastern, portions of the country. Eighty per cent of the total rail mileage lies east of 100 degrees W. longitude.

There is a substantial movement of goods and people between the United States and Canada, by both landways and airways, and each country has its north–south communications, but the main lines of route run from east to west, especially in Canada. Both countries share one important waterway, the Great Lakes–St Lawrence shipping route, and both find the Panamá Canal advantageous as a means of linking Pacific and Atlantic ports and regions.

COMMUNICATIONS

RAILWAYS

Canada, with a population of about 21 millions, has approximately 60,000 miles of railway track, while the United States, holding ten times as many people, has more than 200,000 miles. While Canada claims to have more rail lines per head than any other country, and an expanding network, its neighbour draws attention to the fact that her mileage is as great as that of Europe, and that she carries a third of the world's rail freight. In her case, however, as in that of Britain, the railway mileage is now less than it was in 1916, owing to the effective competition of road

vehicles and aircraft, which has resulted in the closing down of some uneconomic branch-lines. Nor is there any need in the United States to
build new railways, since, unlike Canada, she no longer has any large
pioneer areas to develop.

Nearly all the railways of Anglo-America have been built on the
standard gauge (4 ft 8½ in), but whereas only two significant companies
are active in Canada, a very large number of fiercely competing concerns
operate the U.S. lines.

No company in the United States runs a coast-to-coast service, and
most rail passengers who wish to cross the continent must generally make
changes, certainly of trains, perhaps also of stations. Most of the eastern
lines terminate at Chicago or St Louis, most western lines originate from
there. In Canada the privately owned Canadian Pacific Railway, con-
ceived in 1880, runs through services from Montreal to Vancouver via
Ottawa, Sudbury, Winnipeg, Calgary, and the Kicking Horse Pass; a
loop-line serves Toronto, and there is an alternative track through British
Columbia via the Crowsnest Pass. The Canadian National Railway, a
State-owned company formed in 1922–23, mainly by the amalgamation
of various private lines which did not pay, carries traffic from Halifax to
Vancouver or Prince Rupert via Montreal, Winnipeg, Edmonton, and
the Yellowhead Pass across the Rockies.

The Union Pacific Railway was the first in North America to link the
eastern part of the United States with the Pacific coast (1869). Several
other companies, e.g. the Great Northern, North Pacific, Santa Fé, and
South Pacific systems, now also have lines which cross the Rocky Mountains en route to the Pacific (see Fig. 101).

Canada's mileage is still overwhelmingly single-track, and railways in
that country are spreading only very slowly and tenuously into the north,
where the only existing lines lead to a few valuable mineral deposits, e.g.
the iron of Schefferville, or to the small Bay ports of Churchill and
Moosonee. The volume of freight traffic on Canadian railways doubled
between 1939 and 1958, but is increasing less rapidly than that carried by
lorries or trucks, especially in the field of high-value merchandise. The
C.P.R. itself has recently entered the trucking business, with the establishment, in the busy Montreal–Toronto area, of a "piggyback" service,
whereby trains of flat rail cars are loaded with truck trailers so as to maintain a door-to-door service at rail freight charges.

In the United States there are more double-tracked lines than in Canada,
but only in a few parts of the north-east, the greatest trading area, are
there any three- or four-track lines. The size of the average locomotive
and freight-car is, however, greater than in Europe, which has more
double-tracked lines. The U.S. railway companies are losing even more
traffic to the roads than the Canadian ones, and increasing numbers of

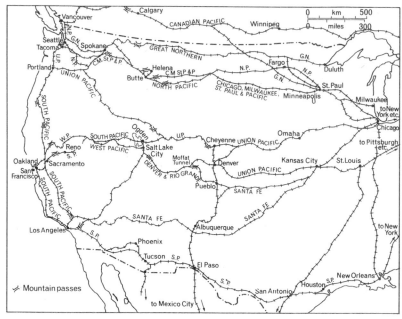

FIG. 101.—Main railways of western U.S.A.

passengers are using long-distance coaches and especially private cars for their journeys. In both countries long-distance passengers are tending to choose air transport because of its speedy operation. The New York Central Railroad, utilising the Hudson–Mohawk corridor, leads in passenger traffic among American railways, but the Pennsylvanian Railroad, linking Pittsburgh to Philadelphia and New York, carries more goods traffic. Not surprisingly, the two companies have recently merged. Among western lines, the double-tracked Union Pacific has the heaviest freight.

ROADS

Both Canada and the United States are proceeding vigorously with the extension of all-weather, well-surfaced roads, and in densely peopled areas are building highways specially designed for express transport. Both, however, and especially the United States, are finding it difficult, in urban areas, to cope with the recent immense growth of motor traffic, despite the construction of by-passes, clover-leaf crossings, and parkways. Already the United States has over 100 million vehicles on her roads. Each U.S. family averages more than one private car, and in Canada there is one car for every three people.

As compared with railway transport, of course, roads have the advantage of greater flexibility, door-to-door service, and even, in some cases, cheaper fuel, and the maintenance of roadways is usually undertaken by public bodies, not private users. Therefore, although the unit of transport (the lorry or truck) carries less than the goods train, it is often preferred by business men and also by other individuals.

The United States has now completed a number of transcontinental roads, but Canada possesses only the Trans-Canada Highway, which covers the 3640 miles between Vancouver and Sydney (Nova Scotia) with extensions to St John's (Newfoundland) and Victoria (British Columbia). The Canadian Government, moreover, with the assistance of provincial authorities, still has the task of driving roads into her great northern pioneer areas. Ottawa has lately agreed to give more help to the provinces in order to provide highways "that adhere to the pioneer principle of opening up a promising area," while Quebec and Ontario have embarked upon the construction of toll roads, similar in conception to the four- to eight-lane turnpikes of the United States, which have become a marked feature of the transport network of the north-eastern states, and are also being laid down elsewhere. In 1961 the United States embarked on a twelve-year project (the National System of Interstate and Defence Highways), designed to link together by broad, toll-free freeways, totalling 41,000 miles, virtually every city of 50,000 inhabitants.

AIR TRANSPORT

It is natural for such large, economically advanced countries as Canada and the United States to have well-developed airways, which not only speed up internal transport but also link these countries with each other and with foreign lands. The United States now has more than twice as many civil aircraft as railway engines, and the volume of her internal air traffic, expanding yearly, is more than ten times that of her international traffic. In all, U.S. airlines carry about 60% of the world's air passengers and 50% of the air freight.

Airways are even more valuable to Canada than to the United States, because her ground communications are inferior. In northern Canada aircraft are essential for almost all long journeys. Here, there are many independent operators who carry on the traditions of the famous "bush pilots" of the 1920s and '30s. They serve the new mining localities as well as isolated Indian and Eskimo communities, who may never have seen a railway engine. The strategic value of Arctic Canada as regards world airways was referred to in Chapter VIII.

WATERWAYS

Canada and the United States share the Great Lakes–St Lawrence waterway. Even before the completion of the St Lawrence Seaway this was the world's greatest inland water route. It is now being increasingly used by both countries, especially for the carriage of low-cost, bulky merchandise

FIG. 102.—Traffic on Mississippi River. Three barges and a tug-boat are shown
passing through an open bridge span at Hannibal, childhood home of Mark
Twain, who was once a Mississippi steam-boat pilot. The area shown here
was severely flooded in 1973.

such as iron ore, coal, gravel, limestone, pulp-wood, and grain.

Canada makes some use, too, of the Mackenzie River system in the
north-west, but as it occupies a poorly developed region, it produces little
traffic. Much more important is the Mississippi system in the United
States, which provides a well-used 9-ft channel from the Gulf of Mexico
to Minneapolis (River Mississippi), Pittsburgh (River Ohio), Knoxville
(River Tennessee), and Sioux City (River Missouri) (see Fig. 102). In the
north these river routes are joined to the Great Lakes at Chicago by an
equally deep channel connecting the Illinois River to Lake Michigan,
while in the south Mississippi navigation gives way to the Intra-Coastal
Waterway along the Gulf shores. The Ohio is the busiest section of the
Mississippi waterway. Along it many modern barges carry large quantities of oil, coal, coke, ore, sand, gravel, pig iron, grain and steel.

In the north-east of the United States the New York State Barge
Canal, in competition with parallel roads and railways, transports
many typical water-borne goods between Lake Erie and the navigable
Hudson River.

CANADIAN TRADE

INTERNATIONAL TRADE

Canada probably leads the world in respect of the volume of foreign
trade *per capita*. It amounts to more than $1 million annually, compared
with $350 for the United States; in both cases the figure represents more
than a six-fold increase over 1938. In 1959, for the first time, Canada's

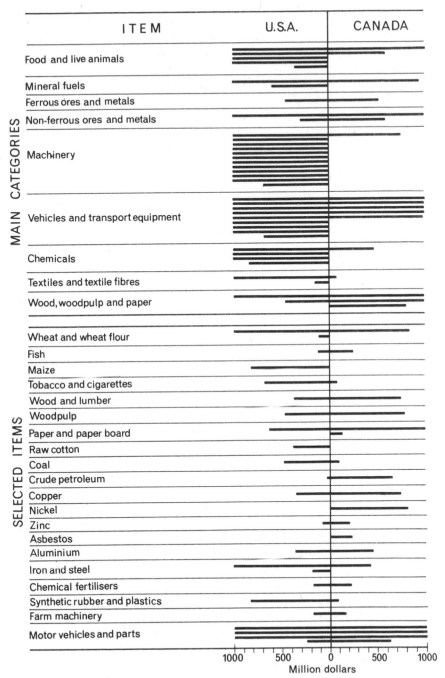

FIG. 103.—Exports of Canada and U.S.A., 1970, compared.

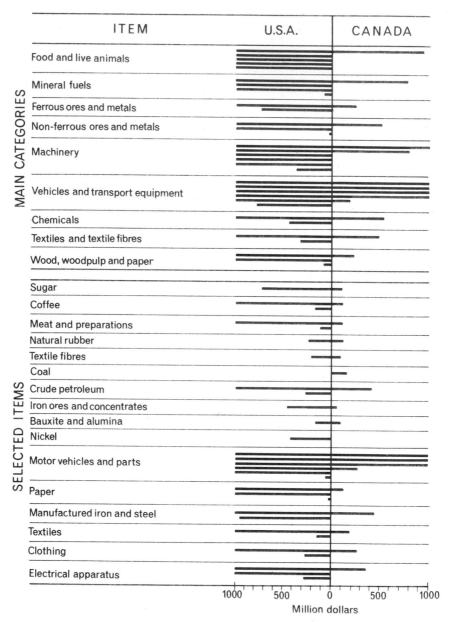

FIG. 104.—Imports of Canada and U.S.A., 1970, compared.

exports exceeded $5000 million, and were surpassed only by those of the United States, United Kingdom, and West Germany. By 1970 they approached $17000, but were exceeded by those of Japan as well as by those of the afore-mentioned countries. This figure represents about a quarter of her national product. By contrast, the United States exports only about 5% of her national output.

In most years Canada spends roughly the same sum on the import of goods and services as she derives from her exports. As an exporter, she makes considerable use of her mineral, agricultural, and forest resources, many of which are processed prior to shipment. Hence 40% of her outgoing products are classed as "manufactures." Among individual exports, the largest single group consists of motor vehicles, closely followed by timber, wood products like pulp and plywood, and newsprint. Grain, especially wheat, may come third, but is now being successfully challenged by various non-ferrous metals and products made from them, e.g. uranium, nickel, aluminium, copper, asbestos, lead and zinc. Other large exports include iron ore, farm and other machinery, meat and dairy products, fish, petroleum and chemicals (see Fig. 103).

Over 60% of Canada's exports find a market in the United States, the chief customer for paper, nickel, aluminium, meat and petroleum. Less than 15% go to Great Britain, which takes, in particular, wheat, timber, aluminium, pulp and paper, copper, and barley. Other countries importing large quantities of the Canadian commodities include West Germany and Japan. Recently the U.S.S.R. and China have bought much of her wheat.

As a young country, Canada naturally imports many industrial goods, notably from the United States, to a much lesser extent from Britain. The most important are machinery, including motor-car engines and farm equipment, iron and steel, electrical apparatus, woollens and worsteds, cotton textiles, ships and chemicals (see Fig. 104). Her Atlantic areas import petroleum, and southern Ontario buys Pennsylvanian coal. Canada's climate makes her dependent upon warmer lands for the purchase of such agricultural products as cane-sugar, coffee, tropical fruit, cotton, and rubber.

The United States is able to supply Canada with 70% of the goods she imports. Other countries satisfying her needs include Great Britain, Japan, Belgium, France and West Germany (manufactures), Venezuela and Saudi Arabia (petroleum), Brazil (coffee), British West Indies (sugar and bananas), and Malaya (rubber).

SEA-PORTS

Most of the trade which passes between Canada and the United States is carried either by landways or by Great Lakes shipping. But the greater part of the traffic she transacts with other countries goes from either Atlantic or Pacific sea-ports. Montreal, though open for less than eight months, conducts most foreign trade, but Vancouver, completely ice-free even if more isolated from Europe, has tended to approach Montreal fairly closely in recent years. Seven Islands, the new iron-shipping port on the St Lawrence estuary, has shown a remarkable advance, and in 1958 exported a greater volume of goods than other important Great Lakes–St Lawrence ports, e.g. Thunder Bay, Hamilton, Toronto and Quebec. Halifax is the chief winter port of eastern Canada. On the Pacific side, Vancouver has no real rival, and the country has only one significant port on her northern coast: Churchill.

Of the total freight handled at Canadian ports, about half represents foreign cargoes, the remainder coastwise loadings and unloadings.

UNITED STATES TRADE

INTERNATIONAL TRADE

Both in volume and in value, the foreign trade of the United States amounts to very much less than her internal trade. Yet since the Second World War the country has transacted more foreign trade than any other.

When considering the United States' trading partners, pride of place goes to Canada, which, indeed, is concerned with a quarter of the United States' foreign trade. Hence the mutual trade of these two countries is the greatest in the world. The United Kingdom and Japan generally head the list of overseas trading partners. Brazil (coffee) and Venezuela (petroleum), West Germany (manufactures) are among the chief suppliers of goods to the United States, and Cuba (sugar) was high on the list of suppliers before 1960. Among the nation's most valued customers, besides Canada and Britain, are Japan, Mexico, West Germany, the Netherlands, India, and Venezuela.

The commodities exported from the United States are extremely varied owing to the breadth of the country's economy (see Fig. 103). Most of them fall into the following categories: (a) manufactures, especially motor vehicles, aircraft, machinery, steel, cotton and synthetic textiles, chemicals, electrical equipment; (b) agricultural products, e.g. raw cotton, wheat, maize, soybeans, meat and dairy produce, tobacco, fruit; (c) minerals and non-agricultural raw materials, especially coal, petroleum, molybdenum, base metals, phosphates, potash, sulphur, and timber. In nearly every case the value of individual export commodities is very much less than the domestic consumption of those commodities.

Despite the fact that U.S. exports are often worth far more than her imports, the United States buys many of the world's surplus commodities. They include: (*a*) foodstuffs, *e.g.* sugar, coffee, bananas, cacao, whisky; (*b*) raw materials, *e.g.* wood-pulp, rubber, tropical fibres, wool, petroleum, nickel, tin, manganese, bauxite, copper, iron, asbestos and diamonds; (*c*) manufactures, especially those of high quality, *e.g.* newsprint, sawn timber, motor cars, porcelain, textiles.

The United States is a much more self-sufficing country than Canada, and, but for the high living standards of her population, the extent of her foreign trade would be much less than it is. She is lacking in relatively few commodities, *e.g.* natural rubber, silk, certain metals, and tropical fruits and oilseeds, but even for some of these she produces substitutes, *e.g.* synthetic rubber, nylon, temperate and sub-tropical fruits, and vegetable oils. She also possesses the largest merchant fleet in the world, a fleet which accounts for about one-third of the global tonnage.

MAJOR SEA-PORTS

The Atlantic, Pacific, and Gulf shores of the United States all provide many harbours for U.S. ships, and the country has a large number of busy sea-ports. It is, therefore, somewhat surprising to find one port—New York—handling so much both of the foreign and coastwise shipping of the country. As an overseas port, it completely dominates the rest, and may conduct more than 30% by value of the entire overseas trade of the nation. Supporting its activities, especially on the North Atlantic run, are Philadelphia, Baltimore, Boston, and the Hampton Roads ports. On the Gulf coast, Houston and Corpus Christi have advanced phenomenally during the last generation owing to the extension of petroleum-drilling, cotton-growing, and manufacturing in the Gulf coastal region and its hinterland, and their harbour facilities have been improved to allow them to deal with the increased traffic of Texas. New Orleans, a more general port, is still an important trading city. On the Pacific coast, San Francisco, Los Angeles, Seattle, Tacoma and Portland continue to dominate the trading scheme, and are growing in significance with the expansion of the West's population and the development of its economy. All of them have benefited from the opening of the Panamá Canal.

It must not be forgotten that the United States, like Canada, has a fourth coast, viz. the shores of the Great Lakes–St Lawrence Waterway, where a number of great inland ports, *e.g.* Duluth, Chicago, Detroit, Conneaut, Toledo and Ashtabula (*see* p. 226) are located. Though principally concerned with more or less local shipments of coal, iron ore, and grain, they are developing increased contacts, not only with Canada but also with overseas destinations. These ports, alone among U.S. shipping centres, are closed by ice for four to five months yearly.

Chapter XXIX

POLITICAL AND SOCIAL PROBLEMS

A SUMMARY OF THE PROBLEMS

Like all other countries, Canada and the United States are beset with both internal and external problems. Even before they expanded westwards to achieve their present dimensions, both laid up future trouble for themselves by adopting federal constitutions. In these the work of the central government (at Ottawa and Washington respectively) is supported by the work of regional administrations (10 provincial governments in Canada, 50 States' governments in the United States, including those of Alaska and Hawaii). This dichotomy of control, though difficult, perhaps impossible to avoid in any very large country, may weaken national unity, because regional and federal executives may have divergent views, and may have reason to complain about the extent of each other's powers. Overriding such a political division is the disunion which may result from an undue allegiance to sectionalism. Should a man of Maine, for example, consider himself primarily an American, a New Englander, or a subject simply of his own State?

Aside from these internal political problems, there is the question of the civil rights that are to be accorded to aboriginal and minority populations. What should be the attitude of white Canadians and Americans to their Eskimo and Indian populations? How should the majority of Canadians treat the French element in their midst, and what place should the negro citizens of the United States hold in their country?

Also to be considered briefly in this chapter are the relations between Canada and the United States, and the relations between these two countries and the outside world, in particular, their attitude towards Europe and the Soviet Union, and the policy of the United States towards Latin America.

INTERNAL UNITY AND DISUNITY

Within both the United States and Canada, political cohesion remains pretty strong despite the problems posed by distance, the physical barrier of the Western Cordillera, the existence of large minority groups, the polyglot origins of their people as a whole, and the federal system of government. Factors which have encouraged the attainment of political and national unity are the development of nation-wide transportation, the establishment of mass-communication media, the possession of a common language, and the threat of external aggression.

"States' Rights" continue to be among the most disruptive elements. Disputes between Federal and States' governments are persistent. Recently there have been quarrels about the right to work offshore oil deposits, and about the position of negroes in the community. From time to time, the central executive has found it difficult to undertake regional planning because of opposition from the affected States, which fear the abrogation of their rights. For instance, the Tennessee Valley Authority, whose creation involved some degree of federal control over seven different States, was set up only after fierce attacks from the several administrations concerned. The main threat to the political cohesion of the United States, of course, was removed by the Civil War (1861–65), when eleven southern States, covering a quarter of the nation's area and containing 18% of the population, were baulked of their intention to secede from the Union and establish a separate Confederacy.

Sectional interests cut across both Federal and States' Rights. These are chiefly a product of the disparity between the administrative and the geographical region, a disparity common to large countries whose internal frontiers have been artificially drawn. It poses the question: which, to mankind, is the more significant grouping, that which comes from living in the same geographical region, or that which comes from living under the same government? What common interests have the Pacific peoples of the United States and Canada, cut off from the rest of the continent by the Cordillera, with, for instance, the extensive grain farmers of Saskatchewan and the Dakotas, even though they are subject to the same laws? And how far can one expect these farmers to have the same outlook as their fellow nationals in the large Atlantic cities?

In Canada all provincial boundaries cut across essential geographical divisions, and most Provinces include parts of several distinct natural and economic regions, therefore even provincial unity is difficult to achieve. To avoid the central council being dominated by Ontario and Quebec, the largest as well as the most populous political units, individual Provinces often present a common front, e.g. the four eastern Provinces unite as the Atlantic section, and Manitoba, Saskatchewan, and Alberta may speak together as the Prairies. Even so, the Atlantic Provinces can only muster 33 seats in Parliament and the Prairie Provinces only 48, against 75 for Quebec alone and 70 for Ontario.

In the United States the primary division between the North and the South—based on both climatic and human divergencies—nearly broke the nation. Today, with the increasing northward migration of the negroes, and the extension of manufacturing in the South, the division is becoming more blurred, and is being partially replaced by another, *i.e.* the division between the humid, industrial, intensively farmed East and the arid, pastoral, and mining West. From the latter section, the Pacific coastlands, now fast developing their human and economic resources, stand apart.

Within each of these large sections, North, South, East, and West, there are smaller ones whose interests do not always coincide with the rest, *e.g.* the Middle West, New England, and Florida. Finally, as we have seen, there are individual States, with their own constitutions, fostering their own loyalties. Some are very large, like Alaska, Texas, and California, some are very small, like Rhode Island and Massachusetts; some are very prosperous like California and Pennsylvania, others, *e.g.* Nevada, have very few resources, and have very little money available for development.

RACIAL PROBLEMS

THE NORTH AMERICAN ESKIMOS

In the North American tundra live between 50,000 and 60,000 Eskimos. Canada has about 12,500, Alaska 25,000, Greenland 20,000. Most live by hunting sea-mammals, fishing, and trapping Arctic fauna. Though racially akin, they live in separate groups, divergent in language and custom, even in their way of building houses. Their numbers fell considerably after they had come into contact with white people, mainly due to the introduction of new diseases, *e.g.* measles, smallpox, and influenza, but medical services are now reducing the incidence and severity of these complaints.

Some Eskimos have now been integrated with white people, for example, through the construction of defence works, and some are now employed as wage-earning mechanics. The introduction of the reindeer into Alaska and north-western Canada, and of the sheep into Greenland, has changed the lives of others. Generally speaking, the Eskimos, whether under American, Canadian, or Danish tutelage, are slowly being helped to make as easy a transition as possible from a self-sufficient Stone Age culture to a modern commercial civilisation. Teachers, doctors, missionaries, traders, radio men are all actively concerned in this transition, and all are doing their best to make it as painless as possible.

How far should the unique culture of the Eskimos be permitted to die out? Is there nothing in it worth preserving? Should the well-meaning efforts of strangers to hasten a revolution in the Eskimo way of life, even though supported by the erection of schools and hospitals, be extended to every group, however well able it may be to support itself by traditional means?

THE AMERINDIANS

Prior to the European discovery of the New World, native Indians, having their earliest roots, like the Eskimos, in Asia, ranged widely through the forests and grasslands of North America, south of the tundra. Some were farmers, most hunters and fishers. Their languages and customs, like those of the Eskimos, varied widely. When Cabot reached Labrador in 1497 the continent probably supported between 1 and 5 million Indians. Gradually, however, they were decimated by the more numerous European immigrants, and had no effective answer to the new weapons and diseases which confronted them. No attempt was made by the newcomers to assimilate them.

Today there are about 800,000 Indians in the United States, 180,000 in Canada. Very few of them live in the east or in any of the economically more desirable parts of the continent. Most dwell in reservations, set aside for their exclusive use by various treaties, and scattered through the arid west and the cold, forested north. The majority make their own living by farming, ranching, trapping, and fishing, but some have left their homelands to work on white peoples' farms and also in commercial fisheries and salmon canneries. On the whole, their living standards are lower than those of white people, and even where the will exists, their integration with Anglo-Americans is far from easy. What should be the attitude of the American and Canadian Governments towards their wards? Should the aim be to assimilate them and to allow them to be detribalised? Or should they be permitted to become increasingly fossilised in their reservations? The growth noticeable in their numbers since the beginning of the present century poses a challenge. Ought Canada and the United States to be more active in stimulating the self-development of the Indians?

Some advance was made among the Canadian aborigines in 1960 when the Government extended to its reservation Indians the right to vote in national elections, and more than 20% of all the Indian children in Canada now attend non-Indian schools.

THE FRENCH CANADIANS

Citizens of French origin are to be found in many parts of North America, e.g. New Brunswick (where about one-third of the population is of French stock), New England, especially Massachusetts and Vermont (12%), and Louisiana, particularly New Orleans. There are very few survivals, even cultural ones, in the old interior French domain of Louisiana.

The core of the French realm is Quebec, which for more than 150 years was entirely under French control. In 1774, eleven years after the British had acquired Lower Canada, Parliament in London passed the Quebec Act, which guaranteed to the inhabitants of the colony religious freedom, the right to retain their own language, the privilege of using their own civil law, and the liberty of running their schools in their own way. These freedoms were confirmed in the British North America Act of 1867, to which the French Canadians adhere tenaciously. The Quebec coat-of-arms still bears the fleur-de-lis, the symbol of pre-Revolutionary France, and displays the motto "Je me souviens." Clearly the people of Quebec do not forget the proud place they once held in North America, and they stubbornly cling to their language, traditions, and Roman Catholic faith. Yet they are as Canadian as the English-speaking majority in the country, perhaps more so; certainly they do not regard themselves as "French" Canadians, but simply as "les Canadiens." Immigration from France had almost ceased even before 1763, and the French Canadians never look to France for the redress of any grievances they may have, but rather to the Government in either Quebec or Ottawa.

They have tended to be the most conservative element in the Canadian population, and among the most rural, but they have also sent out young men as pioneer farmers into the Clay Belt of Ontario and into the more remote parts of the Prairies, and in Quebec itself they have become far more industrialised and urbanised during the present century. Nowadays, the agricultural techniques used by the majority are as advanced as those used by the British Canadians in Ontario, and Quebec factories are equally productive, though still less numerous.

Though the French Canadians derive their culture from feudal, Roman Catholic, seventeenth-century France, the younger people are slowly being drawn into the mainstream of Anglo-American culture. They remain, however, true to their language and faith, and the Church still, for the most part, controls their education. Though they form a minority of the Canadian population, it must be remembered, not only that the French Canadians outnumber the British in Quebec by four to one, but that they form 30% of the total population of Canada as a whole. Moreover, their birthrate is higher than that of English-speaking groups. Also, they have considerable political power, and any government in Ottawa, to function effectively, must have their support.

Anglo-Saxon people, already less than 50% of the total Canadian population, fear that ultimately the French element in the population may come to exceed their own. They also feel that the existence of a second official language in Canada detracts from national unity, and they observe with alarm the increasing demand for political separation expressed by a section of Quebec's extremists.

THE AMERICAN NEGRO

The first negroes were introduced into the United States in 1619 by the tidewater colonists of Virginia, following the example of the Portuguese in Brazil and the Spaniards in the West Indies. They were brought in as plantation labourers and domestic servants, at first from the West Indian realm, later from West Africa. They were to prove invaluable in the tobacco- and cotton-fields, where well-bred white people did not feel inclined to work with their hands, owing partly to their upbringing, partly to the hot, humid climate. In 1808 the importation of fresh slaves was prohibited, and the practice of slavery itself was abolished in 1865, at the end of the Civil War.

There are now about 22 million negroes in the United States. Their numbers are growing relatively more rapidly than those of white American groups, even though they suffer from a higher death-rate and are not now being reinforced by immigration. In 1760 they formed 40% of the entire southern population, now barely a quarter. A generation ago more negroes than whites were to be found in Mississippi and South Carolina, but no state today has a negro majority. However, in Mississippi, South Carolina, Louisiana, Georgia, and Alabama more than a quarter of the population even now is of negro origin, and there are continuing large

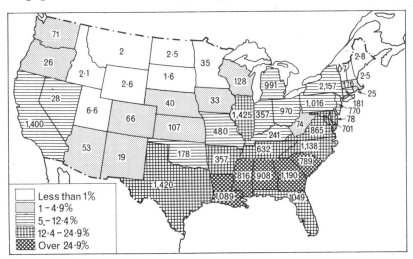

FIG. 105.—Negro population of the U.S.A., 1970.

1. Shading shows the percentage of negroes in the total population.
2. The figures give the *actual* number, in thousands, of negroes in each State.
3. The State of Alaska had 9,000 negroes (3% of the total population) in 1970, while the District of Columbia had 538,000 (71% of the capital's population).

minorities in North Carolina, Arkansas, and Virginia.* There are relatively few in the Western States and in the Middle West, but recently their numbers have been growing rapidly in the central areas of many north-eastern cities, e.g. Chicago, Detroit, Philadelphia and New York and there are now Negro majorities in Washington (D.C.), Newark and Atlanta. This urban migration has been stimulated by: (a) the demand for unskilled and semi-skilled labour in industry, a demand which became urgent after 1924, when the American Government virtually halted the further immigration of poor, ill-educated white people from eastern Europe; (b) the growing mechanisation of cotton-growing and the decline in cotton acreages; (c) the discrimination everywhere practised against the negro in the South. In the North itself, however, social prejudice has led most urbanised negroes to live in quarters distinct from those occupied by whites, and a Civil Rights Commission, reporting in 1959, drew attention to the fact that even in such enlightened states as New York and Illinois an element of discrimination persisted in housing, transportation, and education, in restaurants, and even in the administration of justice.

In the South racial discrimination, marked by a rigid colour bar and segregation, goes much further. In Mississippi, for example, only 4% of the negroes were registered as voters in 1959. Prejudice, backed up by demands for rigid segregation, is being slowly overcome as the educational and material standards of these "second-class citizens" rise, and as their percentage of the total southern population falls. Economically, it is clearly very expensive for the Government of the southern States to provide two, legally equal, sets of everything, e.g. schools and universities, and recent decisions of Federal Courts are inexorably leading to the integration of negro children in educational establishments attended by white boys and girls.

The slave tradition left the southern whites with an enduring conviction of the inferior racial characteristics of the negro. They have not wished to believe that negroes may be as morally fine and as mentally able as themselves. Even the richest and best educated negroes, fully Americanised as they are, find it impossible to find acceptance in white society. Only very gradually, following in part the Army's experience in the Second World War, are the whites coming to concede that when provided with the same opportunities, these darker-skinned Americans are not inferior to themselves, but are equally deserving of the best educational, civil, and political opportunities. There is still, however, a long way for the whites and negroes to go in their efforts to improve mutual relationships. The most enlightened whites still jib at the idea of mixed marriages, and there still exist a number of poor whites, now fortunately

* In 1970, in the District of Columbia, 71% of the total population was negroid in origin. (See Fig. 105.)

less numerous than a generation ago, who fear the economic competition that might result from the full recognition of the innate capacity of the negro.

Just over half of all the negroes in the United States still live in the South, half still depend upon agriculture to give them a livelihood, and their income per head continues to be lower than the national average. With few exceptions, negroes are still allowed to perform only the most poorly paid factory jobs, and there is little scope for high places in either State or Federal Government offices.

It is difficult for the United States to preach the doctrine of racial equality overseas effectively if she continues this illiberal treatment of the negro element in her population. Can she effectively lend her support to the claims of the native peoples of South Africa to equality while her own people continue to curb the aspirations of their kinsfolk?

RELATIONS BETWEEN CANADA AND THE UNITED STATES

Geography, and, generally speaking, history also, make allies of Canada and the United States. They share a frontier of about 4000 miles which has not been altered for more than a century, a frontier completely un-fortified and capable of being crossed by citizens of both countries with-out the need to produce passports. They share the same geographical zones, *e.g.* the Pacific coastal region, the Western Cordillera, the Prairies, the Great Lakes, part of the St Lawrence valley, the Shield, and the Appalachians. Both derive the major elements of their population from the Anglo-Saxons, and English is the official language of each (though the Canadians also employ French). The heaviest population concentrations in both countries are near the frontier, and there is a constant exchange of goods and people across it. Both have democratic forms of government and similar standards of living and education.

Neither has fought against the other since 1812, both are now members, not only of the United Nations but also of NATO, and they usually speak with the same voice in international councils. They combine in continental defence works, designed to meet a possible Soviet attack, of which they are equally fearful, and they have co-operated successfully—after some early misgivings by the United States—in the construction of the St Lawrence Seaway. They have agreed to the use that can be made of the upper waters of the River Columbia, a river which rises in Canada, but enters the sea in U.S. territory.

On the whole, therefore, relations between Canada and the United States are cordial and their needs and fears complementary. Canada, how-ever, remains a loyal member of the British Commonwealth, and recalls that the United States broke away from Britain in 1776. The Dominion entered both World Wars of the present century at the outset, while her neighbour bided her time. Her people, while nowadays regarding themselves primarily as Canadians, with a nationality of their own, are apt to feel that their own ideas and desires are too often either ignored by the Americans or, perhaps even worse, taken for granted. In fact, they sometimes complain that as a people they are looked upon by the British as Americans, and by the Americans as British. Yet the United States has never tried to persuade Canada to merge with her politically.

The root of the Canadian–American problem, if there is one, springs, of course, from the fact that the United States has ten times the population of Canada. Having only a relatively small population, therefore, Canada has come to depend upon her neighbour for much of her culture. Most of the magazines, books, radio and television programmes, for example, which circulate north of the 49th parallel originate south of it. Moreover, the United States has invested so much money in Canada that the latter feels herself to be economically dominated, even though she recognises that her resources could not have been developed without American capital.

Canada, therefore, while in sentiment closer to Europe and the United Kingdom in particular than her continental partner, is very dependent upon the United States, while the latter relies upon Canada to assist her in defence and values her for the minerals and forest products which she can, as a friendly country, make available to her. Their mutual differences are outweighed by the community of their interests, and each is respected by the other. Canada can often act as a "hinge" to smooth relations between the United States and the United Kingdom, and from time to time she acts towards both in an independent way. The Communists are wrong to regard Canada as no more than a satellite of the United States simply because the latter is demographically and economically dominant in North America.

EXTERNAL RELATIONS

THE UNITED STATES, EUROPE AND THE SOVIET UNION

In the nineteenth century, with her "Pax Britannica" policy, Britain claimed to stand for all that was best in the world. Since the Second World War the United States has tended to assume her mantle, and, assisted by her tremendous economic power, her undoubted financial strength, and her large population, has come to regard herself as the defender of the democratic way of life, the moral as well as the economic leader of the "Free World," and the principal bastion against the spread of Communism.

Between the Wars her attitude tended to be one of "isolationism" in world affairs. She never became a member of the League of Nations, even though this world forum was so largely a creation of one of her own Presidents, and she did not even become a fighting participant in the Second World War until Japanese aircraft bombed her fleet at Pearl Harbor, Hawaii, in December 1941. Since then, however, she has come to realise, like Canada, the narrowness of both the Atlantic and Pacific Ocean, and she has grown to recognise the threat of world domination by a power (the Soviet Union) whose political and spiritual ideals are widely removed from her own. Though frequently accused thereby of imperialism, she has been very active since 1945 in aiding other countries, whether devastated by war or economically and educationally underdeveloped, by granting them financial and technical assistance. With the aim of pursuing more effectively her policy of containing the power of the Soviet Union, she has persuaded a number of other friendly countries to allow her to establish military bases, or at least to make mutual assistance pacts with her.

Though apparently now desirous only of extending her influence through the world, the United States has acquired a small overseas empire, composed, in the main, of insular territories of strategic significance, notably the following: (a) Midway Island (annexed 1867); (b) American Samoa (obtained 1872); (c) Hawaii, now a State within the Union, Puerto Rico, now an American "Commonwealth," and the Philippines, now granted independence (all gained in 1898 following the Spanish-American War); (d) the Panamá Canal Zone (secured in 1903); (e) the American Virgin Islands (purchased from Denmark in 1917); (f) the former Japanese-mandated islands in the west-central Pacific (over which the United States was granted trusteeship rights in 1946).

THE UNITED STATES AND LATIN AMERICA

While the United States, for so long aloof from European affairs, was engaged principally in expanding and consolidating her hold on North America, she did not forget what she regarded as her duties and responsibilities towards Latin America. As early as 1823, when the Spanish and Portuguese colonies in the New World were successfully striving to achieve independence, her President (Monroe) enunciated his famous doctrine, repudiating the right of any European government either then or in the future, to intervene in the "American continents" and assume political control. Successive American governments have stood by this policy of regarding the Americas as prohibited areas as far as other Powers are concerned.

Generally speaking, the United States has tried to establish in Latin America a "Pax Americana" system, supported by a "good neighbour" attitude, partly so as to maintain her own influence in the region, partly so as to make Latin America a fruitful and stable field for U.S. investment. From time to time, however, the United States has felt impelled to send troops into at least the northern parts of Latin America, in order to maintain law and order. For instance, she fought a war with Mexico in the 1840s for the acquisition of her present south-western territories, *i.e.* New Mexico, Arizona, and California, and as recently as 1960 she felt it incumbent to sever diplomatic relations with a near-Communist government which had been set up in Cuba, and to support a revolt against that government in the following year.

On the whole, Latin American governments have had reason to be thankful for the interest the United States has shown in their affairs. Currently, the United States is supplying about half their total imports and is taking over 40% of their exports. Her investments in Latin America total several billion dollars, and she has, especially since 1945, provided large amounts of economic and technical assistance, *e.g.* for agricultural and industrial progress, for improved housing, water supply, and sanitation. She is also doing her utmost to prevent what is to her the pernicious doctrine of Communism from spreading in the New World.

STUDY QUESTIONS

1. Examine the wealth and deficiencies of Anglo-America in agricultural and mineral resources.

2. What contribution do the forest resources of North America make to the wealth of Canada and the United States?

3. What effect did the discovery of gold in various parts of North America have upon the development of Canada and the United States?

4. Discuss comparatively the basins of the following rivers: (*a*) Colorado and Mackenzie; (*b*) Columbia and Tennessee.

5. Describe in relation to the relief the routes taken by the principal railways in the western halves of Canada and the United States.

6. Compare and contrast the River Mississippi and the River St Lawrence as waterways.

7. Compare Vancouver and Montreal as commercial ports.

8. In its export trade Canada still concentrates upon the shipment of raw materials and foodstuffs, while the United States chiefly exports manufactures. Why?

9. How far are differences in climate responsible for the small population of Canada as compared with the United States?

10. Outline the problems caused by the existence of a large negro population in the United States.

11. How much geographical significance attaches to the 49th parallel in North America?

12. Do you consider that Canada possesses national unity? What is the nature of the disruptive forces she has to contend with?

PART FIVE

MIDDLE AMERICA AND GREENLAND

Chapter XXX

MEXICO : GENERAL PHYSICAL AND HUMAN GEOGRAPHY

PHYSICAL ASPECTS

GENERAL CHARACTERISTICS

Physically, Mexico belongs to North America, but culturally to Latin America (*see* Fig. 106). It owes much to the influence of the pre-Columbian civilisations of the Maya, Toltec, and Aztec peoples, to three centuries of Spanish rule, and to recent American importations from the north. But it is now transmuting these cultural ingredients into a distinctive social geography of its own.

Though it shares the Western Cordillera with the United States, it is largely cut off from its powerful neighbour on the north both by a political frontier (following the Río Grande for 1200 miles) and by a broad stretch of arid, thinly peopled land.

Only Brazil and Argentina are larger countries in Latin America. Mexico itself could engulf eight Great Britains in its three-quarters of a million square miles.

Politically, the country is a United States, just like the United States itself. It embraces 29 states, two undeveloped territories, and the capital Federal district.

PHYSICAL FEATURES

Often described as a horn-shaped country (without at present being a cornucopia of plenty), Mexico consists essentially of an upraised intermontane plateau, broadening and descending northwards, and enclosed by high Cordilleran ranges—the Sierra Madre Occidental (exceeding 10,000 ft) in the west, the lower, less compact Sierra Madre Oriental in the east. In the latitude of Mexico City the tableland averages 6000–8000 ft in height. It is crossed by a rather tangled skein of east–west ranges, many of which are surmounted by lofty, snow-capped volcanoes, *e.g.* Citlaltepetl or Orizaba (over 18,000 ft) and Popocatepetl (nearly 18,000 ft). Many of these spectacular cones are of recent origin; the new-

377

est—Paricutin—only began to rear itself in 1943, but in eight months it
grew to a height of 1500 ft, and is still rising, though more slowly than at
first.

Between the Sierra Madre and the marginal seas are coastal lowlands.
The eastern Gulf coast—bordered by lagoons and offshore bars recalling
those of the United States Gulf coast—is backed by a much broader lowland than the generally more rocky Pacific coast. In the north-west of

FIG. 106. Mexico: general features.

Mexico, across the Gulf of California, lies the rugged, batholithic peninsula of Lower ("Baja") California, a physical continuation of the Californian Coast Ranges, in the United States, while in the south-east, beyond the gap formed by the Isthmus of Tehuantepec, the Central American Highlands begin their onward march into Panamá. Isolated from the
rest of the country is the low limestone platform of Yucatán, one of the
relatively few significant north-facing peninsulas in the world.

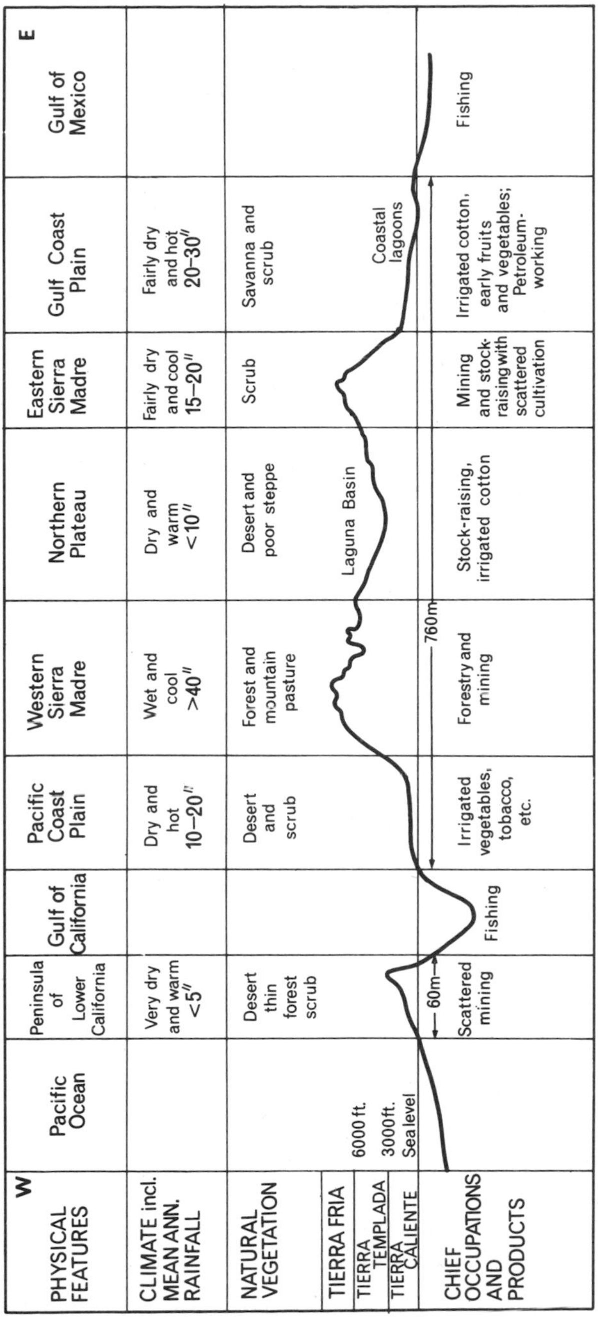

PHYSICAL FEATURES	Pacific Ocean	Peninsula of Lower California	Gulf of California	Pacific Coast Plain	Western Sierra Madre	Northern Plateau	Eastern Sierra Madre	Gulf Coast Plain	Gulf of Mexico
CLIMATE incl. MEAN ANN. RAINFALL		Very dry and warm <5″		Dry and hot 10–20″	Wet and cool >40″	Dry and warm <10″	Fairly dry and cool 15–20″	Fairly dry and hot 20–30″	
NATURAL VEGETATION		Desert thin forest scrub		Desert and scrub	Forest and mountain pasture	Desert and poor steppe	Scrub	Savanna and scrub	
TIERRA FRIA / TIERRA TEMPLADA / TIERRA CALIENTE						Laguna Basin		Coastal lagoons	
CHIEF OCCUPATIONS AND PRODUCTS		Scattered mining	Fishing	Irrigated vegetables, tobacco, etc.	Forestry and mining	Stock-raising, irrigated cotton	Mining and stock-raising with scattered cultivation	Irrigated cotton, early fruits and vegetables; Petroleum-working	Fishing

FIG. 107.—Generalised section across Mexico, lat. 25° 30′ N.

CLIMATE AND NATURAL VEGETATION

Mexico displays as great a diversity of climate and plant associations as of relief features. The Tropic of Cancer bisects the country, but the climate is mainly controlled by the wide variations in altitude, which produce many temperature zones, and also affect the rainfall distribution.

It is common to divide up the country into the following temperature zones: (a) the *Tierra Caliente*, or hot land, up to about 3000 ft—characteristic of the coastal lowlands; (b) the *Tierra Templada*, or temperate land, between about 3000 and 6000 ft or upwards: the northern plateau area, and lower slopes of the Sierras; (c) the *Tierra Fria*, or cool land, between about 6000–8000 ft and the snow-line: the high central plateau, and the highest slopes of the Sierras. Thus Vera Cruz (at sea-level), Oaxaca (5000 ft), and Mexico City (7400 ft) have the following temperatures respectively:

	Coolest month (° F)	Warmest month (° F)
Vera Cruz . . .	71	81
Oaxaca	63	74
Mexico City . . .	54	65

Though in habitable Mexico, temperatures are never very low on average, it should be noted that occasional cold "northers" from the United States (locally known as *papagayos*) may bring short spells of quite intense cold. Everywhere, the diurnal, if not the seasonal, range of temperature is marked.

Most of Mexico lies within the Trade Wind belt, and is therefore well watered on the eastern side. Sheltered by the Sierras, and generally subject to high-pressure conditions, the northern plateau is arid, and there is true desert in Sonora and Baja California. But the more southerly Pacific coastlands experience a kind of monsoonal indraught from the south-west in summer, and therefore have a distinctly rainy season. The higher, southern parts of the plateau, because of their more southerly latitude and their greater height, are wetter than the northern parts. On the eastern shores of Mexico the rainfall shows the same summer maximum as it does on the Pacific side, and similarly increases southwards (to more than 80 in. yearly), but parts of the low-lying tableland of northern Yucatán have less than 30 in. No part of Mexico has much precipitation in the cooler months, but in summer, when the inter-tropical front is farthest north, rainfall may be excessive in places, and on steep slopes may lead to serious soil erosion and periodic flooding.

The natural vegetation of Mexico is in keeping with its climate. Again, there are "many Mexicos." Most of the plateau consists of semi-desert country, degenerating into true desert and creosote bush in the north-west. The Sierras climb up to forests of pine and cedar, and in the higher parts to alpine flora. The southern coast plains, south of about latitude

21 degrees are generously clothed with tropical rain-forests and wood-land savanna, but northwards shed many of their trees and take on a covering of sub-tropical chaparral and grassland not unlike that which drapes the southern coast ranges of California (*see* Fig. 107).

HUMAN AND ECONOMIC GEOGRAPHY

HISTORICAL AND POLITICAL GEOGRAPHY

When the Spaniards reached Vera Cruz *en route* for the Mexican Plateau in 1519 the core of the country, *i.e.* the south-central highlands (or Central Plateau), was dominated by the highly civilised Aztec Indians, successors to the equally cultured Toltecs. In Yucatán the bloom of the once-flourishing Maya civilisation had already faded (*see* Fig. 108). The Spanish conquest was followed by three centuries of foreign rule, during which time many of the Latin immigrants inter-married with the native Indians to produce a *mestizo* population. The Spaniards gave the Mexicans their present tongue (though several Indian tribal languages are still spoken in remote rural areas), their Roman Catholic faith, and their now

[*Courtesy: Mexican Embassy.*

FIG. 108.—Maya ruins, Yucatán. Pyramidal Mayan structures such as these near Mérida are survivals of the once extensive Mayan culture of Middle America.

traditional architecture. They established themselves as a ruling class, dispossessed most of the Indians of their lands, and introduced an agrarian system based on large estates (*haciendas*) and a landless peasantry (*peons*), and did something to develop the mineral wealth of the country, albeit for their own ends.

Encouraged by the French Revolution and averse to the acceptance of Napoleon's brother as their sovereign, the Mexicans revolted against colonial rule between 1810 and 1821, and ultimately managed to secure their independence. The glory of their achievement, however, was tarnished by: (i) the War with the United States (1836–54), which took from Mexico almost as much territory as she retained, and (ii) a succession of internecine struggles for power. Hence economic and social progress were alike retarded.

In the late nineteenth and early twentieth centuries foreign capitalists were encouraged to establish plantations in Mexico, to exploit its mineral wealth, and to build railways and ports. A change of policy between the wars led to the nationalisation of foreign oil companies and railways, and much was done to divide up the existing large estates and to parcel them out among the erstwhile landless peons. The Church was disestablished and most of its secular property taken over by the State. Today, the republic, now politically stable, is expanding its economy, and is again inviting foreign (mainly American) investment. It is also benefiting from large loans from the World Bank, but is trying to ensure that there shall be no overseas exploitation of its resources. Industrialism is making headway, air and road communications are being actively developed, and education is being extended. While the country remains more backward in a material sense than the United States, it is certainly more advanced now than the majority of Latin American republics.

SOCIAL GEOGRAPHY

Present-day Mexico is chiefly a land of mestizos, who probably form about 55% of the total population of more than 50 millions. Most of them have more Indian blood in them than white. More or less pure Indians form 30% of the population, while nearly 10% are *creoles* (or *criollos*), *i.e.* descendants of Spaniards born in Mexico. Americans, Europeans, and negroes form a very small minority.

The population has been increasing rapidly during the present century: it has doubled itself in the last 50 years. This demographic expansion has been in part responsible for the crowding of many of the people into the towns, especially Mexico City; it has led the Government to press on with irrigation and industrial programmes; and has been a factor behind the demand for the breaking-up of the large estates and the intensification of agriculture. Farm holdings now tend to average little more than 40 acres, though most of Mexico is suited by climate and relief rather to grazing than to cultivation. Many farmers work part-time only on the land, and take other jobs if they are available. Increasing numbers are participating in government-controlled *ejidos*, modelled on the pre-Columbian community farms, formed by the pooling of land by individual proprietors.

AGRICULTURE

Although 60% of the gainfully employed Mexicans still work on the land, less than 15% of the country's total area is cultivated. 40% of the remainder is used for grazing, though only in a few areas are the pastures nutritious and the animals of high quality. Slowly the cropped area is being extended by irrigation. For example, along the Río Grande on the American border Mexico and the United States completed the Falcon Dam in 1953 and have been able to expand their production of cotton and vegetables in the frontier region. Other dams have since been built on the same river. South of Vera Cruz on the Caribbean lowlands, the rivers Papaloapan, Grijalva, and Uzumacinta are being taken in hand. On all four rivers the schemes are of the contemporary multipurpose type, designed to produce hydro-electric power and control flooding as well as to furnish irrigation water. Another 100 dams, mainly in Yucatán, Lower California and Sonora, are being built in the early 1970s. Older irrigated areas in Mexico include: (i) the Laguna district in the northern plateau, the republic's chief cotton-growing area; (ii) the Mexican portion of the Colorado delta in the far north-west, where truck-farming and the growing of alfalfa and wheat are characteristic; (iii) several of the Pacific valleys, *e.g.* the Yaqui, where vegetables and other crops are grown (*see* Fig. 106).

Taking Mexico as a whole, most of the present crop yields are low, much land, in the absence of suitable rotations, fertilisers, and water supplies, is under fallow, and techniques, especially among Indian farmers, are backward. However, in the more progressive areas, especially in the Central Plateau region, farmers may well plough their land with oxen or tractors, apply fertilisers to their fields, spray their crops with insecticides, adopt a scientific crop-rotation plan, sow specially selected seeds, and breed improved strains of animals. Elsewhere, especially in the north and east, farmers still commonly approach their fields by footpaths or mule-tracks, and they continue to cultivate the ground with a hoe or even a simple digging-stick, at best a poor wooden plough. They know nothing of the arts of fertilisation or disease-prevention, they have no electricity and must carry their domestic water from streams or springs in hand-made pots. Neither elementary nor technical education is yet widespread, and custom still dominates much of the life of the country, especially in the remoter areas peopled by primitive Indians.

Maize, wheat, and beans are the principal food-crops, cotton and coffee the principal cash-crops. In rural districts and the poorer quarters of the towns the diet normally consists of hot *tortillas* (*i.e.* griddle-cakes made from maize), beans, fruit, sugar, and coffee, but in middle- and upper-class families wheat is being increasingly consumed.

Apart from poultry, which are ubiquitous, cattle are the most numerous domestic animals. They number about 15 millions. Altogether, sheep, goats, horses, asses, and mules approach 20 millions in number. Both cattle and sheep are raised mainly in the north, and are valued chiefly for their flesh. Some dairy cattle are kept on the Central Plateau, where pigs are also well distributed. As with cultivation, so with livestock: the Government is inviting progress by introducing artificial insemination as a means of improving strains, and by taking measures to reduce disease.

MINERALS AND POWER SUPPLIES

Mexico is richly endowed with a great variety of economically useful minerals, many of which, particularly gold and silver, have been worked for several centuries. Today, minerals contribute about 20% of the earnings the republic derives from her exports. Their widespread distribution makes it difficult to generalise about their particular provenance, but it is true to say that the chief mineralised zones lie in and along the flanks of the Sierras bordering the plateau. Most ores are associated with meta-morphic, extrusive, and intrusive rocks, but the large petroleum and natural gas fields—a continuation of those of Texas—are located in the sedimentary strata of the Gulf Coast lowlands near the sea. The petroleum industry has been under State control since 1938, but most of the other mining operations are still conducted by foreign companies.

Mexico is not badly off for power supplies. She has petroleum deposits in relative abundance, but no longer holds second place in the world as a producer as she did in the 1920s, when only the United States boasted a larger output. Venezuela, for instance, now produces ten times as much as Mexico, and several Near Eastern countries have overtaken her despite a continuing programme of exploration and exploitation. Three pro-ducing localities are notable, all along the lowland margins of the Gulf of Mexico:

1. A central area, including fields: (i) near Tampico, which have been productive since 1901; (ii) near Tuxpan, where newer fields have been opened, *e.g.* the Poza Rica field, which is now the most outstanding field in Mexico; (iii) 50 miles inland from Vera Cruz, still more re-cent.

2. A southern area, in Tehuantepec, where oil has been worked round Minatitlan since 1911.

3. A northern area near the Texan border, of fairly recent origin.

Most of Mexico's petroleum is refined domestically, chiefly in and about Tampico, but also at Minatitlan and in and near Mexico City. The latter is linked to the oilfields by pipeline. Natural-gas supplies associated with several wells are being vigorously developed. Gas pipelines from the Tampico–Tuxpan area reach Mexico City and Guadalajara, and Monterrey is served by a line from the Texan border district.

Mexico's coal deposits are more scattered than the petroleum supplies, and the total output is small (less than 2 million tons a year). The chief producing area is the Sabinas Basin in Coahuila, north of Monterrey, but small amounts are raised in Oaxaca.

Mexico's terrain favours the generation of hydro-electricity, and she has now gone farther than any other Latin American country, with the exception of Brazil, in the development of this form of power. Many of the textile industries in the Central Plateau are dependent upon it.

Iron ore has been found in several localities. Particularly notable are the ores of Cerro de Mercado near Durango City which have been instrumental in the development of the iron and steel industries of Monterrey and Monclova. New deposits have recently been broached in the state of Colima.

Silver, lead, zinc, and copper, however, have long been Mexico's principal metals. Indeed, for many years Mexico has led the world in the production of silver, and currently accounts for about a fifth of the global output. Her chief mines are : (i) in the Pachuca district, 60 miles northeast of Mexico City, where, despite 400 years of exploitation, there are still considerable reserves; (ii) near the cities of Chihuahua and Hidalgo de Parral, on the edge of the Sierra Madre Occidental, where the deposits are generally associated with lead and zinc; (iii) in Fresnillo (Zacatecas). Lead and zinc mines are numerous in many plateau states, including San Luis Potosi and Zacatecas. Mexico produces more of these two metals than any other country in Latin America.

Copper extraction remains important, though the deposits of this metal are now being fast depleted. The chief sources are in Sonora and Baja California. Gold mining is not now very significant. The largest mines are in the south-central highlands and in western Durango.

The chief mineral base of Mexico's small chemical industry is sulphur, which is obtained from the Poza Rica extraction plant and also from the salt domes of the Minatitlan petroleum-producing area (cf. the Gulf Coast region of the United States).

Other Mexican minerals include cadmium (a by-product of zinc and copper production), in the production of which Mexico stands second only to the United States, antimony (worked mainly at Huitzuco, 80 miles south of Mexico City), tungsten, manganese, vanadium, tin, and mercury.

Mexico has important base-metal smelters and silver refineries at Monterrey, Chihuahua, San Luis Potosi, and Torreon, and there is a copper smelter at Cananea (Sonora). Lead is mostly refined in Mexico, but considerable quantities of zinc and copper are treated in the south-western United States. Lead takes first place (by value) among mineral exports, and is followed by copper, zinc, petroleum, silver, and sulphur.

MANUFACTURING

As in Canada, but to a lesser extent as yet, Mexico has been developing manufacturing industry on a fairly broad scale since the early part of this century, the two World Wars each giving a fillip to factory work. She has a number of useful raw materials, *e.g.* metals and cotton, much petroleum and natural gas, some coal, and several hydro-electric power undertakings, and a growing net of roads and railways fanning out from the capital, but she is not yet industrially mature, and remains a market for foreign manufactures. Few of her people possess much technical skill, and the purchasing power of most of them is very limited.

While manufacturing still, therefore, concentrates upon consumer goods, *e.g.* textiles and clothing, footwear and furniture, soap, food and drink, heavy industries, such as the production of iron and steel, petro-chemicals, and cement, have made their appearance. The first is concentrated in Monterrey, and expansionist plans are going forward; the second is making progress following the erection of petroleum-cracking plants at Mexico City and elsewhere, and the third is contributing much material for modern, largely American-style building projects. A quarter as many people are now engaged in manufacturing as in agriculture, and industrial production is currently rising by about 10% a year.

TRADE

Mexico, as a rather poor country, has only a small amount of trade *per capita*. Her chief trading partner is the United States, and most of her trade goes overland. Western Germany, Britain, Japan, and Canada are other countries which have a fair measure of trade with Mexico. Exports include metals, petroleum, cotton and coffee, shrimps (from Campeche, Yucatán), henequen (from Yucatán), tomatoes (from irrigated areas in the north-east and north-west), and cotton textiles. Among imports are machinery and industrial equipment, wool and rubber, vehicles, chemicals, steel, and wheat.

Chapter XXXI

MEXICO : REGIONAL GEOGRAPHY

The regions into which Mexico is divided in this chapter (*see* Fig. 109) are fundamentally based on relief. Each, however, also displays its own particular climate and usually has a distinctive type of natural vegetation and

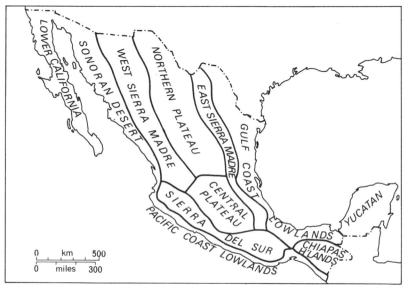

FIG. 109.—Geographical Regions of Mexico.

land-utilisation pattern. Hence, as Jones and Bryan state in their book, *North America*, "for once the 'physiographic division' is the 'Natural Region.'"

CENTRAL PLATEAU

This is the culminating southern section of the great intermontane plateau of Mexico. It is higher than the basins and ranges of the northern interior, and generally exceeds 6500 ft. Though it covers only one-seventh of the total area of the country, it supports half the population, therefore it may be justly regarded as the economic and political core of the republic.

The Central Plateau consists in the main of a collection of fertile, level, lacustrine basins and valleys around which rise lofty volcanoes and hill ranges. Permanent streams from the surrounding, well-watered highlands provide water for irrigation, for industrial power, and for domestic needs, and the soils, mostly of volcanic ash, alluvium, and lake deposits, are the best in Mexico. Moreover, there is a temperate climate, with winter temperatures averaging about 55° F (with altitudinal variations), and summer ones of about 65° F, a rainfall in the basins of 20–30 in., with a summer maximum, and a combination of warm or hot days and cool nights: a climate which is healthy for man and suitable for a diversity of plant and animal forms.

Nearly half Mexico's farmers live in this highly favoured Central Plateau. Maize, the chief staple, is supported, mostly at higher levels, by wheat (consumed in the cities), barley, fruit, potatoes, and other vegetables appropriate to the Tierra Fria. The pastures support dairy cattle as well as beef herds, pigs, sheep, and goats, and alfalfa and other fodder crops are grown to supplement the natural grasses. *Maguey* (a Mexican agave) yields fibre and also *pulque*, an intoxicating drink which is widely consumed in Mexico.

Mining is an important economic activity in many places. Silver remains one of the chief metals, but lead and zinc are also worked in quantity, and there is some production of copper, antimony, and tin.

Manufacturing activity is much more significant than anywhere else in the republic. A wide range of handicrafts, *e.g.* lace and embroidery, gaily coloured blankets, tooled leather, hand-beaten silver, has long been produced. Newer factory industries have been established, but these also mostly use local resources, *e.g.* cotton and wool, hides, tobacco, and foodstuffs. Mills are served by hydro-electric power-stations, though domestically produced petroleum is also used. The chief settlements—Mexico City, Guadalajara, Puebla, and León—are all significant industrial cities as well as market centres. Though their manufactures are becoming more varied, Guadalajara, Puebla, and León are all chiefly noted for their cotton-textile works, the first two also for their pottery industry.

Mexico City, the political capital and principal commercial and cultural centre of Mexico, is one of the greatest cities in the New World (*see* Fig. 110). Its metropolitan population now exceeds 4 millions, a fourfold increase in the last 30 years. The city is located at a height of about 7400 ft in one of the most fertile of Central Mexico's many basins (50 miles by 30 miles), close to the lake-site of the former Aztec capital. From it radiate the country's principal highways and railways, which link it with the coast (at Vera Cruz, Manzanillo, Mazatlan and, recently, Acapulco), the United States (at Nuevo Laredo, Piedras Negras, Ciudad Juarez—facing El Paso—Nogales, and Mexicali), Yucatán, and Guatemala (*see* Fig. 106).

Its industries—the greatest and most varied in the country—include the processing of foodstuffs and drinks, the manufacture of machinery, cement, silverware, tobacco, glass, textiles and clothing, printing and

[*Courtesy: Mexican Embassy.*

FIG. 110.—Columbus Circle, Mexico City. The Anglo-American skyscraper influence and the spacious trafficways should be noted. The hills surrounding the basin in which the capital lies can just be discerned in the background.

publishing. The River Necaxa furnishes hydro-electric power. Mexico City has many fine buildings, including a cathedral, art galleries and museums, skyscraper office-blocks, flat-roofed family dwellings grouped round open patios, broad avenues, and spacious plazas, in which one notes North American as well as Spanish influences. An underground railway system is now being installed and a start has been made with the fanning out of modern motorways.

THE NORTHERN PLATEAU

This region, averaging 4000–6000 ft in elevation, covers nearly a third of the total area of the country. Unlike the higher Central Plateau, it suffers from overall aridity, especially near the U.S. frontier, where the mean annual rainfall is no more than 8 in. though it fluctuates widely. Most of the rainfall, too, is of undesirably high intensity, and is concentrated in the months of July, August, and September. Rivers such as the Conchos reach the Río Grande and ultimately the sea, but there is much interior drainage, many intermittent streams, and numerous shallow depressions ("bolsons"), punctuated with salt-lakes and salt-flats. The existence of many tilt-blocks as well as faulted depressions suggests that this region is a southerly extension of the U.S. "Basin and Range Province."

Irrigation facilities are being increasingly provided. Notable among these is the area round Torreón in the Laguna basin, which is fed by the Ríos Nazas and Nievas, rising in the fairly well-watered Western Sierra Madre. Here most of Mexico's cotton is grown on lacustrine soils. Maize, wheat, beans, and alfalfa are also cultivated here and in scattered plots elsewhere, generally with irrigation water, but in places by dry-farming methods. Istle and guayule, two drought-resistant plants, are valued for their fibre and rubber respectively. But most of the ground—covered as it is with coarse grasses and xerophytic yucca and cactus scrub—is used for grazing. Large cattle-ranches exist, and sheep and goats are numerous. The lack of permanent water and good forage, however, as well as the general inadequacy of communications, hampers the development of a well-organised and intensive livestock industry.

Mining is probably the most advanced activity. Near the Sierras there are concentrations of gold, silver, copper, lead, and zinc. Among important mining and commercial centres are San Luis Potosí, long renowned for its silver, and well equipped with smelters and refineries, Durango, with iron and copper mines, and Chihuahua, located in an important silver-mining area. One of the largest towns is the resort of Aguascalientes, an old colonial settlement well known for its warm mineral springs.

Life is uncertain and hazardous in the Northern Plateau. Mining is a wasting asset, and farming is often at the mercy of a low, fickle rainfall. The population density is low and there is much migration from rural areas into the south-western states of America and also into the Central Mexican Plateau.

THE SIERRA MADRE OCCIDENTAL

This highland region, many of whose rocks have been vulcanised and metamorphosed, approaches 100 miles in width. It extends from the American frontier to the western end of Mexico's high Central Plateau. Its flanks, especially those on the west, are seamed with steep-sided canyons or *barrancas*, which impede movement in a north–south direction just as the mountains themselves hinder east–west travel. The higher parts carry good forests of pine, cedar, and oak, but the lower slopes are dry, especially in the north, and are covered with nothing more than sparse grass and scrub. On fairly level ground above the tree-line good pasturage is available for grazing, but the region is too inaccessible for an economically valuable livestock industry. Indeed, the rugged and broken terrain has deterred all but a few people: mostly backward Indians and mine-workers. The minerals—gold, silver, copper, lead, zinc, and antimony—are exploited chiefly on the mountain slopes, where railway transport is available. Some timber is cut for use in the mine-workings.

THE SIERRA MADRE ORIENTAL

The ranges making up the Eastern Sierra Madre run from the Río Grande to the Sierra del Sur. They are, on the whole, lower and narrower than their counterparts on the western side of the Mexican Plateau, and are more easily surmounted. On the whole, too, they are wetter, at least in the south, and their vegetation is richer. But they remain rather thinly peopled, at least in comparison with the Central Plateau.

Though mostly used for subsistence-farming and grazing, these highlands have two notable crop-growing areas, largely devoted to commercial cultivation: (a) east and south of Monterrey, where wheat, sugar-cane, tobacco, and citrus fruits are grown in addition to the almost ubiquitous maize and beans; (b) round Orizaba, where, at low levels (i.e. in the Tierra Caliente) rice, cacao, sugar-cane and bananas are grown, somewhat higher up (in the Tierra Templada) coffee, maize, and tobacco, and above about 7000 ft (in the Tierra Fria) potatoes, onions, and temperate fruits. Markets include not only local cities but also coastal settlements and Mexico City.

Among the metals worked in the Sierra Madre Oriental are copper, lead, zinc, and silver. The Sabinas coal basin—producing over 80% of Mexico's coal—and the Durango iron mines support the iron and steel industries of Monclova and Monterrey. The latter, the chief steel-producing city in the republic, and also an important producer of lead, commands a pass through the Sierra. Orizaba, the only other important city in this region, has a sub-tropical setting. It displays a happy blend of tourist attractions and factories turning out cotton, jute, silk, and rayon textiles. It also has railway workshops, breweries, and paper mills.

BAJA CALIFORNIA AND THE SONORAN DESERT

This dual region forms a Mexican extension of the hot desert of the south-western United States. It is more remote, and, generally speaking, less productive, than any other part of Mexico.

Baja (Lower) California consists of a long, mountainous, rocky and often cliff-girt peninsula 700 miles long. It is separated from the Sonora desert by the down-warped Gulf of California. Its aridity is largely attributable to the prevalence of north winds, though the cool waters of the Californian current play a part: there are often offshore fogs (as on the Californian coast in the United States), but rain may be absent for more than a year at a time. The prevailing desert vegetation is relieved by the presence of a few pine-trees on high ridges, but neither climate, flora, nor relief have attracted more than a few groups of copper miners, fishermen, Indian farmers, and seasonal tourists to this area. The landward and seaward extremities of the peninsula are the most productive parts. In the extreme south, just south of the Tropic, slight summer rains and mountain streams are utilised for the growing of tomatoes and vegetables. There is also a modest production of irrigated alfalfa, wheat, cotton, olives, melons, and grapes, especially in the far north, where Mexico shares the Imperial Valley with California. Mexicali, near the U.S. border, is the largest city in Baja California. La Paz, near the other end of the peninsula, is the chief town in the southern part of the peninsula, but enjoys only territorial status. Lobsters, shrimps, tuna, and sardines are caught off the Pacific coast (cf. southern California). There are small-scale copper workings at Santa Rosalia on the east coast.

Climatically and vegetationally, the Sonora Desert is comparable with the peninsula of Lower California. But the Western Sierra Madre are high enough to receive a fair orographic rainfall, and longer, stronger, aggrading streams are available for lowland cultivation than in the peninsula. It is in such alluvial valleys as the Yaqui and Fuerte that the bulk of the small population lives. They have made of their environment a number of "little Egypts," which are productive of a variety of crops; among them are winter vegetables, melons, and tomatoes, which, as "earlies," find a ready market in the United States via the frontier town of Nogales. Other irrigated crops include sugar-cane, rice, linseed, bananas, tobacco, cotton, and maize. The largest towns are Hermosillo and Guaymas, both winter resorts and oasis settlements, and Mazatlan, Mexico's chief Pacific port, largely engaged in the export of metals. The main settlements are linked by rail and road with both Mexico City and the United States. In the far north, on the U.S. border, principally at Cananea, Mexico's most valuable copper mines are located.

THE PACIFIC COAST LOWLANDS

South of Cape Corrientes (lat. 20° 30' N.), the Pacific coast of Mexico is backed by an extremely narrow lowland which does not broaden much until the Isthmus of Tehuantepec is approached. In many parts mountain spurs come right down to the sea; between them are the valleys of short, swift streams which add to the difficulties of movement. In fact, there is no railway along this coast between Cape Corrientes and Salina Cruz, except for lines joining Manzanillo with Colima and Guadalajara, and a new one from Acapulco to Mexico City.

The rainfall, though heavier than farther north, is usually less than 40 in., and there is drought in the cooler season. Irrigation is normally needed for assured production, and even then the amount of flat land available is very restricted. Round Acapulco—an old port and now a growing tourist resort with fine beaches and good fishing—and Manzanillo—a small commercial outlet—some rice, maize, fruit, and cotton are grown, as in the "little Egypts" of Sonora.

East of Salina Cruz, the Pacific terminal of the Tehuantepec railway, the coastal lowlands broaden out, the population density increases, and the farm output rises. Here are scattered banana and sugar plantations as well as subsistence plots, coconut groves, and fishing strands.

THE GULF COAST LOWLANDS

The Gulf Coast lowlands—wider, more level, and wetter than most of the Pacific lowlands of the republic—display the Tierra Caliente climatic type better than any other Mexican region. Though fairly dry in the north, near the Texan border, where they are mostly covered with savanna, scrub, and coastal swamp, they become very wet near the Isthmus of Tehuantepec, where there are luxuriant, tropical rain-forests in which some mahogany, rosewood, logwood, and ebony are cut, either for cabinet-making or for the dyestuffs they contain. Some native rubber, chicle, and sarsaparilla are also obtained from these steaming forests.

The immediate coastal margins are mostly ill-drained and insalubrious, and largely remain sources of malaria, yellow fever, and dysentery. Inland, the forest has been sporadically cleared to make room for tropical crops, notably bananas, rice, sugar-cane, tobacco, and vanilla, which, however, occasionally suffer from cold "northers." Cotton is cultivated on parts of the northern savanna, and Mexico to some extent shares in the agricultural productivity of the lower Río Grande valley, a notable irrigated district especially well-developed on the Texan side (*see* p. 271). Here cotton, early fruits, and vegetables are intensively cultivated, and irrigation facilities are being extended by both riparian countries as a joint operation.

As we have seen (Chapter XXX), the Gulf Coastlands are noted for their production of petroleum and natural gas as well as for their contribution to Mexico's supplies of food and timber. Tampico, 7 miles up the River Pánuco, and unfortunately inaccessible to very large tankers, is the principal oil-producing, oil-refining, and oil-exporting city in the country. It is now very much an Anglo-American town in appearance, the older Tampico having been largely destroyed by a hurricane in 1933.

Vera Cruz, the chief general port of Mexico, is 250 miles south of Tampico and at the terminus of an important railway to Mexico City which has to climb nearly 1½ miles on its journey to the capital. The coast at Vera Cruz is encumbered with silt and reefs, but a good artificial harbour has been constructed. A number of mills produce cotton textiles. The area south of the city should benefit considerably from the multipurpose Papaloapan project (*see* p. 383).

THE SIERRA DEL SUR

This region, lying between the Central Plateau and the Pacific, is severed from the former by the deep trench of the River Balsas and its headwaters. It forms a highly dissected highland-region, in which flat agricultural land is at a premium. Indian farmers practise primitive subsistence tillage in narrow valleys and small internal basins, but there is little commercial cultivation. A little silver and mercury are mined. The only sizeable settlement is Oaxaca, on the Inter-American Highway.

THE CHIAPAS HIGHLANDS

In their general physical character these highlands, near the Guatemalan frontier, resemble the Sierra del Sur. Again, backward farmers grow subsistence maize and beans and graze a few cattle. More progressive cultivators pay some attention to coffee—a very suitable crop for sloping tropical terrain—and, on the lower Pacific and Tehuantepec slopes, to bananas and cacao. Material conditions may be improved when the proposed hydro-electric station is built on the Grijalva River, which bisects these highlands in a longitudinal direction.

YUCATÁN

This north-facing peninsula is quite distinctive from other parts of Mexico, and is isolated from them. Like Florida, it consists mainly of a somewhat desiccated, low-lying platform of Tertiary limestones. Its rainfall, under 30 in. on the north-west coast, rises southwards. The northern part of the region, from which the summer rains are quickly evaporated even when they do not drain down through the jointed limestone, is an area of thin, stony soil and karst topography supporting only xerophytic scrub and patches of savanna. Southwards, however, the vegetation increases in luxuriance, and dense rain-forest—almost obliterating the ancient Maya monuments—establishes itself. This southern part of Yucatán is scantily peopled and today yields little of economic value save chicle, a basis for chewing-gum, and timber, worked largely by forest Indians.

A number of other Indians, using water drawn from *cenotes*, *i.e.* deep-water wells, scratch a living by growing maize on the poor northern soils.

They use the shifting or *milpa* system of cultivation. Commercially, however, northern Yucatán is best known for its large production of henequen, a native yucca whose leaf-fibre is used in the manufacture of binder-twine and other tying material. Plantations send their produce mainly to Mérida, the State capital, for onward transmission to the port of Progreso, whence U.S. and other markets may be reached.

Campeche, on the west coast, is an old city noted for its native pottery and tortoise-shell, its Panamá hats and shrimps. Near it, bananas, sugar, oranges, and copra are produced.

Chapter XXXII

CENTRAL AMERICA

GENERAL ASPECTS

CENTRAL AMERICA may be regarded as a land-bridge, nowhere more than 300 miles wide, between Mexico and South America (*see* Fig. 111). Its continuity is broken by the Panamá Canal. Politically it embraces six republics (Guatemala, El Salvador, Honduras, Nicaragua, Costa Rica, Panamá), one European colony (British Honduras), and an American leased territory (the Panamá Canal Zone).

FIG. 111.—Central America: general features.

Each of the political units has a share of the 1000-mile long highland backbone of the region, and also a strip of the Pacific or Caribbean coast, or both. The highlands, which consist of folded, faulted, and dissected ranges, are cut in two by the broad Nicaraguan depression, which can be traced north-westwards as far as the western frontier of El Salvador.

Close to the Pacific coast, but diverging inland in Costa Rica, and extending eastwards as far as western Panamá, is a chain of high volcanic cones, many of which are still active (*see* Fig. 114). This vulcanised area and its Pacific margin is also from time to time the scene of earthquake activity, which may be devastating. On the Atlantic side of central America there is a broad coast plain, including the wide Miskito (Mosquito) coast of Nicaragua, and El Petén, a limestone platform in northern Guatemala. The Pacific shore carries a much narrower lowland.

Climatically, Central America is influenced both by its isthmian character and by its relief. The Atlantic littoral is generally wetter than the Pacific coastlands, and the dry season (occurring between November and April) is usually shorter. Autumnal hurricanes may cause damage to crops and property on both shores, but especially on the eastern. Virtually the whole region lies within 15 degrees of the equator; therefore the lowlands are very hot as well as humid, and experience only a small mean annual range of temperature. Parts of the highlands, however, are quite cool, and it is possible to distinguish, as in Mexico, a number of temperature zones based on altitude.

Central America is a region of marked vegetational as well as physiographic and climatic contrasts. The wetter coastlands carry a natural cover of swamp or tropical rain-forests; drier areas, such as many of the interior basins, are clothed with savanna and scattered woodland, while the higher, exposed parts are decorated with forests of pine and oak.

ECONOMIC AND SOCIAL GEOGRAPHY

Central America is primarily an agricultural region, mining being much less important than in Mexico. Manufacturing, save for the preparation of foodstuffs and timber, and the fabrication of handicrafts, *e.g.* blankets and pottery, is little developed, partly owing to the lack of coal, iron, and petroleum, partly to widespread poverty, and economic backwardness. Many goods are still carried by pack animals and human porters, as communications are inadequate: there are no extensive railway links between the various countries, and the Inter-American Highway (a part of the Pan-American Highway) is not yet quite complete. It should, however, be noted that a Common Market, expected to grow into a Customs Union, was set up in 1966 by all the republics save Panamá, with the object of augmenting both their gross trade and their Inter-State trade.

The main exports of Central America are such plantation products as coffee (especially important on the volcanic soils of Guatemala, Costa Rica, and El Salvador) and bananas (most notably on the plains of Honduras and Panamá). Most of the people, however, are subsistence farmers, although only about 10% of all the land is cultivated. As in Mexico, maize is the main basis of their economy, though they also grow, largely by the *milpa* system of shifting cultivation, beans and other vegetables, and, especially in Panamá, rice, yams, and manioc. In all, Central America supports over 17 million people, who are most numerous on the Pacific slopes and in the more fertile western plateau basins. The average population density is about 85 per square mile (*cf.* the United States), but El Salvador has the comparatively high density of over 400. Almost everywhere, the population is growing more quickly than the world average.

Except in Costa Rica, which has a preponderance of white elements in its population, Guatemala, where native Indians outnumber all other groups, and British Honduras, where half the population is negro or mulatto (*i.e.* a mixture of white and black), the majority of the people are mestizos.

The table on p. 399, indicating the variety of population densities and racial elements, and the export crops, etc., of Central America, will be found useful for reference.

POLITICAL GROWTH

In some ways, at least in comparison with more materially-advanced regions, Central America is more retarded than it was during the pre-Columbian period, when the Maya civilisation of Guatemala, Honduras, and Yucatán had its home there. Some of the monuments left behind by the highly cultured Maya speak of their skill not only in architecture but also in mathematics and astronomy. Why their civilisation broke down is the subject of much argument. Was it due to the decimation of the people by malaria, the increasing wetness of the climate and the advance of the jungle, the unanswerable problem of soil erosion which developed as the population grew so as to outstrip its food-producing capacity, or conquest by a better-armed, more-numerous population with lower cultural attainments?

The Maya culture had already declined when Central America, like Mexico, came under the Spanish yoke. For three centuries the Spaniards ruled. Most of the region, excluding British Honduras, was officially part of the Mexican viceroyalty and formed the Captaincy-General of Guatemala, but after the successful revolts of 1810–24 it proved impossible to maintain political cohesion, and the independent Central American Federation lasted for little more than a decade. Gradually, each of its constituent republics withdrew. Panamá, meantime, had become part of "Gran Colombia"; not until 1903 did it revolt against the Colombian Government to achieve its present independent status.

The Federation broke down for three main reasons. Firstly, Central America lacked interconnecting communications, a lack the region still labours under despite the spread of Pan-American air routes and the virtual completion of the Pan-American Highway. Secondly, the rivalry

Central America—Demographic and Economic Data

Political unit	Area (sq. ml.)	Population (1970 or 1971) and density (per sq. ml.).	Main population elements	Capital city and population	Main exports
Costa Rica	19,695	1,710,083 (87)	97·5% white and mestizo 2% Negro	San José (205,000)	Coffee Bananas Cocoa
Guatemala	42,042	5,347,787 (127)	66% Indian 33% mestizo and mulatto 1% white	Guatemala City (731,000)	Coffee Cotton Bananas
Honduras	43,277	2,669,100 (62)	90% mestizo 7% white 2% Indian 1% Negro	Tegucigalpa (316,000)	Bananas Coffee Timber
Nicaragua	57,143	1,975,000 (40)	75% mestizo 12% white 9% Negro 4% Indian	Managua (381,000)	Cotton Meat Coffee Sugar
Panamá	28,753	1,474,910 (50)	65% mestizo 14% Negro 11% white 9% Indian 1% Asiatic	Panamá City (373,000)	Bananas Petroleum products Shrimps
El Salvador	8,260	3,564,656 (440)	80% mestizo 10% Indian 10% white	San Salvador (368,000)	Coffee Cotton Cocoa
British Honduras	8,867	120,000 (13)	63% creole (mostly Negro and mulatto) 17% Indian 10% Black Caribs 10% white Europeans	Belmopan (1,000) Formerly Belize City (40,000)	Sugar Citrus fruits Timber
Panamá Canal Zone	558	44,650 (80)	—	—	—

(Data mainly from *Encyclopaedia Britannica Book of the Year*, 1972. It should be noted that the percentages of different population elements are very approximate, since the degree of racial mixture varies greatly from family to family. For instance, it is not always easy to distinguish a negro from a mulatto, or an Indian or white from a mestizo.)

between the various political leaders was too keen. Thirdly, the population was, and remains, a dissemination of local clusters mostly concentrated in small upland basins and lowland pockets divided from each other by empty highlands or forests.

Inter-republican strife, however, is now rare, and there is a growing sense of economic unity. The main bone of contention at present is the continued existence within this realm of independent republics of an Old World colony, British Honduras. Guatemala has periodically laid claim to this territory since the 1820s. Its possession would extend her Caribbean coastline, which is at present very restricted, and would remove from Central America what the several republican governments tend to regard as an unwelcome anachronism.

The relations between Central America and the United States are important. Ever since her enunciation of the Monroe Doctrine in 1823, the United States has supported Central America's claims to independence, but has occasionally asserted her right to step in as a "big brother" and "put things to rights." It was because of her failure to persuade Colombia to grant her the privilege of building a canal through the Isthmus of Panamá that she connived at the revolutionary movement in Panamá in 1903. Its successful outcome allowed her to take over the constructional work from Ferdinand de Lesseps and his French company, and to lease the present Canal Zone (in perpetuity) from the new republic. The strategic, as well as the commercial, value of the Canal has been one reason for the enduring interest the United States takes in Central American affairs.

The United States is generally regarded by the Central American republics as a friendly power who can usually be relied upon to provide financial and technical aid for development projects. But from time to time, in their indebtedness to her, various republics charge the United States with attempting to impose a form of imperialism upon them. "Dollar diplomacy," they argue, may lead to political tutelage.

THE COUNTRIES OF CENTRAL AMERICA

GUATEMALA

Guatemala, the westernmost of the Central American republics, is intermediate in size between Nicaragua and Panamá. It stretches from the Pacific to the Caribbean, but the existence of British Honduras denies it all but a few miles of Caribbean coast.

Over half the population of $4\frac{1}{2}$ millions is Indian, most of the rest mestizo. There are small but important minorities of whites, chiefly of Spanish origin, who dominate many political and economic affairs, and of negroes and mulattoes, who are chiefly plantation-workers.

The rather narrow Pacific coast plain of Guatemala rises fairly sharply to a broad highland region, reaching nearly 14,000 ft and trending west-north-west to east-south-east. Eastwards and northwards, the land falls away more gradually. The northern lowland, like the plain of the adjacent Yucatán peninsula, is mainly floored with limestone; known as El Petén, this area is characterised by underground drainage.

Like other Central American republics, Guatemala receives a heavy mean annual rainfall, exceeding 80 in. on the windward slopes of the highlands and on the Caribbean ("trade-wind") coastlands, though everywhere there is a marked summer maximum. The Pacific coastlands are distinctly dry in the cooler season, when winds are generally offshore. Temperatures widely exceed 70° F even in January, but altitude reduces them to produce, as in Mexico, marked altitudinal zones, viz. Tierra Caliente, Tierra Templada, and Tierra Fria. Tropical hurricanes, most common in autumn, periodically damage crops and property on both coasts.

Ninety per cent of the Guatemalans are engaged in agriculture, but—owing partly to soil poverty (e.g. in the limestone tableland), the widespread forest cover, and the occurrence of much steep slope—only 14% of the country is under cultivation, and part of that is farmed by shifting practices.

On the coastal plain bordering the Gulf of Honduras bananas and abacá are sporadically cultivated and chicle (the latex of the sapodilla tree, used as a basis for chewing gum) is collected in the forests. Peasant farmers in the cooler highlands grow subsistence crops of maize, beans, wheat, and potatoes on their small-holdings, and may keep cattle and sheep. A few large commercial estates produce coffee, sugar-cane, and henequen. The chief money-crop—coffee—is obtained chiefly from the rich volcanic soils of the Pacific slopes of the highlands. On the Pacific littoral the United Fruit Company owns banana plantations, but some irrigation is needed here for successful growth. Cacao, sugar-cane, rice, maize, and cotton are also cultivated on the Pacific plain, and the best cattle-ranches in the country are located there. The republic possesses small lead and silver mines and a start has been made with the mining and refining of nickel in the Lake Izabal area.

Most people live on the healthy plateau and its slopes, i.e. in the Tierra Fria and Tierra Templada. At least half are illiterate, and most are very poor. But slowly, some of the larger under-cultivated estates are being broken up, and social improvements have been initiated.

Towns are few and communications inadequate for intensive economic development. The capital, Guatemala City, located in the highland zone at about 5000 ft, is a modern city with an important airport. It was founded after the destruction of the former capital by the eruption of the still active Mt Agua. It is linked by rail to Puerto Barrios, the main Caribbean port, and San José, the chief Pacific outlet. Coffee (easily first), cotton and bananas are the dominant exports, and manufactured goods and petroleum are among the leading imports. Nearly three-quarters of the total foreign trade is with the United States.

EL SALVADOR

El Salvador, the smallest independent state in the Americas, has its only shore on the Pacific, cutting off a large part of Honduras from that Ocean. It extends along this coast for about 160 miles, and inland for half that distance. Two parallel, east–west mountain ranges enclose a narrow inter-mont plateau breached by the transverse valley of the River Lempa. Volcanic eruptions and periodic earthquakes disturb the serenity of this densely populated land.

The combination of rural population pressure, torrential summer rain-fall, and steep slopes has produced serious soil erosion in many areas, although the remaining volcanic soils are very fertile. Over 25% of the land is under crops, in marked contrast to the low percentage in its less thickly settled neighbours, and much of this cultivated land is quite in-tensively cared for. Nevertheless, many of the people find it necessary to migrate across the frontier into Honduras.

The economy is even more narrowly based on coffee than that of Guatemala. In fact, this crop until recently accounted for 80% of the export values of El Salvador. Most of the trees have been planted in small estates on the volcanic slopes of the Tierra Templada. They yield a high-grade, mild variety of coffee which can be speedily transported to the coast at La Unión or other, smaller ports.

The basis of the economy is being broadened and increasing amounts of cotton, henequen and oilseeds are grown. Some water power has been harnessed on the River Lempa, and there are more factories and workshops than in other Central American republics. Among industrial products are cotton (the chief), sisal bags (for coffee), leather and footwear, cigarettes, soap, and sawn timber.

As in other Central American countries, however, most people do not engage in commercial production. The majority—mestizos and Indians —simply tend their plots of maize, beans, and other vegetables, and per-haps look after a few head of cattle. Subsistence farming remains the most widespread means of family support.

The capital of El Salvador, like those of adjoining countries, is located in the healthy highland zone. Called San Salvador, it is a clean, modern metropolis, linked by road or rail to the coffee ports of La Unión, Aca-jutla, and La Libertad, to the inland "coffee capital" of Santa Ana, and even to the main Guatemalan railway.

The overseas trade of El Salvador is less markedly orientated towards the United States than that of most Central American republics. Recently, large exports have gone to Western Germany and Japan, and the United States has been taking less than half its surplus products. The latter, however, supplies half its imports.

HONDURAS

In marked contrast to El Salvador, Honduras has a low population density—just over 60 against 440. It is a rather backward country; even its capital, Tegucigalpa, has no railway link with the outside world.

Like Guatemala, Honduras has one long coastline (in this case the Caribbean) and one short one (the Pacific). The Cordilleras, which traverse all these Central American republics, exceed 10,000 ft in parts of central Honduras, but within them lie many small sunken basins and valleys, and broad plateaus, where most of the people live. Penetrating the highlands are the Comayagua plains, which reach inland from the northern alluvial plains.

The climate, vegetation, and economy are not unlike those of Guatemala, but since the country has had a much more disturbed political history, its people are even poorer and its trade smaller. 90% of the population is mestizo, and there are probably nearly as many West Indian negroes as pure-blooded Indians. The percentage of negroes, however, fell as a result of an attack of sigatoka disease which afflicted the Caribbean banana plantations in the 1940s, and the near collapse of the banana trade in the Second World War. There has since been a marked recovery. (Negroes, as elsewhere in Latin America, are mostly plantation-workers.)

Less than 10% of Honduras is cultivated. Maize is, as usual in this realm, the staple foodstuff. Bananas still form the principal export crop, but do not dominate the economy. Coffee—produced on smaller plantations at higher altitudes—and coconuts, tobacco, and sugar are other significant cash crops, and the West African oil-palm has been introduced into the Caribbean lowlands. Timber is fairly extensively worked and the country has both timber-processing plant and a paper- and pulp-mill.

The cattle industry is being steadily improved, and each year animals are sent into other republics. Disease has reduced the scope of the sponge fisheries, but the offshore shrimp industry is significant, and the skins of alligators and peccary are taken and exported to the United States, where they supply some of the needs of the leather-using industries.

Mining is a more significant activity in Honduras than in most of the Central American countries, though lead and zinc have been worked intermittently in Guatemala since colonial days, and gold is produced in

Nicaragua. Silver—mined about 16 miles north-east of the capital—is the chief mineral worked in Honduras, but small quantities of gold and lead are also raised.

It will, however, be impossible for Honduras to develop its economy to any considerable extent until more railways and metalled roads are laid down. Even the capital cannot really be described as a route focus, though it should be noted that it possesses a large airfield. It is smaller than either Guatemala City or San Salvador, and is, in fact, little more than a large market town. The chief ports are Puerto Cortes, Tela, and La Ceiba, all of which ship bananas from the United Fruit Company's plantations near the coast, and a new deep-water Pacific port is being constructed on the Gulf of Fonseca.

As is the case with Guatemala, the bulk of the overseas trade is with the United States, though Honduras and El Salvador themselves have more inter-republican trade than most Central American countries. Among imports, textiles and manufactured metal goods figure prominently.

NICARAGUA

Nicaragua, the largest country in Central America, is almost the same size as England and Wales. It has more lowland than any other republic, the most notable feature of its build being a depression in the south and west, consisting of Lakes Managua and Nicaragua and the valley of the San Juan River—a depression which has often been seriously considered as a possible basis for an inter-oceanic canal to supplement the Panamá route. There is the usual narrow range of volcanoes near the Pacific coast and an interior zone of highlands, broadening northwards towards the Honduran frontier.

The population density (barely 30 per square mile) is the lowest in Central America, excluding British Honduras. The people—mostly mestizos—are markedly concentrated in the west, on the narrow coast plain, on the volcanic slopes, and on the Pacific shores of the two large lakes. Managua, the capital, devastated by both fire and earthquake in the 1930s and again in 1972, is a modern city on the southern shore of the lake of the same name.

As in other Central American republics, most of the Nicaraguans earn a livelihood either by subsistence farming or by plantation labour. Once notorious for their extremely unhealthy character, parts of the eastern plains were utilised early this century by the United Fruit Company of America as a suitable area for banana plantations, but in 1949 the industry was transferred to the Pacific coastlands following the ravages of siga-toka disease. The old banana fields near the port of Puerto Cabezas are now being planted with cacao trees.

About 12% of Nicaragua is cultivated. The main money crop, as in most republics, has until recently been coffee, which is mainly grown south of Managua, but cotton, which is mainly cultivated round León, has taken the lead in the last few years. Comparatively large amounts of maize and sugar, and smaller quantities of sesame, rice, and tobacco are also raised, and there are important cattle-farms in the lower, more southerly upland areas. Frozen beef, hides, and live animals are shipped out of the country.

More timber is cut than ordinarily in Central America. Mahogany, the chief wood, is a product mainly of the eastern forests and is exported from Puerto Cabezas and other small Caribbean ports.

Off the Miskito coast, shrimp-fishing has recently, as in Honduras, become an important prop of the economy. Packing plants have been established on offshore islands and markets secured both in Central America and the U.S.

Gold may account for up to one-third of the total export trade, and the only significant copper mine in Central America is located in this republic. But manufacturing industry is almost as slow in developing as in Honduras and Guatemala. The advance of cotton-growing has given a fillip to the expansion of a small textile industry, and a few sugar refineries, a cement plant, and small factories producing consumer goods have been erected in and near Managua. The country's only railway serves the capital and the small Pacific port of Corinto.

Only about a third of the exports, a decreasing proportion, go to the United States, which, however, sends two-thirds of Nicaragua's imports. Many goods are shipped to Western Germany, Japan, and the Netherlands.

COSTA RICA

This country—the "Rich Coast"—has the reputation of being politically the most mature, socially the most cultured, and economically the most advanced, of all the Central American republics. How far this is due to the fact that 80% of the population is white (mainly Spanish) may be disputed. Certainly political stability and democratic government are largely responsible.

The country has a highland backbone dominated by two parallel ranges surmounted by volcanoes, the highest one exceeding 13,000 ft in elevation. Between these ranges, as in El Salvador, there is an intermontane plateau, part of which, known as the Central Valley or Meseta Central, is the core of the republic. The Tierra Caliente is represented by the humid Caribbean and Pacific lowlands. The drier Pacific side is not entirely covered with hardwood forest, but carries wide stretches of savanna.

On the temperate plateau many small-holders utilise the rich volcanic soils for coffee-planting, *e.g.* round the capital, San José. The beans are valued for their high quality, and find a ready market in Europe as well as the United States. More dairying is undertaken on the plateau than in other republics, and mixed farming has gained a foothold. There was a setback in both the coffee and cattle industries in 1963 when Mt Irazu violently erupted and ash covered the surrounding land within a 250-mile radius.

Lowland bananas, at first grown on the hot, moist lands of the Caribbean plain, as in Nicaragua, but transferred to the Pacific lowlands again when blight struck, form the second dominant export crop. Other commercial products include abacá, and cacao (largely cultivated on the abandoned banana plantations), tobacco, and sugar-cane. The West African oil-palm is a recent introduction. Maize, beans and potatoes, and rice are grown at various altitudes as food-crops. Yet only 7% of Costa Rica is under cultivation. Cattle are raised on large estates on some of the Pacific savannas, but over three-quarters of the country is still classed as forest.

Manufacturing has advanced a little further than in other Central American countries excluding El Salvador, but most of the factories are small, mainly based on locally produced foodstuffs and raw materials, and designed to satisfy merely a consumer market. Hydro-electric power-plants are being installed, the decision has been taken to work the bauxite deposits of San José province, and petroleum has been lately discovered; consequently, Costa Rica's future appears to be fairly rosy.

Numerous small settlements in the well-populated central tableland are joined together by the Inter-American Highway, and the capital, San José, like most of the chief cities of Central America a blend of recent American and older Spanish architecture, is linked to both coasts by rail. Puerto Limón is the Caribbean terminal, Puntarenas the Pacific. About half Costa Rica's overseas trade is with the United States, but Western Germany is also an important trading partner.

PANAMÁ

Panamá is a narrow, isthmian country in the middle of which the highland spine of Central America breaks down sufficiently to have allowed U.S. Army Engineers to build the Panamá Canal without facing crippling constructional problems. To the west of the Canal Zone is the Cordillera de Talamanca, to the east the San Blas Range. Both enclose small, fertile basins, and each is bordered by a coastal lowland.

The population of Panamá—nearly 1½ millions—is about 65% mestizo in origin, 14% Negro. Most of the people live in clearings cut out of the tropical forests, which still dominate most of the landscape, especially on the wetter Caribbean side. Only small areas have been removed for cultivation. The main commercial crops are bananas, cacao, and sugar-cane, while rice, so characteristic of hot, wet lowlands, rivals maize as a subsistence crop. Some mahogany is cut, and there are significant shrimp fisheries. Recently, a deposit of bauxite has been located, and a beginning has been made in its exploitation by a U.S. Company.

Panamá, however, depends chiefly upon the income she receives from the Canal Zone, and the earnings of her shipping, to bring her foreign exchange. The economic core of the country, in fact, is at present outside her jurisdiction: it is the American-leased Canal Zone (*see below*).

THE PANAMÁ CANAL ZONE

This strip of territory, flanking the Panamá Canal—one of the world's two great inter-oceanic crossings—is 10 miles wide (*see* Fig. 112). It was acquired by the United States in 1904, when she took over from the New Panamá Company the construction of the Canal. Though the United

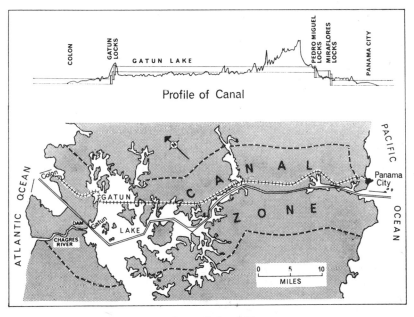

Profile of Canal

FIG. 112.—Panamá Canal Zone.

States has the right of sovereignty in the Panamá Canal Zone, and though she owns and operates the Canal (actually through a company created in 1951), she pays the Republic of Panamá nearly $2 million a year for the privilege and intends to ratify a new treaty giving Panamá sovereignty and a share in the operation of the Canal.

The Canal was opened to commerce in 1914. It was built across the narrowest part of the isthmus of Panamá, where the highest point is only 285 ft. Here a hill had to be sliced through, an operation which produced the Culebra Cut, and which led the American Engineers to decide upon a canal with locks at either end (the three Gatún Locks at the northern end, the Pedro Miguel and two Miraflores Locks at the southern), rather than a sea-level canal like Suez (*see* Fig. 113). The completed waterway ex-

[*Courtesy: U.S. Information Service.*

FIG. 113.—Gatún Locks, Panamá Canal. The Atlantic Ocean end of the Canal is shown in the foreground, the three Gatún Locks in the right centre, and Gatún Lake in the background. Compare Fig. 112.

tends 50·5 miles from deep water near Cristóbal (the Caribbean terminal) to deep water near Balboa (the Pacific terminal), and provides a passage 45 ft deep and, except in a few places, at least 500 ft wide. Close to the Canal ports are the two chief cities of the Panamá Republic: Colón, in the north, and Panamá City, the capital, in the south. Both are linked by an isthmian railway.

One of the reasons for the anxiety of the United States to build the Panamá Canal was to enable her to concentrate her fleet easily in either the Atlantic or the Pacific, but it has been of inestimable value commercially as well, not only to the United States but to countries all over the world. Indeed, it has revolutionised sea-communications between the Atlantic and the Pacific, and has led to the virtual abandonment of the stormy passage "round the Horn." It has enabled ships on the west coasts of the Americas to communicate easily and rapidly with ports in eastern North America and Europe, and has assisted New Zealand's trade with the United Kingdom as well as Australia's commerce with the eastern United States. Between 12,000 and 15,000 ships pass through each year compared with about 20,000 using the Suez route before its closure.

Because of the ever-increasing size of ships, especially tankers, and the delays involved in negotiating the Canal locks, the United States has for some years investigated the feasibility of building a second canal through Central America. After examining possible lines of route across Colombia, Nicaragua and Costa Rica, she has now decided that the best route would be only 10 miles west of the present Canal Zone. Here it should be practicable to construct, over a fifteen-year period, a sea-level waterway requiring only single tidal gates near each end. In return for Panamá's consent to the proposal, the U.S. might well be prepared to finance the closing of the remaining gap (of 400 miles through Darien and northern Colombia) in the Pan-American Highway. Meantime, some relief is being afforded to international traders by the laying of an oil pipe-line across the isthmus only a few miles east of the Canal Zone for the transport of petroleum from Colombia and Ecuador (and ultimately from Alaska?) to the east coast of the U.S.

BRITISH HONDURAS

British Honduras, often referred to as Belize, the name of its chief city, is a Caribbean colony only about as large as Wales. In its political status, it is quite distinct from the other countries of Central America, which threw off the shackles of imperial enchainment more than a century ago. The first Europeans to occupy it were a group of ship-wrecked freebooters under the leadership of a Scottish buccaneer who settled there in the seventeenth century. It has been British ever since, but has been somewhat neglected, and never achieved economic importance. It has now been accorded a large measure of independence.

The low-lying coastal plain, backing mangrove swamps, is still densely forested, but patches of savanna diversify the scene in the rather drier, higher interior. Offshore there is a coral reef marked by a line of small islands known as *cays* (cf. the Florida "keys"). Between this reef and the mainland, as in Nicaragua, the catching of both lobsters and shrimps has recently assumed importance and processing plants have been built.

The land has never attracted much settlement owing to its hot, humid, disease-ridden character, though it is quite possible for Europeans to live healthily in the interior highlands, as they do in other Central American countries.

For three centuries British Honduras has been noted for its mahogany production. Despite the unsocial nature of the species, and its occurrence in very luxuriant forest country, where any physical work is arduous, cutters find it worth while to fell a number of trees each year and to float the logs in autumn down the swollen rivers to the coast, where "boom-men" assemble them ready for export. Considerable numbers of Indians and also West Indian negroes and mulattoes are engaged in this work. There is a small export of other timber, e.g. logwood, rosewood, and ironwood, as well as mahogany, and recently attention has been paid to the felling and export of highland pine-trees. Chicle and vegetable ivory (from the Cohune nut palm) are other forest products.

Agriculture is backward, and only 6% of the total area is under crops, despite the relative fertility of certain of the upland soils. The chief commercial crop of the lowlands is sugar-cane. Citrus fruits, especially grapefruit and oranges, are grown for export in the Stann Creek valley, and canning and juice-bottling plants have been established, but the former banana industry, ruined by Panamá disease, has not been fully restored. There are some cattle-ranches in the interior.

Most of the people live in the river valleys and on the upland slopes. Many still practise shifting cultivation. The only town of any size, Belize, is situated on a low-lying sand-spit guarding the mouth of the Belize River. It is the main port and until 1970 was the seat of colonial adminis-tration. It supports a few saw-mills and small factories producing furni-ture and other consumer goods. Unfortunately, its harbour has a shallow entrance, and large vessels have to anchor offshore and discharge or receive their cargoes by barge. Belize was virtually destroyed by a violent hurri-cane in 1961, but is now undergoing partial renewal. A new capital, named Belmopan, is being laid out 50 miles away. It has a higher, more central location than Belize City, and is already attracting Government departments. It is joined by road to the former capital, has a healthier site, and is in little danger of either hurricane or flood.

About one-third of the trade of British Honduras is with the United Kingdom, and the same fraction with the United States. The West Indies form a valuable market.

Chapter XXXIII

THE WEST INDIES AND BERMUDA

GENERAL ASPECTS

PHYSICALLY the West Indies comprise a broken arc extending from Yucatán to the mouth of the Orinoco, and separate the Atlantic from the more enclosed Gulf of Mexico and Caribbean Sea. The largest islands, *i.e.* the Greater Antilles (Cuba, Jamaica, Hispaniola, and Puerto Rico) lie in the west, the smaller, *i.e.* the Lesser Antilles (comprising mainly the Leeward and Windward Islands), in the east. Belonging also to the West Indies, but to neither of these main groups are: (*a*) Trinidad and Tobago, and a number of other small islands north of Venezuela; (*b*) the Bahamas and other islands north-east of Cuba and north of Hispaniola. While Cuba, Haiti, and the Dominican Republic (the two latter sharing Hispaniola) are independent, most of the rest form part of the British, French, and Dutch realms. Puerto Rico is an American "Commonwealth."

European influences in the West Indies date from their discovery by Columbus in 1492. Gradually, beginning in the seventeenth century, Spanish control was whittled down in favour of interlopers from northern Europe. The United States stepped in during the Spanish–American War of 1898, and since then has played a very active part in Caribbean affairs, especially in Cuba (virtually an American protectorate, 1898–1934) and Puerto Rico (whose people are American citizens). In 1917 she purchased most of the Virgin Islands from Denmark.

Recently, further political changes have taken place. Cuba is now ruled by a government with a Communist programme and an anti-American bias, and the British West Indies, having formed an abortive Federation (1958–62), have now split up into a number of independent or semi-independent states, though they retain their British connections. Since the Second World War many people, desirous of better living standards, have migrated from Puerto Rico to the United States, and from the British West Indies to the United Kingdom, a vastly different movement from that which drew so many negro slaves into this region from West Africa in the seventeenth and eighteenth centuries.

In contrast to the mainland of Central America, most of the West

The West Indies—Demographic and Economic Data

Political Unit	Area (sq. ml.)	Population (1970) and density (per sq. ml.)	Main population elements	Capital city and population	Main exports
Cuba	44,218	8,553,395 (193)	73% white 14·5% mestizo 12·5% Negro	Havana (1,008,500)	Sugar Tobacco
Haiti	10,714	4,969,113 (436)	95% Negro 5% mulatto	Port-au-Prince (386,000)	Coffee Bauxite Sisal
Dominican Republic	18,681	4,011,589 (214)	73% mulatto 16% white 11% Negro	Santo Domingo (671,000)	Sugar Coffee Cocoa Bauxite
Puerto Rico	3,435	2,712,000 (789)	75% white Rest mainly mulatto	San Juan (463,000)	Textiles & clothing Sugar Tobacco
U.S. Virgin Islands	133	63,200 (475)	Mainly Negro	Charlotte Amalie (12,000)	Sugar Cattle
Jamaica	4,411	1,861,300 (421)	77% Negro 18% mixed 1% white	Kingston (117,000)	Alumina Bauxite Sugar Bananas
Cayman Is.	100	10,560 (105)	Mainly Negro and mixed	George Town (4,000)	Rope Turtle shell
Leeward Is.:	356	145,000 (407)	Mainly Negro and mulatto	—	—
Antigua	108	60,000 (555)	—	St. John's (21,000)	Petroleum products
St. Kitts-Nevis and Anguilla	155	62,000 (400)	—	Basseterre (13,000)	Sugar Cotton Salt
Montserrat	33	12,300 (372)	—	Plymouth (3,500)	Fruit and vegetables
Br. Virgin Is.	60	10,500 (175)	—	Road Town (2,200)	Fish Livestock

Indian islands are populated by people of negro or mulatto origin, not by native Indians or even mestizos. Birth- and death-rates are normally high, the masses are mostly illiterate and poor, and welfare services are

The West Indies—Demographic and Economic Data (contd.)

Political Unit	Area (sq. ml.)	Population (1970) and density (per sq. ml.)	Main population elements	Capital city and population	Main exports
Windward Is.:	826	355,000 (429)	Mainly Negro and mulatto	—	—
Dominica	305	70,000 (229)	—	Roseau (10,000)	Bananas Fruit juices
Grenada	133	95,000 (714)	—	St. George's (8,600)	Bananas Cocoa Nutmeg and mace
St. Lucia	238	101,000 (424)	—	Castries (5,000)	Bananas Copra and coconut oil
St. Vincent	150	89,000 (593)	—	Kingstown (5,000)	Bananas Arrowroot Copra
Barbados	166	238,000 (1433)	93% Negro and mulatto 7% white	Bridgetown (8,800)	Sugar Petroleum products
Trinidad and Tobago	1,864	945,000 (507)	43% Negro 36% East Indian 16% mixed 5% white	Port-of-Spain (68,000)	Petroleum and products Sugar Cocoa
French West Indies:	1,073	667,000 (621)	Mainly Negro and mixed	—	—
Guadeloupe	688	327,000 (475)	—	Basse-Terre (15,500)	Sugar Bananas
Martinique	385	340,000 (883)	—	Fort-de-France (100,000)	Bananas Sugar Canned fruit
Netherlands Antilles	382	224,000 (586)	Mainly Negro	Willemstad (43,500)	Petroleum products
Bahamas	4,404	169,000 (38)	83% Negro	Nassau (100,000)	Petroleum products Cement Salt
Turks and Caicos Is.	166	5,675 (34)	Mainly mulatto	Grand Turk (2,300)	Crayfish

not yet widespread. Most of the people are subsistence-farmers, small commercial farmers, or plantation-workers. A growing number, however, live by work in the cities, mostly ports, where they take part in petty trade, small-scale factory production, and dock-work. Mining is important only in Cuba, Jamaica, and Trinidad, though the great oil refineries of the Netherlands Antilles provide much employment in the islands of Aruba and Curaçao off Venezuela. Most of the islands suffer economically from too great a dependence on one product, e.g. sugar in Barbados and others, oil in Trinidad.

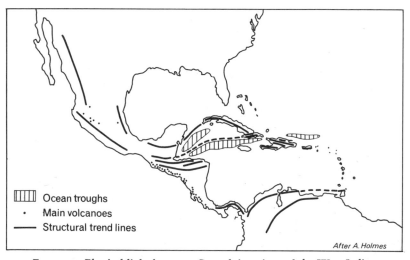

Ocean troughs
· Main volcanoes
—— Structural trend lines

After A. Holmes

FIG. 114.—Physical links between Central America and the West Indies.

The table on pp. 412 and 413 may be found useful for reference.

Structurally, most of the West Indian islands are distinguished by their mountain backbone, often volcanic, and are tectonically connected to the Central American mainland (*see* Fig. 114). But the Bahamas and the outermost members of the Lesser Antilles are of low relief and owe their origin mainly to the growth of coral.

In the Trade Wind Belt the rainfall of the islands is generally very heavy on the windward (*i.e.* north and east) sides and much lighter in the lee of the mountains. It generally exceeds 40 in. yearly, even on the lowlands, and shows a summer maximum. Temperatures, except at high altitudes, normally exceed 70° F in January, 80° in July. Tropical rain-forests clothe windward mountain slopes and valleys, but in the higher mountainous districts are often replaced by pine–cedar stands. Drier areas, especially those based on permeable limestone, carry savanna and scrub.

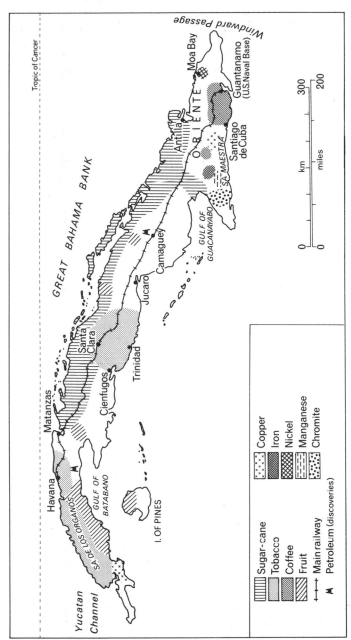

FIG. 115.—Cuba: general features.

THE ISLANDS OF THE WEST INDIES

CUBA

Eight hundred miles long, and by far the largest island in the West Indies, Cuba is about the size of Honduras (*see* Fig. 115). Apart from the high, rugged, Sierra Maestra in the south-east (exceeding 6000 ft), a lower central ridge, and the slightly elevated Sierra de los Organos in the north-west, the island is fairly low-lying, and its relief is so gently undulating as to make it suitable over wide areas for agriculture. Moreover, most of its soils are of limestone origin and are more fertile than average tropical soils. Into this island, thus favoured by nature, and also well placed to trade easily with her, the United States poured large investments during the present century, for it is able to produce sugar-cane and other tropical produce which cannot be extensively grown in the United States. Consequently, Cuba became, economically speaking, the richest of the numerous West Indian islands.

The total population exceeds 8 millions, and equals that of Venezuela. In contrast with the demographic pattern of most of its neighbours, more than half the people are white: they are mainly descended from Spanish colonial settlers and later immigrants. An eighth are negro or mulatto, 15% other racial mixtures, and there is a small minority of Asiatics, chiefly Chinese. Half the inhabitants are urban-dwellers, and over a million live in the one metropolis of Greater Havana. Spanish is the official language, and most people are Roman Catholics. Attachment to Spanish customs, traditions, and architecture remains fairly strong, but the mode of life in the cities and their skyscraper buildings reveals powerful American influences. Until the recent political troubles, 75% of the exports of Cuba went to the United States, and 80% of her imports came from the same country. Now the bulk of the trade is with the Communist world, and Cuba is a member of "Comecon."

The Economy. Cuba's economy, long geared to supply the needs of the United States, has, largely for that reason, been also geared to the production of a few commodities only, of which sugar is dominant. Indeed, nearly two-thirds of the total cultivated area (one-sixth of the whole island) is devoted to this single plantation crop, and only in the mountains and in the far west is it unimportant. Cuban production is about 20% of the entire world output, and Cuba leads all other countries as an exporter. In fact, 85% of its exports normally represent sugar and its derivatives. In the past the United States offered it preferential treatment in its markets, and took up to two-thirds of the output, but new markets have now been found, especially in Russia, by the new Communist régime.

The sugar crop benefits greatly from Cuba's climate, and also from its well-drained limy soils and rolling topography. Temperatures rarely fall much below 70°, 45–60 in. of rain can usually be relied upon each year, and there is generally a dry spell which favours the concentration of sucrose and also facilitates the harvesting of the crop and its transport— by bullock-cart or tractor-drawn trailer or light railway—to the mill. Unfortunately, periodic autumnal hurricanes may damage the crop, at least locally, and more money is now having to be spent on fertilisers, a common price to pay for monocultural techniques.

Both sugar-growing and milling make heavy demands on labour. Planting, hoeing, and cutting are still mainly performed by hand, as in other West Indian islands where labour is plentiful and cheap. The large mills, or *centrals*, are normally operated by the State, which owns the plantations, but most of the cane they receive is actually produced by small-holders (*colonos*). The chief by-product—molasses—is used in the manufacture of rum and treacle and may also be consumed as an animal feedstuff.

Tobacco is a second product of value to the Cuban economy. It is mainly grown by farmers in the western part of the island, where there are few sugar plantations, and in the west central province of Las Villas. Most is exported as leaf, or is made into the renowned Havana cigars, which are packed in boxes fashioned from Cuban cedar.

Winter vegetables, including tomatoes, and also grapefruit and pineapples, are intensively cultivated and used to find a ready market in the United States. Subsistence crops include maize, beans, plantains, and rice. Small acreages are devoted to bananas, henequen, and coffee. The latter crop is confined to the slopes of the Sierra Maestra.

Cuba has more than twice as much land under pasture as she has under all her crops. Most small farmers keep a working bullock, a pig or two, and a few chickens. Large areas in the central and eastern parts of the island are occupied by savanna and are used for livestock-grazing. Beef cattle are the most numerous animals (apart from poultry), but dairying is growing more important near urban areas, and many Cubans, following the example set by Americans, now enjoy their daily drink of milk. On the coasts fishing-boats are a frequent sight in Cuba's numerous "pocket bay" harbours. Besides edible fish, their owners collect turtle-shells, mother-of-pearl, and sponges, though, as in Floridan waters, fewer sponges are now obtained than formerly.

Cuba has several minerals of economic importance, particularly in the easternmost province (Oriente). Iron ore (of both high and low grade), nickel, and manganese occur in quantity. Small amounts of copper are worked, salt is extracted from sea-water round the coasts, and deposits of petroleum have been located. Nickel and chromite are exported from Moa Bay.

Communications and Settlements. Cuba has a much better network of communications than other islands in the West Indian archipelago. A new highway, threading the length of the island, has in recent years drawn many touring motorists to the country, while Havana, the capital, principal port and main manufacturing city, has a major airport.

Havana is by far the largest city in the West Indies. It has a fine, well-protected harbour, capable of shipping large quantities of sugar, tobacco, and winter vegetables. In winter it used to be thronged with visitors from the United States and almost became another Miami. But it no longer depends entirely upon tourists and shipping. It turns out several manufactured products, *e.g.* tobacco, tinned fruit, cement, textiles, and footwear.

Among other Cuban cities are Santiago de Cuba, magnificently sited on an almost land-locked bay at the eastern end of the republic, close to a productive agricultural and mining area; Camagüey, a market centre for cattle and sugar; Santa Clara, another agricultural distributing centre; and Cienfuegos, the seat of what is claimed to be the largest sugar-mill in the world, and an important exporter of sugar and tobacco.

HISPANIOLA

The island of Hispaniola, divided from Cuba by the Windward Passage, through which some shipping passes from the Atlantic to Jamaica and the Panamá Canal, is, politically speaking, a "split island," like Ireland, Tierra del Fuego, and New Guinea. The western third is occupied by the "Black Republic" of Haiti, the eastern two-thirds by the "Mestizo Republic" of Santo Domingo, now more often called the Dominican Republic. The whole consists of a number of mountain blocks, aligned east–west, and separated by fairly broad, down-faulted plains. In the north-east (in the Dominican Republic) are the Northern Cordillera or Sierra de Monte Christi, succeeded southwards by the Plaine du Nord of Haiti and the Cibao and Vega Real valleys of the Dominican Republic. The more central parts are taken up with the Massif du Nord (Haiti) and the Cordillera Central (Dominican Republic), which exceed 10,000 ft. South again are plains, including the Artibonite valley and Plaine du Cul de Sac of Haiti and the Plain of Seibo (Dominican Republic). Finally, in the south of the island rise the lofty Massif de la Hotte and the Massif de la Selle, chiefly in Haiti. Rather narrow plains border the Caribbean.

As elsewhere in the West Indies, the climate and vegetation vary with altitude and exposure. The mountains are usually rain-drenched but fairly cool, the lowlands, especially in the south, somewhat drier, and much hotter. More of the rainfall comes from May to October than from November to April, though only the south-west has a prolonged drought. Tropical rain-forest and highland cedar-forest are widespread, but savannas are found in some sheltered, low-lying districts. Most of the people live on the lowlands or on the coast, and are engaged in either subsistence farming or plantation agriculture.

HAITI

Haiti, for long a French colonial possession, revolted against foreign domination in the name of the French Revolution, and under its negro leader, Toussaint L'Ouverture, established a black republic. The erstwhile slaves, celebrating their victory by a blood-bath, massacred most of the French citizens in the island. Today, the population, numbering about 5 millions, is 95% black, 5% mulatto; the latter group forms the main ruling class. The official language remains French, and most people are Roman Catholics, but Voodooism is still practised in rural areas.

Since the Revolution, the republic has been far from peaceful, but a 20-year period of American occupation (1915–34) helped to set it on its feet economically. Some roads and a railway were built, irrigation slightly developed, water supplies and modern sanitation introduced into the cities, and a number of schools and hospitals erected. Rurally, however, the country remains backward: less than 15% of the ground is cultivated, soil erosion has become a serious problem in places, agricultural techniques are generally primitive, and most of the small-holding farmers grow little more than foodstuffs (cassava, yams, maize, and fruit) and keep a few chickens. They live in crude wood-and-thatch huts with no modern conveniences, 90% of them are still illiterate, and both yaws and malaria are rife.

The only important commercial crop, coffee, furnishes two-thirds of the exports. Small amounts of sisal, sugar, cotton, cacao, and bananas are also produced for sale, chiefly in the north coast plain and the Plaine du Cul de Sac and some bauxite is mined. The bulk of the foreign trade is with the United States, which sends Haiti foodstuffs as well as textiles and machinery.

The capital, chief port, and only large city is Port au Prince at the western end of the Plaine du Cul de Sac. Both it and Cap Haïtien, serving the Plaine du Nord, have suffered severely from earthquakes.

THE DOMINICAN REPUBLIC

The Dominican Republic has fewer people than Haiti on nearly twice as much land. It did not become independent until 1844, following a long period of Spanish domination, and shorter spells under French and Haitian overlords. Since then, like Haiti, the republic has suffered from long periods of economic stagnation and political unrest, and was temporarily occupied by the United States between the two World Wars. Since 1930, however, under the effective but very autocratic leadership of Generalísimo Trujillo, which lasted until his assassination in 1961, it has made much more progress than its neighbour, and today conducts over twice as much foreign trade. Its chief trading partner is again the United States,

[*Courtesy: Embassy of Dominican Republic.*

Fig. 116.—Sugar plantation, Dominican Republic. A modern method of mechanical loading is shown. The caterpillar wheels of the tractor on the left, a response to the muddy ground conditions, should be noted.

though the United Kingdom takes a quarter of its exports. The population, numbering 4 millions, is predominantly mulatto and mestizo, but there is a large white minority. Spanish is the official language.

Plantation agriculture is much more characteristic than in Haiti. Sugar is the dominant crop, and the output has doubled since 1950 (*see* Fig. 116). A number of large government *centrals* have been established in the last few years, and the general efficiency of the industry has greatly improved. The principal growing areas are the richly alluvial Cibao–Vega Real depression and the Plain of Seibo. Other commercial crops include coffee, cacao, and tobacco. Many areas of savanna are devoted to cattle-raising. The Dominican Republic has made rather more progress with the development of its mineral endowment than Haiti, though most deposits remain untouched in the absence of adequate transport facilities. The chief ores are iron, gold, copper, nickel, chromite, and bauxite; deposits of petroleum and rock salt have been located. A large ferro-nickel project is under way in the Yuna valley.

The capital—a larger city than Haiti's Port au Prince—is the port of Santo Domingo (or Ciudad Trujillo), largely destroyed by a hurricane in 1930, but since rebuilt on modern lines. Though a fine-looking city, and with a new steel foundry and rolling-mill, it is at present accessible only by ship and road. The only railway in the republic links the small port of Sánchez to the chief inland market, Santiago.

PUERTO RICO

Puerto Rico, the smallest of the Greater Antillean islands, and easily the most densely populated, is much more varied in its economy than most West Indian islands.

As we have seen, it was acquired by the United States as a prize for its success in the Spanish–American War of 1898. Since 1952 it has been a free Commonwealth associated with the United States, and, when given the chance in 1967 to apply for Statehood, rejected it in favour of a continuance of the *status quo*. Seventy-five per cent of its 2¾ million people are white, most of the rest negro or mulatto. They are increasing in numbers too rapidly for comfort, and the island already has a density of 800 persons per square mile. About 40,000 emigrants leave the country each year for the parent republic, where they take up residence mainly in New York.

Physically, Puerto Rico forms a continuation, across the Mona Passage, of the three main ridges of the Dominican Republic, but here they are crowded as a horst into a 40-mile width of land, and the dividing valleys are almost non-existent. The highest mountains are in the south-central part of the island, where the altitude reaches 4000 ft. In the north-west karstic features are notable, and in the mountain core there are volcanic landforms.

The mean annual rainfall exceeds 180 in. in parts of the highlands, but declines to less than 30 in. on the southern, leeward, coast plain. As in other islands, the natural vegetation is part forest, part savanna and scrub. Much of the forest has been cleared in the interests of cultivation.

Sugar, grown mainly on large estates, and its by-products, molasses, rum, and industrial alcohol, make up a large percentage of the total exports. Cane occupies about a third of all the cultivated area, and dominates the agrarian economy of the coast plain and many of the small alluvial valleys. Coffee—the chief staple at the beginning of the century—

has come to be relegated mainly to the western highlands, where it is rivalled by oranges. Tobacco, vegetables, fruit, e.g. grapefruit and pine-apples, and subsistence crops are grown mostly on small mixed farms, often by sharecroppers. Cattle are fairly numerous, and milk is produced for urban markets.

Pressure of population on the land, coupled with deforestation, has been a cause of soil erosion, which has become severe on many slopes. In com-bination, population pressure and soil erosion have made it necessary for Puerto Rico to import food from the United States. But they have also stimulated the broadening of the economy, in particular the development of industry, notably the manufacture of clothing, rayon, fine needlework (a notable export), cement, glass, paint, hardboard, tobacco, and a variety of miscellaneous consumer goods. A large oil refinery and petro-chemical plant have been built, and hydro-electric power-stations are being erected. Alongside this industrial development, promoted mainly by the United States, is a growing programme of welfare services, including health and education, and an expanding tourist trade.

The chief cities are the large ports of San Juan, on the north coast, and Ponce on the southern. The former, situated on a fine land-locked har-bour, is the capital, and conducts most of the trade, which is mainly aligned towards the United States. Air services link it with Havana, New York, Bermuda, and Trinidad.

THE U.S. VIRGIN ISLANDS

To the east of Puerto Rico, rising from a submarine bank, are the Virgin Islands, more than three-quarters of which have belonged to the United States since 1917. They produce cattle, pineapples, and fish, and are of some strategic value. St Thomas, the chief town, exports cattle, both from these islands and from the adjacent British Virgin Islands. To the south, above another submerged bank, lies the American island of St Croix, pro-ducing sugar. The small population of all these islands is mainly negroid.

THE BRITISH WEST INDIES

In 1958, following years of discussion, most of the British West Indian islands were temporarily integrated into a Federation. On grounds of mutual security, the economic strength that might be expected to result from co-operation, and administrative efficiency and economy, federal union had everything to recommend it. But this merging together of over 3 million people in Jamaica, Trinidad and Tobago, Barbados, and the smaller islands in the Lesser Antilles was not effected without opposition and without qualms, and neither British Guiana nor British Honduras, despite pressing invitations from Britain, were willing to adhere to it.

The main reasons for the delay in establishing political unity were:

1. The physical disunion of the constituent parts, which are strung out over a distance of 2000 miles.
2. The absence of regular inter-island communications.
3. The varied ethnic composition, religion, outlook, and customs of the island peoples.
4. The fears expressed by folk in the wealthier and less densely populated islands that they might be overrun by migrants from the poorer and more thickly settled.
5. The threat of administrative domination by far-away officials felt, for instance, by the 250,000 inhabitants of Barbados *vis-à-vis* the $1\frac{3}{4}$ millions in Jamaica, the leading partner in the Federation.
6. The very novelty of the idea, which did not recommend itself to many conservatively minded individuals and groups.

Assisting the establishment of the Federation were, *inter alia*, the following factors:

1. The development of air transport, which is yearly diminishing distances.
2. The advantages of a common customs union and of regional planning of the economy.
3. The advantages of a greater degree of mutual co-operation in the strategic sphere, made evident by the Second World War.
4. The creation in Jamaica (1947) of a University College of the West Indies, which is drawing together many of the intellectually minded young men and women, who were expected to become the economic, social, and political leaders of the new organisation.

Among the difficulties the Federation had to handle were those concerned with broadening and developing the islands' economy so that the current low standards of living, characteristic of a majority of the population, might be raised. Connected with these problems were others concerned with the improvement of health and education. The selection of a suitable site for a federal capital was not easy. The choice finally made, largely to placate those who feared Jamaica's undue dominance, was one in Trinidad. Even then, there was the fear that a site so far removed from the central and western islands of the Federation would create problems. When Jamaica and Trinidad withdrew from the Federation in 1962 there arose the additional question as to whether a smaller Federation could survive. This hope proved illusory, and by 1966 Barbados, following the lead of Jamaica and Trinidad, embarked on an independent career within the Commonwealth. By 1967, most of the small islands in both the Windward and Leeward groups were individually granted the status of associated Commonwealth states, Britain retaining temporary rights over defence and external affairs and bolstering up their economies with financial and technical aid.

JAMAICA

Jamaica, though only one-tenth the size of Cuba, is the largest of the British West Indian islands. In shape somewhat like Puerto Rico, it measures nearly 150 miles from east to west and nearly 50 miles from north to south (see Fig. 117).

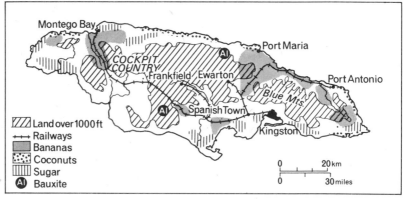

FIG. 117.—Jamaica: general features.

Its population, already approaching 2 millions, is increasing almost as rapidly as that of Puerto Rico, largely owing to improved medical services. Many of its people—accustomed to migrate seasonally to the sugar plantations of Cuba and the banana fields of Central America—are now coming to Britain, but in rural areas population pressure remains acute. There are too many small and uneconomic farms and, despite the growing diversity of the economy, there is much unemployment and underemployment.

Ninety-five per cent of the people are either descended from negro slaves or are of mixed breed, mostly mulatto. The chief minorities are: (a) East Indian, i.e. descendants of indentured labourers from Asiatic counties encouraged to enter Jamaica in the early nineteenth century when slavery was abolished; (b) Chinese, most of whom are petty retailers; (c) whites, largely of British origin, who run the plantations and mines and control most of the administration. The island has been British since

1655, and the previous Spanish occupation has left little impress save in some place-names. The Jamaicans speak English and play cricket, and their principal institutions are derived from the United Kingdom.

Like Puerto Rico, Jamaica rises from comparatively low coast plains to high mountains: in the east the Blue Mountains reach 7400 ft. The highlands are seamed with deep river valleys, most of which are thickly forested, but 80% of the total area consists of rolling limestone uplands, with few surface streams and karstic landscapes. In the north-west is the "cock-pit" country, pitted with deep and often wide solution-hollows.

As in neighbouring islands, the windward side of Jamaica, especially the mountains, receives an excessive trade-wind rainfall, but the leeward side is much drier, and parts of the south and west receive less than 30 in. a year. Port Antonio, on the north-east coast, for example, receives 130 in. a year, Kingston, on the south-east coast, only 36 in. Natural vegetation is as varied as the relief and precipitation. The karst lands are mostly lightly covered with scrub: elsewhere there is either forest or savanna, depending on the amount of rainfall.

The Economy. Despite occasional setbacks produced by hurricanes like that of 1951, earthquakes, like that which ruined the capital in 1907, periodic drought in the south, the incidence of banana-disease, and variations in commodity prices, Jamaica has made many material advances during the present century. Its economy, now reasonably diversified, is based not simply upon commercial crops but also upon bauxite-working, light manufacturing, and tourism. Many of its people, however, still depend primarily upon crops of maize, rice, yams, fruit, and vegetables, which they merely sell locally in a restricted market. In dry, hilly areas they rear sheep and goats, and travel to market either on foot or donkey. They live in airless villages composed of rude shacks of timber and thatch, like so many rural people in the West Indies, or else in town-slums.

About half of the gainfully employed men and women in agricultural occupations labour on sugar plantations or other large estates. Except for the period between the two World Wars, when bananas supplanted it, sugar, with subsidiary molasses and rum, has always been the chief commercial product. It is mainly grown on large holdings in the southern coastlands, where it needs irrigation, and in the north-western lowlands, where overseas corporations have invested much capital both in land and mills. The banana industry slumped badly after 1939 owing to the shortage of shipping and the ravages of disease, but growers still operate lowland plantations, mostly in the north, whence the fruit is shipped in specially designed vessels from such ports as Port Antonio (*see* Fig. 117).

Jamaica also produces, mainly for export, fair quantities of high-grade "Blue Mountain" coffee, cacao (grown chiefly by small-holders in humid but sheltered interior basins in the north-west), pimento or allspice (a speciality of this island), ginger, and tobacco (mainly cultivated in the central limestone districts), citrus fruits, especially oranges and grapefruit, and coconuts (a product mainly of the sandy coastlands of the north and east).

Dairy cattle, as well as beef cattle, have recently assumed increased

Fig. 118.—A banana plantation. Note the very large leaves of the banana trees and the prolific nature of the undergrowth.

importance, and a special breed of cattle—"Jamaica Hope"—has been evolved to suit not only Jamaican but also other tropical conditions. But more striking even than this advance has been the establishment in the central part of the island, since 1942, of a bauxite-mining and alumina-producing industry, which has led to the export of large quantities of raw material to Canadian (Kitimat) and American refining plants. In fact, Jamaica now ranks first in the world as a bauxite producer and new railways and ports have been built to facilitate exports. There are also deposits of manganese, iron, copper, and gypsum.

Tourism has made headway: a result of the delightful coastal climate, varied and beautiful scenery, including coastal cliffs, and coves, skilful propaganda, and good roads. One of the most popular centres is Montego Bay, with fine bathing beaches, a well-served airport, and a railway to Kingston. Nearly half a million tourists now spend nearly £50,000,000 a year on the island.

The advance of manufacturing in Jamaica is shown by a 20% rise in employment between 1952 and 1958. Besides traditional processing industries like sugar and rum, new ones, including textiles, clothing and footwear, pharmaceuticals, plastics, cement, and furniture, are growing and are contributing to a considerable rise in the national income.

Kingston, the capital, though smaller than the other government centres in the Greater Antilles, is worthy of its country. On the sheltered southern coast, it possesses a magnificent natural harbour protected by a long sand-spit ("The Palisados"), and is well laid out on a gridiron plan. Behind it ascend the Blue Mountain slopes adorned with country mansions, whose wealthy inhabitants may enjoy the sea-breezes. Fifteen miles west of Kingston stands the now small, but once-proud capital, Spanish Town.

THE CAYMAN ISLANDS

These small, low-lying coral islands lie over 100 miles north-west of Jamaica, of which they were dependencies until 1959. They are inhabited by about 10,000 seafaring people who voyage as far as the Honduran and Nicaraguan banks in search of turtles. They commonly make their own boats and ropes and sell their catch in Jamaica, where it is either used as a basis for turtle soup or the extraction of tortoiseshell. The sale of the latter is now suffering from synthetic substitutes, but the islands are expanding their tourist trade to recoup their losses.

THE LEEWARD ISLANDS

The Leeward Islands, which have a total population of nearly 150,000, consist of: (*a*) two British "Associated" territories (p. 423): Antigua (with the unimportant Barbuda and the uninhabited Redonda), and St Christopher or St Kitts-Nevis; (*b*) three British dependencies: Anguilla (which broke away from St Kitts-Nevis in 1967), Montserrat, and the British Virgin Islands (*see* p. 422).

Antigua, the largest and most populous of the Leeward Islands, has a volcanic hill in the south-west, but is mostly a low-lying limestone plain. Summer rain, supplemented by well-irrigation, has encouraged the production of sugar, the leading crop, and Sea Island cotton, of which it is the largest producer in the Lesser Antilles. Onions and tomatoes are also grown and exported. The capital is the port of St John's with a new deep-water harbour and oil refinery.

St Kitts and *Nevis* are volcanic islands separated by a strait only two miles wide. As in Antigua, sugar (especially important on the former) and cotton (on the latter, which is less fertile) are the main crops. Some cattle are raised and vegetables are grown. Basseterre (St Kitts) and the smaller Charlestown (Nevis) are the principal towns. *Anguilla* is a coral island producing a little cotton. Salt, however, obtained from sea-water by solar evaporation, is the leading product.

Montserrat, as its name implies, is a mountainous volcanic island of serrated summits. The rich soil produces good crops of Sea Island cotton, sugar (for rum), limes (for lime juice), and vegetables, including tomatoes. Plymouth, with only an open roadstead, on the leeward side of the island, is the chief settlement.

THE WINDWARD ISLANDS

The Windward Islands, wetter than the Leeward as might be expected from their not entirely appropriate title, lie south of the latter. They are larger than the Leeward group and support more than twice their population (about 350,000). They are all mountainous, volcanic islands, with generally rich soils, and produce a greater variety of agricultural products than their neighbours to the north, but again, the chief cities are ports. Fishing is a significant subsidiary occupation, and the population is predominantly negro or mulatto. Individually, their names are Dominica (capital Roseau), St Lucia (capital Castries, with the best harbour in the group), St Vincent (capital Kingstown), and Grenada (capital St George's). All are associated British Commonwealth states. Their main cities lie on the sheltered, western sides of their respective islands.

Dominica, the largest island, as well as the highest, suffers from an overabundant mean annual rainfall of 300 in. on the wet (eastern) side, but is much drier on the west, where soils are very fertile. It is noted for its bananas, limes (valued for their juice), cocoa, copra and vanilla. It still houses about 100 Caribs, remnants of a once numerous cannibalistic aboriginal population scattered through many of the eastern Caribbean islands when the Spaniards first erupted into the region.

St Lucia, which the French held until 1814, is distinguished, like Dominica, by the French patois still spoken by its people, and by their adherence to the Roman Catholic faith. Bananas, grown on large estates, form the chief crop, but it also produces cacao, sugar, lime juice, coconuts and vegetables.

South of St Lucia is the island of *St Vincent*, notorious for the eruption of the volcanic La Soufrière in 1902, when much havoc was caused. Sea Island cotton, bananas, and arrowroot, of which it is the world's chief source, are the dominant crops and exports, but sugar, cacao, sweet potatoes, cassava, and coconuts are also produced. Associated with St Vincent are the rocky, northern Grenadine Islands.

The southern Grenadines are politically attached to *Grenada*, the most

southerly of the Windward Islands, and the one with the greatest proportion of lowland. Small-holders produce a wide diversity of crops,
including cacao and nutmegs (the chief), sugar, coconuts, cotton, limes,
citrus fruits, and a variety of subsistence foods; there are again banana
plantations.

BARBADOS

Barbados, lying east of the Lesser Antillean arc, is a rather isolated pear-
shaped island of coralline origin and rolling relief. It is a little larger than
the Isle of Wight. It is notable for its high proportion of cultivated ground
(two-thirds of the whole) and for its extremely high population
density (nearly 1500 per square mile). In the north, stripped of their
limestone cover, are older sands and shales in which petroleum has been
discovered and worked on a small scale.

Half the cultivated ground is under sugar, which does well on the
productive limestone soils though well-irrigation and fertilisers are often
applied to increase the value of the crop. It is grown both on family
estates and on smaller holdings. Around the cane-fields, many food
crops are raised, e.g. yams, cassava, plantains, maize, beans, bread-fruit,
squashes. Coconuts are of some importance round the coasts.

Barbados was never occupied by Spain, but has been British continuously since 1627. Its capital, from which each year there is an export of
people as well as of sugar, molasses, and rum, is the port of Bridgetown,
spanning a small creek, and controlling the south-eastern approach to the
Caribbean Sea. It supports a number of small industrial estates, a fleet of
shrimp trawlers, and a growing tourist industry. Round it, a wide range
of market vegetables are cultivated.

TRINIDAD AND TOBAGO

Trinidad is less than half the size of Jamaica, but is nevertheless next to
it in area among British West Indian islands. It lies south of the Lesser
Antilles, only 7 miles away from the Orinoco delta in Venezuela, with
which it has structural connections, and is only 10 degrees from the
equator.

Unlike other West Indian islands, over a third of its population (nearly
a million in all) is of Hindu, Chinese, and East Asiatic origin, and its
economy is based principally, not upon crops, but upon minerals. Nearly
half the population, however, is of African ancestry, and tropical plants
grow well. One-third of the country, in fact, is cultivated, the main non-
agricultural areas occupying parts of the high northern ridge (a continuation of the coastal ridge of Venezuela), the lower southern ridge, and
certain swamp lands on the west and east coasts.

Sugar and cacao are the leading money crops. Both are mainly grown on large company-owned estates. The former is especially important on the flat, low-lying western coastal plains facing the shallow Gulf of Paria, the latter in the moister, though sheltered valleys of the Northern Range. Coconut palms do well on the sandy shores of the coastlands, and there is a small production of coffee, rice, grapefruit, and other citrus fruits.

The chief minerals are petroleum and natural gas which are worked in the Tertiary sedimentaries of the southern hill country and in offshore waters. Petroleum normally accounts for 80% of the colony's total exports, the output being about two-fifths that of Mexico. Trinidad refines most of its own oil, and also a proportion of the much vaster Venezuelan supply. Asphalt, a bituminous kind of petroleum, has been produced for nearly four centuries at the Pitch Lake, near La Brea. At first used for caulking the seams of wooden sailing ships, it is now valued chiefly for road-surfacing. Despite an annual shipment of well over 100,000 barrels, the lake shows no signs of exhaustion, and fresh supplies constantly well up to replace what is removed. Manufacturing is becoming more important. There is a car assembly plant, and tyre works, and both fertilisers and domestic appliances are made.

The capital, and easily the largest city in Trinidad, is Port of Spain, which is nearly as large as Kingston, Jamaica. It has a long, well-equipped wharf, extending 3300 ft into the shallow Gulf of Paria, and acts as an entrepôt for many other West Indian islands and for Guyana, as well as serving Trinidad itself. Twenty-five miles farther south, and similarly located on the west coast, is the second largest settlement, San Fernando, an outlet for the principal sugar-growing district.

Tobago, integrated with Trinidad in 1888, is a small, rugged, forested island 20 miles north-east of Trinidad. Cacao and coconuts are grown commercially, but the island is best known as a tourist centre. The main resort and largest settlement is the aptly named Scarborough.

THE FRENCH WEST INDIES

France retains two colonial territories in the West Indies: Guadeloupe, with a number of adjacent islands, including Marie Galante, and Martinique. Though remaining colonial in character, constitutionally they are both overseas departments of metropolitan France, and send deputies to the French Assembly. They are separated from each other by the British island of Dominica. Each has a population of about ⅓ million mainly of negroid origin.

Guadeloupe is a twin-island, its two parts being very narrowly divided by a sea channel. The misappropriately named Basse-Terre, in the west, is of volcanic origin and culminates in the still active La Soufrière (4870 ft), while Grande-Terre, in the east, is coralline and nowhere surpasses 450 ft in altitude. Basse-Terre may well be flooded during the torrential summer rains, while Grande-Terre may be drought-stricken.

Sugar, grown mainly on Grande-Terre, is the chief crop and finds a ready sale in the preferential French market. Bananas, cotton, coffee, cacao, citrus fruits, and vanilla are the main subsidiary cash crops. These products are for the most part handled at Pointe-à-Pitre, which boasts a fine harbour. The capital is the smaller town of Basse-Terre.

Martinique is somewhat akin to Basse-Terre. Its highest point is the volcanic Mt Pelée (4430 ft), which suddenly erupted with explosive violence in 1902, to destroy the fine old city of Saint-Pierre, which has never recovered from the disaster. Hurricanes are another hazard to which the people of Martinique are occasionally subject.

Sugar-cane growing dominates the economy of Martinique to a less extent than that of Guadeloupe. Fruit, *e.g.* bananas and pineapples, are also cultivated, and small acreages are devoted to coffee and cacao. All these products are shipped to the home country from Fort de France, the seat of government, which is located on the sheltered, leeward side of the island.

THE NETHERLANDS ANTILLES

The Netherlands Antilles, which enjoy domestic autonomy within the Dutch realm, fall into two groups over 500 miles apart: (*a*) Curaçao, Aruba, and Bonaire, off Venezuela; (*b*) Saba, St Eustatius, and St Martin (shared with France) in the volcanic zone of the Lesser Antilles.

Agriculture is not very important, though small amounts of Sea Island cotton, sugar-cane, and maize are grown in the Lesser Antillean group. St Martin has a small salt industry, and some fishing is undertaken along the shores of all the islands.

The main reason for the economic importance of the Netherlands West Indies lies in the association of Curaçao and Aruba with the oil-producing industry of Venezuela. Both these islands support large refineries which prepare crude Venezuelan oil for export. The refinery at Willemstadt, the capital of Curaçao, is, indeed, one of the world's largest. As a port, the city is well served by a commodious deep-water harbour capable of handling big tankers. On Aruba, a large new "hydro-desulphurisation" plant is beginning to turn out large quantities of sulphur products.

Among other activities worthy of note in Curaçao are the following: (*a*) phosphate-mining; (*b*) the collection of divi divi pods, which supply tannin to the leather industry; (*c*) the preparation of orange peel for flavouring the renowned Curaçao liqueur.

THE BAHAMAS

The Bahamas—a former British colony recently granted self-rule—are an archipelago of about 700 coral islands, rising from a number of shallow banks south-east of Florida, with which they have structural affinities. Only just over 20 of the islands are inhabited. About half of the 170,000 people occupying them live in the capital, Nassau, on New Providence, a strikingly beautiful city shaded by trees, decorated with gardens, and embellished with splendid hotels. Its proximity to the United States, the tropical warmth of its sunny, winter climate and also of its sparkling seas (washed by the infant Gulf Stream), have combined to make it a very attractive holiday resort. About 1½ million visitors enter the Bahamas as a whole each year, and most of them spend their time in and about Nassau. In all, tourism employs two-thirds of the working population of the Bahamas.

Though Columbus is believed to have made his first landfall in the New World in San Salvador or Watling Island, in the Bahama group, the archipelago was settled by the British, not by Latin people. Thanks to the slave trade, however, the main element in the resident population (83%) is of African origin.

Although only just over 1% of the archipelago is cultivated, enough tomatoes, cucumbers, and pineapples are grown to have made it worth while to establish canneries for their preservation and export. Some people live by lumbering: there is an export of pulpwood, and of yellow pine for pit-props; others by fishing, in particular for crawfish, turtles, and lobsters; a few by extracting salt from sea-water by solar-evaporation processes. There is little manufacturing, but an industrial area is now being laid out at Freeport on Grand Bahama Island where there is already an oil refinery and some factories.

THE TURKS AND CAICOS ISLANDS

South-east of the Bahamas is a former dependency of Jamaica known as the Turks and Caicos Islands. Physically, these deposits of coral belong to the Bahamas. About 6000 people inhabit them. They are chiefly noted commercially for their crawfish, salt, and sisal.

BERMUDA

Though not part of the West Indies, this may be a convenient place to refer to the Bermudas, as they share many of their characteristics with the Bahamas. They form a cluster of about 300 small coral islands, of which (as in the Bahamas) about 20 are inhabited. Though situated 600 miles north of the Tropic, they enjoy an almost tropical climate owing to their insular character and their position relative to the warm Gulf Stream. They are only 600 miles distant from the populous mainland of North America, from which they draw numerous visitors by air and sea. Hamilton, the capital, located on Main Island, is only a small town, but may be compared with Nassau as a health resort. Air passengers from New York can reach it in three hours, and its harbour provides a safe anchorage for ships.

The Bermudas have been British since 1609, but have a resident population of only 50,000. Nearly two-thirds of the people are coloured. Apart from fish and vegetables, most food is imported, and is largely paid for out of the income the islanders derive from their tourist earnings. There is, however, an export of lilies and bulbs to North America, for the very equable climate favours many flowers.

Both Britain and the United States maintain air bases on Bermuda on account of its strategic position in the open North Atlantic.

Chapter XXXIV

GREENLAND

GEOGRAPHICAL BACKGROUND

GENERAL ASPECTS

Greenland is one of the largest islands in the world, but among the most thinly peopled. Lying north-east of Canada, it covers about 840,000 square miles, and is nearly 1700 miles long and 700 miles broad in its widest part (see Fig. 119). It extends from about 60 degrees N. (Cape Farewell) to 83° 40' N. (Cape Morris Jesup), which brings it to within 450 miles of the North Pole. Most of it, therefore, lies well within the Arctic Circle. Eighty-five per cent of it is permanently covered with ice, and the rest is no better than tundra. Not surprisingly, its population in 1970 was less than 50,000, mostly of mixed Eskimo and Danish blood. Not very long ago it was a Stone Age survival, but, under recent Danish and U.S. influences, it is being quickly thrust forward into an age dominated by commerce, strategy, and nuclear power.

While the life and outlook of its people are being thus revolutionised, especially in and near the west coastlands, the great ice-cap of the interior and the desolate northern and eastern shores are still imperfectly known and continue to attract exploratory expeditions, in which British, French, Danes, Swedes, and Norwegians are the chief participants.

PHYSICAL GEOGRAPHY

The Greenland ice-cap is the largest surviving remnant of the once very extensive Pleistocene ice-sheets of the northern hemisphere. Even this seems now to be shrinking, if only temporarily, as the climate during the last half century has been ameliorating somewhat and the snowfall decreasing. Throughout the interior, however, the ice is still over 6000 ft thick, and in places recent seismic records suggest a depth of 10,000 ft. This central ice-bearing area appears to rise from a land-surface depressed below sea-level. Near the coasts there are mountain ranges which exceed 12,000 ft in elevation on the east side, where they consist mainly of Archaean gneisses and schists. Their steep slopes and exposure to high winds keep parts of them free of permanent snow: they form, in fact, *nunataks.* Below their frost-riven peaks and arêtes are cirques and U-shaped valleys down which glaciers descend, generally to the sea, by way of long fiords, *e.g.* Scoresby Sound in the east, and Sondre Strømfiord in the west. Except in the south-west, where most nowadays have their snouts above sea-level, Greenland's numerous glaciers calve icebergs in

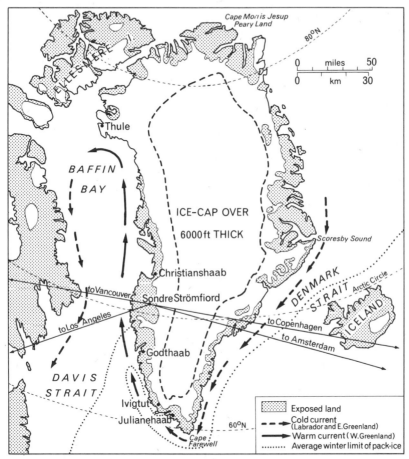

FIG. 119.—Greenland: general features.

summer which are carried southwards into the North Atlantic by the East Greenland and Labrador currents. The coastal ranges are highest in the east, they descend more sharply to the sea than in the west, and they usually overlook deeper fiords. In fact, on the western side fairly extensive coastal lowlands are evident, especially in the vicinity of the Arctic Circle. Here, between the interior ice and the sea, there is an ice-free strip up to 120 miles in width, interrupted only locally by sea-reaching glaciers. Paradoxically, also, parts of Peary Land in the far north of Greenland are ice-free: not because of favourable temperatures in this case, but because of a very low precipitation.

As the air over Greenland is usually too cold to hold much moisture, precipitation is nowhere excessive, and may take the form of rain in summer. At this season some of the crevasses in the ice-cap, which in winter are concealed by a thin ice-crust, may open and make travel even more difficult than it is during the long, dark, severe winter, when snow-blizzards frequently rage. The mean annual temperature in the interior is usually well below 0° F, and in the warmest months may not exceed 32° F, but summer averages of over 40 are not uncommon on the west coast, and in the sun the thermometer may record more than 80° F, while in lowland areas covered by water-logged tundra mosquitoes may become pestiferous. The summer days are long as well as briefly kind, and coastal crops of potatoes, turnips, radishes, broccoli, and lettuce are not unknown as far north as the Arctic Circle on the relatively mild, western coast. Greenland, however, despite its name—given to it by Eric the Red, doubtless so as to encourage immigrants—is at best a land which takes on the character of a Dartmoor or Grampian Plateau. It is not a country where settlement can ever be more than sporadic.

GREENLAND AND THE OUTSIDE WORLD

Greenland was sparsely-inhabited by Eskimo hunters and fishermen when Icelanders, led by Eric the Red, began to make their homes there shortly before A.D. 1000. For the ensuing 200–300 years, a republic was maintained; about 200 stock farms were established, and trade relations with both Iceland and Norway were kept up. The latter assumed political control in 1261; shortly afterwards the European population began to decline, perhaps due to attacking Eskimos inspired by climatic deterioration, or to the failure of Iceland and Norway to maintain their food exports to the country. Denmark secured possession in 1721 and continues to exercise its sovereignty. In 1953 the island became an integral part of the Kingdom of Denmark, though only western Greenland, where over 80% of the population resides, sends representatives to the Folketing in Copenhagen.

Since 1941 the United States has played a significant part in Greenland affairs. In that year, following the German occupation of Denmark, it was feared that Hitler might order the island to be used as a base for submarines, surface ships and aircraft, and from it launch attacks upon allied shipping in the North Atlantic. Its possession would also yield the enemy valuable advance information about the weather which usually progresses towards Europe from this north-west Atlantic area. For these reasons, the United States assumed responsibility for the defence of Greenland, and later began to use the island from time to time as an intermediate stop on oceanic flights. She also established there a naval base and weather stations to assist Britain. In 1951 the United States agreed to share, with

[*Courtesy: U.S. Information Service.*

FIG. 120.—Thule, Greenland. The massive steel radar screens rising from the tundra are part of U.S.A.'s first Ballistic Missile Early Warning System station. The background glacier and the ice-strewn water should be noted.

Denmark, the defence of Greenland under the North Atlantic Treaty Organisation. Near Thule, in the north-west, in lat. 76 degrees N., she built a large military airfield, well equipped with aluminium buildings, radio and radar towers, supported on piles deeply driven into the ground to prevent disturbances due to frost-heaving of the soil and damage which might result from summer thawing (*see* Fig. 120). Thule is 1900 miles from New York, barely 2500 from Moscow, and only 1250 from Soviet bases in Franz Josef Land.

TRADITIONAL ECONOMY AND MODERN
DEVELOPMENTS

The Greenlanders—traditionally hunters of sea-mammals and musk-ox, subsistence fishermen and catchers of spring and summer game such as eider-duck, auks, ptarmigan, guillemots, and sea-gulls—used, like the Eskimos of Canada and Alaska, to be an entirely self-sufficient people. Some animals, birds, and fish are still taken in the traditional manner, a number of old, scattered peat and stone igloos remain, especially on the more remote and harsher north and east coasts, and such equipment as the kayak and dog-sledge have not been entirely discarded, but one cannot ignore the revolution this century has wrought in the life of most of the people, especially those who live in the favoured south-west. For example, most of the larger settlements have shops at which food, cloth, and tobacco may be bought, as well as a church, school, and post office. New houses, rapidly replacing the old, less-sanitary dwellings, are mostly made of wood; they rest on rock foundations and are brightly painted in green, white, red, or blue. Education to the age of fourteen is now compulsory, more than a dozen hospitals have been erected, and tuberculosis, which once menaced the whole population, has been brought under control. The capital, Godthaab, with a population of about 6000, has a technical college as well as a restaurant. The Danes have done well for the Greenlanders, of whom they have much understanding, and the population is now rising steadily as sanitation and other health measures, including piped water supplies, are being developed.

The chief sources of wealth are fish and minerals. Since the First World War the waters of the North Atlantic have become warmer, and many cod and other edible fish have migrated northwards into Greenland seas. From the northern settlements, the people continue to hunt seal and walrus, but farther south, in their new, motor-powered craft, they now join foreign visitors, e.g. Norwegian and British trawlermen, in commercial fishing. Besides cod, they catch catfish, halibut, mackerel, salmon, and shrimps. Fish filleting, freezing, and canning plants have been opened at such places as Christianshaab and Julianehaab, and many harbours now carry oil supplies from which even foreign vessels may replenish their stocks. The Greenlanders have not yet, however, been introduced to trawling, and they confine their activities to inshore waters. Also, except in the extreme south-west, their harbours freeze up in winter and their vessels lie idle.

The chief commercial mineral is cryolite, quarried on a big scale at Ivigtut, on Arsukfiord, in the south-west, since 1856 (see Fig. 121). Here are the only cryolite mines in the world, and since the mineral plays an essential part in the electrolytic refining of aluminium, its sale contributes significantly to the revenues of the country. Other minerals include low-grade coal, of which enough is raised in the west each year to satisfy local demands, and lead and zinc, which are now beginning to be exploited following their discovery in the north-east in 1948.

[*Courtesy: Royal Danish Ministry for Foreign Affairs.*

FIG. 121.—Ivigtut cryolite mine, Greenland. Cryolite is an essential raw material in the aluminium industry.

Reindeer have been introduced into the Godthaab district, and sheep into the Julianehaab area. The latter have to be fed indoors in winter, but local farmers have undertaken the storage of native grasses, turnips, and willows, and the drying of fish for this purpose.

Among the many developments that have taken place in Greenland in recent years, those arising from its strategic location in respect of air transport have already been touched upon. Many of the shortest air routes between North America and Eurasia traverse Arctic regions. The Scandinavian Airlines System, already accustomed to the maintenance of cold-weather routes, took advantage of this fact in 1954, when they inaugurated the first commercial air service between Europe and the west coast of America. With terminals at Copenhagen and Los Angeles, they have made the new airport of Sondre Strømfiord one of their landing stages. The same halting-place is now also used by a Canadian Pacific Airways service from Vancouver to Amsterdam, and the airport is also being utilised as a U.S. Air Force base. Thule (*see* p. 436) has become a port of call for the Trans-World (U.S.) Airlines operating between London and California. Further services are being considered.

Striking an even more contemporary note than these airway developments is the news (announced in 1960) that Greenland's first nuclear reactor has come into operation. It is located at Camp Century, a new American scientific base about 140 miles inland from Thule. Generating about 2000 kw, it supplies the living-quarters, shops, and hospital with heat and power.

Greenland, therefore, still physically and climatically a forbidding land, is today acting in large measure as a scientific laboratory in which man's ingenuity is revealing how effective use can be made of a region which many would still class as one of privation. Fifty years ago, it sent little save icebergs into the outside world, and few people except Danish administrators knew very much about it. Now it exports cryolite and fish in increasing amounts, the United States is vitally concerned with its strategical aspect, and travellers from widely separated parts of both America and Europe are coming to know it at first-hand. Its people, growing in number, are no longer, save in very remote places, quaint survivals, but full members of our modern commercial and nuclear age. They are still, however, for the most part confined to the margins and heads of coastal fiords, to the leeward margins of the western skerry guard, and to the sheltered side of peninsulas on or close to river-mouths. The interior of their country still belongs to the ice and the wind.

STUDY QUESTIONS

1. Draw a map to illustrate the relief and climate of Mexico.

2. Discuss, and illustrate by reference to specific areas, the altitudinal zoning of climate and agriculture in Mexico and Central America.

3. Estimate the role of agriculture in the economy of Mexico.

4. Account for the marked concentration of population in the Central Plateau of Mexico.

5. Is there any likelihood that Mexico will one day rank as a major power? What difficulties has she to overcome?

6. Discuss Ottawa, Mexico City and Washington as national capitals.

7. Examine the difficulties of bringing under one goverment: (a) the Central American republics; (b) the West Indies. What advantages might you expect to accrue from such a political union?

8. Summarise the advantages the Panamá Canal has brought to its users.

9. Give a reasoned account of the distribution of sugar and banana plantations in Central America and the West Indies.

10. Draw a political map of the West Indies.

11. Compare the physical and human geography of Cuba and Jamaica.

12. Write an essay on the aboriginal populations of North America.

13. Discuss the concept of the terms "undeveloped areas" and "underdeveloped areas" as it might be applied to parts of North America.

14. Write an account of the geography of Greenland as you might expect to find it in 50 years' time.

SHORT GUIDE TO FURTHER READING

BOOKS

Pounds, N. G. *North America*. Murray, 1955.
Smith, J. R., and Phillips, M. O. *North America*. Harcourt Brace, 1942.
Jones, L. R., and Bryan, P. W. *North America*. Methuen, 1957.
Miller, G. J., Parkins, A. E., and Hudgins, B. *North America*. Wiley, 1954.
Paterson, J. H. *North America*. O.U.P., 1960.
Carlson, B. *North America*. U.T.P., 1963.
Adams, D. K. and Rogers, H. B. *An Atlas of North American Affairs*. Methuen, 1969.
Dury, G. H. and Mathieson, R. *The United States and Canada*. Heinemann, 1970.
Sealy, K. R. and Rees, R. *Regional Studies of the United States and Canada*. Harrap, 1968.
Watson, J. W. *North America*. Longmans, 1963.
Young, E. *North American Excursion*. Arnold, 1947.
White, C. L., and Foscue, E. J. *Regional Geography of Anglo-America*. Prentice Hall, 1953.
Wright, A. J. *United States and Canada: An Economic Geography*. Appleton-Century-Crofts, 1948.
Shaw, E. B. *Anglo-America*. Wiley, 1959.
Taylor, G. *Canada*. Methuen, 1947.
Newbigin, M. *Canada: The Great River, the Lands and the Men*. Christopher, 1926.
Putnam, D. F., and Kerr, D. P. *A Regional Geography of Canada*. Dent, 1956.
Putnam, D. F. and R. G. *Canada: a regional analysis*. Dent, 1970.
Gilmour, J. P. (Ed.). *Canada's To-morrow*. Macmillan, 1954.
Roberts, L. *Canada: the Golden Hinge*. Harrap, 1953.
Various authors. *Canada: Nation on the March*. Harrap, 1954.
Estall, R. *A Modern Geography of the United States*. Penguin, 1972.
Haystead, L., and Fite, G. C. *The Agricultural Regions of the United States*. Methuen, 1955.
Fenneman, N. M. *Physiography of Eastern America*. McGraw-Hill, 1938.
Fenneman, N. M. *Physiography of Western America*. McGraw-Hill, 1931.
Atwood, W. W. *The Physiographic Provinces of North America*. Ginn, 1940.
Butland, G. J. *Latin America*. Longmans, 1960.
Robinson, H. *Latin America*. Macdonald and Evans, 1961.
James, P. E. *Latin America*. Cassell, 1959.
Jones, C. F., and Darkenwald, G. G. *Economic Geography*. Macmillan, 1954.
Alexander, L. M. *World Political Patterns*. Murray, 1957.

JOURNALS

Baker, O. E. "Agricultural Regions of North America," *Economic Geography*, Vols. II–VIII, 1926–32.
Watson, J. W. "The Pattern of Canada's Post-war Growth," *Geography*, Vol. XXXIX, 1954.
Chevrier, L. "The St. Lawrence Seaway and Power Project," *Geogr. Journal*, Vol. CXIX, 1953.

Usborne, J. "The St. Lawrence Seaway," (two articles). *Geogr. Mag.*, Vol. XXXII, 1959.

Adams, R. G. "Developments in Electric Power Generation in Ontario," *Geography*, Vol. LVII, 1972.

Birch, J. W. "The Expansion of the Canadian Aluminium Industry," *Geography*, Vol. XLII, 1957.

Humphrys, G. "The Railway Stimulus in Labrador-Ungava," *Geography*, Vol. XLII, 1957.

Hattersley, P. E. "The French Element in the Population of Eastern Canada," *Geography*, Vol. XXXV, 1951.

Falardeau, J. C. "French Canada To-day," *Geogr. Mag.*, Vol. XXXII, 1959.

Dunlop, J. S. "Changes in the Canadian Wheat Belt, 1931–69," *Geography*, Vol. LV, 1970.

Rogge, J. R. "Some Recent Developments in Northern Manitoba," *Geography*, Vol. LVII, 1972.

MacKinnon, T. J. "The Forest Industry of British Columbia," *Geography*, Vol. LVI, 1971.

Barbour, G. B. "Kitimat," *Geogr. Journal*, Vol. CXXV, 1959.

Drummond, J. "Moving Day for an Arctic City" (Aklavik), *Unesco Courier*, May 1960.

Davis, J. F. "United States Population Changes, 1960–70," *Geography*, Vol. LVII, 1972.

Ullman, E. J. "The Railroad Pattern of the United States," *Geogr. Review*, Vol. 39, 1949.

Huxley, E. "Farms from the Desert: Land Reclamation in the U.S.A.," *Geogr. Mag.*, Vol. XIII, 1941.

Stern, P. M. "New York City," *Focus*, Vol. II, 1952.

Estall, R. C. "The Changing Industrial Patterns of New England," *Geography*, Vol. XLVI, 1961.

Eyre, L. A. "Land Reclamation and Settlement of the Florida Everglades," *Geography*, Vol. LVII, 1972.

Wrathall, J. E. "The Arkansas River Basin Development," *Geography*, Vol. LVI, 1971.

Wrathall, J. E. "Recent Developments in the Ohio River Valley," *Geography*, Vol. LIV, 1969.

Zelinsky, W. "The Changing South," *Focus*, Vol. I, 1951.

Morris, F. G. "The Human Geography of the Cotton Belt," *Geography*, Vol. XXXIV, 1949.

Hart, F. J. "Cotton Goes West in the American South," *Geography*, Vol. XLIV, 1959.

Parsons, J. J. "Recent Industrial Development in the Gulf South," *Geogr. Review*, Vol. 40, 1950.

Underhill, R. "The Modern Indian of the American South-West," *Geogr. Mag.*, Vol. IX, 1939.

Balchin, W. G. V., and Pye, N. "Recent Economic Trends in Arizona," *Geogr. Journal*, Vol. CXX, 1954.

Mason, P. E. "Nuclear Power Stations along the California Coast," *Geography*, Vol. LVI, 1971.

Curti, G. P. "The Colorado River: Its Utilisation in Southern California," *Geography*, Vol. XLII, 1957.

Parsons, J. J. "Californian Manufacturing," *Geogr. Review*, Vol. 39, 1949.
"San Francisco," *Focus*, Vol. 9, 1959.
Glendinning, R. M. "Desert Controls illustrated by the Coachella," *Geogr. Review*, Vol. 39, 1949.
Paterson, J. H. "The Columbia Basin Revisited," *Geography*, Vol. LV, 1970.
Ullman, E. L. "Rivers as Regional Bonds: the Columbia–Snake Example," *Geogr. Review*, Vol. 41, 1951.
"Alaska," *World Survey*, 1971.
Hart, J. F. "Oil Rush on the North Slope of Alaska," *Geography*, Vol. LV, 1970.
Sugden, D. E. "Piping Hot Wealth in a sub-zero land" (Alaska), *Geogr. Mag.*, Vol. XLIV, 1972.
Lewis, G. M. "The Distribution of the Negro in the Conterminous United States", *Geography*, Vol. LIV, 1969.
Jones, D. "Panama's non-transit Attractions," *Geogr. Mag.*, Vol. XLIV, 1971.
Jones, D. "Belize Hovers on the Brink of Independence," *Geogr. Mag.*, Vol. XLIII, 1971.
Furley, P. "A Capital Waits for its Country" (British Honduras), *Geogr. Mag.*, Vol. XLIII, 1971.
Momsen, J. D. "Crisis in the Caribbean Sugar Industry," *Geography*, Vol. LVI, 1971.
Wordie, J. M. "Ice in Greenland," *Geogr. Mag.*, Vol. XXVII, 1955.

OFFICIAL PUBLICATIONS AND OTHER SOURCES

Canada, Fact Sheets, Dept. of External Affairs, Ottawa.
Canada Handbook, 1971, and earlier years, Canadian Govt. Bureau of Statistics.
Canada Yearbook, 1971 and earlier years, Canadian Govt. Bureau of Statistics.
Various "Canada" Supplements: *Times, Guardian, Financial Times*.
The Canadian Arctic, Dept. of Mines and Technical Surveys, Ottawa. 1951.
The North West Territories, Lands, Parks and Forests Branch, Ottawa, 1943.
The Yukon Territory, Lands, Parks and Forests Branch, Ottawa, 1944.
Journal of Commerce: "St. Lawrence Seaway" Supplement, 25 July 1958.
Statistical Abstract of the United States, 1972, U.S. Bureau of the Census.
Oil in the U.S.A., Petroleum Information Bureau, 1960.
The T.V.A. Today, U.S.I.S., 1961.
Greenland, Royal Danish Ministry for Foreign Affairs, 1957.
The Statesman's Year-Book, 1972.
The Oxford Economic Atlas and *Oxford Regional Economic Atlas of the United States and Canada*.
Encyclopaedia Brittanica, Books of the Year.
Keesing's Contemporary Archives.
Philip's Digest, 1972, and earlier years.

INDEX

Main references are indicated by figures in *italics*